From Requirements to Java in a Snap

Michał Śmiałek · Wiktor Nowakowski

From Requirements to Java in a Snap

Model-Driven Requirements Engineering in Practice

Springer

Michał Śmiałek
Warsaw University of Technology
Warsaw
Poland

Wiktor Nowakowski
Warsaw University of Technology
Warsaw
Poland

ISBN 978-3-319-35719-5   ISBN 978-3-319-12838-2   (eBook)
DOI 10.1007/978-3-319-12838-2

Springer Cham Heidelberg New York Dordrecht London
© Springer International Publishing Switzerland 2015
Softcover reprint of the hardcover 1st edition 2015

Printed on acid-free paper

Springer International Publishing AG Switzerland is part of Springer Science+Business Media (www.springer.com)

*To Maria and Mieczysław who helped
to choose the right path, and to Grażyna,
Magda, Zosia and Wojtek who constantly
motivate to keep the right path.*

—Michał Śmiałek

*To my wife and children for being the true joy
of life.*

—Wiktor Nowakowski

Foreword by Juan Llorens

Dear candidate reader, it is simple: read this book! As I am not the author, my duty when writing these words is to describe the impressions I got when I read the manuscript. And I have discovered that I have many positive impressions.

Software engineering is—slowly but steadily—converging with the rest of the domain-specific "engineerings" (civil, industrial, aero-space, etc.). The convergence is, of course, not based on the variability of the different domains, but on the commonalty of the engineering processes applied to all of them. Even if it seems to be a straightforward assertion, information systems are starting to be considered as key elements within the other engineering disciplines. We can find large software components in contemporary complex technical systems like aircrafts, trains, cars or medical devices. The influence of software engineering in the development of such systems is becoming clearer daily. The new standards for system development and management include now the fundamentals of software engineering: separate the problem from the solution, and test the solution with the needs described by the problem statement.

More and more, engineering disciplines start to understand that in order to develop a system (including information systems) it is necessary to declare and describe what the stakeholder needs are. These needs allow to define stakeholder requirements, which are turned into system requirements. And system requirements are the basis for subsystem requirements. This decomposition in the specification process should end only when the complexity of the system is properly "tamed".

Thus: requirements, requirements and more requirements. They have to be fulfilled by tracing them into design artefacts and code (in case of software); they must satisfy higher level requirements; they must be verified from the product side; they must be used for validation; they must be the means for certification purposes; and, of course, they must be used to communicate humans with humans during the software and system engineering life-cycle stages. Everything starts, and consequently ends, in requirements.

On the other hand, it seems to be trendy in some sectors of the Software Engineering community to attempt at producing software products by exclusively applying models and model transformations. For its proponents, Model-Driven

Engineering (MDE) seems to become equivalent with the whole Software Engineering. Some want to define the silver bullet for modern software development by drawing graphical models, assuming that smart computers will produce exactly the software the customer wants. The real issue, the real problem, is to include requirements in this trend of model-based Software Engineering. MDE offers real benefits to increase traceability, quality control, defect reduction and explicit automation, but still calls for requirements to properly define needs, capabilities, operations, properties and restrictions.

This book deals with one of the real problems of today: how to apply requirements-based Software Engineering while not forgetting MDE. This is called Model-Driven Requirements Engineering. Until now, requirements engineering has always been outside the kernel of application for MDE; it was, perhaps, too complicated to connect both worlds. But now, this book really contributes to change this situation, by describing and presenting a clear methodology to tackle the problem. The methodology includes definition of a process, concrete methods, technology and also tools. This book has the attributes to offer a solution to existing problems under research today, particularly regarding the integration of requirements engineering within the discipline of automated software engineering.

Long live executable requirements, and enjoy your reading!

Madrid, September 2014   Juan Llorens, Ph.D.
                                        Professor, Universidad Carlos III de Madrid
                                                       CTO, The REUSE Company
                                           Technical Director, NCOSE Spanish Chapter

Foreword by Audris Kalnins

Model-Driven Software Development (MDSD) is at crossroads now. In recent years, the question asked at many major software engineering events is whether MDSD—started in 2001 as Model-Driven Architecture (MDA)—has reached its goals in providing a new road for industrial software development. The answer is typically mixed—success stories are contrasted with observations that MDSD is predominantly ignored by practitioners. This leads to tendencies to change the form in which MDSD is practiced. The classical form of MDSD is a successive chain of models, mainly in standard UML, finally leading to the system code. Intermediate models are improved manually, which causes model synchronisation problems and is seen as a key obstacle. In many successful cases, this form has given way to approaches that use model-based Domain Specific Languages (DSL). DSLs with their "one-stop" approach from initial model to the system code seem to have more chance to be accepted in practice.

Fresh ideas in the area are sought eagerly—how to really proceed further. In that sense, the book proposed by Michał Śmiałek is a real breakthrough. It originates in the ReDSeeDS project, where the main innovative aspect was the introduction of a suitable content for the first model in the MDSD chain—the CIM model. Specifically, this involves requirements specified as use case models, refined with scenarios written in controlled natural language and linked to the conceptual data model of the system to be built.

Now, in the book, this idea has reached its coherent and complete form. It offers a consistent language RSL for requirements specification, which can be applied in classical MDSD approach, or more precisely, in the step of Model-Driven Requirements Engineering (MDRE). However, at the same time, this language can be treated as a DSL. The book presents methods to transform automatically code for the application layers from precise requirements. The language thus serves as a broad domain-universal DSL for typical web-based systems—more precisely, for the whole user-system interaction control aspects to be implemented in the Controller layer of the MVC design pattern (or Presenter in the MVP pattern). RSL covers also the basic elements of the screen forms (View in MVC) which then can be extended for a specific framework. In addition, the language can easily be combined with a narrow-domain DSL for describing also the data processing aspects of the system (Model in MVC), thus enabling complete code generation for the system. As a result, the book is a very promising further development of the ReDSeeDS project, initiated by Michał Śmiałek, where me and my colleagues participated so enthusiastically.

Another especially interesting aspect of the book is the use of MOLA model transformation language developed at the IMCS University of Latvia. The language was intensively used throughout the ReDSeeDS project which was one of its major use cases. Now, the book shows how to apply MOLA (and other similar languages) to obtain even more interesting results than were achieved in ReDSeeDS: generation of Java code directly from RSL models. By presenting extensive and detailed examples, the book can also very well play the role of a MOLA textbook. The language is explained so clearly and precisely—all this based on M. Śmiałek's significant experience as an educator in the area of software development.

Riga, September 2014   Audris Kalnins, Ph.D.
                                              Senior Researcher, IMCS University of Latvia

Preface

Back in 1988, Gerald M. Weinberg, in his seminal book "Understanding the Professional Programmer" [180] has formulated the following statement: "...programming computers is by far the hardest intellectual task that human beings have ever tried to do. Ever." We can discuss this statement and argue with it but we have to admit that software development is an extremely complex task, and this is so for various reasons. Probably the most concise summary of these reasons was given by Fred Brooks in his famous essay "No Silver Bullet" [26]. He has pointed out that software is composed of two types of complexity: essential and accidental. The essential aspect is inherent for the problem at hand and cannot be reduced. This complexity has to "be there" in software so that it would be able to solve the actual problem. The accidental aspect is associated with the computer technology and includes things like programming language constructs, distributed calls, middle ware, UI technologies and so on. This kind of complexity resides within the software systems due to the complexity of computer technologies themselves.

The general diagnosis might be that "it has to be complex and we cannot do anything about it". Or maybe we can? We certainly cannot reduce the essential complexity, because the reality is complex and we need to solve complex problems in our reality. However, what we can try to do is to "tame" the accidental complexity, or more specifically—hide this complexity from the software developers. How could this be done? The first step would be to define ways of specifying precisely the essence of the solution to the problem at hand. The second step would be to build programs that would transform this essence into a working software system. The more we automate this transformation, the better we hide the accidental complexity...

It can be noted that the essential complexity of software is closely related to requirements for software. Requirements define the problem to be solved but often— at a more detailed level—they also offer essential descriptions of this problem's solution. Let us assume that we have a notation that can describe the various aspects of the essential solution with "high precision" (whatever this means). With enough precision we would have the potential to transform these detailed requirements descriptions automatically into executable artefacts. In other words: we elaborate requirements with fine precision, and in a "snap" we obtain working code.

This scenario has one important obstacle: we somehow need to cater for the accidental complexity. To implement the "snap" we immediately face the question of where this complexity goes. For hints on answering to this question we can refer to the bygone era of the domination of assembly language programming. Assembly language programmers needed to deal with the complexity of computer architectures which included such elements like processor registers, arithmetic logic units, memory locations and so on. This complexity was abstracted away with the advent of Third Generation Languages (3GLs) like FORTRAN, Algol, Pascal, and later—Java or C#. Compilers for such languages contain specific rules that are "injected" into the 3GL code to produce equivalent assembly and machine code. By analogy, we can thus imagine "injecting" technology-related aspects during transformation from requirements into more detailed software artifacts and finally—executable code.

The process of translating from a 3GL code to assembly/machine code (or other executable code) through a compiler, is completely automatic. What is more, we can also apply automatic translation (transformation) to higher-level artefacts, like design specifications. The main idea is to be able to create precise artefacts (models) at certain levels of abstraction (or: complexity) and transform them to artefacts (models) that are more detailed and complex, which finally includes also code. This idea was formally formulated around the year 2000 and led to the concept known as Model-Driven Architecture (MDA) [111]. Later, somewhat more general names of Model-Driven Software Development (MDSD) and Model-Driven Software Engineering (MDSE) emerged. Currently, this concept can certainly claim maturity with more and more tools supporting it.

Still, it has to be noted that practically all the tools concentrate on transformations between various design-level models and generating code from these design models. Moreover, these transformations have to be interlaced with manual interventions of software developers. For example, high-level architectural models cannot be translated directly into code. They need to be transformed into detailed design models and then adapted manually to cater for certain aspects not covered by the automatic transformation engines. Only then can they be transformed into code, which can be compiled and executed.

Can the model-driven concepts be extended onto requirements? Requirements are usually seen as much less subject to formalization and thus not really suitable for model transformation. Despite this, recently a new area of MDSD has emerged in the form of Model-Driven Requirements Engineering (MDRE). It concentrates on defining ways to formulate requirements as precise models and transforming these models into various more detailed models with technology details "injected" (design models, test models, etc.). It can be noted that the ultimate goal would be to be able to transform requirements directly and automatically to executable code. Though the question arises whether we can make requirements precise enough to reach this goal, yet retaining their comprehension by customers...

Purpose and Scope

There are many books that deal with issues of requirements engineering and the role of requirements in the software engineering process [5, 13, 32, 93, 130, 136, 164, 173, 183]. Most of these books concentrate on eliciting and formulating requirements of good quality (unambiguous, consistent, understandable, complete, verifiable,...). Some of the books propose to use modelling notations like use case models, class models or data flow models. Such requirements are then placed within a process in which requirements are the basis for implementing a software system.

Furthermore, there are also several books on Model-Driven Software Development/Engineering (MDSD/E) [18, 25, 66, 92, 106, 127, 167, 178]. These books concentrate on defining models and transformations between them. This includes explaining the precise meaning of models (semantics) and using this meaning to develop automatic transformations to other, more precise models. These transformations are usually performed using various model transformation languages. Some of the books present ways to define new modelling languages that can be used to formulate problems in a specific domain. This particular area of MDSD is called Software Language Engineering (SLE) [91].

This book is meant to provide the reader with a coherent approach to combine both of the above worlds [187]. It presents systematic treatment of requirements within the realm of modelling and model transformations [102], i.e. Model-Driven Requirements Engineering. What is important as the aim of the book is to treat MDRE as comprehensively as possible. The basic assumption in this comprehensive treatment is that detailed requirements models are used as first-class artefacts playing a direct role in constructing software. For this purpose, the book presents the Requirements Specification Language (RSL) that enables precision and formality, at the same time retaining end-user comprehensibility. This is important for typical requirements engineering tasks like requirements elicitation, formulation and usage.

In the book, we assume that requirements engineers use typical ways to elicit requirements from the users and from the stakeholders, and we do not provide any special guidelines in this respect. However, we provide the means to formulate these elicited requirements in the form of precise RSL models. These models facilitate assuring good quality of requirements, including coherence, unambiguity (clarity) and completeness.

Good quality requirements models, expressed in RSL can be used in a standard ("manual") way, to produce design models and implementation. Yet, the book offers a much broader use of requirements models. The ultimate goal of the book is to give the reader the means to automate the process of turning requirements into a working system. To achieve this, the book presents techniques to write and apply model transformations and code generation to RSL. What is crucial, this is supported by a state-of-the-art tool suite that accompanies this book. The suite contains an RSL editor with an integrated transformation engine (code generator)[1] and a transformation development environment.[2] Together with this set of tools, the book supplies the reader with what it promises: the means to get very quickly from requirements to code (i.e. "in a snap").

The transformations described in this book focus on processing two main types of requirements: functional requirements and vocabulary requirements (domain definitions). The reader will notice that quality requirements (or: non-functional requirements) are left aside. We do not provide a specific notation or semantic rules for them, but we discuss their influence on the final system architecture [23]. This is definitely a very interesting topic that deserves further intensive research [55, 90]. However, currently we need to assume that the quality requirements are specified using informal natural language. Such specifications are taken into account by the transformation developers when writing the transformation programs.

Who is this Book for?

When writing this book, we concentrated on presenting many technical details of requirements modelling and model transformations for requirements. This should make the book suitable for researchers, graduate students and practitioners from the industry. Researchers will find insight into possible research directions that stem from the presented approach to MDRE. Students and practitioners will find knowledge and practical techniques in several areas, including general requirements engineering, architectural design, software language construction and model transformation.

Our main goal was to present a comprehensive approach to MDRE that leads beyond the current state-of-the-art and state-of-practice. We are convinced that the presented technologies form good grounds for a very interesting field of research and innovation. This new field could concentrate on overcoming the accidental complexity of software through moving development efforts from 3GL programs towards formalised requirements models. The results presented in this book are meant to encourage the readers to join the effort of building research fundaments for such a next-generation development framework. This effort encompasses research on new ways to code application and domain logic at much higher levels of abstraction. The book already presents some of the solutions that involve semantically precise scenario notations and coherent development of domain models.

The research efforts can lead to important innovations in the area of software development tools. This area seems to be in stagnation in terms of innovative features and support for software developers. This particularly pertains to

---

[1] The ReDSeeDS tool is presented in Sect. 7.1 and can be downloaded fromhttp://www.redseeds. eu/.

[2] The MOLA Tool is presented in Sect. 6.1 and can be downloaded from http://mola.mii.lu.lv/.

requirements engineering tools [50]. Evaluations of such tools made more than 15 years ago [182] and recently [30] show little (or: practically no) progress in terms of automatic handling of requirements and assuring their formal precision. In general, it can be noted that software development tools generally do not form a coherent framework that integrates requirements directly with implementation activities [71]. This is mainly because of clearly visible mismatch between representations for user requirements and software requirements versus representations for architectural and design models and code. This book aims at changing this situation, by proposing a tooling environment that offers the means to bridge this gap through automatic transformations.

Our second goal was to show how the techniques of MDRE could already now support and increase productivity and quality in a typical software engineering project. What is important, the presented techniques can be used in various contexts, for different purposes. Requirements engineers will certainly benefit from the presented systematic approach to formulating requirements. RSL, as a notation, can be used even without the tooling environment to keep high quality of requirements, which includes precision, coherence and unambiguity. When the appropriate editor is applied, the RSL notation gains additional support through syntax checking and automatic domain model synchronisation. The editor can also support using requirements-based patterns, thus increasing productivity in creating high quality requirements models.

The presented techniques will also benefit software developers (architects, designers, programmers). They will be able to work out their models and code at a significantly higher level of abstraction—close to the problem domain. The developers will be able to work on semantically precise (code-like) requirements models in close cooperation with requirements engineers and end-users. This book shows how they can be then relieved from caring about many of the "accidental" aspects of software development which are encapsulated in the automatic transformations from requirements to code. What is important is that the transformations always generate high quality code with uniform architecture, well documented with the generated UML models.

Apart from supporting these traditional roles in software engineering, the book promotes the role of transformation engineer. This book provides the grounds for readers interested in constructing and evolving model transformations, specifically those operating on requirements. These skills are becoming very important in the current world of changing software technologies. Having fast changing targets of the transformations and code generation, we need skilled transformation developers. The book concentrates on applying MDSD to requirements models but the presented techniques can be used for any kind of model transformation task.

Finally, the book can benefit project managers through defining a clear path from requirements to code. The managers receive guidelines on how to efficiently organise software development effort around automatic model transformations from requirements to code. This includes iterative development of software applications with evolving functionality and with evolving implementation technology.

Recommended Prerequisites

This book assumes at least some basic to intermediate knowledge of various aspects of software engineering. The overall goal was to maintain it accessible for those not yet familiar with MDSD, SLE or requirements modelling. At the same time, the book goes far beyond the basics and covers several research-level topics and shows possible research directions.

Generally, it is assumed that the reader is familiar with the software development process and its phases like requirements specification, design and implementation. Thus, it is recommended that student readers have already taken a course in Software Engineering Fundamentals or similar, or alternatively—study a good book on that topic [132, 159]. The book frequently presents UML and UML-like diagrams. The reader is thus expected to understand some of the commonly used UML notations: class and object models, interaction models, activity models and use case models. Good understanding of UML syntax and semantics of these five model types is highly recommended. This is part of any good course or book on UML [24, 52, 128].

The book includes many examples and specifications that use Java or Java-like code. It is thus recommended that the reader knows at least fundamentals of Java programming, accessible through various courses and books like the widely known "Thinking in Java" [42]. Readers familiar with other similar languages like C# or C++ should also find the code parts easy to understand. Knowledge of imperative programming (like in Java or C#) will be also needed to understand model transformation programs. These programs use graphical notation similar to UML's activity diagrams.

The book treats the topics of use case development, software language development and metamodelling. Readers familiar with them should find certain parts of the book easier to understand. However, the book aims at explaining these topics also to unfamiliar readers.

Structure of this Book

The book is divided into eight chapters with two appendices. The first two chapters present the main concepts and give an introductory guide to requirements modelling in RSL. The next two chapters concentrate on presenting RSL in a formal way, suitable for automated processing. Chapters 5 and 6 concentrate on model transformations with emphasis on those involving RSL and UML. The transformations are presented using the model transformation language called MOLA. Chapters 7 and 8 provide a summary in the form of a systematic methodology with a comprehensive case study. The book is supplemented with two appendices containing short summaries of RSL and MOLA notation.

Chapter 1 introduces the main concepts of the book. It presents rationale for formulating requirements as precise models and explains approaches to use such models as "first-class citizens" in the software development process. This chapter also gives an introduction to MDRE as a new but already established and promising branch of Model-Driven Software Development.

Chapter 2 explains how to formulate precise requirements using RSL. It presents all the relevant RSL constructs using an example specification. All the important details of the RSL concrete syntax are outlined and its usage shown in practice. Also, good practices in formulating requirements using RSL are given. The main purpose of this chapter is to provide an RSL tutorial for requirements engineers and software developers. It should also be read as an introduction to reading the next chapter on the RSL metamodel.

Chapter 3 gives a more formal definition of RSL forming the basis for performing transformations from RSL to other modelling languages (mostly UML) and code. An important purpose of this chapter is to give the reader practical introduction to metamodelling. Consecutive sections present the language's abstract syntax in the form of a metamodel. For each of the syntactic elements, concrete (visual and/or textual) syntax is presented through examples. The explanation of the syntax is supplemented by informally presented semantics (meaning) of the various language elements. At this level, semantics is given in reference to the concepts of business modelling and requirements engineering.

Chapter 4 presents the translational semantics of RSL using Java. This consists in a set of rules that translate RSL constructs into equivalent Java constructs. In order to construct the rules, a specific architectural framework (pattern) with specific technological assumptions (UI framework, data passing model, etc.) is chosen. This framework is expressed in plain Java for all of its components. The selected target code structure is used to explain RSL runtime semantics (semantics for executing RSL specifications). Based on this, the translation rules are generalized in order to be applicable to various technological contexts. This chapter should be read by RSL developers to understand precisely RSL semantics for the working system. Moreover, this chapter is important for transformation engineers. It shows the initial steps in designing a transformation from RSL to a specific technology.

Chapter 5 presents an introduction to model transformations. It explains intricacies of operating on models which are nonlinear graphs in contrast to text (cf. programs) which is linear. The whole presentation in this chapter is accompanied by various examples from the simple "Hello world" to more advanced transformations using the MOLA model transformation language. This chapter should give the reader the basis to understand model transformation and develop non-trivial transformation programs.

Chapter 6 extend the previous introductory chapter with guidelines for developing complex transformations based on complex metamodels. The basis for this is the RSL metamodel, the UML metamodel and the syntax of Java. This chapter thus also gives some more details of the UML formal specification and the Java syntax. For the chapter to be practical, the presentation is backed by a short introduction to a MOLA development environment. After reading this chapter, the reader should be able to understand the rules for developing complex transformations originating in requirements models, and be able to tailor them to specific target technologies (including those emerging in the future).

Chapter 7 summarizes the book by offering a methodology and tools to apply its contents in practice. It gathers all the presented elements and places them in a coherent software development framework. This framework complies with modern iterative approaches, including agile software development. Software project managers and software developers will benefit from this chapter by organizing MDRE-based software projects according to its guidance.

Chapter 8 presents a comprehensive case study. Within the study, a specific target platform with detailed technology solutions is applied. The case study involves an example requirements model in RSL. The chapter presents some details of the model and the system (UML, Java code, UI layouts) generated from this model. It also discusses important details of the transformations that lead to generating this system.

Finally, there are two appendices. Appendix A offers a short reference of the RSL concrete syntax and Appendix B does the same for MOLA. Each of the syntactic elements is shortly summarized and an example given. The aim of the appendices is to provide the language users (requirements engineers, software developers) with an easily accessible and complete reference of the syntax.

Acknowledgments

The tool suite that accompanies this book has been developed within two projects partially funded by the European Union: ReDSeeDS[3] and REMICS.[4] We would like to thank all the Partners that have cooperated with us within these projects, especially in developing the RSL language and the ReDSeeDS tool.

Warsaw, August 2014   Michał Śmiałek
                                                                                        Wiktor Nowakowski

---

[3] http://www.redseeds.eu/.
[4] http://www.remics.eu/.

Contents

Acronyms

3GL	Third Generation Language
CASE	Computer Aided Software Engineering
CMOF	Complete MOF
CRUD	Create-Read-Update-Delete
DAO	Data Access Object
DSL	Domain Specific Language
DTO	Data Transfer Object
EMOF	Essential MOF
IDE	Integrated Development Environment
MDA	Model-Driven Architecture
MDRE	Model-Driven Requirements Engineering
MDSD	Model-Driven Software Development
MOF	Meta Object Facility
MOLA	MOdel transformation LAnguage
MVC	Model-View-Controller
MVP	Model-View-Presenter
OMG	Object Management Group
QVT	Query/View/Transformations
RDB	Relational DataBase
RSL	Requirements Specification Language
SPEM	Software and Systems Process Engineering Metamodel
SPL	Software Product Line
SQL	Sequence Query Language
SVO	Subject-Verb-Object
UI	User Interface
UML	Unified Modelling Language

Chapter 1
Introducing Requirements-Driven Modelling

Requirements play a pivotal role in software development because they express the needs of the customer. A quality software system can emerge only when the real needs of the client are discovered. However, this is not enough. A typical software development project faces the problem of translating the user needs into a working system. These problems are dealt with by hundreds of books on various aspects of software design and pertaining to the plethora of software development technologies we can choose from. Related activities produce important artefacts that are treated as primary in software development: design models and code. Software design and coding directly contributes to the final system, and thus their results are treated as first-class citizens in the world of software development.

By contrast, requirements engineering is treated as a much less crisp and precise field of software development [33]. Requirements are treated as secondary artefacts for software developers as they cannot be translated directly into code. They are formulated as paragraphs of text structured to some extent, but still usually quite ambiguous and necessitating disambiguation during the later stages of development. They are obviously important but they do not contribute directly to the final effect. Their contribution is indirect and is treated like a craft rather than as a discipline of engineering. Various books on requirements engineering concentrate a lot on communication with the client and the psychological aspects of requirements elicitation (which is obviously good). This also includes notations (languages, templates, guidelines) with different levels of precision. However, there can be seen a lack of approaches to formulate requirements in a way that would allow for automation in their translation into code.

In this chapter, we introduce an approach to requirements engineering where requirements are treated as first-class citizens [70], contributing directly to the production of the final code. In this approach, requirements are formulated as models [17]. These models are intended to be comprehensible even by "ordinary" people (not software developers). At the same time, these models are formulated in a language that is precise enough (has precise semantics) to be able to generate meaningful and usable design models and code.

© Springer International Publishing Switzerland 2015
M. Śmiałek and W. Nowakowski, *From Requirements to Java in a Snap*,
DOI 10.1007/978-3-319-12838-2_1

1.1 Why Model Requirements?

If we could try to imagine an ideal dream of a software project manager, it would most likely look as in Fig. 1.1. In this dream, requirements agreed-upon with the user and written down in whatever format, would automatically transform themselves into ready executable code of the target system [37, 148, 155, 179]. All that is needed is an automaton that would encapsulate all the knowledge on the target executable environment, logical and physical architecture, user interface design and so on. Moreover, this automaton would need to be able to process natural language and disambiguate it. Having such a tool, we would only need to press a button ("make a snap") and voilà—here come the executables of the system.

Of course, this is just a dream... Or maybe not? Maybe we can bring this dream closer to reality? First, let us take a look at Fig. 1.2. It shows a similar situation but at a much lower level of abstraction. Here we transform a program written in a 3rd Generation Language (3GL; like C++, Java or C#) into executable code. This is done by an automaton known to all programmers and is called the compiler [3]. This automaton encapsulates the knowledge about the hardware and the execution platform (machine code, bytecode, registers, memory access, basic I/O access and so on). During compilation, this knowledge is automatically "injected" into the executable program and merged with the programming constructs that could be expressed in the specific 3GL. The resulting code can be executed directly by the execution environment (in a specific operating system, processor type, virtual machine, etc.). The knowledge of this execution environment is to a large extent abstracted away in the 3GL code. As a result, the source code is significantly less complex (or: easier to comprehend) than the machine code.

We can argue that the two situations are different. The 3GL code has precise syntax and semantics (meaning) that determines its interpretation for execution (during runtime). By contrast, the requirements are too ambiguous. They do not use a syn-

Fig. 1.1 From requirements to code: ideal scenario

Fig. 1.2 From 3GL code to executable code

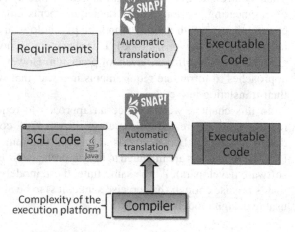

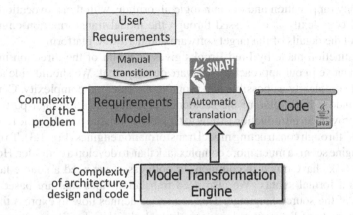

Fig. 1.3 From requirements to code: a more realistic scenario

tactically and semantically precise language. Thus, it is not possible to develop an automaton that would be able to process requirements and produce executable code. Obviously, this is true for requirements written in natural language and using semi-formal diagrams, even when certain templates and constraints on the requirements structure are applied. However, we can think of a much more realistic scenario, as illustrated in Fig. 1.3.

In this scenario, the less structured user requirements are manually transformed into syntactically and semantically precise requirements models. These models capture the complexity of the problem using a high-level modelling language. This includes the desired functionality of the system (application logic, user interface) and a detailed description of the problem domain. The main issue here is to be able to capture all such knowledge using this high-level language with "enough" precision. Provided that the precision is satisfactory, we will be able to develop a model transformation engine (cf. a compiler) that produces a full code of the desired system. This engine, by analogy to the compiler, would encapsulate the technological details of the target programming platform. This includes the target architectural solutions, detailed design decisions and intricacies of specific coding guidelines. Such technological knowledge is injected during translation and is combined with the description of the problem (the requirements models) to produce fully operational code.

This last scenario (see again Fig. 1.3) refers to a clear separation of two kinds of software complexity formulated by Fred Brooks [26, 27]. Back in the 1980s, Fred Brooks distinguished the "essence" from "accidents" in programming. His definition was that "the **essence** of a software entity is a construct of interlocking concepts: data sets, relationships among data items, algorithms, and invocations of functions" and "**accidental** tasks arise in representing the construct in language". In our case, the essential complexity is expressed through the requirements models. These models contain the definition of the problem domain (data and relations) and the desired functionality (application and domain logic algorithms with their invocations). The accidental complexity is expressed through the model transformation engine and contains all the details of the target software and hardware platform.

The distinction made by Fred Brooks gives us a hint of the direction in which we should move in our approach to software development. We should hide as much accidental complexity as possible and promote the essential complexity. Compilers (Fig. 1.2) indeed hide some of the accidental complexity. In the later parts of this book, we provide an introduction to how to tackle the problem of hiding the remaining "accidents" through constructing model transformation engines (Fig. 1.3). To develop such an engine seems a much more complex task than to develop a compiler. However, these two tasks have much in common. In both cases, we need a source language which has a formal syntax. We also need translation rules that are based on the semantics of the source language. This semantics defines how to express the (high level) constructs of the source language through the (low level) constructs of the target language.

3GL compilers allow us to express programming constructs at a significantly higher level than machine/assembly code. However, this is done at a cost of less programming freedom and usually worse performance. This is because the compilers apply uniform translation rules to all the 3GL constructs and produce uniformly structured and often not perfectly optimised output code. All the detailed decisions on how to structure the output code were made by the compiler constructors. Despite this, we do not really want to go back to the era of assembly language programming. The advantage of abstracting away the complexity of the execution platform is much higher than the minor disadvantages that were mentioned. Though, in some cases, whenever it is necessary (e.g. for performance reasons), some subroutines can be programmed in assembly language.

Still, we can try to move up the ladder of abstraction in software development. We would like to define a language that abstracts away not only the execution platform but the whole software technology platform. This includes the architectural design (physical and logical architecture), approaches to persist data, ways to exchange data through the user interface, divisions into programming units (packages, classes), approaches to pass control between programming units (class dependencies) and so on. The appropriate translator for this language would need to capture and unify specific decisions in these areas. Thus, the developers that would use the new high-level language would have a lot less freedom in making these decisions than when they would program in Java or other 3GL. This would be the cost of "programming" at the level of the problem domain (or: requirements [31, 69, 150]). The question would be whether this cost would pay off just like in the case of 3GL to machine code translators. Another question is how to develop such new translators and this is what we want to answer in this book.

In the meanwhile, the reader would probably appreciate some more concrete justification on why we should bother about modelling requirements in a semantically precise way. Let us illustrate what we mean, through an elementary example. In Fig. 1.4, we can see a tiny requirements model. This model uses a notation that should be familiar to many requirements engineers. It contains a single use case

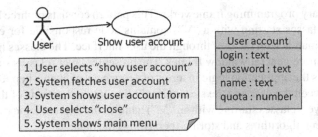

Fig. 1.4 Tiny example: source requirements model

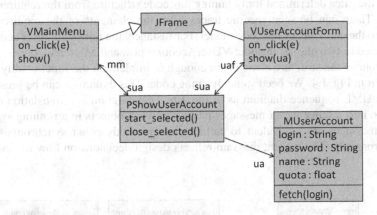

Fig. 1.5 Tiny example: target code structure model

(the oval) and a single actor (the sticky figure). This simple notation was invented by
Ivar Jacobson and dates back to the beginning of the 1990s [2, 12, 34, 44, 78, 96, 137,
141]. The use case diagram is supplemented by a textual scenario (sentences 1–5)
and a single definition of the domain notion ("user account") used in this scenario.
The notion definition uses standard UML class notation [24, 52] and contains four
attributes (information components) of the notion.

The diagram in Fig. 1.4 is a requirements model that we claim is precise enough
to generate working code. Obviously, this generated code should be governed by
certain design decisions that would be uniformly and automatically applied. Here
we do not explain these rules in detail, instead we describe code that we would like
to have as an implementation of the source requirements model. The structure of this
code is presented in Fig. 1.5. This is a UML class diagram that depicts four classes
with their operations and relationships between them. A careful reader might notice
right away that we have applied an architectural pattern to this code structure.[1] It is
the Model-View-Presenter (MVP) pattern that is becoming more and more popular

---

[1] The examples in this chapter use very simplified Java with an imaginary programming framework.
Here we want to abstract away from any specific Java technology.

in contemporary programming frameworks. This pattern consists of three layers. The view layer (classes starting with a "V") contains code responsible for exchanging data and commands with the user through the user interface. The classes in this layer specialise in more general window frames. The presenter layer (classes starting with a "P") handles the application logic in terms of sequences of events happening in the dialogue between the user and the system (including internal actions of the system). The model layer (classes starting with an "M") handles the domain logic that includes data processing algorithms and storing (persisting) the data.

The code structure in Fig. 1.5 should be substantial enough to handle the simple functionality defined in Fig. 1.4. Moreover, we may intuitively feel that there can be specific rules determined for obtaining this code structure from the requirements model. There can be seen specific traces from the elements of the requirements model to the elements of the code model. For instance, the notion of "user account" is reflected in two classes in code: VUserAccountForm and MUserAccount.

Of course, the structure alone is not enough to implement the functionality (scenario) from Fig. 1.4. We need some dynamic code. This dynamics can be presented using a UML sequence diagram as in Fig. 1.6. This diagram is a translation of the scenario into a sequence of messages passed between objects in a running system. These messages are equivalent to calling class methods either synchronously or asynchronously. The current diagram reflects design decisions on how to structure

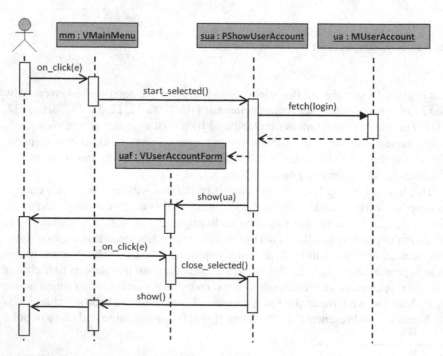

Fig. 1.6 Tiny example: target code dynamics model

code within individual methods in code. For instance, the method "start_selected" in PShowUserAccount contains a call to "fetch", a constructor call for VUserAccountForm and a call to "show". Similarly to the case of the code structure, we can intuitively see certain traces from the sequence of sentences in our example use case scenario to the sequence of messages in the sequence diagram. For instance, the sentence "User selects 'show user account'" can be traced to the sequence of two messages: "on_click" and "start_selected".

The class diagram from Fig. 1.5 and the sequence diagram from Fig. 1.6 already contain much of the target complexity. However, the final code has more details, as presented in Fig. 1.7. The presenter ("PShowUserAccount") code is a direct translation of the dynamics from the sequence diagram. However, the other class methods contain code that adds more details. The view classes have specific code to show individual widgets on the screen (here: a very simplified widget rendering framework). The model class contains code to fetch persisted data from the database (here: a very simplified inline SQL). In reality, this code would be significantly more complex but we have removed much of the technical details for the sake of simplifying this example. Despite this simplification, it can be seen that at this stage, the target platform (technology) details were introduced. However, the individual instructions in code can be intuitively traced back to the initial requirements model.

In the remainder of this book, we show that it is possible to automate the path sketched in this simple example. The main prerequisite for this automation is the ability to define the source requirements models precisely. This means using precise syntax that allows to assure the coherence of the models similar to the coherence of code. Moreover, we need a precise definition of the semantics that would explain the

```
class VMainMenu extends JFrame{
  PShowUserAccount sua;
  void on_click(Event e) {
    sua.start_selected();
  }
  void show() {
    show_option("Show User Account");
  }
}
```

```
class VUserAccountForm extends JFrame{
  PShowUserAccount sua;
  void on_click(Event e) {
    sua.close_selected();
  }
  void show(ua: MUserAccount) {
    show_text(ua.login);
    show_text(ua.name);
    show_number(ua.quota);
  }
}
```

```
class PShowUserAccount {
  VMainMenu mm; VUserAccountForm uaf;
  MUserAccount ua;
  String login;
  void start_selected() {
    ua.fetch(login);
    uaf.show(ua);
  }
  void close_selected() {
    mm.show();
  }
}
```

```
class MUserAccount {
  String login, password, name;
  float quota;
  void fetch(String l) {
    "SELECT * FROM user_accounts
        WHERE login=l"
  }
}
```

Fig. 1.7 Tiny example: target code

translation of requirements elements into specific code constructs. Assuring strict precision of requirements involves additional effort in this phase of software development. However, this effort should pay off with the possibility to apply automatic translation into fully working code. In the above example, we have not considered many other aspects of this translation which are explained in detail in the subsequent chapters. Thus, although considerable effort is needed to develop the transformation, this transformation can be reused many times similar to how we "reuse" transformations into machine code within compilers.

So, how do we answer the question "why model requirements?" There can be at least two reasons (see Fig. 1.8). First, requirements models have very good communication capabilities. Using visual models, we can make requirements more comprehensible to the business people who order and use software. Visual models can thus be used by less formal human readers. The second reason is more important, as its effects can have a significant impact on the productivity of the developers. Requirements models can be made formal enough to be able to transform them automatically into other artefacts like design models and code. Also, we can assure their coherence through implementing certain automated validation mechanisms. The possibility to generate code directly from requirements means a significant rise in abstraction for activities that produce running code. This rise of abstraction is similar to that of 3GL programming in relation to assembly language programming.

However, a significant problem we face is to design a language that is comprehensible to "ordinary people" and at the same time gives enough "power" to serve as high-level code for software developers. This language must have a precise but understandable syntax (grammar) and its constructs must possess strict meaning (semantics) in terms of code generated from them. The following two sections provide an overview of these two aspects.

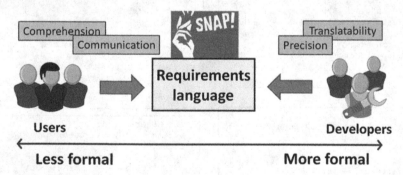

Fig. 1.8 Combining good communication with precision

1.2 Making Requirements Precise

1.2.1 Writing Good Stories

To answer the question of how to make requirements precise we start with an analogy that may look odd at first sight. We start by explaining how to write a good adventure novel. First, we have to have a good story. It should have an exciting action with many possible resolutions. Preferably, the story should end with a happy ending but there always has to be a possibility of the story ending sadly. Moreover, we should place this action in an interesting environment. This should include the characters that take part in the story, placed within the nature (forests, animals, etc.) and the products of technology (buildings, vehicles, etc.) that surround them. The best novel writers try to create a coherent new (future, alternative, sci-fi) environment, or try to reflect the real environment existing some time in history or at the present.

One of the best examples of a coherent environment created by a talented writer is the Middle-earth. J.R.R. Tolkien has described it in much detail throughout several of his works like "Hobbit", "The Lord of the Rings" and "Silmarillion". The environment of the Middle-earth consists of many different intelligent species (men, hobbits, dwarfs and so on), a specific landscape with different landmarks (cities, mountains, rivers), specific technical capabilities (weapons, means of transport, etc.) and other features of the characters like their extra-natural capabilities. Being a good novel writer, Tolkien gradually reveals to us the whole environment of the Middle-earth. This is done along with the different stories being told. A good novel is thus a balanced combination of stories and the description of a coherent environment. This is illustrated in Fig. 1.9 where the descriptions of various events (forming the story) are interweaved with the descriptions of the environment.

In order to be able to understand the environment of the Middle-earth better, Tolkien provides us also with a sketch of its map. However, his text is so precise and

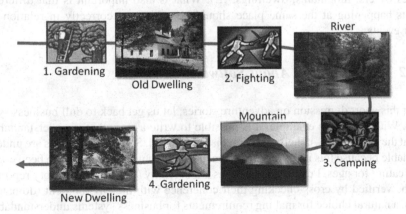

Fig. 1.9 Story and environment combined in a novel

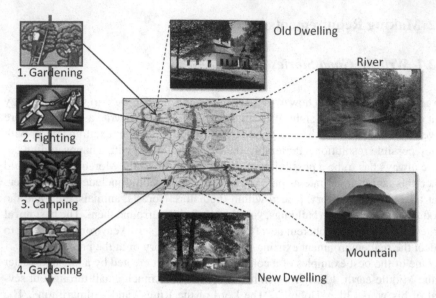

Fig. 1.10 Making the environment coherent with the story

coherent that many other authors have developed various other descriptions of the Middle-earth. This includes atlases with detailed maps of various areas of Middle-earth, encyclopaedias explaining all the notions, and vocabularies explaining all the terms in various Middle-earth languages. In fact, from Tolkien's various works on the Middle-earth, there has been "extracted" a coherent (quasi-historical) description of the whole environment. This can be generalised in that a good adventure novel should provide an environment that can be described with a coherent conceptual framework, e.g. using a map. An illustration of this can be found in Fig. 1.10. Now, all the events from Fig. 1.9 are extracted to form the story. The events refer to specific places on a coherent map of the territory. Each of the places is described in a vocabulary of places (rivers, mountains, dwellings, …). What is also important is that different events happening at the same place should be positioned correctly in relation to other events.

1.2.2 Writing Stories About Software

After this short digression on adventure stories, let us get back to dull business systems. With the above example, it is possible to write a story that is understandable and at the same time—coherent and precise [147, 181]. Stories themselves are understandable because this is the most fundamental way in which people have been communicating for ages. Furthermore, stories about reality (testimonies, history reports) can be verified by cross-checking their coherence with the environment (domain). Thus, a natural choice for making requirements for business systems understandable

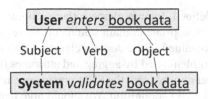

Fig. 1.11 Sentences in a story

and precise would be to base them on stories. How can we write such stories for software [7, 147]?

We can write them from the point of view of the system's user. Then, the story should tell about the dialogue between the user and the system. The story can consist of simple sentences, as those shown in Fig. 1.11 [20, 61]. These sentences are indicative and contain a subject, a verb and an object. We call them Subject-Verb-Object (SVO) sentences. The SVO structure should be sufficient to present the interactions between the users (when the subject is a user) and the system (when the subject is the system). However, it is obviously not sufficient to explain the context for the interactions. Thus, requirements specifiers often tend to insert such explanations as continuations of sentences with such (or similar) structure. For instance, we receive a complex sentence like, "The user enters book data, where book data contains the book title and the author". This can be compared to writing an adventure novel where the story is interweaved with the descriptions of the environment. In another part of the story (e.g. 20 pages later in the requirements document), we can have a sentence like, "The system validates book data (author, title, issue date) by comparing the issue date with the author's lifespan". This leads to significant confusion when we want to define "book data". Both definitions do not match—is it the same kind of data we are talking about in both cases? To make things coherent, we need to use the same technique as Tolkien and his followers did—create a detailed map of the territory, coherent with the story.

Note that we have clearly emphasised the three sentence parts—the subject is in bold, the verb is in italic and the object is underlined. This emphasis is important, because we want to relate the verbs and the nouns to their centralised definitions. This will make the "environment" coherent with the "story" as in our discussion on the Middle-earth, as illustrated in Fig. 1.12. It can be seen that both sentence objects

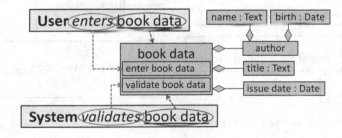

Fig. 1.12 Extending story sentences with domain definitions

refer to one centrally defined domain element (here: "book data"). Moreover, the sentence verbs refer to appropriate domain statements (here: "enter book data" and "validate book data") contained in the domain element (verb phrases). The domain element definition is complemented by aggregated attributes (here: "author", "title" and "issue date"). The references from the SVO sentences can be seen as hyperlinks [82] leading to a central "wiki" definition. We should note that this "wiki" contains definitions of not only the nouns ("book data") but also the verb phrases associated with the nouns ("validate book data").

Several SVO sentences can be formed into a story which we can also call a scenario. An example can be found in Fig. 1.13. There we find in fact two scenarios. One of them ends with a "happy end" (the book data are saved) while the other one ends with a failure (an error message is shown). Both scenarios have the same beginning (sentences 1–5) and what distinguishes them are the condition sentences (book data either valid or invalid). These condition sentences can be compared to the dilemma of a scenario writer for a TV "soap opera" (or an adventure novel writer). She might wonder how to resolve a specific key scene in an episode. Depending on this resolution, the plot might go into several different directions. The issue for software system scenarios is that we need to specify all the possible "plots"…

When writing scenarios, we maintain their coherence with the domain definition [10, 20–22, 152, 165]. This definition grows through adding new notions and new verb phrases. The notions are taken not only from the problem domain (like "book data") but also from the domain of the user-system dialogue [177], which includes window frames (see «frame» in Fig. 1.13), button triggers (see «trigger») and message boxes (see «message»). This forms a vocabulary of notions to be used coherently within

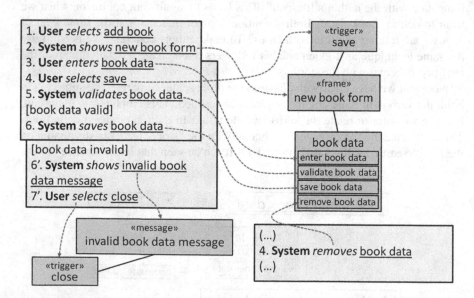

Fig. 1.13 The stories and their vocabulary

various scenarios throughout the whole requirements model. This is illustrated in Fig. 1.13 by showing another (perhaps distant) scenario (at the bottom) which also refers to the same domain notion as that referred to from the first two scenarios. We can associate the various notions through relationships which makes also the vocabulary internally coherent. For instance, we can indicate which of the domain data elements (here: "book data") should be presented in which of the window frames (here: "new book window").

Several similar scenarios can be combined to form a use case. Use cases were introduced earlier in an example in the previous section but here we present them more formally. There can be found many definitions of what use cases are in the literature. Our definition tries to summarise them and concentrates on three main features of use cases.

Definition A use case is a complete piece of functionality that possesses the following characteristics:

1. It starts with the interaction of an outside actor with the system or assumes the possibility of such an interaction to start it.[2]
2. It contains several scenarios that constitute sequences of interactions of an outside actor (or actors) with the system, and replies (or requests) of the system.
3. It ends by reaching a goal of some value to the outside actor or failing to reach that goal (despite trying).

Use cases are defined in relation to outside actors. Outside actors represent roles that groups of people or outside systems play in relation to the currently considered (specified) system. A representative of an outside actor can come into interaction with the current system in accordance with the use cases related to this outside actor. Note that the definition speaks of "outside actors" and not simply "actors" (as is done in the literature and software engineering practice). This is due to certain confusion that can occur for less-experienced modellers. They sometimes model actors as internal elements within the modelled system (or even as the system itself). The word "outside" makes it unambiguous that actors are never part of the current system.

This definition can be analysed through the example found in Fig. 1.13. We did not name the use case in the figure, but it is obvious that the name could read as "Add new book". This name also specifies its goal. The use case (all of its possible scenarios) starts with a specific interaction (selecting the "add book" button). It contains several SVO sentences forming a sequence of interactions between the user (cf. outside actor) and the system. It ends either by reaching the goal (saving "book data") or failing to reach it (presenting an error message). Note that after reaching the goal, the system is in a stable state from the point of view of the user interface and internal system transactions. This means that—for instance—the user can start the use case again.

---

[2] The assumption of possible initial actor interaction is explained in Chaps. 2 and 4. This pertains to use cases invoked from within other use cases (see Fig. 2.27 and rules P9 and P10).

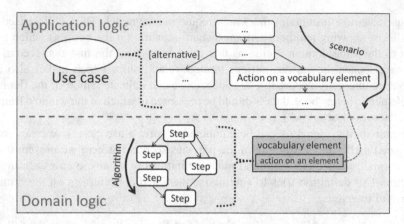

Fig. 1.14 Use cases: stories forming the application logic that refers to domain logic

The functionality defined through use case scenarios can be also called the application logic. This is in contrast to the domain logic illustrated in Fig. 1.14. The application logic contains all the possible alternative scenarios of user–system interaction. Actions in the application logic refer ("hyperlink") to specific actions in the domain logic. The domain logic is organised around the vocabulary of notions as presented above. The verb phrases (actions) that are contained in the notions can be defined in more detail to form the domain logic. This includes specific notations to denote data processing algorithms (e.g. how to "validate book data" or how to "calculate mean book price"). We do not discuss these notations in detail here because they are specific to the considered domains (cf. domain-specific notations mentioned in the next section).

It should be emphasised that the presented notation for the requirements models is domain agnostic. This means that it can be applied to any typical business domain, thus making it universal. The domain vocabulary is constructed within the specification and is then used to define the domain logic [47]. The notation is simple and understandable by a "layman" (not proficient in software engineering, e.g. a business person). It consists mainly of simple SVO sentences and domain element definitions. Its main characteristic is strict relation between the application logic (use case scenarios) and the domain logic (verb phrases). We call this notation the Requirements Specification Language (RSL) [83, 118].[3] This language allows us to implement the "realistic" code translation scenario described in the previous section. For this purpose, we need to define the meaning of RSL constructs in terms of application logic and equivalent code. This is introduced in the next section.

---

[3] The idea of requirements modelling started with the Requirements Modelling Language proposed by Greenspan et al. [63, 64]. More recently, Helming et al. proposed the Unified Requirements Modelling Language [16, 68]. Yet another approach was proposed by Beatty and Chen [13].

1.2.3 How About Quality Issues?

Note that use cases and the vocabulary identify two types of requirements: functional requirements and vocabulary requirements (domain definitions). For a requirements specification to be complete, we need to define quality requirements (known also as non-functional requirements). The first two types of requirements define the way the system functions, as seen by the outside user and defines what data are processed and exchanged with the user. The quality requirements influence the internals of the system. Architects use specific design solutions based on the required performance, reliability or security. Moreover, they might need to apply certain constraints to the target technology (e.g. a specific operating system or UI framework has to be used).

Quality requirements may highly influence the "accidental" aspects of the target code. Thus, they need to be carefully considered when developing translation rules for functional and vocabulary requirements. For some of the quality requirement types, we can determine precise guidelines as to which architectural patterns or specific software development frameworks should be applied. For instance, the requirement that the application should be used on mobile devices determines many elements of its architecture and various detailed design solutions. In case of other types, some general guidance can be applied, and only later verified when some parts of the system are ready. This is typically the case for performance requirements. Experienced architects can use specific design solutions that are known to fulfil the desired system performance (e.g. response time). However, there is no way to assure this in advance at design time.

In this book, we assume the average quality requirements that influence the translation from requirements models to code. In particular, we assume that the system is available through the Internet and thus a web application is needed. We also assume that the response time can be average, and typical architectural solutions for web application will be satisfactory. In case there are special quality constraints set on the target system, the translation rules presented throughout this book should be updated. This may, for instance, influence the code structure and its distribution between processing nodes (physical/virtual machines). It may also involve developing code for different UI platforms or using a certain security framework.

In general, this may be reflected in several variants of translation programs that produce code from requirements, selectable depending on the specific quality requirements. We may also think about automating this process, and selecting appropriate transformation procedures depending on the values of the quality requirements. For this purpose, we would need a precise modelling language for quality metrics and a schema for parameterising code generation depending on these metrics. This topic is still well beyond the current state-of-the-art and thus we will not elaborate on it in this book. However, it seems a promising direction worth a significant research effort in the future.

1.3 What Is the Meaning of Requirements Models?

Being a language (and specifically—a modelling language), RSL communicates some meaning. To understand this meaning we need to define its semantics. Semantics is a necessary complement of the indexsyntax syntax (grammar) for any language (including natural languages). To explain the semantics of a software language, we can use various methods. In all of these methods, we need to specify the given language in terms of simple concepts which have a known meaning (semantics). For instance, to explain the semantics of a programming language, we can introduce a simple automaton (with memory, processing capabilities, etc.). Then we can show how specific constructs of the given language work during runtime in terms of operations of this automaton (called operational semantics). However, this approach—although precise and formal—is usually hard to understand and use in practice.

A practical way of defining the semantics of a language is to specify the rules of translating specifications (programs) in this language into specifications (programs) in another language. Obviously, this other language has to have its semantics already defined. This way of defining semantics is called translational semantics [91, 146]. We use this approach to specify the semantics of RSL in Chap. 4. We offer rules for translating RSL into Java (also explaining some constructs using UML). This is helpful for constructing language translators. At the same time, it allows to understand the meaning of specific language constructs by software engineers proficient in 3GL programming.

However, it is also important to explain the meaning of RSL to domain experts not proficient in software development. In this case, we should provide some account on RSL constructs in terms of the behaviour of the specified systems as seen from the outside. This would include the navigation and appearance of the user interface and changes in the system state related to the domain (business) model. Again, these semantics can be defined through some target language understandable to the reader of the semantics definition (translational semantics). Yet, this definition might not necessitate the level of precision as that for translating into, e.g. Java.

1.3.1 Requirements Explained Through Observable Behaviour

In this introduction to semantics, we start with the approach based on defining the system's observable behaviour. It allows us to be less formal. We explain use cases, scenarios and vocabulary elements by translating them into sequences of user interface elements that would appear to the user and changes in domain objects handled by the system. A summary of this approach can be found in Fig. 1.15. It consists of three parts: (1) control flow semantics, (2) individual sentence semantics and (3) vocabulary element semantics. The first two parts pertain to the application logic of the system to be built. The third pertains to the domain logic (see the previous section for explanation of the distinction between application logic and domain logic). Control

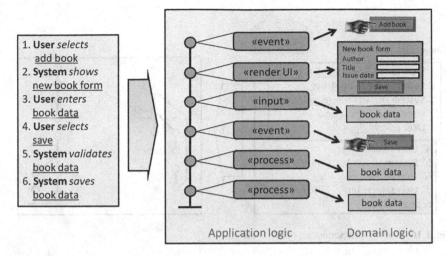

Fig. 1.15 Software language semantics explained through observable behaviour

flow semantics defines the sequence in which the individual interactions are to be executed. In Fig. 1.15, it is depicted with a series of dots along a line, ending with a "stop bar". In our simple example, we have only one straight line because there are no alternatives: we have a single scenario. Each of the dots represents a single action equivalent to a single sentence in a scenario. Each of these sentences has a specific meaning, which can be a user-triggered event, a UI rendering action or a data processing action. Detailed semantics of each of the actions can be determined by examining the vocabulary elements linked from the associated scenario sentences. These details include, e.g. the specific button to be pressed, the layout of a window frame to be displayed or the specific data processing algorithm to be executed.

The semantics of use cases and especially their control flow semantics was not the first concern of the literature on this subject [143, 170]. This is because use cases were not intended for automatic translation into design and code. However, for our purposes we need to be clear about this. The "use case language" has to define precisely how a set of use cases may be "executed" in a running system. This is illustrated in significant detail in Fig. 1.16. We can see two use cases related through a relationship denoted with «invoke». This is complemented by two scenarios of the first of the two use cases ("Show book list"). The second use case is the already presented "Add new book". Note that we do not use the well-known «include» and «extend» relationships because of their ambiguous control flow semantics, criticised in the literature [57, 97, 108–110, 143]. Instead, we use a new kind of relationship for which we introduce precise control flow semantics.

The control flow of this RSL model is explained through the diagram on the right of Fig. 1.16. It shows how the individual scenario actions can be executed. There are two alternative paths for "Show book list" starting after sentence 3 (see the left part of the diagram). Two SVO sentences denote two alternative decisions by the actor—to

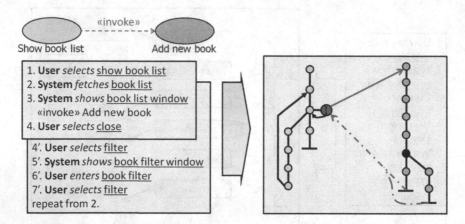

Fig. 1.16 Control flow semantics of use cases

either select "close" or "filter". In "Add new book", there are also two possible paths (compare with Fig. 1.13) but the alternative is of a different kind. This time it does not depend on the user's decision but on the system's state and data processing. This is denoted by the black dot in the right part of the control flow diagram. The dot can be expanded into several (here: two) alternative conditions (here: data are valid or invalid) leading to selection of one of the outgoing paths.

The control flow diagram in Fig. 1.16 also presents the semantics of «invoke». An invocation relationship exists between two use cases whenever an appropriate «invoke» sentence is present in a scenario. In our example, "Add new book" is invoked within sentence 3 of "Show new book". The control flow semantics of this RSL construct resembles a procedure call. Control is first passed to the first sentence of the invoked use case. After reaching one of the final sentences of the invoked use case, control is passed back to the invoking use case. However, the return of control repeats the action associated with the invocation sentence. In our example, the action to "show book list window" is performed after returning from "add new book".

Having explained the control flow, we need to explain the meaning of individual actions, associated with SVO sentences. In general, we can distinguish four types of sentences as presented in Fig. 1.17. Their general meaning depends on their subject and their object. Syntactically, the subject of an SVO sentence can be either one of the outside actors or the system. Moreover, the object of an SVO sentence can be a trigger or a domain element. Based on this division, we can define the four types of SVO sentences.

1. **User-to-system-event**. These sentences denote interactions of an actor that passes control to the system. This includes selecting menu options, pressing buttons or other such events.

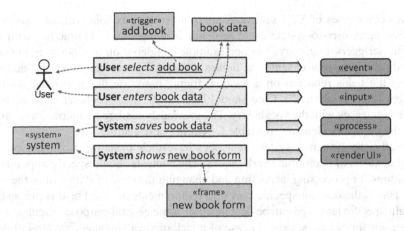

Fig. 1.17 SVO sentence semantics

2. **User-to-system-input**. These sentences denote passing data from the user to the system. These data are compliant with some domain element and its components (attributes).
3. **System-to-user**. These sentences denote presenting some message or data to the user. Most often, these data are rendered through some graphical user interface. These data can be read-only or editable in some part (subject to a further user-to-system-input sentence).
4. **System-to-system**. These sentences denote performing some processing related to specific domain elements that may include performing calculations, changing system state or retrieving persistent data.

The exact meaning of a specific SVO sentence depends on the actual vocabulary elements that are linked from this sentence. This is illustrated for system-to-user sentences in Fig. 1.18. This example shows the effect of executing "System shows new book form", having a specific definition of "new book form". This «frame» has an associated domain element ("book data") and a «trigger» ("save"). These two elements are rendered on the window frame as shown on the right.

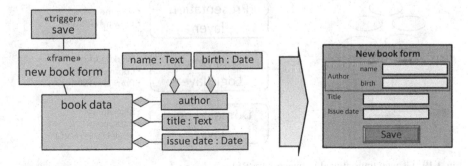

Fig. 1.18 Vocabulary element semantics

Two other types of SVO sentences are quite easy to explain without a separate illustration. A user-to-system-event sentence is a reaction to interacting with the specific «trigger» (e.g. "save" in our example) rendered on a window frame in a preceding system-to-user sentence. In turn, a user-to-system-input sentence denotes editing the fields rendered on a window frame, based on the associated domain element (e.g. "book data"). Care should be taken to assure coherence of user-to-system sentences with the vocabulary. The previously rendered window frame must have the necessary elements available for editing or triggering.

Finally, the system-to-system sentences have their meaning dependent on the actual contents of appropriate verb phases. The contents should specify appropriate algorithms for processing, accessing and changing the state of data within the system. This is the domain-specific part of a requirements model. For this purpose, a domain-specific language can be developed or some general-purpose language with known semantics can be used. In case of a lack of such language, we are left with specifying the domain logic algorithms informally and leave them out of the automatic transformation path. This is a very broad topic of domain-specific languages and is out of the scope of this book. However, all the techniques for defining software modelling languages that we describe can be used also for such domain-specific languages.

1.3.2 Requirements Explained Through Translation into Java

So far, we have used elements observable by the user to explain the meaning of requirements models. Now let us get back to the idea of defining requirements semantics by offering equivalent 3GL (Java) code. This approach is fully formal and can be used directly to construct automatic transformation engines. In this introductory section we present the basics of the approach, and the details are given in Chap. 4.

The first step is to define the translational framework, illustrated in Fig. 1.19. The translational framework assumes a certain code structure to which the requirements

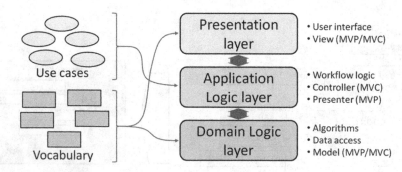

Fig. 1.19 General translational framework for RSL

models are translated. Here we choose a standard three-layered architecture consisting of Presentation, Application Logic and Domain Logic. This division is equivalent to the architectural patterns of Model-View-Controller (MVC), Model-View-Presenter (MVP), etc. This approach was earlier informally introduced in Sect. 1.1. The presentation layer is responsible for accepting and presenting data to the user. The application logic layer contains code that pertains to the workflow of the application which includes different flows of user-system interaction. The domain logic contains code that does the actual data processing (algorithms) and accesses persistent data.

Figure 1.19 shows that use cases with their scenarios are translated mostly into the code within the application logic layer. This is obvious in the face of what we have already explained about the semantics of use cases. Use case scenarios can serve as good controllers of the application logic. In turn, the vocabulary requirements influence mostly the other two layers. This is also obvious from the previous descriptions of their semantics. The domain logic layer reflects the realisation of verb phases with the associated algorithms. These algorithms process data as defined by domain elements and their attributes. The presentation layer reflects the visualisation of the same data to the user. The data are shown within specific UI elements that are also defined in the vocabulary and relate to the domain elements.

Figure 1.19 provides an informal overview of the translation; more details are required. A summary of several formal translation rules is presented in Fig. 1.20. Here we use a UML class diagram to present the code structure. Moreover, the class operation methods are expanded to show their code (in this example—only one of the methods). The arrows with numbers show how RSL constructs are translated into code constructs.

1. Use cases are translated into classes of the Presenter (application logic) layer.
2. User-to-system-trigger sentences are translated into operations of the Presenter class translated from the current use case.

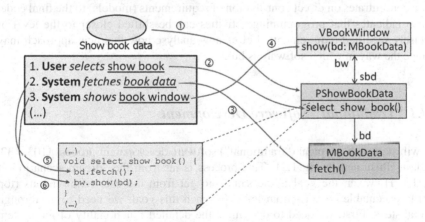

Fig. 1.20 Use case translational semantics

3. System-to-system sentences are translated into operations of the Model (domain logic) class associated with the given domain element.
4. System-to-user sentences are translated into operations of the View (presentation) class associated with the given UI element.
5. System-to-system sentences are translated into procedure calls referring to appropriate operations in the Model layer. These calls are generated within the method generated with rule 2.
6. Stem-to-user sentences are translated into procedure calls referring to appropriate operations in the View layer. These calls are generated within the method generated with rule 2.

Note that the presented translational framework uses simple programming constructs. It is not scalable for larger systems and was meant only for these introductory notes. Our rules were also not presented in full detail and precision. In the actual detailed presentation in Chap. 4, we use a more sophisticated framework, which will also contain more rules and consider various configurations of RSL scenario sentences and domain elements. However, even with the current simple introduction, we can see that the intuitions from Sect. 1.1 can be substituted with very specific translation rules.

1.4 Towards Model-Driven Requirements Engineering

All the elements presented in the previous sections lead to constructing a new approach to software engineering. We call this approach Model-Driven Requirements Engineering (MDRE) [15, 114–116], although perhaps it would be more apt to call it Requirements-Oriented Programming. The first name emphasises the way we specify requirements—through constructing requirements models. The second name concentrates on direct contribution of requirements (models) to the final code. It also indicates that programming activities can be shifted closer to the level of precisely specified requirements. Let us now analyse how this new approach may change the way in which software is built.

1.4.1 "Traditional" Software Development

We will start with a typical ("traditional") software development process [103, 132, 159], as illustrated in Fig. 1.21. This process is far from the "dream scenario" of Fig. 1.1. However, the goal is the same—to get from the user requirements (top left) to executable code (bottom left). To reach this goal, we need to go through several steps. First, we need to determine the detailed functionality of the system and describe the problem domain in terms of the data that need to be handled by the system. This forms the detailed software requirements. Having these details, we can

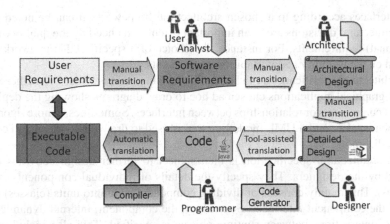

Fig. 1.21 Traditional software development

start design activities. We develop the high-level architectural specifications, and then determine the details of the individual components. This detailed design can then be implemented in 3GL code. Finally, we obtain the executables through compiling this code. This ends a typical path—user requirements to software requirements to architectural design to detailed design to 3GL code to executable code. The cycle can be repeated several times throughout a single project resulting in an iterative lifecycle. Of course, we have greatly simplified the lifecycle, leaving out important activities like quality assurance (testing) and deployment. Instead we concentrate on representing a gradual shift from artefacts at a high level of abstraction (user requirements) to those at the lowest level of abstraction (executable code).

This briefly sketched process involves various roles which use different techniques and tools to produce intermediate and final artefacts. Software requirements are normally created by analysts that cooperate with the users. This is usually a manual transition from less precise user requirements. Often, some elements of modelling are used, like use case diagrams to denote units of functional requirements and class diagrams to denote domain elements. However, most often such specifications rely on standard templates and natural language descriptions with some rigour in terms of the structure of use case descriptions. Moreover, it is not often that the vocabularies are made fully consistent with the functional specifications. The most frequently used tools to specify requirements are traditionally word processors. In many cases, this is supported by special-purpose CASE (Computer Aided Software Engineering) tools for requirements management [29, 30]. These tools can facilitate the management of requirements units, assigning attributes to requirements and tracing between user requirements and software requirements. To draw use case diagrams, another group of CASE tools is used—UML modelling tools [184].

The software requirements are taken by architects and turned into architectural specifications [40]. This is again traditionally a manual process. During this step, architects "inject" their knowledge on architectural frameworks and technological solutions. This knowledge turns use cases and domain elements into, e.g. components and interfaces according to a chosen architectural framework. It can be noted that the architectural decisions are to an important extent influenced by the quality (non-functional) requirements. For instance, the choice of a specific UI framework can depend on the usability and portability requirements.

Architectural specifications can be developed using various tools. Often, these are simple graphical applications chosen ad hoc to draw diagrams showing the deployment of components or relationships between interfaces. Sometimes, a more rigorous approach is taken and a UML modelling tool is used to draw deployment and component diagrams.

The architectural specification is then subject to further design activities performed by the designers. They specify the details of individual components (subsystems). This mainly consists of dividing component code into units (classes) that realise the component interfaces. Sometimes, the component, internal dynamics in terms of interactions between runtime objects is specified. This also includes the design of detailed algorithms for especially complex data processing code. Detailed design specifications are more and more often developed using UML CASE tools [129]. This is due to their capability of generating code skeletons from class models. Class diagrams are used for documentation purposes (as a visual "map of code") and thus their role becomes significant.

Designers are often the same people as the programmers. Thus, they often simultaneously design and program their components. This is obviously done using typical IDEs (Integrated Development Environments) [88] that contain code editors, compilers, debuggers and execution environments. The compilers form the final, most automated step in "traditional" software development. Sometimes, the IDEs are integrated with UML editors and generators. In this way, design models and code can be developed hand-in-hand, thus making code more visual and understandable.

1.4.2 Model-Driven Software Development

Typical software development can be seen as mainly a manual process. There exist some elements of code generation but we would certainly desire much more automation. This has changed with the advent of Model-Driven Software Development/Engineering (MDSD/E) [18, 25, 178]. Originally, the idea of MDSD was launched by the Object Management Group (OMG)[4] and called Model-Driven Architecture (MDA)[5] [56, 66, 92, 106, 111, 127, 167]. The underlying principle is that the intermediate artefacts in the software development process are models that are transformed to produce other, more detailed models. For example—generating the user interface models from higher-level domain model [73]. MDA introduces three basic levels at which models are produced.

---

[4] http://www.omg.org/.

[5] http://www.omg.org/mda/.

- *Computation-Independent Model (CIM).* "A computation-independent model is a view of a system from the computation-independent viewpoint. A CIM does not show details of the structure of systems. A CIM is sometimes called a domain model and a vocabulary that is familiar to the practitioners of the domain in question is used in its specification".
- *Platform-Independent Model (PIM).* "A platform-independent model is a view of a system from the platform-independent viewpoint. A PIM exhibits a specified degree of platform independence so as to be suitable for use with a number of different platforms of similar type".
- *Platform-Specific Model (PSM).* "A platform-specific model is a view of a system from the platform-specific viewpoint. A PSM combines the specifications in the PIM with the details that specify how that system uses a particular type of platform".

MDA in its specification is not precise as to what the exact boundaries are between these layers. This also pertains to defining what a "platform" is. The definition offered by the MDA Guide [111] is rather imprecise, although it gives some important hints. "A platform is a set of subsystems and technologies that provide a coherent set of functionality through interfaces and specified usage patterns, which any application supported by that platform can use without concern for the details of how the functionality provided by the platform is implemented". It can be argued that the division between platform-independent and platform-specific design is quite foreign to "traditional" software developers. Thus, the postulate to create an artefact that is "platform-independent" sounds somewhat artificial to them. This might be the reason that MDA did not really spread widely in software engineering (at least not as widely as it was initially expected and hoped for).

Nevertheless, the MDA approach introduces a fundamental concept of gradual and automated transition from models that are close to the problem domain to models that are close to the target code. This transition is made by means of model transformation, as illustrated in Fig. 1.22. The less detailed (general) models (e.g. at the PSM level) can be transformed to more detailed (specific) models (e.g. at the PIM level) by adding certain details inserted through the transformation. What is important is that these inserted additional details can be configured to some extent—the models can be marked with additional information. If several PSMs are the

Fig. 1.22 General model transformation scheme

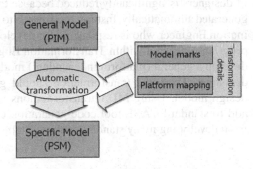

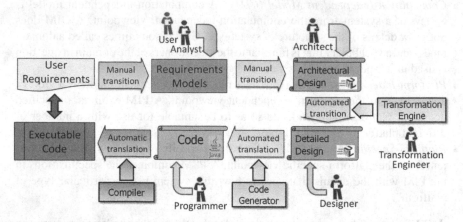

Fig. 1.23 Model-driven software development

potential targets of the transformation, it can be configured based on these markings. This configuration determines the kinds of mappings to the target platform elements that will be used in the transformation. In this way, models leading to code for different target platforms can be produced.

MDA transformations can be used in the software development process and thus form the MDSD lifecycle as shown in Fig. 1.23. We retain the same process structure as in Fig. 1.21. The MDA layers of CIM, PIM and PSM can be mapped onto Software Requirements, Architectural Design and Detailed Design respectively. This is not an exact mapping but such division into layers and phases is familiar to software developers not acquainted with MDA. In the MDSD approach, we concentrate on using models during all of these three main phases of software development. However, note that we have not introduced any automation in the transition from Requirements Models (cf. CIM) to Architectural Models (cf. PIM). Such transitions are not supported in industrial reality. Practically all of model transformation approaches concentrate on transitions from PIMs to PSMs. This means shifting between design-level models and not reaching as far back as the requirements models.

MDSD activities are performed by Architects and Designers. However, the role of designers is significantly reduced because the design models are to a large extent generated automatically. Instead, there needs to be introduced the role of the Transformation Engineer who is responsible for developing and maintaining transformation programs executed within Transformation Engines. The role of the Architects is to develop a general (platform independent) model and mark it with platform-specific decisions. Then, the transformation should generate a platform-specific detailed design model. Using MDA transformations we can also generate code. This can add to standard CASE tool code generation capabilities and relieve Programmers from developing many standard and repeatable code fragments.

MDSD can be practiced using various tooling environments. The most popular are probably the various model transformation engines embedded into UML modelling environments. Being the most widely used modelling language, UML is the obvious choice for developing models also in the MDSD process. Thus, UML tool producers have developed various model transformation modules. They introduce model transformation languages usually specific to a given tool. Moreover, there can be found several model transformation environments that are based on standardised model transformation languages [38]. These environments are external to modelling tools but interface with their model repositories [168]. We discuss this in detail in Chap. 5.

When discussing the applicability of MDSD in practice, we can compare Fig. 1.23 with Fig. 1.21. The complexity of both processes is similar or one may even infer that MDSD is in fact more laborious. This impression can be argued as incorrect [112, 113] but it may be one of the reasons for the limited success of typical MDSD approaches. MDSD would need to remove some phases in software development in order for software developers to see the real benefits. This necessitates much more automation and transformations coming right from requirements.

1.4.3 Software Development with DSLs and Model-Driven Requirements

To shorten the path from requirements to code, we can try to remove or simplify some of the phases. This is usually done when agile methodologies are applied. Often, the detailed requirements are simplified to informal user stories combined with sketched domain models as the exact requirements are worked out during an iterative development process when the actual system is examined by the users. Moreover, the design activities are also reduced and most of the design decisions are made directly during coding. The great advantage is that we result with a system that is developed precisely according to what the user needs—this is verified on-the-go in very short validation cycles. However, this approach certainly influences scalability and maintainability of systems. Further maintenance and extensions are compromised due to lack of proper documentation and diagrams showing the code structure and "how it works".

Software developers consider detailed requirements and design documentation as overhead. Writing code directly contributes to the final effect, while writing models does not. However, it is obvious that for large systems to be maintainable, we need design documentation. The model-driven approach brings a solution to this dilemma, where the design models become first-class artefacts and not overhead. Developing a model pays off through automatic transformation down to code. But, we would like to have even more: to be able to construct a single model at a high level of abstraction (as close to requirements as possible) and translate it directly into code.

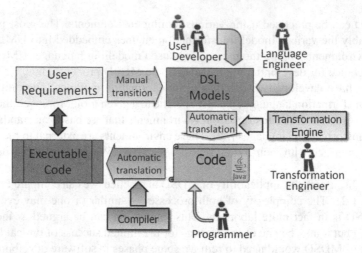

Fig. 1.24 DSL-based software development

The desire to shorten the software development path is reflected in the idea of Domain-Specific Languages (DSL) [36, 54, 89]. Such languages allow us to create models that are specific to a given problem domain and quickly transform into working code. This significantly reduces the number of steps in the process, as illustrated in Fig. 1.24. We no longer need architects and designers, instead, we have only the Developer role that cooperates with the User to produce DSL models. Also, the role of 3GL programmers is significantly reduced or even not needed as most or all of the target code is generated automatically through the transformation engine.

In the DSL-driven process, two additional roles are important. This is the Transformation Engineer and the Language Engineer. We have already discussed the first. The second role is necessary to develop and maintain the language in which the users and developers create their domain-specific models. This is crucial because the language has to be expressive and understandable but also formally precise (cf. language semantics). Such languages are distinct for specific problem domains and develop together with these domains. Moreover, they usually combine elements of domain logic and application logic. A specific DSL may be created for only a single system, and within the domain of a single business organisation.

The greatest advantage of the DSL approach is that in the realm of a suitable problem domain, significant productivity gains can occur [62]. This is mainly achieved when a family of similar systems is needed (e.g. for different clients), leading to the idea of Software Product Lines (SPL) [60, 131, 138, 171]. A fast process to generate similar (variable) systems can be established through defining similar source models based on a DSL. For isolated systems, productivity gains are not very impressive as additional effort is needed to develop a DSL (Language Engineer) and then to develop model transformations to the target platform (Transformation Engineer). This effort pays off significantly only when several similar systems using the same DSL and transformation are developed. To develop a DSL and associated transformations is also a significant investment which forms a barrier for using this approach.

For the above reasons, it would be beneficial if we had a general-purpose (unified) language that would be able to substitute the plethora od domain-specific ones. This language could be used in a wide range of domains and for various application types. Moreover, we could develop many transformation variants for different target platforms. These transformations could be reused many times and thus a unit cost of their development could be spread among many projects throughout many business organisations. This idea finally brings us to Model-Driven Requirements Engineering. In this approach, we want to develop models in a unified Requirements Specification Language and transform them directly to code.

Figure 1.25 illustrates this kind of process. It is similar to the previous one, driven by DSLs. This time RSL is the source language for automatic transformations. Moreover, the Language Engineer is not needed because RSL is a unified language and is maintained across many projects and many organisations. The main consequence of using RSL is that not all the code is generated from requirements models. This is due to lack of constructs to express the domain logic (data processing). In DSLs, these constructs were developed as part of a specific language. As a result, three possible scenarios for data processing formulation are possible: (1) it is coded directly in 3GL; (2) it is expressed using a DSL integrated with RSL; (3) it is formulated in an RSL algorithmic extension (which necessitates additional research). These three scenarios are discussed in detail in Chap. 7. In this book, we mostly concentrate on the first one, where the generated code is clearly marked with places where data processing code should be supplied by 3GL programmers. The marking can be performed using detailed design models showing the map of necessary updates. This means a compromise between full code generation, limited

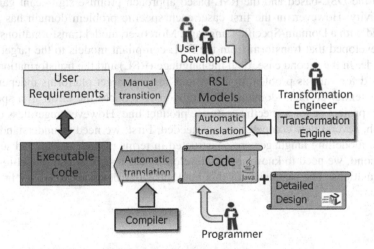

Fig. 1.25 Model-driven requirements software development

Fig. 1.26 RSL to code
transformation scheme

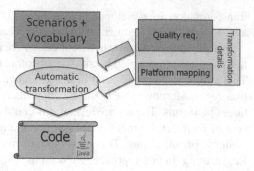

to specific domains (DSLs) and universality of approach with a more sophisticated
process (standard MDSD).

Technically, an RSL-based MDRE transformation can be implemented as a typical MDA transformation according to Fig. 1.22. The big shift however is that the
transformation source is equivalent to a CIM. A PSM together with working code is
thus generated directly from the CIM. This was not even present in the DSL-based
approach where the source models expressed in a DSL should be placed somewhere
between a CIM and a PIM (they are predominantly too technical to call them "requirements"). Instead of model marking and platform mapping, the transformation can
be controlled with quality requirements models as indicated in Fig. 1.26. This is an
important characteristic of this transformation. The architectural and detailed design
decisions pertaining to the target platform are embedded in the transformation and
marked through the values of quality metrics. For instance, a different target platform
may be chosen by the transformation if a mobile interface is required and a different
one for a web-based interface.

Both the DSL-based and the RSL-based approach promise significant gains in
productivity. However, in the first case, each specific problem domain has to be
equipped with a Domain-Specific Language. Moreover, model transformations have
to be developed that transform from the DSL-compliant models to the target platform code. In the second case, both the language (RSL) and the transformations are
developed for various problem domains and various target platforms independent
of the potential problem domains. This obviously reduces the effort in a specific
software project or for a specific software product line. However, regardless of the
approach, several new competences are needed. First, we need to understand how
software modelling languages are constructed in terms of their syntax and semantics. Second, we need to know how to develop model-to-model and model-to-code
transformations. The remainder of this book provides detailed guidelines in these
two areas.

Chapter 2
Presenting the Requirements Specification Language

The key to any modelling activity is a modelling language. For a model-driven approach that involves model transformations, we need to define this language precisely. Here, we present such language specific for requirements modelling, called the Requirements Specification Language (RSL). In the previous chapter, we have given some glimpses of its syntax and semantics and in this chapter we present it in detail.

2.1 How to Define a Modelling Language?

For a language definition to be complete, it should consist of three parts: (1) the abstract syntax, (2) the concrete syntax and (3) the semantics. The abstract syntax specifies the possible language constructs and their correct arrangements and thus determines the language grammar. Note that the grammars for visual modelling languages have to be defined differently from the grammars for natural languages or programming languages. Generally, models are graphs and they need to be defined as such. A model normally consists of model nodes (e.g. classes in a UML class diagram) and model edges (e.g. associations between classes) that can be arranged spatially in various ways. Thus, a modelling language grammar is graph-based and determines a possible arrangement of nodes, connected through edges. Compared with grammars for typical textual languages (e.g. context-free grammars), in this case, the language constructs (lexemes, e.g. keywords, identifiers) are arranged linearly (in a sequence). The grammars for such languages determine the possible linear sequences of these elements.

The abstract syntax of a modelling language defines all the possible graphs that would form correct models in this language. It is called abstract as it abstracts away the visible (graphical, textual) elements of the language. Using the abstract syntax we could build the persistent storage (repository) for models but not necessarily their editors for which, we need the concrete syntax. This part of a language definition defines the language constructs in terms of their visual appearance.

© Springer International Publishing Switzerland 2015
M. Śmiałek and W. Nowakowski, *From Requirements to Java in a Snap*,
DOI 10.1007/978-3-319-12838-2_2

- For graphical language elements, the concrete syntax defines arrangements of boxes, lines and other graphical shapes that are visible to the language user. For instance, the concrete syntax for classes in UML is a rectangle with a textual name inside.
- For textual language elements, the concrete syntax defines arrangements of textual units (lexemes) that form larger structures (sentences, expressions, etc.). For instance, the concrete syntax for class attributes in UML is a sequence consisting of a visibility marking, an attribute name, a colon and an attribute type (e.g. "- name : String").

The difference between abstract and concrete representation is illustrated in Fig. 2.1. It shows a typical class diagram in its concrete form (see right), containing two classes (one with an attribute) and an association between them. The same model is presented in an abstract form through a UML object diagram (see left).[1] The abstract version shows the possible arrangement (connections) between elements and their information contents, and is suitable for data storage. The concrete version is suitable for rendering it to users through, e.g. an editor.

In this chapter, we concentrate on presenting the RSL concrete syntax. We give examples of various language constructs as seen by its users. We also present the abstract syntax of RSL models, but only informally, through examples of possible RSL element arrangements. The formal definition of the abstract syntax is discussed in the next chapter.

For many of the RSL elements we also explain their semantics (meaning). As indicated earlier, this can be done in different ways. At this initial stage, we do this rather informally. Having a requirements language to explain, we concentrate on presenting how the system should behave or how it should look for its users. We can call this the "observational semantics". For requirements engineers, this is the most fundamental element in a requirements language. They need to assure that their specifications will mean to everyone precisely what they want to express in terms of the desired observable system behaviour. For instance, it has to be clear how use case

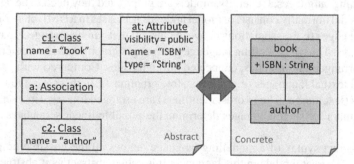

Fig. 2.1 Abstract versus concrete model

---

[1] This object diagram is a simplification for illustrative purposes. The official definition of UML would necessitate a slightly more complex arrangement of objects.

scenarios and domain elements translate into sequences of user interface forms and data presented in these forms. In Chap. 4 we introduce the formal way of defining semantics by translating RSL constructs into well-understood Java constructs.

When presenting RSL, we show examples of the various RSL constructs. For the examples to be consistent and comprehensible, we use the library domain, which should be familiar to all readers. We assume a simple Library Management System that consists of functionalities like catalogue management, reader management and loan management. The system handles the library collection and the reader data. It also records loans. We want the system to work in a web environment and have typical application logic with menus and forms.

This simple library system is presented in small fragments throughout this chapter to Chap. 4. It is not meant to form a complete case study, instead, we offer a full summary example in Chap. 8. The reader can refer to this example when studying the consecutive RSL constructs and their semantics.

2.2 Structuring Requirements Specifications

Any rigorously written requirements specification has to conform to certain rules. Often, these rules are codified through requirements document templates. In the modelling world, an equivalent of a document template is a model structure template. Having a well-structured model we should be able to easily move around it. The model organisation is usually done within well-familiar tree browsers. If necessary (and it most often is), the model can be turned into a linear document for documentation and legal purposes. Many modelling tools allow for quick generation of documents and thus working on models does not conflict with typical habits of average business readers.

Analysis of typical requirements specification templates shows that they generally concentrate on two main issues: (1) how to determine and specify requirements units and (2) how to group and classify requirements units. Compliance with such a template can be assured using minimum tooling with only a word processor in place. However, quality of requirements specifications does not only consist in compliance with the templates. An important aspect is that of coherence, which is usually assured through maintaining relationships between requirements units. The most effective way to assure coherence is to use specialised requirements management tools or general-purpose modelling tools as it is difficult to trace relationships between requirements using only a linear word processor. We need mechanisms to visualise the links and to trace them. Also, keeping coherence using even specialised tools is laborious, as the links need to be maintained and analysed manually.

RSL goes beyond the above typical approach to assure the requirements quality. Unlike for most typical requirements modelling approaches, it introduces a mechanism to assure coherence of requirements automatically by introducing a central domain vocabulary. Unlike for manually maintained links between requirements units, the vocabulary is created and attached automatically. For this reason, RSL models distinguish between requirements specifications and domain specifications in a precise way.

2.2.1 Basic Concepts

Any RSL model consists of two distinct parts: a requirements specification and a domain specification. Requirements specifications can be composed of requirements packages and domain specifications—of domain element packages. The notation is similar to that found in UML and uses familiar folder icons. Figure 2.2 presents the specifics of this notation. The icon for a requirements specification is adorned with a thick line on the left side (a), and the icon for a requirements package—with a double line (b). The domain specification has an additional rectangle inside the icon (c) and the domain elements package is denoted with a plain folder icon (d). Obviously, each of the packaging elements has its name placed inside or near the package icon.

Packages can contain other packages of the same type and thus form a tree structure. The leaves of the tree are the requirements and domain elements. Requirements can be placed only inside requirements packages while domain elements can be placed only in domain element packages. The notation for generic requirements shown in Fig. 2.2e is a rectangle with a double line on the left side. Requirements have

Fig. 2.2 Notation for
a requirements specifications,
b requirements packages,
c domain specifications,
d domain packages,
e requirements,
f use cases, **g** domain
elements and **h** actors

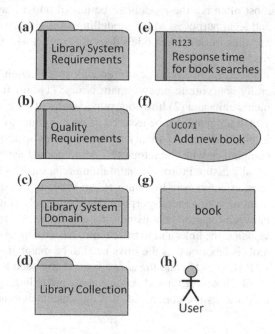

short names and can have identifiers. The most important special type of requirements are use cases. Their notation is taken from UML and use familiar oval icons
(Fig. 2.2f). Also, similar to that in UML is the notation for domain elements. The
rectangles with names (Fig. 2.2g) resemble UML classes. A special kind of domain
elements are actors (Fig. 2.2h) whose notation is also taken from UML.

In RSL, requirements "as such" have just short names and identifiers and
their purpose is to divide the specifications into distinguishable units suitable
for handling. For project management, they can be additionally adorned with
attributes. Attributes are name–value pairs that specify project-specific information. For instance, they can specify who is responsible for a particular requirement
(responsible = "John"), what is the version (version = 5) or what is the importance
(importance = HIGH)? Attributes can be placed inside notes attached to requirements icons, as illustrated in Fig. 2.3 (see left). The requirements attributes do not
have any effect on the target system code. In this book we will not go into the details
of this aspect of RSL.

Requirements "as such" with their attributes are good for dividing work and managing projects. However, we need to specify the details. This is done within detailed
specifications of requirements which in RSL are called "requirement representations". The basic form of requirements representation is simply a piece of natural
language text attached to the given requirement. Figure 2.3 (see right) gives a couple
of examples—one for a quality requirement and another for a functional requirement
(use case). Note that also domain elements can have their representations.

So far, the basic constructs of RSL seem standard allowing for specifying typical
text-based requirements specifications with some graphical elements. The specificity
of RSL begins at the level of requirements representations. The language offers constructs which provide much more precision than the natural language. The first step
towards precision constitute the so-called "natural language hypertext" representations. The relevant syntax is illustrated in Fig. 2.4 using an example of a use case
textual representation.

Note that the illustrated representation contains hyperlinks to domain elements.
This includes an actor ("User"), a business domain element ("book") and a system

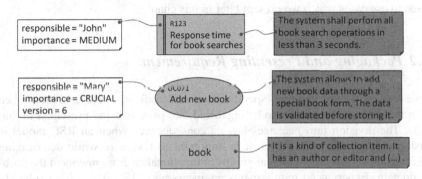

Fig. 2.3 Requirements, their representations and attributes

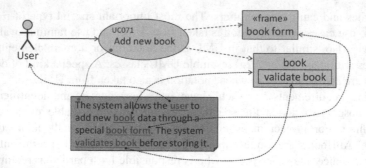

Fig. 2.4 Relationships at the requirements level versus hyperlinks in requirements representations

domain element ("book form"). Moreover, one of the hyperlinks points to a verb phrase ("validate book"). To make text consistent with the domain model (because of using the specific verb phrase), it had to be changed slightly in comparison to that in Fig. 2.3. However, it still retains the characteristics of unconstrained natural language.

The hyperlinks to domain elements contained in a requirement representation can be reflected also in a diagram at the requirements level. In Fig. 2.4, the hyperlink to the actor has its counterpart in the actor-to-use case relationship (a solid line arrow). Similarly, the hyperlinks to domain elements and phrases can be summarised through relationships between the given requirement (here: the use case) and domain elements (a dashed arrow).

The hyperlinks make requirements specification more coherent through consistent use of domain terminology. This is similar to structuring hyperlink-based knowledge bases like wiki dictionaries or the Wikipedia. This feature of RSL can be easily introduced into its editor environments. However, hypertext still does not offer enough precision. We cannot apply techniques of model transformation on natural language text even when it is adorned with some hyperlinks. For this reason, RSL introduces requirements representations with strictly controlled grammar. In addition to structured text, they also include graph-based notations. These representations are mainly related to use cases which we present later in this chapter.

2.2.2 Packaging and Presenting Requirements

As we can see, the requirements specifications in RSL form a coherent, interlinked structure. This structure needs to be organised into packages and presented in diagrams. The division into packages has its consequences when an RSL model is transformed down to code. Thus, it is important to take care while determining packages that should reflect logical groups of functionality or fragments of the problem domain. Experienced requirements engineers have their worked-out rules. In a traditional setting, the task of structuring a requirements specification is done through determining document chapters and sections and this is captured in document templates. In RSL this is very similar but chapters and sections are substituted by a hierarchy of packages. As we have already seen, the fundamental division between requirements and domain elements is made at the level of language definition. Thus, the two top level elements of the hierarchy are the requirements specification and the domain specification. Underneath these two major specification-level packages, the requirements specifiers are free to define their own package structure.

Here, we present simple rules that assure good structuring of the model, necessary for future model transformations. Of course, this structuring is meant not only for facilitating MDRE but follows the best practices for structuring requirements specifications as such. An example of our library system is shown in Fig. 2.5. The requirements specification package ("Library System Requirements") is divided into "Vision" and "Software Requirements". The vision part is not meant for model transformation as it contains only generic requirements with natural language representations. It contains generally formulated features of the system, describing its overall functionality and quality characteristics. The details of how these features should be included in the target system are provided by detailed software requirements.

Following the typical classification of requirements we can divide software requirements into two packages: "Functional Requirements" and "Quality Requirements" (also called: non-functional requirements). The functional requirements package contains all the use cases that define individual units of functionality as seen by the outside actors (users). This functionality is usually complex and needs further division into sub-packages. In case of our library system we decided to introduce three packages of functionality (see again Fig. 2.5): "Catalogue Management", "Reader Management" and "Loan Management". This division can be done using various criteria. Here, we have concentrated on identifying crisp areas of application logic centering around the management of certain types of data. Other methods might

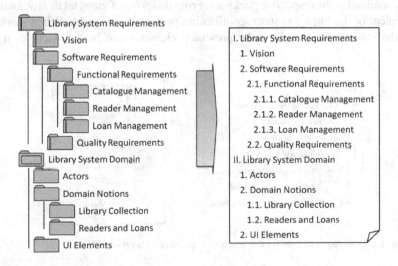

Fig. 2.5 Typical division into packages in a requirements model

concentrate on division from the point of view of actors (user types) or menus in the user interface. Each of the packages in our example do not contain more than 7–10 use cases and this is seen as a general rule-of-thumb. Packages containing more they 10–15 elements tend to become less manageable and understandable.

The quality requirements package contains all the aspects of a system that define the criteria to evaluate the way it operates, but not its functionality (application logic or domain logic). These requirements are important from the point of view of the requirements model transformation as they influence the quality characteristics of the target code. Such requirements can be further divided into more detailed classes. A good way to approach this is to use a standard like the ISO 9126 [74] or ISO 25010 [76]. According to ISO 9126, quality requirements are divided into Functionality (not to be confused with functional requirements), Reliability, Usability, Efficiency, Maintainability and Portability. A similar classification is offered by the FURPS model (Functionality, Usability, Reliability, Performance, Supportability). As in packages containing use cases, quality requirements can be placed in packages under the main Quality Requirements package. For brevity, this is not shown in Fig. 2.5.

The second part of every RSL specification is the domain model. For our example system, this model was called the "Library System Domain". Every such model should be divided into three main packages: "Actors", "Domain Notions", and "UI Elements"; the names indicate clearly the purpose. The Actors package is distinct in that it can only contain actors. The other packages can contain domain elements of various kinds which are introduced later in this chapter. They can be further divided into sub-packages as illustrated in Fig. 2.5.

With a well thought-over model structure we can easily transform an RSL model into a linear document. As shown in Fig. 2.5, the package hierarchy is a good basis for structuring the chapter and section headings in the document. The contents are filled with diagrams, requirement representations and domain element representations contained in the respective packages. From this point of view, let us now analyse a fragment of the library system specification presented in Fig. 2.6. When working with the specification, each of the presented elements can be accessed from the

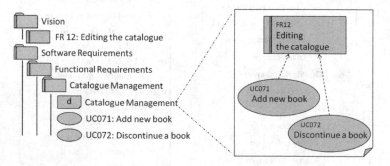

Fig. 2.6 Example requirements specification with requirements relationships

project tree. Moreover, the individual requirement representations can be accessed and traversed by following the various links between requirements and hyperlinks contained within their text. When some version of the model is ready, it can be "frozen" and transformed into a document that can serve legal or other purposes.

Relationships between requirements, seen in Fig. 2.6 are not yet introduced. In Fig. 2.4 we have seen relationships at the requirements level but they connected requirements with domain elements. Here, we notice that requirements can also refer to each other. In our example, two use cases trace back to a vision-level requirement and two other use cases "operationalise" a quality requirement. Such relationships can be visualised in generic requirements diagrams as in Fig. 2.6.

2.3 Specifying the Problem Domains and Their Rules

As indicated in Chap. 1, the key to assuring coherence of requirements is to define their domain with precision. We need to express all the relevant domain vocabulary elements and relationships between them. This should form a model that expresses the "map" (some might say: an ontology) of the reality of the problem domain and of the application that is supposed to support this problem domain. Moreover, it is important that we can easily refer to these coherently related domain elements from within the functional and quality requirements.

For requirements on software, the domain consists of two connected areas: (1) the problem (business) domain and (2) the application domain. This distinction is important, because the problem domain is independent of the actual application to be built. It should have the same properties regardless of the characteristics of various systems that support it. The problem domain is stable, and it changes along with the changes of the reality. The application domain can (and should) be quite dynamic and changes whenever new ideas emerge regarding the properties of the applications.

In RSL, the problem domain consists of domain notions (e.g. "book", "publisher") that can have attributes (e.g. "title", "name"). This is similar to other notations that can serve domain modelling (e.g. UML class models). However, RSL introduces other important elements like verb phrases and data views. Moreover, attributes are treated in RSL as distinct from notions and can be referred to by other elements. This is important for defining the application domain which—in RSL—is composed of UI elements which can present values of individual attributes and a specific combination of such values. Thus, we need ways to organise attributes not only from the point of view of concrete domain notions but also their arrangements within the UI. In this section, we present these various elements of RSL's domain specification.

2.3.1 Defining the Problem Domain

The problem domain is the actual reality that the software system supports and/or reflects. The examples in this section pertain to the library business domain and show the suitability of RSL to define all kinds of business domains. However, we can also define the problem domains for physical phenomena (e.g. the physics of airplanes) or social relationships (e.g. family life). Regardless of the domain, we need to specify a set of related concepts and the possible ways to view and process data related to these concepts. This constitutes the so-called *domain logic* (or *business logic*) of the system to be built.

The basic element of the domain model expressed in RSL is thus a **Concept**. Its notation is simple and resembles that of a UML class. Figure 2.7 shows variants of the Concept's notation (see left). It is a rectangle with a name and the "Concept" tag or the «concept» stereotype.[2] Concepts can also have no tag. The second type of domain elements is **Attributes**. They are denoted with the "Attribute" tag or stereotype (see Fig. 2.7—centre). Attributes can hold elementary data and thus their notation includes additional information about the data type (included in brackets). The data types are not limited by RSL but have to be specified in advance when a transformation from RSL is planned. In our examples we use the following set of data types:

- "text"—string of text;
- "whole number"—an integer number (negative or positive);
- "real number"—any number with a possible decimal;
- "true/false"—a boolean value;
- "date"—a value containing date and/or time;
- "secret text"—encrypted string of text.

Depending on the problem domain, this basic set of data types can be extended with, e.g. sound, graphics and binary data. Of course, for any new data type to be used for code generation, the semantics during runtime have to be defined, as explained in Chap. 4. Also note that attributes are not graphically contained in Concepts, in contrast to how it is done in UML. This has to do with the third type of domain elements—**Data views**.

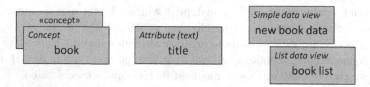

Fig. 2.7 Domain notion types

---

[2] In future examples we will use the tag notation.

Data views are denoted with two types of tags/stereotypes: "Simple data view" and "List data view" (see Fig. 2.7—right). They do not contain attributes but can refer to attributes contained in different concepts thus allowing to present attributes in various configurations. Simple data views serve presenting single instances of combined attributes. List data views, as expected, can present lists, containing many such instances. The exact meaning of data views is explained in further examples below.

The above three types of domain elements should be connected through appropriate relationships as illustrated in Fig. 2.8. The most obvious relationship is the association between concepts. RSL allows for any two concepts to be associated, and the concrete notation of associations is similar to that in UML. Associations can have multiplicities, with notation also taken from UML. In the example in Fig. 2.8 we can see two associations with appropriate multiplicities. The concept 'book' is associated with two other concepts—'author' and 'publisher'. The book should have at least one author and can have many authors ('1..*'). On the other hand, it should have exactly one publisher ('1'). Both the publishers and the authors can be associated with any number of books ('*').

The second type of relationship is containment of attributes within concepts. Its notation is taken from UML's aggregations, where the diamond is placed on the side of the concept (the 'whole' containing the attribute). In the example in Fig. 2.8, the 'book' contains the 'title'. This example also explains why the attributes are graphically placed outside of concepts. This is associated with the attribute relationships with data views. These relationships are denoted with arrows pointing always from the data views to the attributes. Note that the relationships to attributes can have multiplicities on the attribute side. Usually, this multiplicity is '1' but sometimes it might be necessary to indicate that more than one attribute of some type is contained in a concept or referred to from a data view.

A more elaborate (although still quite simple) example of relationships for attributes is presented in Fig. 2.9. From the conceptual point of view, the problem domain consists of three concepts: 'book', 'author' and 'publisher'. These concepts are explained in detail through the attributes they contain. For instance, the 'book' concept is composed of the 'title', the 'issue date', the 'number of pages' and contains information whether it has 'hard cover'. This conceptual model of the domain can be viewed from different perspectives. Different applications (software systems) can view different attributes in different settings and through different user interfaces.

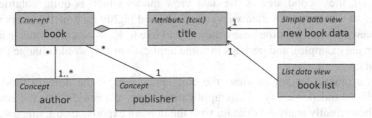

Fig. 2.8 Domain notion relationships

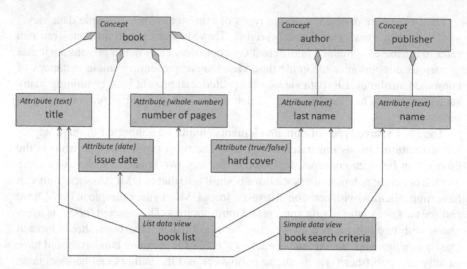

Fig. 2.9 Concepts, their attributes and data views

This can be represented by the data views. They can point to attributes taken from different (but related) concepts and group them together. In other words, a data view groups several attributes under one name that can be used to describe the application logic.

In our example in Fig. 2.9, we have two data views that can be used, e.g. in some user interface that searches through and presents lists of books. The 'book search criteria' view groups three attributes ('title', 'last name' and 'name') that are contained in the three presented concepts. Although the attributes are part of different concepts, from the perspective of the user interface they can be presented together as a single entity. The same situation is for the 'book list' data view. This time it groups four attributes from two different concepts. These attributes can—for instance—form columns in a table listing several books. The specific table will contain four columns associated with the four attributes.

The presented example illustrates the two distinct areas that define the problem domain. One area defines the stable conceptual model. It is unlikely that the presented concepts ('book', 'author', 'publisher'), their relationships and attributes will change. They are tightly associated with how the outside world (reality) is structured. On the other hand, the second area is the data view model which is quite volatile. The attributes to which various data views point depend highly on how the users would like to view the data. In some cases, they would like to view four attributes in a book list (as in the example), and perhaps in some applications this would change to show more data.

From a practical point of view, the conceptual part of the domain model can be developed independently of any application logic. We can discuss the concepts within the currently analysed domain with the domain experts, abstracting away any software systems. For the data view part, we need to consider the application logic. Thus, in practise, the data views emerge along writing the functional requirements—the use case scenarios. This is discussed in detail in Sect. 2.4.

2.3.2 Defining the Application Domain

In most software applications, the problem domain is presented through the User Interface. The UI elements thus form the application domain. Through these UI elements, the *application!logic* is expressed to the users (in general—to the objects outside of the software system). The application logic is tightly related to the domain logic. For this reason, the UI elements have to be related to domain elements.

RSL offers four types of UI elements, as illustrated in Fig. 2.10. Three of them are associated with presenting and handling data, and one is related to handling various interactions from the user. The most comprehensive of the UI elements is the **Screen**. These elements can be presented to the users, who can interact with them. They can contain various data elements and can also serve updating these data elements. Screens can represent various elements in the actual user interface like data forms, list windows or media presentation windows. Screens do not specify the way data are to be communicated to the users. This can be in the form of a graphical user interface or using other methods (e.g. actuators in building/factory automation, printers, light and sound devices and so on).

Screens can contain another type of UI elements—**Triggers**. Triggers are associated with interactions of the user with the system. The most obvious kind of triggers represent buttons in graphical user interfaces. However, they can represent all the elements that the user can interact with like menu items, editable fields, physical buttons or sensors in automation systems. Whenever a trigger is accessed, some application logic—controlled by the software system—is executed. A typical Screen can contain several Triggers that determine various paths through the application logic, depending on the choices of the user.

Fig. 2.10 UI element types

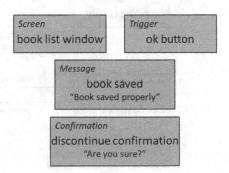

In addition to Screens, RSL offers two other types of presentation elements — ***Messages*** and ***Confirmations***. These elements are included for convenience purposes as their functionality could be realised with Screens and Triggers. These two elements offer simple functionality for presenting information and accepting decisions from the user. The Message element by default has only one option to choose (equivalent to a single associated Trigger, like the 'OK' button) while the Confirmation has more possible options (like 'Yes' and 'No' buttons). In both cases, we can specify the message text as part of the element definition, as shown in Fig. 2.10.

Screens and Triggers should be associated with the problem domain elements. This is done through arrow relationships, as presented in Fig. 2.11. In general, any Screen can relate to one or more Data views (simple or list). There are two kinds of relationships between Screens and Data views. The «present» relationship (arrow pointing towards the Data view) means that a given view (i.e. the grouped attributes) is shown within the given Screen for viewing by the user. This consist in rendering appropriate screen elements to hold the data and showing the actual data values (as retrieved from the system's storage). The «update» relationship (arrow pointing towards the Screen) means that the given view is shown to the user for editing individual values of the grouped attributes and eventually—updating the system's storage. This also means rendering appropriate screen elements but leaving them blank for editing. It is also possible to have both relationships between the same Screen and Data view. In such cases, the system presents the actual retrieved data values of the attributes and at the same time makes them available for editing.

The example in Fig. 2.11 presents two Screens that can handle attributes contained in the associated Data views. The 'book list window' screen can present attributes

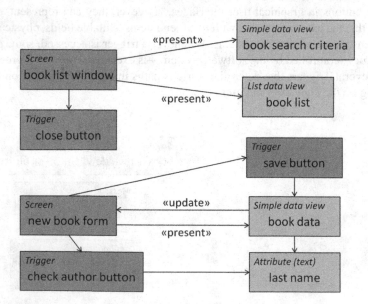

Fig. 2.11 Relations between UI elements and data views

grouped into two data views—'book search criteria' and 'book list'. To determine exactly what data is to be presented within the screen, we can refer to Fig. 2.9. Namely, the screen will show the values of the three attributes grouped by the 'book search criteria' and will contain a list with four columns indicated by the attributes grouped by the 'book list'. The same situation is for the 'new book form' screen. This screen presents the 'book data' view that was not yet introduced (not present in Fig. 2.9) but we can assume that it includes all the attributes found in Fig. 2.9.

Note that the data in the 'book list window' screen is only shown and is not available for editing. If, for example, we would like to change this and allow editing of the 'book search criteria'—we would need to add an «update» relationship. This editing capability is available for 'book data' in the 'new book form'. What is important to observe is that editable data should be associated with triggers. This is because editing causes data to be updated in the system's storage and this update has to be somehow triggered. In Fig. 2.11 we can see one trigger associated with the 'book list window' and two triggers—with the 'new book form'. The RSL notation is simple—triggers are pointed at by arrows coming from screens.

To indicate data that need to be updated when a trigger is evoked, it can point to a data view or to an attribute. In our example, the 'save button' points to 'book data'. This means that pressing this button causes 'book data' to be transferred from the relevant screen for further processing (and possibly—for storage). A similar situation is for the 'check author button'. However, this trigger points only to a single attribute. The meaning is similar to when a whole data view is pointed at by the trigger. Only this time, the single data element is passed for processing.

The best way to explain the semantics of screens and triggers is to translate the RSL constructs into concrete UI elements. This is shown in Fig. 2.12. It shows two forms that are equivalent to the UI elements from Fig. 2.11. The upper form is the 'book list window'. It presents the 'book search criteria' (three attributes) and the 'book list' (four columns). Also, it contains the 'close' button. A similar situation is for the lower form, presenting the 'new book form'. Comparison with Figs. 2.9 and 2.11 shows how RSL constructs can be represented in a real system. It must be emphasised that RSL models are technology-independent and these technological details can be added during transformation into design models and code, as presented in further chapters. The actual type of the user interface (web-based, mobile, desktop, ...) can be determined through non-functional (quality) requirements and constraints.

2.3.3 Defining the Domain Rules

Concepts, data views and attributes define the structure of the problem and application domains. For the description to be complete, we need to define the domain rules. Here, by domain rules we mean the ways in which the data elements are processed. In RSL, this data processing is organised through verb phrases contained within domain elements as illustrated in Fig. 2.13.

Book list window

Book search criteria

Book title [   ]   Publisher name [   ]

Author last name [   ]

Book list

Last name	Title	Issue date	Number of pages

[Close]

New book form

Author last name [   ]   [Check author]

Publisher name [   ]

Title [   ]   Issue date [   ]

Number of pages [   ]   Hard cover ●

[Save]

Fig. 2.12 Semantics of UI elements with data views

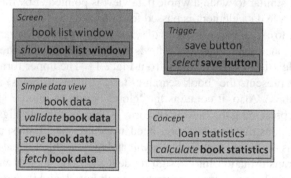

Fig. 2.13 Verb phases within domain elements

A verb phrase consists of a verb ("show", "validate", "calculate") and a noun (more precisely: a noun phrase). The noun reflects the actual domain element that contains the particular phrase. So, for instance, all the phrases with the noun "book data" are contained in the domain element 'book data'. Verb phrases to some extent resemble class operations in UML, the main difference is that the phrases have the defined verb-noun grammar and they have no parameters.

Verb phrases can be contained in most of the domain element types: Screens, Messages, Confirmations, Data views, Triggers and Concepts. There is no limitation as to which verbs and nouns can be used within verb phrases; however, certain standard verbs can be used to denote typical types of domain rules. This reflects typical actions within application and domain logic. The types of predefined actions depend on the types of domain elements. For Screens, we use three predefined actions: SHOW, CLOSE and REFRESH. Messages and Confirmations are limited and only the SHOW action has a defined meaning. Also, the triggers can contain only one type of predefined action: SELECT.

- SHOW—render a UI element in the user interface and (if relevant) present the data view attribute values. The following verbs can be used as keywords for the SHOW action: 'show', 'display', 'present'.
- CLOSE—remove the UI element from the user interface. The following verbs can be used as keywords for the CLOSE action: 'close', 'shut', 'remove'.
- REFRESH—presents updated values of the data view attributes associated with the given UI element. The following verbs can be used as keywords for the REFRESH action: 'refresh', 'renew', 'repaint', 'update'.
- SELECT—evoke some application logic associated with selecting a trigger. The following verbs can be used as keywords for the SELECT action: 'select', 'press', 'push', 'choose', 'click'.

A different set of predefined actions is available for the problem domain elements (Data views and Concepts). They include the popular CRUD operations (CREATE, READ, UPDATE, DELETE) and validation (VALIDATE). Note that these actions cover a vast majority of domain logic in typical business systems.

- CREATE—add new data items to the system's storage, containing values of the given domain element's attributes. The following verbs can be used as keywords for the CREATE action: 'create', 'save', 'add', 'write'.
- READ— retrieve values from data items in the system's storage, according to the definition of the given domain element's attributes. The following verbs can be used as keywords for the READ action: 'read', 'fetch', 'get', 'build', 'retrieve', 'search'.
- UPDATE—substitute data item values in the system's storage with new values, in accordance with the given domain element. The following verbs can be used as keywords for the UPDATE action: 'update', 'modify', 'edit', 'override'.
- DELETE—removes data items from the systems's storage, in accordance with the given domain element. The following verbs can be used as keywords for the DELETE action: 'delete', 'remove', 'destroy', 'erase'.
- VALIDATE—check the values of the given domain element's attributes according to specified validity rules. The following verbs can be used as keywords for the VALIDATE action: 'validate', 'verify', 'examine', 'inspect', 'check'.

Setting one of the above action types, or using one of the keywords has certain consequences for the meaning of a given verb phrase. This meaning is used by the code generation engine, as explained in Chap. 6. If the action type is not specified, the domain logic needs to be specified trough additional means. Namely, some data processing algorithm has to be given. In the current version of RSL, there are no facilities to specify such algorithms. In such situations, the verb phrases serve as

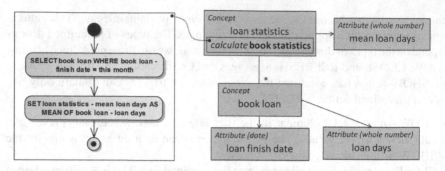

Fig. 2.14 Verb phrases having domain (business) rules

placeholders for specifying the algorithms externally. One possible solution is to use an existing Domain-Specific Language, or to develop one that is suitable for the given problem domain. All the techniques in this book pertaining to defining RSL can be used to define a suitable extension in the form of a DSL.

An elementary example of such an extension to RSL is given in Fig. 2.14. We can see an example activity-based notation for specifying algorithms that involve numerical calculations. In this particular case, a language is developed where one of its capabilities is to calculate mean values. This language uses specific notations to access and set the attribute values and each of the activity-based models is attached to a specific verb phrase.

2.4 Specifying Functional Requirements

Functional requirements in RSL are defined mostly through use case models. RSL's use cases are derived from UML but RSL introduces several new and changed features. There are important modifications made at the level of use cases as such and relationships between use cases and actors. These modifications are associated with ambiguous semantics of the use case model, as defined in the UML specification. RSL still maintains the overall semantics of use cases and actors but introduces much more precision. This precision, at the level of use case units, is realised through new relationships: «invoke», «use» and «participate».

The fundamental enhancement of RSL is that of use case representations (contents). RSL introduces a comprehensive language to model use case scenarios and links them to the domain model elements. This extended language is based on constrained natural language sentences that have strict and simple syntax complying with the syntax of verb phrases described in Sect. 2.3.3 and with the «invoke» relationship. Individual sentences are organised into scenarios and several scenarios form a use case.

Note that the RSL constructs for use cases allow to define the whole application logic of the considered software system. By application logic we mean the observable behaviour of the application as seen by its users (outside actors).

It covers all the user-system interactions through the user interface, system responses and actions of the system with results that affect its users. In this section, we present the detailed RSL constructs that allow specifying the application logic through detailed use case models.

2.4.1 Use Cases and Relationships

According to the definition provided in Sect. 1.2.2, use cases are pieces of observable functionality that lead to goals of some value to outside actors. This general definition is reflected in various RSL constructs. We start with the top level of use cases and their relationship with actors and between themselves. An example notation at this level is presented in Figs. 2.15 and 2.16.

Figure 2.15 illustrates two types of relationships between use cases and actors. The «use» relationship is denoted with an arrow pointing from an actor towards a use case. The «participate» relationship is denoted with an arrow pointing in the

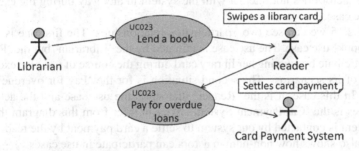

Fig. 2.15 Relationships between use cases and actors

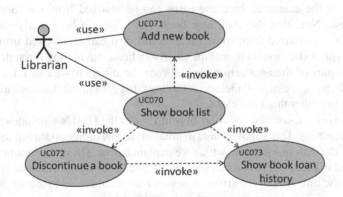

Fig. 2.16 Example use case diagram with use case relationships

opposite direction. We can also use an alternative notation without the arrows but with simple lines adorned with the above stereotypes.

The «use» relationship means that a particular actor initiates execution of a given use case (or: of its scenarios). This actor is also the one who wants to reach the final goal associated with the use case. The use cases that are in the «use» relationship with some actor are accessible from some central place in the user interface for that actor. Normally, in a graphical user interface, this is equivalent to choosing some option in the main menu. Thus, in our example in Figs. 2.15 and 2.16, the actor 'Librarian' will have three options available in the main menu: 'lend a book', 'add new book' and 'show book list'.

The «participate» relationship means that a particular actor is prompted and responds to the system during the actual execution of the use case scenarios. It is important to observe that this interaction has to occur before the use case goal is reached or—in general—before the use case execution terminates. It is a common mistake of inexperienced use case modellers to model a «participate» relationship in situations where the actor is informed about something already after the use case terminates. An example of such an error would be the situation where the use case execution ends with sending some SMS or email message to an actor. Here, the "participating" actor does not interact with the system in any way during the execution of this use case.

In Fig. 2.15 we can see two «participate» relationships. The first one is for the 'Lend a book' use case. The use case is initiated by the 'Librarian' but the 'Reader' has to participate by swiping her library card during the course of use case execution (in some of its scenarios). The second situation is for the 'Pay for overdue loans' use case. In this case, it is the 'Reader' that starts the use case and the actor that participates is the 'Car Payment System'. We can infer from this diagram that this other system is contacted by our system to settle a card payment by the reader. This example also shows how non-human actors can participate in use cases.

Figure 2.16 also illustrates the «invoke» relationship. The notation is simple with a dashed arrow pointing towards the invoked use case, adorned with the «invoke» stereotype. In the example, three use cases can be invoked from the 'Show book list' use case. Note that the 'Add new book' use case can be directly «use»d by the librarian (e.g. started from some main menu) or it can be invoked from 'Show book list'. The invocation relationships clearly indicate navigation through the user interface as part of the application logic. From the diagram we can infer that the 'Show book list' use case will include actions (cf. triggers in the domain model) that would start the other three use cases.

The indexinvoke «invoke» relationship substitutes the UML's «include» and «extend» relationships. This slight change in notation seems unimportant but the important issue is the shift in semantics which we explain below. The difference in notation in illustrated in Fig. 2.17. As we can see, «invoke» can substitute «include» and does not change the direction of the arrow. Whenever we would need to use an «include» relationship in UML, we ca use «invoke» in RSL in the same manner.

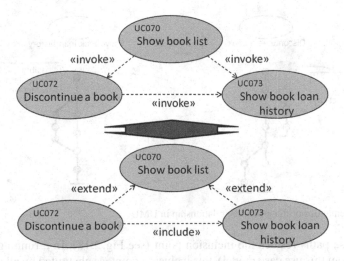

Fig. 2.17 Comparison of «invoke» with «extend» and «include»

A different situation is for the UML's «extend» relationship. We can also substitute it with «invoke» but we need to change the direction of the arrow. In UML, it is the extending use case that points at the extended one. In RSL we cannot extend use cases but we can invoke them. Invocation is directed opposite because the invocation has call semantics in contrast to the extension which has specialisation semantics.

To explain these changes introduced by RSL we need to refer to the official semantics defined within the UML specification. For the «include» relationship it says: "An include relationship between two use cases means that the behaviour defined in the including use case is included in the behaviour of the base use case. The include relationship is intended to be used when there are common parts of the behaviour of two or more use cases. This common part is then extracted to a separate use case, to be included by all the base use cases having this part in common." and "Execution of the included use case is analogous to a subroutine call. All of the behaviour of the included use case is executed at a single location in the included use case before execution of the including use case is resumed."

From this definition we infer that inclusion has macro-like semantics. In other words, all the contents of the included use case are inserted at one point in the including case. This contents can then be executed like if the including use case had all the included use case behaviour substitute the "inclusion point". Unfortunately, the UML's specification of use cases does not specify "inclusion points". Thus, to determine precise semantics of UML's inclusion we need to go beyond the official UML specification as shown in Fig. 2.18.

The including use case (here: 'Discontinue a book') contains an inclusion point. This point is a distinguished action within the use case's scenarios. The behaviour defined by the use case starts when an actor interacts with the system in a specific way (cf. 'initial actor interaction'). Then, consecutive actions occur with possible different paths that lead either to reaching the use case goal or failing to do so. On

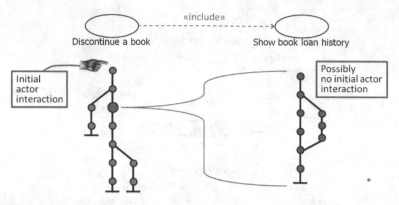

Fig. 2.18   Semantics of the «include» relationship in UML

one of these paths resides the inclusion point (see Fig. 2.18). In a running system (derived from this use case model), this inclusion point is substituted by all the paths defined within the included use case (here: 'Show book loan history'). This resembles macros available in various programming language environments. We can specify a macro as a piece of generic code suitable for inclusion into some other code (cf. an included use case). Before compilation, this code is preprocessed and inserted into the other places in code where the macro is used (cf. inclusion points).

Note that the included use case is usually not fully defined—it lacks the initial user interaction. This is because when the inclusion point is reached, the including use case is usually in the middle of some processing or after some user interaction. Thus, it does not make sense to start the included use case with a user interaction, but rather—begin with some actions performed by the system.

While the semantics of the «include» relationship seems straightforward, the semantics of «extend» defined in the UML specification is much more twisted. The specification says that: "Usually, a use case with extension points consists of a set of finer-grained behavioural fragment descriptions, which are most often executed in sequence. This segmented structuring of the use case text allows the original behavioural description to be extended by merging in supplementary behavioural fragment descriptions at the appropriate insertion points between the original fragments (extension points). Thus, an extending use case typically consists of one or more behaviour fragment descriptions that are to be inserted into the appropriate spots of the extended use case. An extension location, therefore, is a specification of all the various (extension) points in a use case where supplementary behavioural increments can be merged. If the condition of the extension is true at the time the first extension point is reached during the execution of the extended use case, then all of the appropriate behaviour fragments of the extending use case will also be executed."

This leads to interweaving of scenarios of the extended and the extending use case, as illustrated in Fig. 2.19. The extended use case can have several extension points where the functionality of the extending use case is to be merged. The extensions are merged under certain conditions. In the figure, the condition is shown in a note

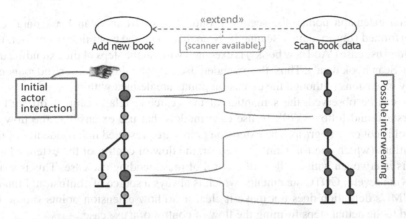

Fig. 2.19 Semantics of the «extend» relationship in UML

attached to the arrow. If the condition is met at the first point, the appropriate extending actions are merged at this point. The same situation is for any other extension point.

In contrast to inclusion points, extension points are part of the official UML definition. Their notation is shown in Fig. 2.20. Each extension point is defined through its name and place of extension. Note that this place is not formally associated with any specific step within a use case. The illustration in the figure is only for comprehension purposes. UML does not offer any constructs to link extension points with the use case "contents".

Figure 2.20 explains the actual extension example. The 'Add new book' use case has two extension points. The first extension can be made after the 'main entry screen' is displayed. If the scanner is available (see the condition in Fig. 2.19), then the appropriate steps from 'Scan book data' are performed (the title pages is scanned). Later, when an 'optional data screen' is displayed (and the condition was met at

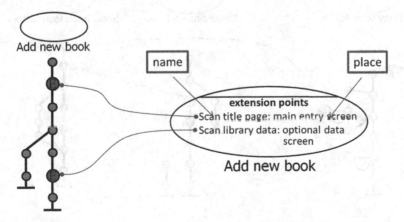

Fig. 2.20 Extension points in UML

the first extension point), the second group of steps from 'Scan book data' can be performed (library data is scanned). Note that when the condition is not met, the extended use case ('Add new book') is executed without the steps of the extending use case ('Scan book data'). Thus, the extended use case should be written independent of any extensions (although the extension points are defined within it).

As can be observed, the semantics of the «extend» relationship is difficult to understand and follow [170]. In use case models that use extensions, the flow of control is not easy to grasp. The extension points are presented independently of the conditions (which control them). Moreover, the flow of control of the extended use case is interwoven with the flow of control of the extending use case. This is close to having several GOTO statements, which is always a source of confusion. Finally, the UML's definition does not make it clear as to how extension points should be linked to the actual steps forming the flow of control of a use case.

For these reasons, RSL has dropped the «extend» relationship and substituted it with «invoke». This move results in removing the possibility to interweave use cases. Instead, the typical procedure call semantics is applied. In some cases, this necessitates some changes in the use case model. However, situations as in Figs. 2.19 and 2.20 are rare and can easily be modified. What is retained from the «extend» relationship is the possibility to define conditions. However, the actual flow of control is organised differently for extensions. Certain instances of «invoke» can behave similarly to «include». However, again, the macro semantics of «include» is substituted by the procedure call semantics of «invoke».

The call semantics of «invoke» is explained through the example in Fig. 2.21. It shows three cases of invocation where two of them can be seen as partially equivalent to UML's extension and one—to UML's inclusion. The 'Show book list' use case contains two invocation points associated with two «invoke» relationships it has

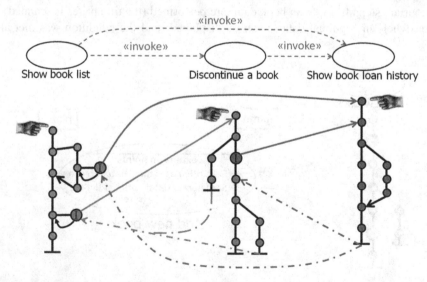

Fig. 2.21 Semantics of the «invoke» relationship in RSL

with the two other use cases. Similarly, the 'Discontinue a book' use case has one invocation point.

The presented diagram shows an overview of control flow for the invocation points. Two situations can be distinguished. The first situation is present in both inclusion points of the 'Show book list' use case. The invocation point is associated with some step in use case execution. When control flow reaches this step, a condition associated with the inclusion point is evaluated. This makes the invoked use case available to the user. The user (more generally: the actor) can then select to start the invoked use case. This is equivalent to performing the first step in the invoked use case (see the hand icons in the diagram), i.e. performing the initial user-to-system interaction. Then, the control flow continues through the steps of the invoked use case until it reaches one of its final points. After the invoked use case finishes its execution, the control returns to the initial step of the invoking use cases with which the invocation point is associated.

To illustrate this in Fig. 2.21, we assume that 'Show book list' reaches some point in one of its scenarios where a list of books is displayed. At this point, some condition is evaluated which is associated with a switch that allows to discontinue books (which normally is not allowed). With this switch on, the window that displays the list of books presents a relevant button. By pressing the button, the user in fact "executes" the first sentence in the 'Discontinue a book' use case. After this second use case finishes (with success or perhaps with failure), the execution flow goes back to the 'Show book list' use case and returns to the step of displaying the list of books. A similar situation is for the invocation of the 'Show book loan history' use case from 'Show book list'.

A different situation is presented in the inclusion point contained in the 'Discontinue a book' use case. This time, the inclusion point is reached directly and unconditionally as one of the steps in the use case control flow. After reaching this step, control goes to the invoked use case (here: 'Show book loan history'). Unlike the previous cases of invocation, this time the user need not select any button. Thus, the first sentence of the invoked use case is not "executed". Control flow goes directly to the second sentence. When the execution of the invoked use case finishes, control goes to the next step after the initial invocation point.

The above explanation of invocation semantics does not go into the details of particular use case steps and their individual semantics. To understand this issue better we need to present more information about structuring individual steps in use case logic and forming complete scenarios out of these individual steps. This includes conditions for invocations that—as it can be noted—are not present at the use case level. These issues are presented in the subsections that follow.

2.4.2 Sentence Types

In contrast to UML, RSL precisely defines the use case contents and provides appropriate notation. We start to present this notation from the basic building blocks, which are individual sentences. In general, RSL uses constrained natural language for the

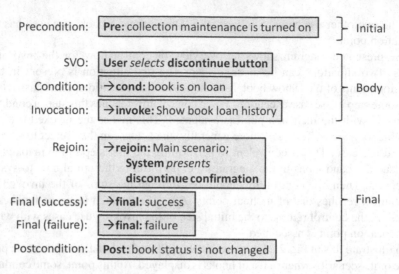

Precondition: **Pre:** collection maintenance is turned on   ] Initial

SVO: **User** *selects* **discontinue button**

Condition: →**cond:** book is on loan

Invocation: →**invoke:** Show book loan history   ] Body

Rejoin: →**rejoin:** Main scenario;
          System *presents*
          discontinue confirmation

Final (success):   →**final:** success   ] Final

Final (failure):   →**final:** failure

Postcondition: **Post:** book status is not changed

Fig. 2.22 Scenario sentence types

sentences. Each sentence denotes either an individual step in the use case logic or controls the flow of steps. In Fig. 2.22, sentences were divided from the point of view of their position within the use case contents. We can distinguish Initial sentences, Body sentences and Final sentences.

A use case can be initiated with one type of sentences: Preconditions. Their syntax is simple and starts with the keyword 'Pre:' which is followed by free text describing the actual condition. The meaning of this sentence is to provide a condition for executing the given use case. If the condition is met, the use case is ready for execution. If it is not met, the use case cannot be executed. In the context of the invocation sentence (see the previous subsection), the precondition is the condition that is checked when a sentence with an associated invocation point is reached.

The precondition sentence in Fig. 2.22 refers to the example in Fig. 2.21. In the 'Show book list' use case, a sentence showing a book list is reached. This sentence has an associated invocation point which refers to the 'Discontinue a book' use case. The condition that is checked at that point is the precondition of 'Discontinue a book' presented in Fig. 2.22. If the precondition is not met (collection maintenance turned off), the option to discontinue a book is 'greyed out' or not visible. If the precondition is met, the user has an appropriate button available and can (if she wishes) start the invoked use case. In case the precondition sentence is not present in the invoked use case, it is assumed that the precondition is always met.

In the current version of RSL, preconditions have no defined syntax for their condition parts. Thus, the appropriate code, checking the condition will not be generated and will need to be updated by hand. This is explained in Chap. 6. However, the condition text can be transferred to code as a comment and thus should be meaningful. We should assume that the precondition specifies some system state and refers to the domain elements.

The precondition sentence can be followed by various sentences that form the use case body. There are three types of such sentences: SVO sentences, condition sentences and invocation sentences. Again, the syntax of these sentences is simple and consists of only a few elements (see again Fig. 2.22). The SVO sentences are normally composed of three parts: the Subject (S), the Verb (V) and the Object (O). In some cases, a more elaborated syntax can be used with an additional (indirect) object together with a preposition. In general, the simple SVO(O) sentences have proved to serve as satisfactory means to express all the possible actions of the application logic.

While SVO sentences define individual actions, the condition sentences and the invocation sentences allow for controlling the flow of these actions. The syntax for conditions sentences starts with the '->cond:' keyword followed by free text, specifying the actual condition. Whenever a condition sentence is reached, the actual condition is checked and if it is met, the flow of control goes to the sentence that follows. If the condition is not met, the flow of control moves to another scenario, which will be explained in the next subsection.

As in the case of preconditions, the conditions sentences in RSL have no specific syntax for the part that follows the keyword. Despite this, code can be meaningfully generated from several corresponding condition sentences. Again, the condition text can be copied into code as a comment.

The syntax for the invocation sentence is also straightforward and consists of the '->invoke:' keyword followed by the name of the specific invoked use case. The meaning of invocation sentences was already initially explained in the previous subsection and when explaining the precondition sentences. More information is given in the next subsection.

The body of each use case scenario has to be ended with one of the final sentences. There are three types of such sentences where two of them can be followed by a postcondition sentence (see Fig. 2.22). The actual final sentences are denoted with the '->final' keyword which is followed either by the 'success' or the 'failure' keyword. The meaning of these sentences is quite obvious. Whenever such sentence is reached, the use case terminates its execution and passes control to where it was called from. The additional keyword signals to the caller the final status of processing within the current use case (whether the use case goal was reached or not). In addition to this, the postcondition sentence can specify the state in which the system should be at the end of the given scenario. The notation for postconditions is similar to that of preconditions and differs in the keyword 'Post:'. The postcondition text can be copied to code similarly to how it is copied for preconditions.

In addition to the actual final sentences, RSL has a third final sentence which is the rejoin sentence. Its syntax starts with the '->rejoin:' keyword followed by the identification of the rejoin point. This point is determined by giving the name of the scenario and the SVO sentence at which the other scenario has to be rejoined. Rejoining can be made only within the current use case. No 'goto' rejoins to other use cases are allowed. Rejoin sentences facilitate writing scenarios which "detour" from some main course of action but after some alternative steps—return control to that main course. Whenever a rejoin sentence is reached, control is passed to the sentence which is pointed at through the rejoin.

After presenting all the sentence types we now return to SVO sentences. Their syntax, despite being simple, allows for various combinations of the three sentence parts leading to their various types. This variety allows to construct complex application logic describing the dialogue between the actors and the system, with references to the domain logic. In Fig. 2.23 we see all the possible SVO configurations.

The main division is between sentences where the subject points to one of the actors, and sentences where the subject points to the system. These are either 'Actor-to-' or 'System-to-' sentences. Obviously, the actor sentences specify possible actor interactions with system—triggering events or entering data. The system sentences specify the system's reactions to the actor's interactions. These various interactions and reactions are specified through the VO (Verb-Object) part of each sentence. Note that these predicates are equivalent to the verb phrases that are part of the domain model as illustrated in Fig. 2.23. We can recall from the previous sections that verb phrases are contained in domain elements. Each SVO sentence predicate is in fact a hyperlink to such a verb phrase. The sentence object indicates the actual domain element, and the sentence verb selects the appropriate verb phrase. In an RSL editor environment, these links should be maintained automatically. Whenever an SVO sentence is created, its parts should be hyperlinked to appropriate phrases in the domain model. If the domain models lacks a phrase—it should then be created.

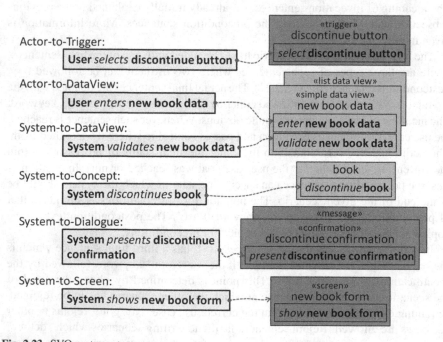

Fig. 2.23 SVO sentence types

Figure 2.23 shows six types of SVO sentences where two are the actor sentences and four are the system sentences. The classification is straightforward and does not need more elaborated explanation. Note that in general, the sentence subject determines the allowed domain elements that can be hyperlinked by the sentence predicate. The actor sentences can pertain to triggers and data views. The system sentences can also pertain to data views but additionally—to concepts, dialogue elements (messages and confirmations) and screens. The example sentences in Fig. 2.23 show the rationale behind such classification of sentences. It is also obvious that these sentences should be combined in a certain order. The rules for ordering sentences lead to forming use case scenarios, which are presented in the following subsection.

The reader has probably noticed that SVO sentences do not contain any articles ('a/an' or 'the'). This can be explained by the desire to simplify the constrained grammar and to concentrate on links with the domain vocabulary and not on specifics of a concrete natural language (here: English). With this approach, various national languages with similar grammar can be used.

2.4.3 Scenarios

Every use case should have at least one scenario that leads to successful reaching of its goal. Use cases with just one scenario are quite seldom and usually there are alternative scenarios that either lead to failure or reach the final goal in a different way than in the main scenario. Before we present example scenarios, we need to explain various rules for putting individual scenario sentences together in sequences. These rules are based on the fundamental notion of *dialogue state*.

The notion is explained in Fig. 2.24. The dialogue can be in one of two states: 'Actor' or 'System'. In the figure, these states are shown as lifelines in a UML-like sequence diagram [6, 152]. The dialogue state is propagated and changed along the scenario sentences. Each of the six SVO sentence types can be placed in a scenario in places where the dialogue state is suitable for this sentence. The 'Actor-to-' sentences can be placed when the dialogue state is 'Actor'. Similarly, the 'System-to' sentences can be placed when the dialogue state is 'System'.

The 'Actor-to-Trigger' sentences shift the dialogue state from 'Actor' to 'System', and the 'System-to-Screen' sentences shift in the opposite direction. Note that the 'System-to-Dialogue' sentences do not shift the dialogue state. This is for convenience reasons. Such sentences relate to either messages or confirmations. The user interactions for these UI elements are limited to selecting a trigger. Thus, it is assumed that the user must select some trigger and this is 'built into' the 'System-to-Dialogue' sentence. This approach saves some work on writing obvious 'Actor-to-Trigger' sentences.

SVO sentences change the dialogue state but cannot change the control flow. With only SVO sentences, the control would go from one sentence to another and only one scenario for a use case could be written. Thus, we need to use condition sentences. These sentences need to be introduced in at least pairs. For every condition

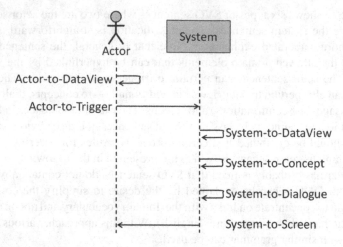

Fig. 2.24 SVO sentences: changing the *dialogue state*

sentence, at least one other associated condition has to exist forming a group of alternative conditions. As shown in Figs. 2.25 and 2.26, there can be two situations where conditions can be used.

The first situation (Fig. 2.25) is when a condition sentence group is placed at a point where dialogue state is 'Actor'. This means that the current actor should make some decision leading to alternative paths through the use case. Thus, immediately following each condition sentence in the group we need to place an 'Actor-to-Trigger' sentence. This situation is explained in the sequence diagram on the right of Fig. 2.25. The two alternative paths of control are depicted with two sections of the 'alt' combined fragment (please refer to UML's combined fragments) equivalent to an 'if' statement in most programming languages. In both cases, some trigger is selected by

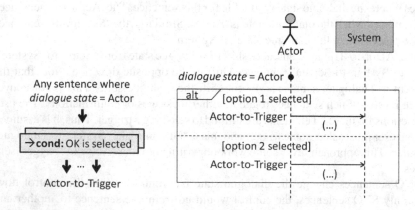

Fig. 2.25 Condition sentences: changing control flow (1)

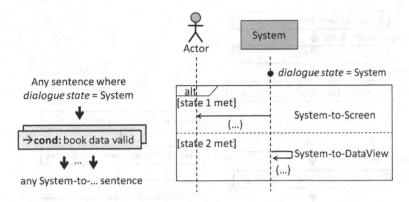

Fig. 2.26 Condition sentences: changing control flow (2)

the actor and thus the state of dialogue is changed to 'System'. However, normally, the two triggers are different (e.g. pressing 'Save' or pressing 'Cancel') and thus the following actions (SVO sentences represented by dots) define different steps.

The second situation (Fig. 2.26) happens when the dialogue state at which condition is situated—is 'System'. Normally, this is equivalent to the system first performing some data validation, checking the state of some domain elements or executing some data processing. This leads to several possible results (e.g. data valid or not valid) which are guarded by several grouped conditions. These conditions can be each followed by any possible 'System-to-' sentence. This might be some further internal processing by the system (e.g. 'System-to-DataView') or presenting a UI element to the user ('System-to-Screen'). As for the previous case, this is illustrated with a sequence diagram containing the 'alt' combined fragment in Fig. 2.26. Again, depending on the result of some system operation (dialogue state = 'System'), control within the use case logic can go through one of the alternative paths.

Having defined the notions of dialogue state and SVO sentences changing this state, we can now proceed to explain how invocation sentences can be situated in scenarios as illustrated in Fig. 2.27. As explained previously, there can be two situations—the invocation is unconditional or the invocation is conditional and depends on the user interaction. For the latter situation, the '–>invoke:' sentence has to be placed at a point in a scenario where dialogue state is 'Actor'. In fact, we can place several consecutive invocation sentences at such a place. These sentences are not executed in sequence but are treated as parallel possibilities to start several use cases.

This can be best explained with the example in Fig. 2.27. Somewhere in a scenario, the dialogue state is changed to 'Actor' through the 'System-to-Screen' sentence **'System** *shows* **book list window'**. Sometimes, this sentence can be followed by some 'Actor-to-DataView' sentences (e.g. **'User** *enters* **book filter'**) which do not change the dialogue state. At this point, we can put one or more '–>invoke:' sentences. In our example, one of these sentences invokes 'Show book loan history'. Other

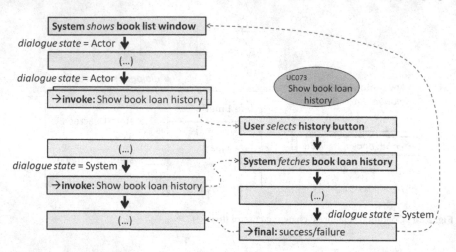

Fig. 2.27 Invocation sentences: passing control to other use cases

examples which refer to Fig. 2.16 are 'Add new book' and 'Discontinue a book'. Initial triggers (e.g. buttons) for these three use cases have to be present in the 'book list window'.

When a running system reaches the point where invocations are situated, the dialogue state is with the user, who may choose to start one of the use cases made available for invocation. So, for example, when the user *selects* the available **history button**, flow of control is taken by the first sentence of 'Show book loan history'. Then, this invoked use case 'executes' until it reaches one of its final points. Following this, control is passed to the invoking use case. The point to which control is passed is the last 'System-to-Screen' sentence before the '–>invoke:' sentence. In our example, this is '**System** *shows* **book list window**' which results in returning control back to the same window from which the last invocation call was made.

This simple standard control flow semantics can be extended to cater for more complex situations. In such case, the invocation sentences have to be combined with condition and rejoin sentences. Each of the invocation sentences in the situation described above could be placed in a separate alternative scenario, guarded by a condition sentence. Then, flow of control after returning from invocation would go to the next sentence in the given alternative scenario. This sentence would normally be a rejoin to the 'System-to-Screen' sentence as explained above. However, in some situations this could involve other actions like refreshing the original window (here: the 'book list window').

Figure 2.27 presents an example of the second possible type of invocation, i.e. the situation when the dialogue state is 'System'. Note, in this situation, the invoked use case is 'executed' beginning from its second sentence and the first 'Actor-to-Trigger' sentence is omitted. This is a reasonable solution, considering that in the dialogue state 'System' the actor has no control and cannot evoke a trigger event.

In this situation, it is the system that starts the invocation without any external actor intervention. The invoked use case executes exactly the same as it would be triggered by the user. The only difference lies in the initiating event.

It has to be stressed that at the final point of any use case the dialogue state has to be 'System'. This means that the invoked use case does not decide to which user interface element control should be passed when it finishes. This is logical because otherwise it would be impossible to invoke the same use case from several use cases. Each of these invoking use cases might start invocation when a different window is displayed. We would thus expect the invoked use case logic not to decide as to which window should be displayed when it ends.

With control flow explained for individual sentences, we are finally ready to assemble sentences of various types into full scenarios. In RSL we can use two alternative notations. The first notation is purely textual, and the second notation uses familiar activity notation taken from UML. These two notations are presented in Fig. 2.28. The lower activity diagram is almost fully equivalent to the upper four scenarios in textual format. The minor difference is that the textual scenarios can have names (e.g. 'Invalid reader id').

Analysing the presented example it can be noted that all the scenarios start with the same set of sentences from 1 to 4. In general, for all kinds of use cases, the first two sentences have to be the same. The first sentence is always an 'Actor-to-Trigger' sentence. Then it needs to be followed by a 'System-to-' sentence as an invocation sentence. Only after this second sentence, the first possible condition sentence group can occur. In our example in Fig. 2.28 a condition group occurs after the fourth sentence. This is the situation where the dialogue state is 'Actor', explained earlier in this section. In the textual notation, presence of a condition group (here: two alternative conditions) leads to having one scenario per indexcondition condition (here: 'Main scenario' and 'Main scenario with swiping'). In the activity notation, the conditions are denoted as guards annotating the appropriate number of control flows (arrows) leading from the previous sentence (here: sentence number 4).

It should be observed that the condition texts that are specified in the dialogue state 'Actor' do not really matter. What matters are the 'Actor-to-Trigger' sentences that follow ('Librarian selects next button' and 'Reader swipes through card reader'). These sentences determine which application logic (i.e. further steps in scenarios) will execute after the specific alternative interactions of the user with the system. A different situation is for the condition sentences that occur at the dialogue state of 'System'. These conditions matter because they directly refer to the preceding sentence ('System validates reader id' in one case and 'System validates reader card' in another). So, the alternative scenarios execute depending precisely on the result of this preceding sentence and evaluation of the following conditions.

The final observation for Fig. 2.28 is related to sentence numbers 8 and 7. We assume that these sentences are 'System-to-Dialogue' and thus the final dialogue state is 'System'. The 'OK message' defined in the domain model is type of «message». If it was a «screen», then sentence 8 would need to be followed by another sentence like '**Librarian** *selects* **OK button**'. The usage of a «message» instead of a «screen» simply saves some work.

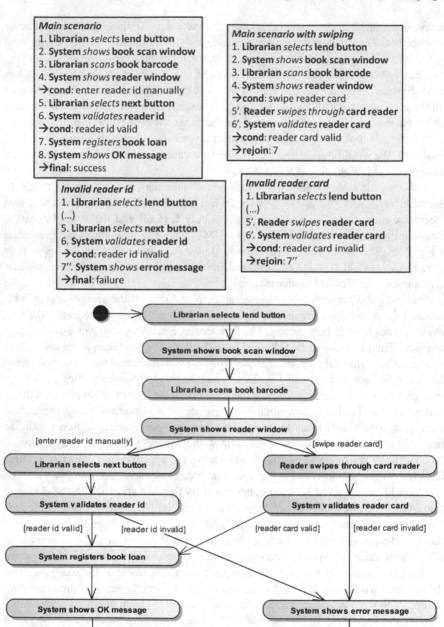

Main scenario
1. **Librarian** *selects* **lend button**
2. **System** *shows* **book scan window**
3. **Librarian** *scans* **book barcode**
4. **System** *shows* **reader window**
→**cond**: enter reader id manually
5. **Librarian** *selects* **next button**
6. **System** *validates* **reader id**
→**cond**: reader id valid
7. **System** *registers* **book loan**
8. **System** *shows* **OK message**
→**final**: success

Main scenario with swiping
1. **Librarian** *selects* **lend button**
2. **System** *shows* **book scan window**
3. **Librarian** *scans* **book barcode**
4. **System** *shows* **reader window**
→**cond**: swipe reader card
5'. **Reader** *swipes through* **card reader**
6'. **System** *validates* **reader card**
→**cond**: reader card valid
→**rejoin**: 7

Invalid reader id
1. **Librarian** *selects* **lend button**
(...)
5. **Librarian** *selects* **next button**
6. **System** *validates* **reader id**
→**cond**: reader id invalid
7". **System** *shows* **error message**
→**final**: failure

Invalid reader card
1. **Librarian** *selects* **lend button**
(...)
5'. **Reader** *swipes* **reader card**
6'. **System** *validates* **reader card**
→**cond**: reader card invalid
→**rejoin**: 7"

Fig. 2.28 Notation for scenarios: text and activity diagram

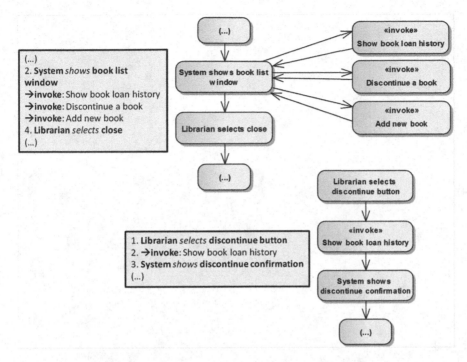

Fig. 2.29 Textual and activity notation for invocations

In Fig. 2.29 we have an example of alternative notations for the invocation sentences. Again, we use both the textual and the activity notation. In the first case (the upper part of the figure), we have the situation with a 'System-to-Screen' sentence ('System shows book list window') followed by several invocation sentences. In activity notation this can be represented as in the shown diagram. Each «invoke» action can be reached through a control flow leading from the action containing the 'System-to-Screen' sentence. Another control flow points back to this initial action. The second case in Fig. 2.29 (lower part) shows an unconditional invocation. The notation is self-explanatory and needs no further comments.

This concludes the introduction to various RSL constructs. In this introduction, we have presented the elements most relevant for further automatic processing and code generation. However, the presented part of the language does not claim to exhaust all the possible twists in the application logic. The language can be extended by introducing other domain element types through adding new stereotypes. Also, certain other configurations of scenario sentences can be introduced. These extensions would then need to be explained in terms of their semantics that influence the generated code. In the next two chapters, we approach RSL in a more formal way to prepare for developing an automatic model transformation from RSL to code.

Chapter 3
Defining RSL

In the previous chapter we presented the various constructs of RSL as they are visible
to the language users. This concrete syntax is important for comprehensibility of
the language but does not offer enough formality. In order to represent this syntax
in a modelling tool, we need a formally precise version of the syntax that allows
for creating storage and processing of RSL models—the abstract syntax. We use a
model to represent RSL models [145, 153], and such a model is called the metamodel
("model of models").

3.1 Introduction to Metamodelling

The notion of abstract syntax was introduced earlier in Sect. 2.1. We know that the
abstract syntax specifies the arrangement of model elements treating them as an
abstract graph. Being graphs, models are composed of nodes (vertices) and edges.
To handle models in a tool we need to be able to store and process the nodes, edges
and the ways in which edges connect the nodes. When storing these elements we
do not include the visual form of the nodes and edges, nor do we store the spatial
relations between these elements. This information is *abstracted* away and specified
elsewhere. The visual forms of nodes and edges form the concrete syntax. The spacial
relations are specified in concrete model diagrams. When we remove the visual forms
and the diagram-related information what is left is called the abstract syntax.

Individual models can form different abstract graphs. However, for models that
conform to a specific modelling language—these graphs have to obey specific rules.
To define these rules we can also use models. The individual abstract graphs become
instances of these models. We thus have now two levels of models: the "actual
models" and the models that define possible arrangements of elements of these "actual
models". Models at this second level of modelling are called metamodels.

Experience shows that the above explanation of metamodels is not enough to
understand to start metamodelling. Thus, we attempt to explain by starting with an

© Springer International Publishing Switzerland 2015
M. Śmiałek and W. Nowakowski, *From Requirements to Java in a Snap*,
DOI 10.1007/978-3-319-12838-2_3

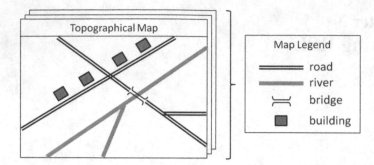

Fig. 3.1 Maps and their legends

analogy that is known to most readers. Although we all know and use various kinds of maps we seldom realise that maps are models of reality. Maps use a specific language to reflect the reality. For readers to understand the map, this language has to be explained. Each "syntactic" element in a map has a definition. Moreover, for a specific type of map, the language should be coherently used. A typical way to present the "map language" definition is to use a legend.

In Fig. 3.1 we see an example of such a legend, defining the language for certain kinds of topographical maps. Our "map language" is simple and consists of only four elements: roads, rivers, bridges and buildings. Note that the legend is also a model composed of these four elements. It is not a complete model, because it only enlists the four syntactic elements of the "map language" and provides a mapping between the abstract form (the element names) and the concrete form (the visual icons).

The legend lacks the information about possible arrangements of the map elements. This is assumed as obvious to the reader who knows the reality represented by maps. However, in a language engineering context, we need to specify these rules illustrated in Fig. 3.2. Here, the rules are expressed through graphical examples (left) that are summarised with textual statements (right). If we remove the graphical examples we are left with abstract statements that specify how the syntactic elements can

Fig. 3.2 Syntactic rules for maps

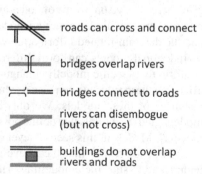

roads can cross and connect

bridges overlap rivers

bridges connect to roads

rivers can disembogue (but not cross)

buildings do not overlap rivers and roads

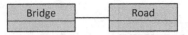

Fig. 3.3 Model representing a syntactic rule

be arranged. These statements abstract away the visual and spatial issues and consist of only element names ('bridge', 'road') and relations between these elements ('connect', 'overlap').

In defining the "map language" we can go a step further and present the above rules through a model. For instance, to show that bridges can generally connect to roads, we could write a simple diagram shown in Fig. 3.3. This diagram is an elementary example of a metamodel. The advantage of using a metamodel is that it can be made formally precise and can contain well-organised information on various other elements of the language syntax.

Modelling languages in software engineering are to some extent similar to our "map language". They are meant to represent a specific domain and are often called Domain Specific Languages. One such language is RSL, where the domain it covers is requirements engineering. Yet, before explaining the metamodel of RSL let us present some general rules for creating metamodels. For this purpose, we use a simple language ('VSL') presented through an example in Fig. 3.4.

The figure contains an example model in its concrete (left) and abstract (right) forms. We can see a circle and a pentagon connected with two arrows in opposite directions. The circle and the pentagon contain three and two dots, respectively. The diagram also contains a square. Note that the abstract form is in fact a UML-like object diagram. The objects have names (e.g. 'd1', 'a2') and types (e.g. 'Circle', 'Arrow'). The arrangements of objects are presented through links where each link is equivalent to a physical connection between two model elements. For example, the link between objects 'p1' and 'a1' is equivalent to the point where the outgoing arrow touches the pentagon. This link is marked by an appropriate identifier ('out')

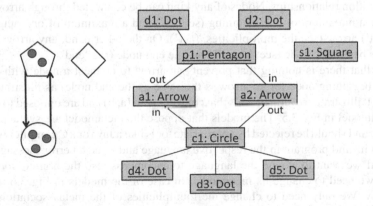

Fig. 3.4 Defining an elementary modelling language

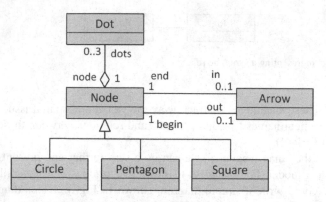

Fig. 3.5 Metamodel for the example modelling language

placed at one of its ends. In this way its role as the beginning of the arrow is clearly determined. The other arrow object ('a2') is also clearly linked with the pentagon at its incoming end ('in').

The presented example model is one of many possible configurations of the elements in 'VSL'. To specify all the possibilities we need to generalise the object diagram into a class diagram. As shown in Fig. 3.5. Each of the classes represent one type of elements found in Fig. 3.4, so the presented set of classes can serve as the "legend" for this model. The syntactic rules are defined through the various relationships between classes—associations, aggregations and generalisations. This class model is the definition of the model syntax in 'VSL'. In other words—it is a model of models, or a metamodel. The classes and associations in the metamodel can be distinguished by calling them metaclasses and meta-associations.

As we can see, the models in 'VSL' generally consist of 'Nodes' and 'Arrows'. The nodes can have up to three 'Dots', but may also not have any dot (see the multiplicity '0..3'). Every dot has to belong to exactly one node. There are three kinds of nodes: 'Circles', 'Pentagons' and 'Squares', which is denoted through the generalisation relationships. Nodes of any kind can be connected through arrows. It can have a maximum of one incoming (see 'in') and a maximum of one outgoing (see 'out') arrow (see the multiplicities '0..1'). On the other hand, any arrow must have one beginning node (see 'begin') and one end node (see 'end').

Note that there is nothing that prevents an arrow to connect a node with itself (i.e. the beginning node for an arrow is the same as the end node) as illustrated in Fig. 3.6. It illustrates several models that conform with (a, b) and are opposed to (c, d) the metamodel in Fig. 3.5. The models that oppose the metamodel are syntactically incorrect and should be rejected by appropriate tools like a Java or a C compiler would reject an invalid program in the respective language and issue an error message. Of course, if we want to extend the language to encompass also the non-conformant models we need to change its metamodel. In case of the models in Fig. 3.6 this is very easy. We only need to change the multiplicities of the metaassociations for

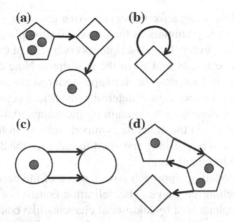

Fig. 3.6 Model conformance to metamodels

'Arrow' from '0..1' to '0..*'. Now the number of arrows coming out and into any 'Node' is unlimited.

Graph-based models can also have textual elements. For instance, the nodes in 'VSL' models can have names and other textual specifications. In Fig. 3.7 we see an example node (a pentagon) with the name (*'Penta27'*) and an additional descriptor ('FIRE'). The descriptor is composed of a keyword, a sequence number (here: '3') and a procedure identifier (here: 'Proc12').

The metamodel for textual elements includes class attributes. These attributes represent atomic texts in the models. Figure 3.7 presents three alternative approaches to model names and descriptors. In the first approach (top) the 'Node' metaclass contains attributes of 'name', 'fire_seq' (fire sequence) and 'fire_proc' (fire procedure). In the second approach (middle) an additional metaclass 'Fire' models the descriptor clearly distinguishing it from the containing node. In the third approach (bottom), the descriptor is modelled simply as a single string metaattribute ('fire'). In such a case we need to supplement the meta-attribute with the definition of the string's

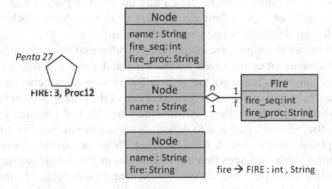

Fig. 3.7 Example metamodels for textual elements

syntax. This can be done using a formal context-free grammar [3]. We will not go
into details of context-free grammars as the presented example is self-explanatory.
The grammar defines that every 'fire' descriptor is composed of the 'FIRE' keyword
followed by consecutive tokens that form the descriptor. Note that while the first
two approaches are purely abstract—the third approach reveals some of the concrete
syntax. In the first two cases, we cannot determine the actual keyword and sequence
of tokens of the 'FIRE' descriptor by examining the metamodel alone. This would
need to be done separately in the concrete syntax definition. In the third approach,
the concrete syntax has to be partially specified in order for the definition of all the
descriptor elements to be complete.

This simple metamodelling approach covers much of the necessary expressiveness to define a modelling language. The definition consists of simple class diagrams, sometimes supplemented by additional elements like context-free grammar
expressions and constraints. This abstract syntax has to be matched with the concrete
syntax. There are numerous possibilities of how elements symbolised by metaclasses
and metaattributes are presented graphically. They can overlap, touch each other, be
placed near each other and so on. In some cases, the elements can be hidden in a
diagram and shown in a separate descriptive element. In the following sections, we
see how this can be applied to RSL. We present the most important elements of its
metamodel and map it onto concrete models.

3.2 Overview of the RSL Metamodel

RSL is a complex modelling language and as such necessitates an elaborate metamodel. If we analyse the RSL concrete syntax presented in the previous chapter, we
will come up with many dozens of metaclasses needed to represent the individual
RSL elements. To make the RSL metamodel manageable we need to divide it. Here,
we also use the familiar construct known from UML—the package. Each of the packages contain a distinct part of the language definition, starting from the most detailed
constructs and ending with the whole specifications. The actual RSL definition [83]
contains more than 20 packages and more than 200 metaclasses. In this book, we
present a slightly simplified version containing the most important subset of RSL
which is substantial enough to demonstrate various metamodelling techniques and
use for developing RSL editors and transformation engines.

Figure 3.8 shows seven packages that can be divided into those defining requirements specifications (four packages on the left) and those defining the domain
specifications (three packages on the right). The relationships between packages
denote usage (inclusion) of elements defined in one of the packages (pointed-at with
the arrow) within another package. For instance, the 'Terms' package uses metaclasses from the 'Phrases' package to define metaassociations that link the various
terms with phrases within which they are used. In the actual definition of RSL,
we have various other packages that are not shown in Fig. 3.8. However, the presented division gives a good overall view of the language structure. In the detailed

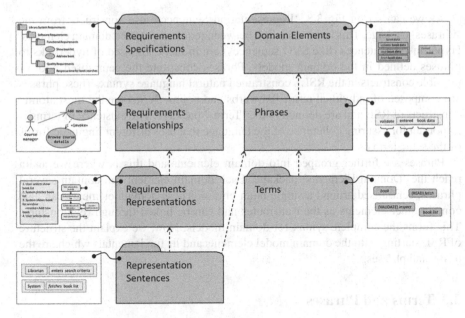

Fig. 3.8 Structure of the RSL metamodel

descriptions in the following sections we refer to some other packages but they all can be treated as sub-packages of the seven presented.

The highest level RSL constructs are defined in the 'Requirements Specifications' and 'Domain Elements' packages. 'Requirements Specifications' defines the most general and structuring RSL elements like packages and requirements-as-such. Elements in this package also refer to domain specifications in 'Domain Elements'. Using the elements defined in these two packages we can build tree-like structures familiar to all that use the various modelling tools and their "project browsers". Within the requirements specifications and domain specifications we can define packages, sub-packages, requirements and domain elements.

Requirements and use cases have relationships and this is defined in the 'Requirements Relationships' package (with a sub-package 'Use Case Relationships'). This package uses the 'requirements' metaclasses from the 'Requirements Specifications' package and introduces additional metaelements that allow for connecting them, like 'usage' and 'invocation'. In this way it allows for creating use case diagrams and other graph-based diagrams composed of requirements units.

The next package—'Requirements Representations' introduces the modelling levels that are below requirements as such. It contains top-level metaclasses for defining requirements descriptions with varying precision. This includes simple textual representations but also structured language scenarios and activity models. The more detailed representations are composed of sentences whose syntax is defined in the 'Representation Sentences' package. This package contains constructs for modelling SVO sentences and various control sentences.

As we can see in Fig. 3.8, 'Representation Sentences' use constructs from the 'Phrases' package. This is the main link between requirements and domain elements. Hyperlinked sentences (like SVO sentences) are in fact composed of hyperlinks to phrases defined in the domain models. Phrases constitute the centralised pool of possible constructs in the RSL's constrained natural language syntax. These phrases are composed of individual terms like verbs and nouns. Terms are the most atomic constructs of RSL and are defined in the 'Terms' package. The existence of terms is important for assuring coherence of the language that uses different linguistic forms of the same terms.

Phrases are further grouped into domain elements and this is where we again reach the 'Domain Elements' package. Each domain element can contain several phrases, centralised around a single noun phrase. These domain elements can also contain other elements as their attributes and can be linked through relationships. This forms the complete syntax for domain models. Now, we explain the structure of RSL starting with the domain model elements and its fundamentals which are the terms and phrases.

3.3 Terms and Phrases

Complex scenarios and sentences in RSL are composed of simple building blocks. The simplest of them are 'Terms' contained in a central 'Terminology'. This part of the metamodel is presented in Fig. 3.9 (up). Examples of concrete syntax are denoted by numbers in circles referring to appropriate metaclasses. The terminology contains many terms and can be filled with their names using various known terminology databases like WordNet [49]. In this way, RSL users can consistently associate their

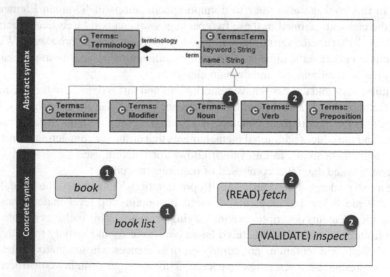

Fig. 3.9 Metamodel for basic terms

specifications with the words available in a given natural language. If a given term is not present it can be easily added to the terminology and extend it.

The term's 'name' constitutes its value that is a string containing its basic linguistic form. There are several types of terms represented by individual metaclasses that specialise the 'Term' metaclass. The most commonly used types are 'Nouns' and 'Verbs' (examples for these types are shown in Fig. 3.9). Term names can consist of several words, like in 'book list'. Moreover, terms can have 'keyword' values that are mostly used for the verbs. These keywords (like 'READ' or 'VALIDATE') can reflect the predefined actions assigned to the specific verbs, as explained in Sect. 2.3.3.

Only one instance of each term can exist in a given RSL model, terms are thus singletons. Whenever a term has to be used in a phrase, a hyperlink to it has to be created. These hyperlinks are called 'TermHyperlinks', as presented in Fig. 3.10. For each term type there is defined a separate class of hypelinks, where appropriate metaclasses specialise from 'TermHyperlink'. Term hyperlinks contain information about the various possible forms of the hyperlinked term (case, gender, mood, number, person, tense). Not all of these form types exist in every natural language but the metamodel is prepared to adapt to various natural languages (English, Polish, German etc.). In the example in Fig. 3.10 we can see that the term 'fetch' is pointed-at by two term hyperlinks. One of them is formulated in the second person, and the other—in the third person.

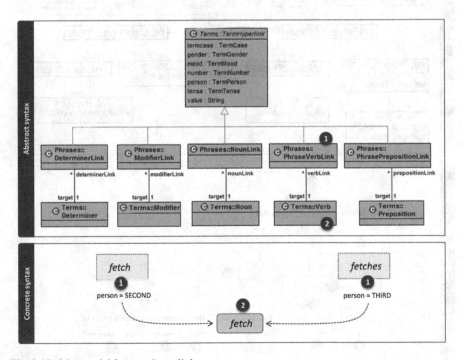

Fig. 3.10 Metamodel for term hyperlinks

Term hyperlinks are the building blocks for phrases. In fact, any phrase consists of just a sequence of term hyperlinks. In the abstract syntax, a phrase does not contain any meta-attributes within its text but is associated with term hyperlinks specific for the given phrase. The metamodel is presented in Fig. 3.11 and defines two fundamental types of phrases:'NounPhrases' and 'VerbPhrases' which

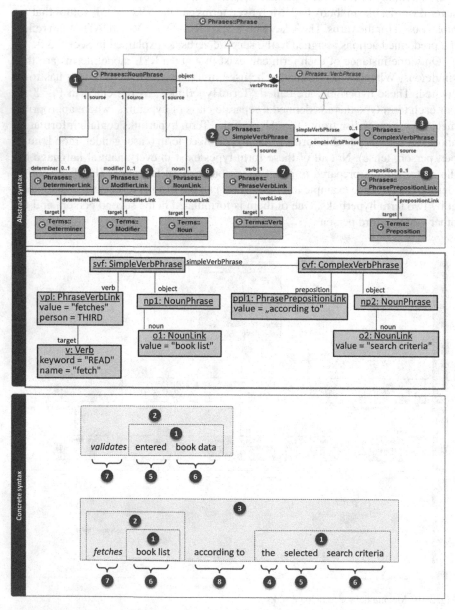

Fig. 3.11 Metamodel for phrases

specialise in general 'Phrases'. 'NounPhrases' are always associated with a single 'NounLink' which constitutes the actual 'noun' of the phrase. Moreover, any noun phrase can contain a 'modifier' and a 'determiner'. This is denoted by appropriate multiplicity ('0..1') in the meta-associations between 'NounPhrase' and 'Modifier-Link' or 'DeterminerLink'. Appropriate examples of noun phrases with their term hyperlinks are presented in the lower part of Fig. 3.11. The noun phrase (1) 'book list' is composed of a single noun link (6). Other two examples show phrases with modifier links (5: 'entered' and 'selected') and a determiner link (4: 'the').

A more complex metamodel is introduced for the verb phrases. RSL defines two types of verb phrases: 'SimpleVerbPhrases' and 'ComplexVerbPhrases'. Their concrete syntax shows that a simple verb phrase (2) consists of a phrase verb link (7) and a noun phrase (1). A complex verb phrase (3) adds to this a preposition (8) and a second phrase verb link (1). Both 'VerbPhrases' contain exactly one 'NounPhrase' in the role of the direct 'object'. A 'SimpleVerbPhrase' contains a 'PhraseVerbLink' which has the role of the 'verb'. Thus, in summary, the 'SimpleVerbPhrase' can be composed of a 'noun' (possibly with a 'modifier' and a 'determiner') and a 'verb'.

The definition of 'ComplexVerbPhrases' extends the syntax of 'SimpleVerb Phrases'. This is not realised through specialisation but through composition. Every 'ComplexVerbPhrase' aggregates one 'SimpleVerbPhrase' and adds a 'preposition'. Note that the 'ComplexVerbPhrase' contains an additional indirect 'object' inherited from the 'VerbPhrase'. Thus, in summary a 'ComplexVerbPhrase' contains one 'verb', two 'objects' (direct and indirect), one preposition and can contain a 'modifier' and a 'determiner'.

To explain how this works, let us analyse object relationships for an example complex verb phrase (see the middle part of Fig. 3.11). The complex verb phrase 'cvf' contains the simple verb phrase 'svf'. This contained phrase is composed of a phrase verb hyperlink 'vpl' with the value of "fetches". This hyperlink points to the actual verb 'v' with the name of "fetch". The simple verb phrase contains also the noun phrase 'np1', because this link is inherited from the generic verb phrase. The noun phrase in turn contains the noun link 'o1' with the value of "book list". The complex verb phrase object contains another noun phrase 'n2' as it also inherits it from the generic verb phrase. Finally, the phrase preposition link 'ppl1' completes the composition of the phrase. Altogether it results in the phrase containing the following hyperlink values: "fetches", "book list", "according to", "search criteria".

We have presented the above values in the order that complies with proper arrangement of sentence parts. However, the abstract syntax (the metamodel) does not enforce this order in any way. For this purpose we need to use another technique which is a context-free grammar. The following expressions define such a grammar for complex verb phrases:

- Start=ComplexVerbPhrase -> SimpleVerbPhrase preposition NounPhrase
- SimpleVerbPhrase -> verb NounPhrase
- NounPhrase -> determiner modifier noun | modifier noun | determiner noun | noun

According to this grammar, every 'ComplexVerbPhrase' starts with a 'SimpleVerbPhrase'. This 'SimpleVerbPhrase' starts with a 'verb' followed by a 'NounPhrase'. The 'NounPhrase' can be in one of four possible configurations which always end with a noun. After returning to the 'ComplexVerbPhrase' we reach a 'preposition' which is followed by a second 'NounPhrase'.

Such grammars are typically used to formally define textual software languages like Java. Here, we use this approach to support the metamodel and specify the ordering of individual sentence parts in concrete syntax for verb phrases.

3.4 Domain Elements and Relationships

Having defined the syntax for terms and phrases we are ready to use this syntax to formulate the domain elements. RSL distinguishes three types of domain elements: 'Actors', 'SystemElements' and 'Notions'. As shown in Fig. 3.12, three correspond-ing metaclasses specialise the 'DomainElement' metaclass. This general metaclass provides the general characteristic of any domain element, to have a 'name' in the form of a 'NounPhrase'. Thus, the syntax of each of the three types of domain ele-ments has to contain a hyperlink to a specific term in the terminology. In the concrete syntax, this hyperlink is seen as the 'value' of the appropriate noun link contained in the noun phrase. Let us take—for example—the "book data" notion shown in Fig. 3.12 (bottom-right). In concrete syntax its name is a string of characters. To see how it is stored we should examine the abstract objects that form this model (see the middle part—left). Now we can see that in fact this string is contained as the 'value' of the 'NounLink' which is the 'noun' contained in the 'NounPhrase' in the role of the actual 'Notion's' 'name'.

Apart from this textual syntax, each of the domain element types has a graphical syntax. For actors (1) this is a stick-man icon, and for system elements (2) and notions (3) this is a (slightly differing) rectangle. These graphical elements can be represented in model browsers (Fig. 3.12, bottom-left) or in diagrams (bottom-right). These two possible representations can differ in the arrangement of the domain elements' graphical layout and position of the textual name. For instance, in diagrams, the notion names are centred inside and at the top of the rectangle icon.

The presence of 'Notions' and 'Actors' in the domain model seems obvious, however, the reader might wonder about 'SystemElements'. In fact, normally we have only a single system element which is the system under development. It is this system's name (e.g. in our ongoing example it is the "Library Management System") that we use in all the relevant parts of the requirements models. Specifically, we can use this name in scenario sentences like "**Library Management System** *validates* **book data**". Normally, we should specify system sub-components during design phases. However, in some situations we need to distinguish certain parts of the system already at the level of the domain model. For this purpose RSL introduces this third type of domain element—'SystemElements', which allows to construct more natural sentences that use vocabulary more understandable to users. For instance, in some

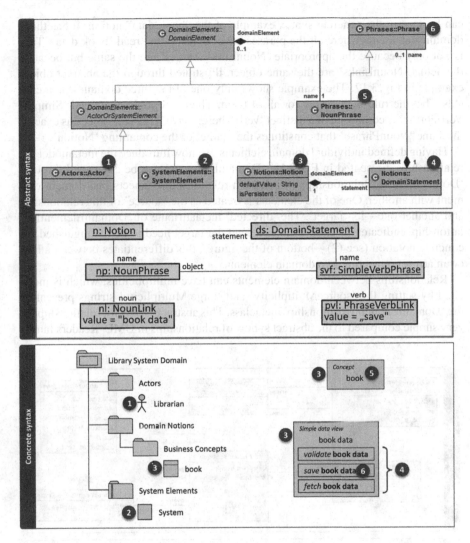

Fig. 3.12 Metamodel for domain elements

contexts it would be more natural to say "**Library Card Scanner** *displays* **scan signal**" instead of using "Library Management System".

'Notions', apart from having names can contain 'DomainStatements'. As the metamodel (Fig. 3.12) shows, this is only the characteristic of notions—actors and system elements do not contain domain statements. Each notion can contain many ('*') such 'statements'. A domain statement is basically composed of a single 'Phrase'. The metamodel may suggest that any phrase will do, but in fact it is important to observe an important constraint. The domain statements in a specific notion must contain phrases that point to the same noun phrase as for the notion's name. This can be seen in the concrete syntax example of the "book data" notion. It has three domain statements where all the phrases have 'objects' that read 'book data'. This is not only because the appropriate 'NounLink' 'values' are the same but because the actual 'NounLinks' are the same object, illustrated through the abstract object example in Fig. 3.12. The example shows only one of the three domain statements ('ds') but the rule is the same for all of them. The appropriate contained 'Simple-VerbPhrase' is composed of a distinct 'verb' (here: "save") but the 'object' is exactly the same 'NounPhrase' that constitutes the 'name' of the containing 'Notion'.

Having defined individual domain elements, we now introduce the metamodel for relationships, presented in Fig. 3.13. 'DomainElements' can be connected through 'DomainElementRelationships'. Each such relationship connects one domain element with another. One of the elements is treated as the 'source' of this relationship and another one—its 'target'. The 'directed' metaattribute of 'DomainElementRelationship' indicates whether the source and the target need to be distinguished. In concrete notation (see (2)—bottom of the figure), this differentiates between a line or an arrow connecting two domain elements.

Relationships between domain elements can have multiplicities, which is modelled by setting the 'sourceMultiplicity' and 'targetMultiplicity' strings present in the 'DomainElementRelationship' metaclass. This abstract syntax for relationships is very simple compared to the abstract syntax of relationships in UML. Readers famil-

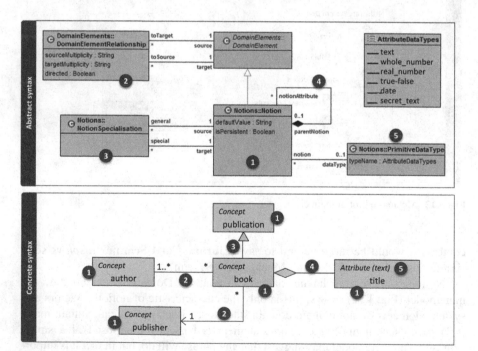

Fig. 3.13 Metamodel for notion relationships

iar with the UML metamodel should remember that e.g. associations are connected to classes through properties that have multiplicities. In RSL this is not necessary because the domain model has sufficient expressiveness without the more complex structures. As a result, the RSL metamodel preserves comprehensibility and provides simple examples for patterns in metamodelling.

Relationships can be modelled between any domain elements (actors, system elements, notions). However, only notions can have specialisations and attributes. The 'NotionSpecialisation' is modelled exactly as the 'DomainElementRelationship'. The 'target' side of the specialisation is denoted with a closed arrowhead (see (3)). The semantics of specialisations are similar to that in UML. In the transformation programs in Chap. 6 we do not use specialisations, so we will not go into the details on this kind of relationship.

On the other hand, attributes are very important for the transformations from RSL to code. Attributes are defined in RSL as regular 'Notions' but with a 'dataType' attached. The data type is defined through the 'PrimitiveDataType' metaclass which holds the 'typeName'. This is an enumerated metaattribute whose possible values can be seen in Fig. 3.13 (top-right). These values reflect the possibilities presented in Sect. 2.3.

Notions can contain many other notions that serve as attributes. In the metamodel in Fig. 3.13 this is defined through a metaaggregation that references from the 'Notion' metaclass to the same metaclass. The contained notions are in the roles of 'notionAttributes'. The concrete notation for this containment is similar to an UML aggregation (see (4)). However, this symbol is not reflected in any metaclass. It can be seen as an extended "joining point" between the composite notion (here: "book") and the contained attribute(s) (here: "title"). This is different from 'DomainElementRelationships' and 'NotionSpecialisations' which, despite similar concrete notation, have their respective metaclasses in the metamodel. This shows different possibilities in shaping the metamodel and its concrete notation.

For the language to be coherent this metamodel has to be extended with some additional constraints. The first constraint says that when a notion is an attribute (has a 'dataType' attached), it cannot contain other attributes. Attributes are atomic and thus cannot be further decomposed into "smaller" attributes. The second constraint says that a notion can have other notions as its 'notionAttributes' only when these other notions are in fact attributes, i.e. have appropriate 'dataTypes' attached. These constraints are obvious but formally have to be specified because the pure metamodel does not prevent certain incoherent situations.

Notions can have attributes but this is often not satisfactory. Thus all the domain elements (and notions) can have additional 'DomainElementRepresentations', as shown in Fig. 3.14. A single domain element can have several separate representations if necessary. A representation is meant to provide detailed specification of some domain element. In requirements specifications this is normally equivalent to a vocabulary-like definition. RSL provides a special construct for this which is the 'NaturalLanguageHypertextSentence'. 'DomainElementRepresentations' are sequences of such sentences, as a result they allow for formulating free text with some hyperlinks inside as shown in the example in Fig. 3.14 (see (2)). The hyperlinks can

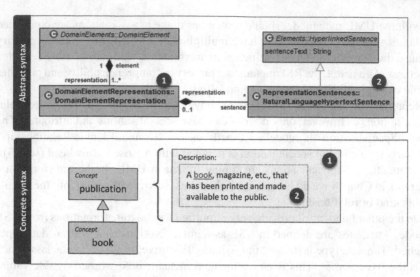

Fig. 3.14 Metamodel for domain element representations

point to domain elements, which makes the whole domain model highly coherent. Natural language hypertext sentences are not used in automatic transformations (see Chap. 6) because of their ambiguous nature associated with free text contents. For this purpose we need more structured sentences which are described in the next section.

3.5 Constrained Language Sentences and Scenarios

The domain model presented in the previous sections provides the building blocks for the actual requirements. Actors, notions and associated phrases define a consistent language which can be used in forming requirements representations. We want the requirements representation language to be very precise, much more precise than the hyperlinked sentences used to represent domain elements. The hyperlinks in these sentences allowed for simple linking between domain elements providing information on semantic relationships between various domain elements. For instance, when a hyperlink to 'book' is used in the definition of 'publication', it necessitates some relationship between these domain elements (see Fig. 3.14). However, the semantics of such a hyperlink in the context of possible code generation is too weak as it is placed within unstructured free text. Thus, appropriate transformation cannot be developed.

For functional requirements representations we want to be able to produce operational code and thus we need strong semantics. This means that the abstract syntax has to be highly structured. We need a constrained language consisting of constrained

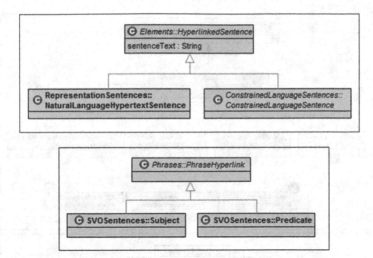

Fig. 3.15 Hyperlinked sentences and phrase hyperlinks

language sentences. RSL provides the necessary constructs through the introduction of the 'ConstrainedLanguageSentence' metaclass, as presented in Fig. 3.15. These sentences are also kind of 'HyperlinkedSentences'. Unlike for 'NaturalLanguage-HypertextSentences', they do not contain free text but their content is composed of only 'PhraseHyperlinks' which form their 'Subjects' and 'Predicates'. If we can write our requirements using only constrained language, our functional requirements specification would contain application logic which is completely defined using the domain phrases contained in the domain model. This gives us good means to define semantics that would translate this coherent RSL syntax into code, as described in the next chapter.

To define the application logic we need several kinds of ConstrainedLanguage-Sentences'. In Fig. 3.16 we can see a complete hierarchy of such sentences. These types reflect the possible concrete constructs of RSL scenarios that we have already presented in Sect. 2.4. Note that there is no separate metaclass for the final sentences. These sentences are joined with postcondition sentences because a post-condition is always associated with a final sentence.

All the constrained language sentences can have free text content. This is because all the appropriate metaclasses specialise the 'HyperlinkedSentence' (see Fig. 3.15), where we can find the 'sentenceText' metaattribute. In concrete syntax this free sentence text is made visual for preconditions (see (6) in Fig. 3.16), postconditions (see (7)) and condition sentences (see (3)). Since this is only free text it is not used for code generation apart from copying it to only code for commentary purposes. For other constrained language sentences this text is not used because their other syntax contains all the necessary elements. For instance, 'RejoinSentences' (see (4)) need only a reference to some other sentence to which control should be passed during rejoining. This is reflected in the metamodel by the appropriate metaassociation

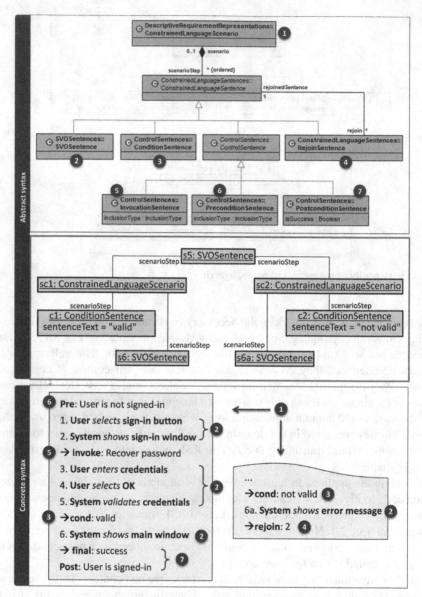

Fig. 3.16 Metamodel for constrained language scenarios

connecting 'RejoinSentence' and 'ConstrainedLanguageSentence'. The syntax for
SVO sentences and invocation sentences is explained later in this and the next section.

Constrained language sentences are grouped into 'Scenarios'. The metamodel
in Fig. 3.16 shows that each scenario (see (1)) can have any number of ordered

constrained language sentences. In concrete notation this is represented by a sequence
of textual sentences, where SVO sentences are numbered (see (2)). The numbers
serve better referencing and readability, but can also be used as labels for the rejoin
sentences. All other types of sentences start with a respective keyword. The concrete keyword syntax was presented in the previous chapter and can also be seen in
Fig. 3.16.

RSL does not specify the actual rules for structuring scenarios. However, for
the purpose of code generation, the rules specified in Sect. 2.4 have to be used as
constraints. These rules define the correct sequences of sentence, that can be checked
by the code generation tools. For practical reasons it is recommended that each
scenario contains pointers to all of its sentences. However, as the example in Fig. 3.16
shows, scenarios can share sentences. In this case the sentences up to number 5 are
identical for both scenarios. Depending on the tool preferences, we could ask to show
or hide the common part. Moreover, for storage optimisation purposes, the actual
sentence objects for sentences up to 5 could be stored once but referred-to by both
scenarios.

An example solution for storing scenarios is shown in the middle part of Fig. 3.16.
This object diagram presents a fragment of the storage for the two scenarios presented
at the bottom in their concrete syntax. This fragment encompasses sentence 5, the
two condition sentences and sentences 6 and 6a. The object for sentence 5 ('s5')
is referred-to by both scenarios, and for the other sentences the scenarios split and
point to their own individual content.

The most often used type of sentence is the 'SVOSentence' (see (2) in Fig. 3.16).
Having all the necessary constructs available in other parts of the RSL metamodel,
the abstract syntax for SVO sentences is extremely simple. It is composed of only
two metaclasses: 'Subject' and 'Predicate', as presented in Fig. 3.17.

Both metaclasses represent phrase hyperlinks (see Fig. 3.15), one pointing at a
'NounPhrase' and the other at a 'VerbPhrase'. These two hyperlinks do not provide
any text that could be combined into the sentence text. Instead, they point to phrases
that have the appropriate text included, illustrated in the middle part of Fig. 3.17. The
example refers to one of the sentences expressed in their-indexsyntax!concrete—
concrete syntax below ('Librarian enters search criteria'). The actual sentence is
composed of the three objects highlighted in the figure with a darker background.
All the other objects in the figure are parts of the domain model. In order to construct
the sentence concrete text we need to follow the links to other objects. The 'Subject'
points at a 'NounPhrase' which is the 'name' of an appropriate 'Actor' defined
in the domain model. This noun phrase has a 'NounLink' that contains the text
("Librarian") to be used in the relevant place in the SVO sentence. The 'Predicate'
points at a 'VerbPhrase' that is contained as a 'name' of a 'DomainStatement' of some
domain 'Notion'. This verb phrase points to a 'VerbLink' (containing "enters") and
indirectly points to a 'NounLink' (containing "search criteria"). Concatenated texts
of these two links finally form the text for the predicate part of our SVO sentence.

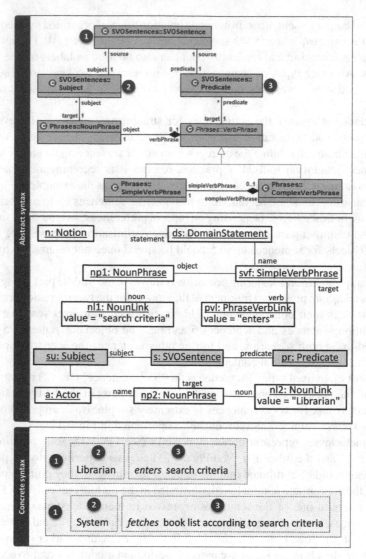

Fig. 3.17 Metamodel for SVO sentences

3.6 Requirements and Use Cases

Scenarios serve describing requirements and they are called 'RequirementsRepresent-ations' in the RSL metamodel. Figure 3.18 shows the appropriate fragment of the metamodel. The official RSL specification provides two groups of requirements rep-resentations: 'DescriptiveRequirementRepresentations' and 'ModelBasedRequire-mentRepresentations'. For the purpose of this book we concentrate on only one of the possible representations, presented earlier in the previous section—'Constrained

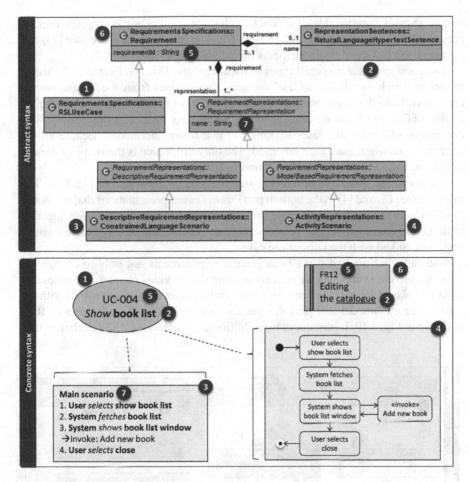

Fig. 3.18 Metamodel for requirements and use cases

LanguageScenarios'. Alternatively, the language users can create 'ActivityScenarios'. We omit this part of the metamodel for brevity and also because it is not used for code generation. Figure 3.18 shows concrete syntax of the two alternative representations (see (3) and (4)) which was presented in the previous sections. The metamodel allows to formulate names for requirements representations. This is often used to name individual scenarios (see (7)).

The 'RequirementRepresentation' metaclass finally brings us to the central element of RSL which is the 'Requirement'. It can be noticed in Fig. 3.18 that every requirement must have at least one representation and possibly can have more (multiplicity '1..*'). There is no restriction on the types of representations and various types can be mixed. Moreover, requirements can have names which are 'NaturalLanguageHypertextSentences' presented in the previous sections. In addition, requirements have identifiers which can be any strings of text (see 'requirementId'). This simple abstract syntax reflects the concrete elements visible to the language user, as presented in the example in Fig. 3.18 (see (6)). The requirement name (see (2)) can contain hyperlinks to domain elements (here: "catalogue").

Use cases in RSL are special types of requirements. This is reflected in the metamodel in which the 'RSLUseCase' metaclass specialises from the 'Requirement' metaclass. Note that the metaclass for use cases is not named simply 'UseCase' to avoid conflicts with the metamodel which we discuss further in this section. The concrete notation for use cases is similar to that for requirements, because all the elements (identifier, name) are inherited. The only difference is the shape of the use case icon, aligned with the notation found in UML.

Use cases can also have different representations as illustrated in Fig. 3.18. The example (see (3) and (4) in the bottom part) shows two representations that are stored together with the presented use case. In tools they are normally not shown together with the use case icon but can be accessed from separate diagrams or textual editor windows, linked with the current use case.

Use cases are made distinct from generic requirements not only to change the icon in concrete syntax. As we remember from the previous chapter, use cases can be in «invoke» relationships between themselves and can be in relationships with the actors. The metamodel that provides the abstract syntax for these features of RSL is shown in Fig. 3.19. It introduces two additional metaclasses: 'UsageRelationship'

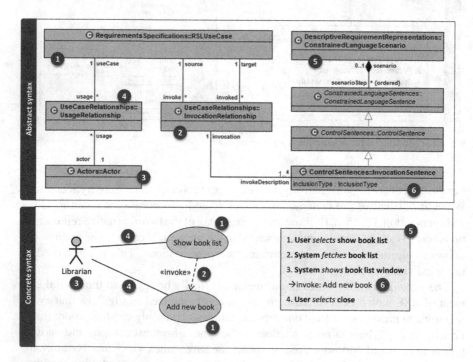

Fig. 3.19 Metamodel for use case relationships

and 'InvocationRelationship'. The abstract syntax is simple and similar to the syntax of relationships between domain elements. The metamodel defines that there can be many invocation relationships (2) coming out or going into a particular use case. The same situation is for the usage relationships (4). For the invocation relationships the metamodel itself does not prevent from self-referencing relations (from a use case to itself). Obviously, such a relationship is not valid and thus we have to explicitly express a separate constraint to prevent this.

An important feature of the invocation relationship is that it is directly attached to invocation sentences in scenarios. Every 'InvocationRelationship' must have at least one corresponding 'InvocationSentence'. On the other hand, every 'Invocation-Sentence' must point to exactly one 'InvocationRelationship'. This feature of the metamodel enforces strict coherence of use cases and their representations. A single use case can be invoked from several use cases and/or from several places of another use case. This only depends on the other use case scenarios and how many invocation sentences are associated with the appropriate invocation relationship. Of course, the metamodel has to be appended with a constraint stating that the invocation sentence attached to a given invocation relationship has to be present in a scenario of the invoking use case, and not of the invoked one.

The RSL's metamodel for use cases and their relationships can be contrasted with the similar metamodel in UML. The UML version is presented in Fig. 3.20. The most visible difference is the presence of the 'Include' and 'Extend' relationships. Note that 'include' is owned by the 'includingCase'. This means that the information about inclusion is defined within the use case that includes another use case. By contrast, the 'extendedCase' is not aware about which other use cases extend it. This information is stored in the 'extension', i.e. in the use case that extends another use case. In RSL, these ownership considerations at the level of use cases are not relevant. This is because 'InvocationRelationships' have to be combined with 'InvocationSentences' which are always contained in the invoking use case.

Despite the extending use case not being aware of the extending use cases, it has to contain appropriate 'ExtensionPoints'. The role of extension points is to denote places where the behaviour of a use case can be extended through the 'Extend' relationships. Extension points serve as 'extensionLocations'. For unambiguous identification, they need to have textual 'names'. This is realised through the 'ExtensionPoint' metaclass indirectly specialising from the 'NamedElement' metaclass. In general, most UML constructs are named elements which is one of the reasons for having quite complex specialisation hierarchies in the UML's metamodel.

There has to be at least one extension point available for any 'Extend' to make sense. Moreover, the extension points have to be ordered. This is necessary to unambiguously associate the extending behaviours with specific extension points. Unlike for RSL's invocations, the extension points need not be associated with any 'Extend' relationship and they can also be associated with more than one of them. By contrast, in RSL, an invocation sentence has to be identified with exactly one invocation relationship.

Note from Fig. 3.20 that there is no equivalent for extension points related to the 'Include' relationship. There are no "inclusion points" in UML. This shows one of

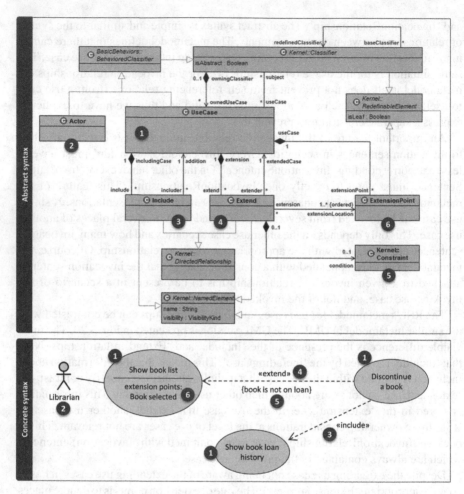

Fig. 3.20 Comparison: metamodel for use cases in UML

the several deficiencies of the UML's metamodel in this area. UML lacks any notation for locating the actual points in the use case logic at which the inclusions are to be made. This makes it impossible to define any control flow semantics in this respect.

To have some level of runtime semantic precision, use cases in UML need to be defined in terms of their application logic. UML gives some possibilities in this area which are realised through the 'UseCase' metaclass specialising in the so-called 'BehavioredClassifier'. This abstract metaclass provides a common ground for various UML constructs that should expose some behaviour. It allows to append 'Classifiers' (like classes, use cases and actors) with behavioural models (like activities, interactions and state machines). However, there are no specific syntactic rules for using these behaviours within the use case models. The UML users are free to define any such model in any possible way. Moreover, there is no syntax for determining the flow of control between different use case behaviours. Although 'Extension-Points' exist in UML, there is no semantically unambiguous way to relate them to such behavioural constructs like actions, transitions or messages. In RSL this is precisely defined through associating invocations with invocation sentences. Invocation sentences are precisely located within use case scenarios. In this way, control flow semantics is very strict and can easily serve to generate operational code.

When examining the UML's use case metamodel in Fig. 3.20, the reader may notice three more issues. The first issue is the 'Constraint' metaclass associated with the 'Extend' metaclass. Constraints are used in UML in various places to denote statements that express some conditions. In this case, the extend relationship can have an additional 'condition' which determines whether the particular extension instance can take place or not. This again raises the question of control flow semantics. It is not certain at which place (or places) in the extended use cases these conditions would be checked and how control would flow within the use case behaviour. In RSL, flow of control is unambiguously determined by condition sentences placed within scenarios.

The second remaining issue is the lack of a metamodel element for relationships between use cases and actors. This can be explained through both modelling elements specialising from 'BehavioredClassifier'. Classifiers in general can be related through association relationships. This part of the metamodel is defined elsewhere and is not shown in this diagram. This however shows complexity of the UML's metamodel which necessitates traversing through complex hierarchies of metaclasses to understand the full syntax.

The third issue is related with the 'Classifier' metaclass which is in two metarelations with the 'UseCase' metaclass. This can be seen as equivalent to what is available in RSL's scenarios and sentences. Every SVO sentence in RSL can have a subject which refers to a 'SystemElement'. This makes it unambiguous as to what system is defined through the use case that contains this sentence as part of its representation. In UML there is no such construct. Yet, we would want to denote which system "owns" the given use case and is the "subject" of its behaviour. The solution in UML was to introduce such relations at the use case level rather than at the use case representation (behaviour) level.

3.7 Domain and Requirements Specifications

To organise and group its various constructs, RSL uses the notion of package, which is used extensively in UML. However, RSL introduces several specialisations of packages and thus provides much more rigour in structuring requirements-related models. A the highest level, this rigour is assured by dividing the specification into two parts: one part holds the domain elements and their representations, and the other part—the requirements with their representations.

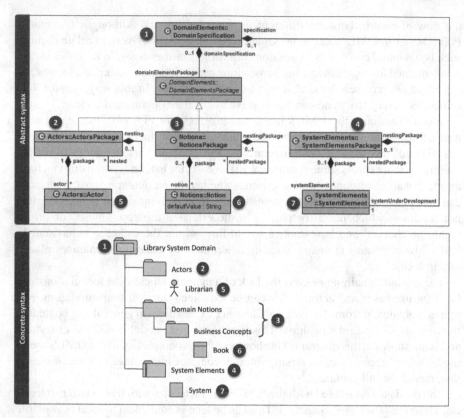

Fig. 3.21 Metamodel for domain specifications

Figure 3.21 shows the structure of the first part. The topmost construct is the 'DomainSpecification' which is normally represented as the root in the specification tree (see (1)). The 'DomainSpecification' metaclass specialises the UML's 'Package' metaclass thus providing one of the links between the two metamodels. The same specialisations are present for other package-related metaclasses in RSL. UML's packages can have names (as they are also specialising 'NamedElements'), and thus also RSL's packages can have names.

Domain specifications can contain several 'DomainElementsPackages'. RSL provides specialised packages for actors ('ActorsPackage'), notions ('NotionsPackage') and system elements ('SystemElementsPackage'). There are no restrictions on the number of domain element packages that can be contained in the domain specification. However, in a tool this can be restricted to just one of each kind. Each of the kinds can contain 'nested' packages of the same kind. Thus, for instance, actors packages can hold only other actors packages. This prevents from mixing concerns and makes the whole specification coherent. Obviously, domain element packages can hold respective domain elements ('Actors', 'Notions' and 'SystemElements').

As for 'nested' packages, the type of the held elements matches the type of the package. As a result, we have a tree with three main branches holding domain elements of the three types.

'DomainSpecification' pertains to a specific 'systemUnderDevelopment' (see Fig. 3.21). This is the top level 'SystemElement' that represents the actual system for which this specification is developed. Domain specifications are local to systems. Each system under development has its domain specification separate from specifications for possible other systems under development. This is important for organisations that develop many systems and prevents from confusing vocabularies. For instance, the notion of "user account" can have varying meanings (and associated attributes) in different systems. On the other hand, the term "user account" can be reused many times as such, in its generic sense. This observation led to introducing the separate global 'Terminology', presented in Sect. 3.3. The terminology can be common for many systems, leading to possible reuse of notions associated with specific terms. Moreover, it allows to compare different domain elements and requirements for possible matching and reuse.

'DomainSpecifications' are tightly coupled with 'RequirementsSpecifications'. In fact, it is a one-to-one relationship, as shown in Fig. 3.22. Thus, for each system under development we have a single domain specification and a single requirements

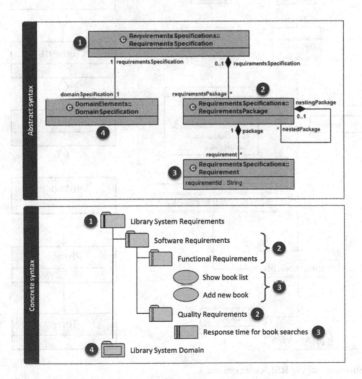

Fig. 3.22 Metamodel for requirements specifications

specification. These two specifications form two roots in the specification tree structure. Just like for their domain counterparts, 'RequirementsSpecifications' specialise packages. They can contain many 'RequirementsPackages' which are nested structures. Finally, requirements packages can contain many 'Requirements' (including 'UseCases'), which makes the metamodel complete. This abstract syntax is reflected in the concrete syntax presented at the bottom of Figs. 3.21 and 3.22. This concrete syntax is familiar to all modelling tool users and was presented in detail in the previous chapter.

With these top level modelling elements we conclude the presentation of the RSL's metamodel. Generally, this metamodel reflects the overall philosophy of stacking more and more complex constructs on top of simpler ones. Specifications are composed of requirements and domain elements. Requirements and domain elements contain representations which consist of sentences. These sentences refer to phrases which link to individual (and atomic) terms as illustrated in Fig. 3.23 (generalised and simplified metamodel to the right, concrete notation to the left). Note that the connection between the domain specification and the requirements specification is at

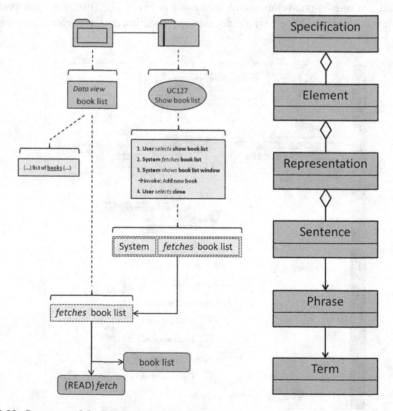

Fig. 3.23 Summary of the RSL's element stack

the level of phrase hyperlinks. These links are a part of sentences in requirements representations (mostly scenarios). The links point to phrases that are a part of domain notions.

3.8 Summary of Metamodelling

When presenting the metamodel of RSL we have used class diagrams composed of classes, associations, attributes and so on. We did this informally, assuming that the reader is familiar with class diagrams. We have used a very limited subset of what can be seen as the UML's class model language. This subset is satisfactory for developing metamodels and we call it a "metamodelling language". As a modelling language (suitable for modelling models), this language also needs to have its definition. Obviously, we should also create a metamodel for this purpose which is a level higher than the RSL metamodel, and we call it a meta-metamodel.

Because the language is simple, its metamodel is also simple. It contains only 7 metaclasses, as presented in Fig. 3.24. In fact, only four metaclasses in this metamodel represent concrete modelling elements: 'Class', 'Property', 'Generaliation' and 'Association' (marked with numbers in circles). The other three metaclasses provide general typing and naming scheme. As we can see, the metamodel is structured similarly to that for RSL, however, there are some interesting features that we explain below.

The 'Generalisation' relationship (see (2)) can link two classes (the 'general' one with the 'specific' one). We can thus notice that our language allows for single generalisation only. Any 'specific' class can have at most one 'generalisation' (multiplicity '0..1'). When we examine all the metamodel diagrams in this chapter, we can notice that single generalisation is followed throughout. Only the use case metamodel taken from the UML specification uses multiple generalisations (e.g. the 'Extend' metaclass specialises two metaclasses, as shown in Fig. 3.20). This metamodel is thus not part of the RSL specification and it uses somewhat extended language. In our meta-metamodel in Fig. 3.24 we could easily update this by changing multiplicity for 'generalisation' to '0..*'.

Another interesting feature of our meta-metamodel is the way it handles associations. The 'Association' metaclass is not connected to the 'Class' metaclass but is connected to 'Property'. To explain this we use the object diagram available in Fig. 3.24. This diagram shows that classes (see 'c1') can contain "simple" properties and properties with associations. Simple properties serve as the class' attributes. Properties with associations serve as the roles of these associations. The object diagram is equivalent to the respective part of the concrete syntax example in the bottom part. The property 'p1' is contained in 'c1' and is connected to its counterpart 'p2' contained in 'c2' through the association 'a'. In concrete notation, property 'p1' ("representation") is visualised at the other end of the association. It also contains the multiplicity string which is derived from two metaattributes: 'lower' and 'upper'. The upper limit is set to -1 which denotes infinity.

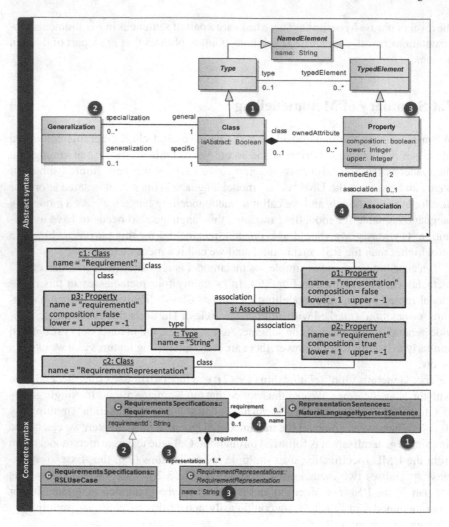

Fig. 3.24 Metamodel for the metamodelling language

Associations in our simple meta-language are binary (have two ends) and not navigable (do not have arrows). To introduce n-ary and navigable associations, we would need to substitute the metaassociation between 'Association' and 'Property'. Instead of one metaassociation with multiplicity '2' we would need two metaassociations with multiplicity '1..*'. In fact, this flexibility in shaping associations is the main benefit of introducing the solution with associations linked through properties. All the information about association ends (the 'lower' and the 'upper' value for multiplicity, presence of the 'composition' diamond) can be contained in the properties instead of in some additional metaelements attached to associations.

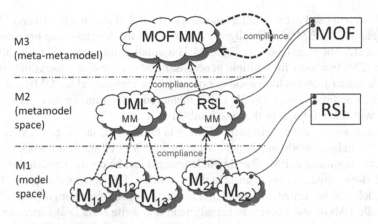

Fig. 3.25 Levels of metamodelling

A careful reader may notice that our meta-metamodel (i.e. the upper part of Fig. 3.24) is also written in some language and this language would again necessitate defining a metamodel (a meta–meta-metamodel?). This would lead us to an infinite regression of metamodels. Fortunately, the meta-metamodel is written in exactly the same language it defines, in other words, it is self-reflective. This limits our meta-modelling hierarchy to only three levels, as illustrated in Fig. 3.25. Level M1 contains individual models written in particular modelling languages (UML, RSL, etc.). Level M2 contains metamodels defining the modelling languages. Models, in order to be treated as correct have to comply with these metamodels. Metamodels are written in a common metamodelling language (called "MOF" in the figure). This common language also has a metamodel (level M3) that defines it and to which it has to comply. This meta-metamodel is written in the same language (MOF) as the metamodels it defines. So, the meta-metamodel complies with itself, providing a "bootstrapping" mechanism.

The above hierarchy of metamodels defines a coherent framework for defining various modelling languages. Using a single meta-language with its meta-metamodel we can define many different languages that are defined using the same techniques. This approach was developed as a continuation of the idea started in the first specifications of UML (versions 1.x). In these early days, UML was defined using UML's class diagrams in the same bootstrapping manner as the meta-modelling language described above. Later, this class model language was extracted from UML and is treated as a separate language dedicated to specifying metamodels—extending its application from just UML to any other modelling language. This meta-language is called Meta Object Facility (MOF, see again Fig. 3.25)[1] [123] and is managed by the Object Management Group. MOF in one of its earlier versions is also standardised by ISO [75].

---

[1] http://www.omg.org/mof/.

MOF is composed of two similar languages—EMOF (Essential MOF) and CMOF (Complete MOF). EMOF only slightly differs from the language we have used to present RSL. The metamodel in Fig. 3.24 is a small simplification of EMOF. For instance, EMOF allows for multiple generalisations and for class operations; it also introduces other features like property ordering. The metamodel for UML use cases in Fig. 3.20 is drawn using EMOF. Other metamodel diagrams in this chapter also comply with EMOF because they use a subset of it.

The most significant counterpart of EMOF is Ecore. This language is extensively used in the Eclipse world and is part of the Eclipse Modelling Framework (EMF)[2] [28]. Ecore is similar to EMOF and both languages can be easily translated into one another. Both languages offer serialisation facilities. This means that graph-based metamodels can be turned into serial text for the purpose of exchanging data. Tools that handle EMOF and Ecore can usually read and write serialized forms for both languages. This serialised form is based on XML and is called XMI (XML Metadata Interchange) [124].

Official specifications of RSL[3] [83] and UML[4] [121, 122] use a somewhat extended metamodelling language. This is CMOF, which has several additional features. It provides constructs for the management of more complex metamodels, constructed by merging many packages at several levels in the generalisation hierarchies. The additional constructs allow for subsetting and redefining metaclass properties. This makes large metamodels more readable and manageable but at the same time does not allow for direct implementation using typical object-oriented languages—no direct mapping from CMOF exists. For this purpose, a metamodel in CMOF has to be transformed into its EMOF or Ecore version. Sometimes (for instance in the case of Java), an even simpler language (with single generalisation) has to be used.

Metamodelling languages are the basis for several tools that allow for creating modelling language environments. Such tools are called language workbenches [46], where the term was introduced by Martin Fowler [53]. There are many language workbenches on the market. Some of them are embedded in modelling tools, while some are stand-alone. Their main characteristic is that they allow for specifying the abstract syntax in the form of a metamodel and the concrete syntax in the form of graphical element designs. Many language workbenches offer capabilities to define the syntax of textual language elements. Using context-free grammars, as in the example for verb phrases in Sect. 3.3. In this sense, language workbenches can be compared to compiler compilers that facilitate the development of compilers for textual languages.

Apart from language workbenches, metamodels are used as a part of model transformation languages and their tooling environments. In order to perform a model transformation, we need to know the metamodels of the source and the target models. A model transformation language can use an external definition (e.g. taken from the language workbench) or can allow to define the metamodel directly.

---

[2] http://www.eclipse.org/modeling/emf/.

[3] See the documentation section at http://www.redseeds.eu/.

[4] http://www.uml.org/.

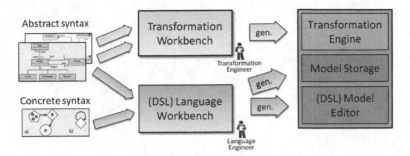

Fig. 3.26 Process of developing a modelling language

A comprehensive solution to develop modelling languages should provide integration of the language workbench and model transformation tools as illustrated in Fig. 3.26. To develop a new language (e.g. a Domain Specific Language) we need to know its abstract syntax (metamodel) and concrete syntax (graphical symbols and textual grammars). These two elements are input by the language engineers to the language workbench which can automatically generate a model editor together with model storage. The abstract syntax of our new language should be also input to a model transformation tool (we also call it a "transformation workbench"). We would also need the abstract syntax of the target language. Having these two metamodels, the transformation engineers can develop transformation programs and then generate transformation engines for the new language that result in a tooling environment that consists of the (DSL) Model Editor, Model Storage and Transformation Engine. This can be compared to IDEs (Integrated Development Environments) for programming languages which contain syntax-checking editors and compilers that transform source languages (e.g. Java) into target languages (e.g. bytecode).

Figure 3.26 lacks an important element which is necessary to build the transformation engine—the runtime semantics of the new language. Only having defined this kind of semantics we can write a sensible model transformation that generates code. The next three chapters are dedicated to this broad issue.

Chapter 4
Explaining RSL with Java

In Chaps. 2 and 3, we presented the concrete (visual) and abstract syntax of RSL. Chapter 2 also contains the conceptual semantics of RSL, which explains it in terms of observable system behaviour. This quite informal explanation is sufficient for the understanding of end-users and domain experts. However, to develop formal transformations from RSL to code we need a much more formal definition of the requirements semantics [144] in relation to the system runtime [154]. This chapter presents all the necessary details.

4.1 Translational Framework

There exist several well-established ways to formally define the semantics of software languages [98, 146, 186]. Many of these approaches use complex mathematical frameworks which are hard to grasp by language implementers. We use an approach that is more "user friendly" and uses a pragmatic engineering approach [174]. This approach is to define the semantics of a language by translating it to the semantics of another (simpler) language with already known semantics [48, 91].

We call this approach the **translational semantics**. Figure 4.1 illustrates the overall concept. To explain a language ("Source language") we introduce another language ("Target language") and define rules for translating from the source language to the target language. Every construct of the source language syntax is translated into certain constructs of the target language syntax. The whole translation involves only the syntax.

The target language is usually a simple language whose semantics is well-defined (using other formal methods or even informally). The semantics of the source language can thus be derived from the semantics of the target language. This is because every source model or program can be translated into a target model or program. This translation changes syntax (from source to target) but does not change the semantics.

© Springer International Publishing Switzerland 2015
M. Śmiałek and W. Nowakowski, *From Requirements to Java in a Snap*,
DOI 10.1007/978-3-319-12838-2_4

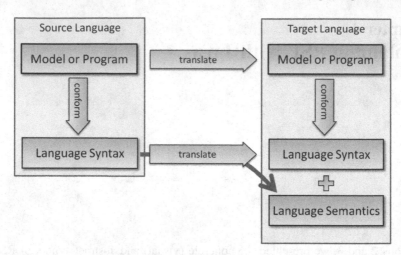

Fig. 4.1 Explaining a language through translation

A typical example of applying translational semantics is the definition of high-level imperative programming language. Such languages can be translated into a simple assembly level language. Every instruction of a high-level language can be translated into several instructions of the assembly language. In this way, the meaning of a particular instruction is well-defined through the meaning of the assembly language instructions that substitute it. This approach is pragmatic in terms of its direct application in compiler construction. The language engineers can take the language semantics and use it directly to generate executable code. This is because the target language in the definition of the translational semantics is easy to map onto the target language of the particular compiler.

To apply translational semantics to RSL we only need to observe that it is a higher level language than the current 3G languages like Java. We can thus propose to translate RSL constructs into 3G language constructs [70]. Semantics of 3GLs is well known and is applied daily by millions of contemporary programmers. Thus, this approach should make the semantics of RSL understandable to them. Explaining the semantics of RSL in terms of a 3GL is also very pragmatic. Based on the translation rules we can relatively easily construct a transformation program that would generate 3GL code and ultimately executable code. We thus do not need to translate RSL into assembly language—it is enough to translate it to a 3GL.

The target language that we use for translation from RSL in this chapter will be a hybrid one. It will partially consist of UML class models and partially of Java-like code. This will allow us to present the code structure in a more comprehensible way than by using only Java. Moreover, this approach is more compatible with model transformations that we introduce in the following chapters. It allows us to define a full transformation from RSL to Java code using largely the UML metamodel (see Chap. 6).

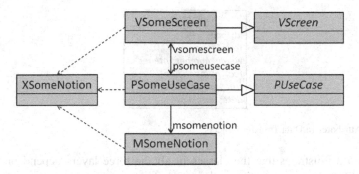

Fig. 4.2 Translational framework structure

The language and its framework that we chose for the translational semantics is arbitrary. The main rationale is pragmatics and further application of translation rules in constructing an appropriate transformation from RSL to code. We chose UML and Java as the overall approach because it is widely known to a vast majority of software developers. However, we also need to decide on more detailed issues like representing application and domain logic, and the user interface elements. This is important because RSL has several constructs that necessitate translation into the system's logic and into the constructs that exchange data with the user through the user interface.

The most appropriate architectural framework for code being the target of translation from RSL seems to be the Model-View-Presenter (MVP) pattern introduced earlier in Sect. 1.1. The variant we use here is presented in Fig. 4.2. The classes in the View layer represent UI screens and they specialise (inherit) from the standard abstract class 'VScreen'. By convention, the names of these classes start with the letter 'V'. Similarly, the classes in the Presenter layer represent use cases and specialise from the standard abstract class 'PUseCase'. By convention, the names of these classes start with the letter 'P'. Finally, the classes in the Model layer represent notions and their names start with the letter 'M'.

Classes in the three layers are related through associations. Associations between the Presenter layer and the View layer are bidirectional, and the associations from the Presenter layer to the Model layer are unidirectional. This is due to the characteristics of the MVP framework which uses the variant with active Presenter. This MVP variant does not introduce any associations between the Model and the View layer classes.

Note that the framework we use refers to an abstract (non-existent) technology. We assume that the View elements specialise from 'VScreen' and the Presenter elements specialise from 'PUseCase' which do not in fact exist in any specific technology framework. Instead of using an arbitrarily chosen technology, we introduce a simplified abstract framework which should be easy to comprehend and at the same time easy to translate to specific frameworks like JavaFX, Echo3, GWT or similar. In fact, the rules presented further in this chapter allow for relatively easy translation into any framework that is based on the MVP (or MVC) pattern.

XSomeNotion
id: long
text: String
whole_number: integer
real_number: float
true_false: boolean
date: DateTime

Fig. 4.3 Attributes in Data Transfer Objects

Figure 4.2 illustrates that the classes in all the three layers depend on certain classes with their names starting with an 'X'. These are special classes called Data Transfer Objects (DTO). Instances of these classes are used to pass data between layers—up from the user down to the database and vice versa. Each DTO has one or more attributes that hold appropriate data values, as illustrated in Fig. 4.3. We assume standard built-in data types like integer, float and boolean. Also, String and DateTime are assumed as built-in. Every DTO class contains the standard 'id' attribute. This attribute is a long integer and it holds the object's unique identifier. These identifiers are used to indicate objects within lists and can serve for organising object retrieval from the database.

The target MVP classes have a specific structure as illustrated in Fig. 4.4. This structure is assumed in the translation rules presented in the following sections. The classes follow strict rules regarding the attributes and operations they possess.

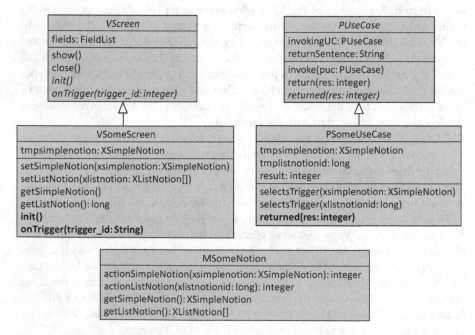

Fig. 4.4 Operations in MVP classes

All the View classes specialise from 'VScreen'. This class defines one attribute, two concrete operations and two abstract operations. The single attribute is of type 'FieldList' which is specific to our abstract UI framework. This is an ordered list of data fields. Each field can represent data of one of the standard types (see Fig. 4.3). The fields can be simple (holding one value) or column (holding many values). The fields can be defined, written and read using operations that are presented further in this section.

The 'fields' attribute is used by the 'show()' operation. This operation opens a new window or page, renders all the fields and presents them to the user. If the fields have their values set, these values are also presented. The actual layout of the simple fields in a window is not determined as this is not covered by the presented semantics definition. Consecutive column fields are presented as one list containing rows with appropriate values taken from the value lists associated with the columns. The opposite of the 'show()' operation is the 'close()' operation which removes the window associated with the current View element. This operation also shows the window that was shown previously. In general, 'show()' and 'close()' operate on a stack of windows. The first operation places a window on the stack, and the second removes a window, showing the one that is at the top of the stack.

The above two operations are concrete and are assumed to be already implemented as part of the framework. The two other operations of 'VScreen' are abstract and have to be implemented by the concrete specialising classes. The 'init()' operation contains code that defines all the fields in a given window. This code should add field definitions to the 'fields' attribute. The 'onTrigger()' operation is a standard event handler operation that is called by the operating system whenever an event occurs within a user interface. Normally, this means pressing a button in a window or selecting a menu option. This operation has to be implemented in a specialising class with code that depends on the 'trigger_id' parameter. This parameter determines the actual trigger (button, option) that was selected.

Each class that specialises from 'VScreen' has to implement the two abstract operations, but also to introduce some other operations and attributes. These operations pertain to setting and getting field values based on DTO attribute values. Figure 4.4 presents an example involving a simple DTO and a list DTO. For simple DTOs there have to be defined two operations and one attribute. The first operation should write the fields from the DTO (here: 'setSimpleNotion()') and the second should read the fields ('getSimpleNotion()') and set the DTO attribute ('tmpsimplenotion'). For list DTOs, we also need two operations but no attribute is needed. The first operation should write the column fields from a DTO table, while the second operation should return only the identifier (cf. 'id' in Fig. 4.3) of one DTO from the associated list—the one currently selected by the user.

Also, the Presenter classes have a strict structure as they all specialise from 'PUse-Case'. This abstract class implements a generic invocation mechanism through two attributes and three operations. This mechanism is in fact an invocation stack that allows to control the flow of logic between the Presenter class instances. The attribute 'returnSentence' is used to remember the context in which the invocation was performed. After returning from invocation, the context has to be restored and control flow should return to a particular "sentence". The attribute 'invokingUC' is used by the invoked Presenter class instance. It is tightly related to the 'invoke()' and 'return()' operations. The first one sets the invoking instance (a derivative of 'PUse-Case') and the second returns control to this remembered invoking instance. Return of control is done by calling the 'returned()' operation of the invoking instance. Its 'res' parameter passes the final state of the invoked use case. Every Presenter class that is involved in invoking Presenter instances should implement the 'returned()' operation. We explain this mechanism in detail later in this section.

Invocation control is only part of the logic contained in the Presenter classes. They must also implement event handlers that contain application logic. These event handlers respond to triggers that are captured by the View classes. Figure 4.4 shows a typical example of such operations. Their names reflect the events of selecting certain triggers in the user interface (buttons, options). When needed, these operations pass parameters. Two types of parameters are possible: simple DTOs or list DTO identifiers. For each parameter in an event handler operation, a separate attribute has to be declared in that class. These attributes are used as temporary storage for exchanging data between the View layer and the Model layer. In addition to these attributes, each Presenter class that calls operations of the Model layer should have the 'result' attribute. This attribute is used to store the results of data processing within the Model layer.

To explain the mechanism that uses the 'result' attribute, we use the sequence diagram presented in Fig. 4.5. This diagram generally serves to explain the presented

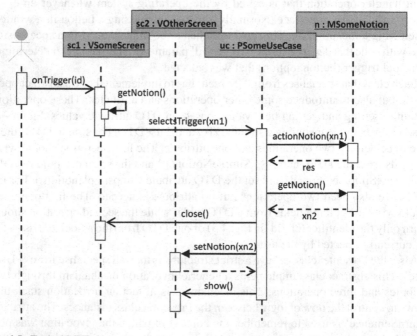

Fig. 4.5 Typical MVP dynamics

variant of MVP in terms of its dynamics. The sequence presented in the diagram implements a couple of steps in a use case scenario. Full implementation of a use case will necessitate several of such sequences.

A typical sequence of actions starts with selecting some trigger by the user and finishes with presenting some screen. After selecting a trigger, the operating system calls the 'onTrigger()' operation of the currently displayed screen (here: 'sc1'). Depending on the trigger 'id', an appropriate event handling operation is called from one of the Presenter class instances (here: 'uc'). In case some data need to be passed, a 'getNotion()' operation has to be called first. This operation collects data from the current screen's fields and places them in a temporary DTO attribute. Then, this attribute is passed as the parameter (here: 'xn1') of the event handling operation (here: 'selectsTrigger()'). Communication between the View and the Presenter is asynchronous, so the 'selectsTrigger()' message does not have a return message; 'onTrigger()' does not wait for 'selectsTrigger()' to finish.

After a Presenter class instance takes control, the sequence depends on the particular logic that is needed. This logic can involve performing some reading, writing or processing data by the Model layer. It also involves calling operations from the View layer. In the example in Fig. 4.5 we see that this particular logic starts by performing some domain logic action ('actionNotion()') on a Model class instance ('n'). The appropriate message is synchronous and thus can return a result. As we can see in Fig. 4.4, the appropriate operations of the Model layer classes return integer values. These values can serve to make certain decisions by the Presenter and branching the flow of control. Our example sequence diagram does not show alternative flows and concentrates on only one of them. After some data manipulation is done by the Model layer instance ('n'), the logic may involve retrieving some data and this is done through an appropriate data passing operation ('getNotion()'). The data passed from the Model can then be transferred to the View through calling the appropriate setter operation in the View layer ('setNotion()'). It can be noted that both the getter and the setter operations are synchronous because the Presenter needs to wait for their completion before commencing other actions. In our particular example, after setting the data within the appropriate View instance ('sc2'), it is then shown to the user. In one of the previous actions, the Presenter can ask the previous screen element ('sc1') to close itself ('close()').

This general structure and dynamics is implemented with detailed code which we denote in a Java-like language. Figures 4.6 and 4.8 present typical implementations of the operations described above. The figures contain only the method contents, and the appropriate operation signature (parameters, return types) can be found in the UML notation in Fig. 4.4.

Figure 4.6 presents the field-related code of the View layer classes. The 'init()' method is called at the beginning and initialises the 'fields' attribute for a given View class. All the instructions in the method's code operate on 'fields' and add respective elements. There are several possible instructions to add fields of various basic types. For simple fields, we can also add an optional label. For example, line 1 in our example adds a new text field (containing a string) with the label "Text".

```
      init()
01:  fields.addLabel("Text"); fields.addTextField();
02:  fields.addLabel("Number"); fields.addIntegerField();
03:  fields.addIdClField();
04:  fields.addTextClField("Text");
05:  fields.addFloatClField("Real number");
06:  fields.addButton("Save");
```

```
   getSimpleNotion()
01:  tmpsimplenotion.text = fields.getTextField(1);
02:  tmpsimplenotion.number = fields.getIntegerField(2);
```

```
   getListNotion()
01:  return fields.getIdClField(3);
```

```
   setSimpleNotion(...)
01:  tmpsimplenotion = xsimplenotion;
02:  fields.setTextField(1,tmpsimplenotion.text);
03:  fields.setIntegerField(2,tmpsimplenotion.number);
```

```
   setListNotion(...)
01:for (int i=1; i<=len(xlistnotion); i++) {
02:     fields.setIdField(3,xlistnotion[i].id);
03:     fields.setTextField(4,xlistnotion[i].text);
04:     fields.setFloatField(5,xlistnotion[1].realnumber);
05: }
```

Fig. 4.6 Typical code for the View classes (init/get/set)

Other possibilities include adding integer fields (see line 2), floating point number fields (Float), date/time fields and Boolean fields.

In addition to simple fields that hold single values, we can add column fields. The respective instructions contain the 'Cl' infix, like in lines 3–5. Possible column types are identical as for the simple fields. A column field can contain a list of values which are ordered in the sequence in which they were set. Several column fields that are initialised together form a list field. Each of the columns in the list has a header text which is specified as a string in a parameter within the 'Cl' instructions. A special type of column is the ID column (see line 3). This column holds object identifiers that should match the 'id' attribute values of the respective list DTOs.

Finally, the screen can hold buttons and these can be added by the instruction 'addButton()' (see line 6). The sequence in which the fields are added determines the layout of the screen. An example is shown in Fig. 4.7. This layout is consistent with the code of the 'init()' method shown in Fig. 4.6. Note that the ID column is not shown—it is only held internally for referencing selected rows in the list, which is explained below.

The next method in Fig. 4.6 is 'getSimpleNotion()'. It is an example implementation of an operation to produce a simple DTO from several fields contained in a screen element. The presented code assumes that the containing class has an appropriate DTO attribute called 'tmpsimplenotion'. The appropriate attributes of this DTO are set with the values contained in consecutive fields. For instance, to get a

Fig. 4.7 Example screen
layout

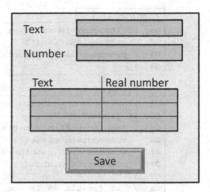

text field value, we need to use the instruction 'getTextField(x)'. This instruction
has one parameter that determines the field sequence number. Fields are numbered
according to the sequence in which they were added to the 'fields' attribute in the
'init()' method.

Attribute values for simple DTOs are retrieved from simple fields. Lists, composed
of several column fields are handled differently as shown in the 'getListNotion()'
method. As we can see in Fig. 4.4, only one long integer value is returned in such
case. This value is taken from the appropriate ID field using the instruction 'getId-
ClField(x)'. This instruction returns one value which is the ID value of the row
currently selected by the user within the current list element.

The remaining two methods in Fig. 4.6 represent the field setters. The first method
('setSimpleNotion()') is used to set the values of the simple fields associated with
a specific simple DTO. This method assumes a single parameter which is a DTO.
The fields are set with appropriate 'set' instructions (see lines 2 and 3) which are
analogous to the 'add' and 'get' instructions presented above. These instructions
have two parameters. The first parameter determines the field id number, like for the
'get' instructions, while the second parameter is the value to be set taken from an
appropriate attribute value of a DTO. This setting is supported by the class attribute
(here: 'tmpsimplenotion') which is assigned with the appropriate DTO parameter
(see line 1, compare with Fig. 4.4).

The second setter method ('setListNotion()') pertains to list DTOs. It uses the
same instructions as for the simple fields (see lines 3 and 4) but applied to the column
fields. These instructions are called in a 'for' loop which iterates over objects in a
DTO table which is the parameter of the method. The 'set' instructions applied to
column fields add consecutive values to value lists held within these column fields.
Of course, also the ID column needs to be set with an appropriate 'set' instruction
(see line 2).

Fields are read and written as a result of certain actions performed by the user.
These actions are handled by the View layer classes through the 'onTrigger()' methods. A typical structure of code in this method is presented in Fig. 4.8. It is a series
of 'if' statements which check the 'trigger_id' passed as the method's parameter.

```
onTrigger(...)
01: if (trigger_id == "Save") {
02:    getSimpleNotion();
03:    psomeusecase.selectsTrigger(tmpsimplenotion);
04: }
```

```
selectsTrigger(...)
01: result = mothernotion.actionOtherNotion(tmpsimplenotion);
02: if (result == 0) {
03:    tmpothernotion = mothernotion.getOtherNotion();
04:    vsomescreen.close();
05:    votherscreen.setOtherNotion(tmpothernotion);
06:    votherscreen.show();
07: }
08: /* if (result == 1) etc. */
```

Fig. 4.8 Typical code for event handling (View and Presenter)

For a particular trigger, an appropriate Presenter layer operation is called (here: 'selectsTrigger()'). Of course, the appropriate role identifier (here: 'psomeusecase') is used to determine the specific Presenter class instance on which the operation is called. If the particular trigger is supposed to pass data to the Presenter, the appropriate local 'get' operation is called which collects data from the screen's fields and puts them into a DTO. Then, this DTO is used as the parameter of the call to the Presenter layer.

Note that this code is consistent with the typical MVP dynamics presented in Fig. 4.5. This also pertains to the method that implements the Presenter layer event handler operation ('selectsTrigger()' in Fig. 4.8). This method contains varying code which depends on the desired application logic. In our example, the first instruction is to call a data processing and retrieval operation in the Model layer ('actionOther-Notion()'). This operation passes the DTO received from the View layer and returns an integer result. Depending on this result, different actions can be taken. Our example code follows the dynamics presented in Fig. 4.5 and performs a sequence of calls. First, it retrieves data from the Model layer object (some result of previous data retrieval/processing in the Model layer). Then it closes the current screen, sets the data in some other screen and shows it to the user.

The above code is suitable for typical situations which involve a single Presenter class instance. The situation where more Presenter classes are involved is illustrated in Fig. 4.9. Such situations implement the invocation relationships and invocation/final sentences in RSL use case models. Invocation is equivalent to passing control of the application logic to the code of another Presenter layer class instance.

The initial sequence of messages for an invocation is similar to the already presented event handling. It involves the 'onTrigger()' method which calls the appropriate 'getNotion()' and 'selectsTrigger()' type methods. The difference is in the contents of the 'selectsTrigger()' method. In the "invoking" class (here: 'PSomeUse-Case'), this method calls the 'invoke()' operation on the "invoked" class instance (here: 'POtherUseCase') and passes reference to the current "invoking" instance

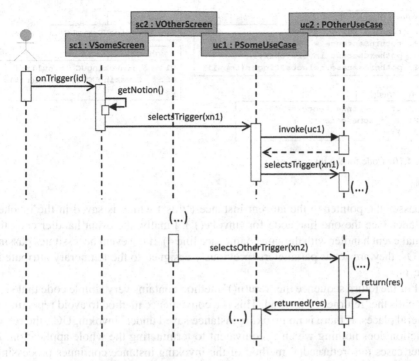

Fig. 4.9 Typical invoke dynamics

(here: 'uc1'). Then, it calls the 'selectsTrigger()' operation on the "invoked" class instance. This second call passes control to the Presenter class instance associated with the invoked use case. The contents of the second 'selectsTrigger()' operation is consistent with the schema presented in Fig. 4.8 and implements appropriate application logic.

When all the actions controlled by the "invoked" instance (here: 'uc2') are completed, control needs to be passed back to the "invoking" instance (here: 'uc1'). This is done in some event handler method which is related to the final sentences in a use case scenario (e.g. pressing the final acknowledgement button). The last part of this method's code contains a return sequence. This consists of calling the local 'return()' method that in turn calls the 'returned()' method in the "invoking" instance. We may remember that this is possible thanks to the 'invoke()' method which appropriately sets the local 'invokingUC' attribute to point back to 'uc1' (see also Fig. 4.4).

Figure 4.10 shows the details of the methods that implement the sequence in Fig. 4.9. The first piece of code is the "proxy" event handler function that starts the invocation sentence (here: 'selectsTrigger()'). It first saves the identifier that marks the place in the original use case scenario to which control should be returned (see line 2). Later, this identifier is used to continue executing the correct application logic after returning from the invocation. Further, the event handler calls the 'invoke()' method on the invoked Presenter class instance (here: 'potherusecase', see line 3).

```
selectsTrigger()
01:  tmpn1 = xn1;
02:  returnSentence = "7";
03:  potherusecase.invoke(this);
04:  potherusecase.selectsTrigger(tmpn1);
```

```
returned()
01:  if (returnSentence == "7") {
02:    /* some code */
03:  }
```

```
invoke()
01:  invokingUC = pUC;
```

```
return()
01:  if (invokingUC != null) {
02:    invokingUC.returned(ret);
03:  }
```

Fig. 4.10 Code for the invocations

It passes the pointer to the current instance ('this') which is saved in the invoked instance (see the one line code for 'invoke()'). Finally, the event handler calls the actual event handler with the same name (see line 4). If the event necessitates passing DTOs, they are set as parameters (previously assigned to the temporary attribute in line 1).

For the return sequence the 'return()' method contains very simple code that simply calls the 'returned()' method. This is a convenience method to avoid repeating in several places. If there is no invoking instance saved under 'invokingUC', the return function does nothing which is equivalent to terminating the whole application. In other cases the 'returned()' method of the invoking instance continues processing. It determines the value of the 'returnSentence' (see line 1) and performs code that is relevant for the scenario that follows the invocation. Note that there can be several possible 'returnSentences' and thus the 'return()' method can have more 'if' conditions.

This completes our definition of the translation framework. All the translation rules presented in the following sections produce code that is compliant with this general scheme. The scheme can be treated as a high-level "virtual machine" that would execute models written in RSL. By translating RSL constructs into code compliant with the scheme, we will define the runtime semantics of RSL. This is divided into three parts, each related to a specific aspect of the translational framework. The first part pertains to the general structural elements of the framework (classes and associations) and the rules will be denoted with the letter 'G'. The second part treats the View layer code and the rules are denoted with 'V'. Finally, the last part deals with the Presenter layer and the rules are denoted with 'P'.

In general, the rules should be applied in the above overall sequence and in the sequence of their numbering. So first, the source RSL model should be subject to translation according to the general rules from G0 to G7. Then the View layer elements should be created according to rules V1–V8, and the Presenter layer elements according to rules P1–P13. All the rules that pertain to sequences of sentences should be applied in accordance with these sequences, observing sentence numbering in scenarios. The code for the sentences placed later in scenarios should be appended at the end of the appropriate code for the sentences placed earlier.

4.2 Semantics Involving the General Structure

The first part of our definition of RSL's runtime semantics includes simple rules that translate top-level RSL constructs into the MVP structure. For each rule we provide a definition which includes (1) types and layout of the source RSL elements, (2) types and layout of the target MVP elements. Each definition is illustrated with an example diagram, where the left-hand side shows the source configuration and the right-hand side the target configuration.

> **Rule G0.** *Every RSL model produces two top-level classes: 'PUseCase'and 'VScreen'.* The PUseCase class contains two attributes: (1) 'invokingUC' of type 'PUseCase', (2) 'returnSentence' of type 'String'. It also contains two concrete operations: (1) 'invoke()' with parameter 'pUC' of type 'PUseCase', (2) 'return()' with parameter 'ret' of type 'integer', and one abstract operation 'returned()' with the same parameter as 'return()'. The VScreen class contains one parameter 'fields' of type 'FieldList'. It also contains two concrete operations: (1) 'show()', (2) 'close()', and two abstract operations: (1) 'init()', (2) 'onTrigger()' with one parameter 'trigger_id' of type 'integer'.

This rule, illustrated in Fig. 4.11, does not specify any source elements. It is applied to any RSL model regardless of its contents. The two created classes are the basis for other classes, created according to rules G1 and G2. The attributes and operations of 'VScreen' and 'PUseCase' are used to control the screen-related logic and the application logic, according to the descriptions in the previous section.

> **Rule G1.** *Every Use Case is translated into a Presenter class.* The translated class specialises from the 'PUseCase' class translated according to rule G0. The class name is derived from the use case name by removing spaces, turning to upper camel case notation and adding the 'P' prefix.

This simple rule is illustrated in Fig. 4.12. Translation according to rule G1 is obvious. Use cases generally define the application logic of the system. Thus, it is natural to turn them into Presenter classes which control the application logic in terms of scheduling the sequences of actions involving the View and the Model. The Presenter classes all specialise from the 'PUseCase' class which is shown as already

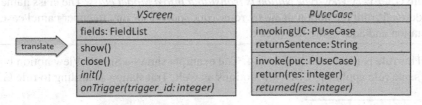

Fig. 4.11 Rule G0: PUseCase and VScreen

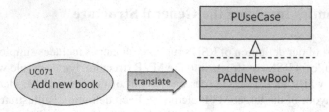

Fig. 4.12 Rule G1: Use cases to Presenter classes

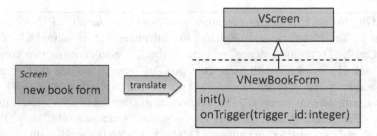

Fig. 4.13 Rule G2: Screen notions to View classes

existing (above the dashed line). Of course, their names have to be written without spaces and the camel case notation is selected as one often used by programmers.[1]

> **Rule G2.** *Every Screen-type Notion is translated into a View class.* The translated class specialises from the 'VScreen' class translated according to rule G0. The class name is derived from the notion name by removing spaces, turning to upper camel case notation and adding the 'V' prefix. The class contains two concrete operations: (1) 'init()', (2) 'onTrigger()' with one parameter 'trigger_id' of type 'integer'.

This simple rule is illustrated in Fig. 4.13. As for G1, translation for rule G2 is obvious. Screen-type notions naturally translate into View layer classes which handle individual screens in the user interface. The View classes all specialise from the 'VScreen' class which is shown as already existing (above the dashed line). Due to this specialisation the View layer classes need to obtain the necessary operations that concretise the two abstract operations of the 'VScreen' class.

> **Rule G3.** *Every View-type Notion is translated into a Model class.* The class name is derived from the notion name by removing spaces, turning to upper camel case notation and adding the 'M' prefix.

This rule is illustrated in Fig. 4.14. The example shows a Simple View notion but the same rule applies to List View notions as well. Translation according to rule G3

---

[1] Upper camel case consists in writing compound words so that each word begins with a capital letter. Camel case differs from upper camel case in that the first letter is small.

Fig. 4.14 Rule G3: Data Views to Model classes

assumes that data processing is divided between several classes and the division is made according to the View notions. For each View notion, a class is defined that can create, read, update and process data associated with this notion.

Rule G3 can also have its variant where the Model layer classes are translated from Concept-type Notions instead of View-type Notions. In this variant, each Data View Notion needs to be related to an appropriate "main" concept which determines the Model layer class that will be used for data processing. This slightly complicates the rules that involve the Presenter layer (see rules P5–P7) and thus we do not elaborate it further in this chapter. The reader is encouraged to formulate the possible alternative rules as an exercise.

Rule G4. *Every View-type Notion with associated Attribute-type Notions is translated into a DTO class.* The class name is derived from the notion name by removing spaces, turning to upper camel case notation and adding the 'X' prefix. The Attribute Notions are translated into the attributes of the DTO class. The attribute names are copied from the Attribute Notion names. The attribute types are translated from the Attribute Notion types ('text' to 'String', 'whole number' to 'integer', 'real number' to 'float', 'true/false' to 'boolean', 'date' to 'DateTime'). In addition, each DTO class obtains the 'id' attribute of type 'long'.

Rule G4 is illustrated in Fig. 4.15. The example shows a Simple View notion with one Attribute but the same rule applies also to List View Notions and to all the View Notions with many associated Attribute Notions. The purpose of this translation is to provide constructs for passing data between the MVP layers. These data are grouped into the various View Notions, thus it is natural to translate these elements into Data Transfer Objects. Note that List Views also produce simple DTOs. However, in code, these DTOs are further grouped into tables (e.g. XBookList[]).

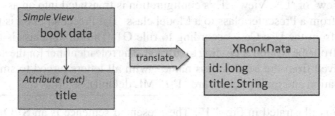

Fig. 4.15 Rule G4: Data Views with attributes to DTO classes

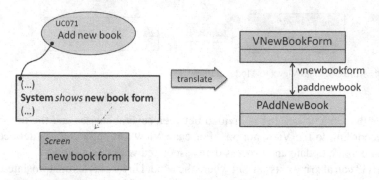

Fig. 4.16 Rule G5: Associations between Presenter and View classes

---

Rule G5. *Every Use Case with a hyperlink to a Screen Notion is translated into a View–Presenter association.* The Use Case contains at least one SVO Sentence where the Predicate is a hyperlink to a Verb Phrase contained in a Notion of type 'Screen'. This configuration is translated into an association navigable in both directions. The association connects two classes. The first class is the class translated from the Use Case according to rule G1. The second class is the class translated from the Notion according to rule G2. The role identifiers for the association are derived from the class names—with all letters turned to small case. The association end multiplicities are '1' (UML default).

Rule G5 is illustrated in Fig. 4.16. The presented sentence is an SVO Sentence, where the Predicate ('*show* **new book form**') refers to a Screen Notion. This means that the Presenter class code will call some operation of the View class (here: to show the screen element). For this purpose, an association from the Presenter to the View is needed. The association has to be also directed in the other direction as the View class code normally contains event handler code that will call some operations of the Presenter class.

Rule G6. *Every Use Case with a hyperlink to a View Notion is translated into a Presenter–Model association.* The Use Case contains at least one SVO Sentence where the Predicate is a hyperlink to a Verb Phrase contained in a Notion of type 'Simple View' or 'List View'. This configuration is translated into an association, navigable from a Presenter class to a Model class. The Presenter class is the class translated from the Use Case according to rule G1. The Model class is the class translated from the Notion according to rule G3. The role identifier for the navigable end is derived from the Model class name—with all letters turned to small case. The association end multiplicities are '1' (UML default).

Rule G6 is illustrated in Fig. 4.17. The presented sentence is an SVO Sentence where the Predicate ('*validate* **book data**') refers to a Simple View Notion. Analogous examples could also be made for a List View notion. The situation here is similar to that in rule G5. The Presenter class code will call some operation of the

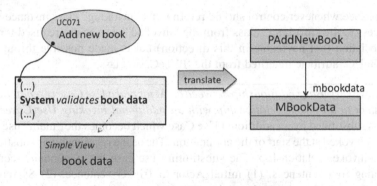

Fig. 4.17 Rule G6: Associations between Presenter and Model classes

Model class (here: to validate some data). For this purpose an association from the Presenter to the View is needed. Unlike in rule G5, the Model class code does not call any operation from the Presenter class, so navigability in the opposite direction is not needed.

> **Rule G7.** *Every «invoke» relationship between two Use Cases is translated into a Presenter–Presenter association and an invoke-related operation.* The association is made between two classes that already exist and were translated from the two Use Cases according to rule G1. The association is navigable in the direction consistent with the direction of the «invoke» relationship. The role identifier for the navigable end is derived from the respective class name—with all the letters turned to small case. The class at the non-navigable end is appended with one operation: 'returned' with one parameter 'ret' of type 'integer'.

Rule G7 is illustrated in Fig. 4.18. The purpose of the added association between the Presenter classes is obvious, where the "invoking" class instances need to be able to access the appropriate operations in the "invoked" class instances. The operation created in the "invoking" class is the concretisation of the abstract operation defined in the 'PUseCase' class (see rules G0 and G1). This operation is called by an "invoked"

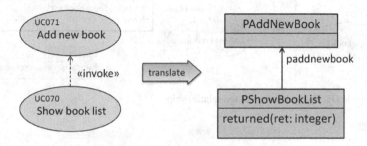

Fig. 4.18 Rule G7: Associations between Presenter classes

class instance whenever control should return to an "invoking" class instance. Note that access to the "invoking" class from the "invoked" class is not realised through the association (not navigable in this direction) but is made possible through the 'invokingUC' attribute inherited from the 'PUseCase' class.

Rule G8. *Every usage relationship between an Actor and a Use Case is semantically equivalent to an invoke relationship with an additional invoking Use Case.* The Actor is substituted by an additional Use Case which becomes the "main" use case which is invoked at the start of the application. The usage relationship is substituted by an «invoke» relationship. The substituting use case has a standard scenario containing four sentences: (1) initial Actor-to-Trigger sentence, (2) System-to-Screen sentence that shows the main application screen, (3) invocation sentence that invokes the original Use Case that is in the relationship with the Actor, (3) rejoin sentence that refers to sentence 2.

Rule G8 is illustrated in Fig. 4.19, where the RSL model to the right of the thick double arrow is the original model. It contains an Actor ('Librarian') which uses a Use Case ('Show book list'). The Actor is semantically substituted by an appropriately named new Use Case ('Start librarian app') and the usage relationship is substituted accordingly. The new use case contains a scenario that generally shows the application's main screen ('librarian main screen'); showing of this main screen is part of the application's startup sequence (equivalent to pressing the 'start' button). The main screen contains appropriate Trigger elements that result from the contents of the invoked Use Case. This equivalent RSL model is subject to other semantic rules which define the target code structure, for instance, from rule V6c we obtain code that generates an appropriate button that starts the invoked use case. In this way, we can simplify the other semantic rules by suppressing the variants that involve actors and usage relationships.

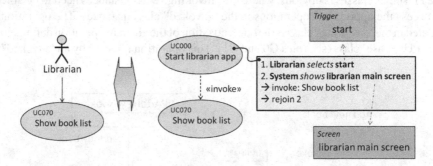

Fig. 4.19 Rule G8: Equivalence of usage relationships

4.3 Semantics Involving the View Layer

The next group of rules involves the RSL constructs that translate into the elements of the View layer. The already presented general rules involved creating UML classes with attributes and operations and associations between them, while the current group of rules mostly pertain to creating detailed Java code of the methods that implement the operations defined in UML classes according to rules G0–G7. However, this also involves appending certain new operations and attributes to the existing classes.

> **Rule V1.** *Every Simple View Notion related with a Screen Notion is translated to field initialisation code.* The relation between the Simple View Notion and the Screen Notion can be directed in either direction. The translation creates code as part of the method of the existing 'init()' operation of the View class created using rule G2. For each Simple View, the respective code is appended to this method. The code consists of the instructions 'fields.addLabel()' and 'fields.Add...Field()'. For every Attribute Notion that the Simple View Notion points to, a pair of these instructions is created. The parameter of the 'addLabel()' instruction is taken from the Attribute name. The type of the 'Add...Field()' instruction depends on the type of the Attribute Notion: for 'text—'AddTextField()', for 'whole number'—'AddIntegerField()', for 'real number'—'AddFloatField', for 'true/false'—'AddBooleanField()' and for 'date'—'AddDateTimeField()'. The translation also adds an attribute to the respective View class. The attribute is typed as a DTO, created according to rule G4. The attribute name is derived from the Simple View with spaces removed and 'tmp' added as prefix.

Rule V1 illustrated in Fig. 4.20 is straightforward. We can see the class 'VNew-BookForm' with the 'init()' operation that was created from the Notion 'new book form' according to rule G2. The method for 'init()' is appended with two instructions that create a single field from the only Attribute of 'book data'—the 'title'. In addition, the 'tmpbookdata' attribute is added to the class definition.

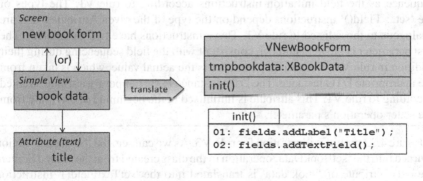

Fig. 4.20 Rule V1: Screens with simple Views to field initiation

It is typed with the appropriate DTO class ('XBookData'), created with rule G4. This attribute is used by the code created according to rules V3, V5 and V7.

Rule V2. *Every List View Notion related with a Screen Notion is translated to column initialisation code.* The relation between the List View Notion and the Screen Notion can be directed in either direction. The translation creates code as part of the method of the existing 'init()' operation of the View class created using rule G2. For each List View, the respective code is appended to this method. The code consists of one instruction 'fields.addIdClField()' followed by one or more instructions 'fields.add...ClField()'. For every Attribute Notion that the List View Notion points to, one of the 'add...ClField()' instructions is created. The parameter of the instruction is taken from the Attribute name. The type of the instruction depends on the type of the Attribute Notion and is analogous to that in rule V1. The translation also adds an attribute to the respective View class. The attribute is typed as a table of DTOs, created according to rule G4. The attribute name is derived from the List View with spaces removed and 'tmp' added as prefix.

Rule V2 illustrated in Fig. 4.21 is similar to the example for rule V2. The difference lies in that the field addition instructions (e.g. 'addTextField()') are substituted with column addition instructions (e.g. 'AddTextClField()'). Also, the respective attribute is defined as a DTO table ('XBookList[]') instead of a single DTO.

Rule V3. *Every Simple View Notion with a relation pointing at a Screen Notion is translated to field setter code.* The relation is in the direction from the Simple View Notion to the Screen Notion. First, the translation creates an appropriate setter operation. The operation's name is derived from the Simple View name by removing spaces, turning to upper camel case notation and adding the 'set' prefix. The operation has one parameter which is of a DTO type, where the DTO is created according to rule G4. The parameter's name is the same as the type but with all letters turned to small. Next, the method for the setter is filled with code that depends on the Attributes that the Simple Notion points at. For each attribute, an appropriate 'fields.set...Field()' operation is added. These instructions are added in the same sequence as the field initiation instructions according to rule V1. The types of the 'set...Field()' instructions depend on the type of the given Attributes, and are analogous to those listed in rule V1. These instructions have two parameters. The first parameter is the field number, consistent with the field sequencing during their addition in rule V1. The second parameter is the actual value, which is taken from the appropriate DTO instance. The DTO instance is the temporary attribute created according to rule V1. This attribute is initialised in the beginning of this code from the setter operation's parameter.

Figure 4.22 provides illustration for rule V3. As we can see, the 'book data' notion is turned into the 'setBookData' operation in the class created from the related Screen. The only attribute of 'book data' is translated into the 'setTextField()' instruction (see line 2). The field is set from the 'title' of the 'tmpbookdata' object. This object is initialised in line 1 with the operation's parameter. This usage of the temporary

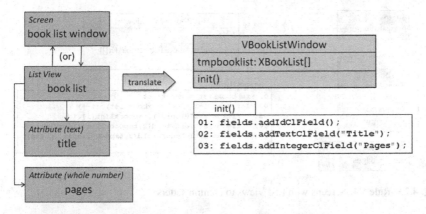

Fig. 4.21 Rule V2: Screens with List Views to column initiation

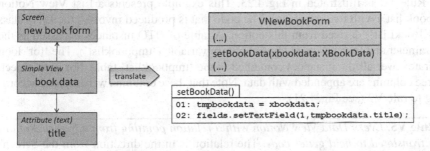

Fig. 4.22 Rule V3: Screens with Simple Views to field setters

variable (here: 'tmpbookdata') is used for convenience reasons and further potential manual optimisation. It is not necessary in the scope of the current translation rules.

Rule V4. *Every List View Notion with a relation pointing at a Screen Notion is translated to column setter code.* The relation is in the direction from the List View Notion to the Screen Notion. First, the translation creates an appropriate setter operation, with the name analogous to that in rule V3. The operation has one parameter, analogous to that in rule V3 but the type is a DTO table. Next, the method for the setter is filled with code that depends on the Attributes that the List Notion points at. The code contains a 'for' loop that iterates through all the elements of the DTO table. Within the loop, for each DTO attribute, an appropriate 'fields.set...ClField()' operation is added. These instructions are added in the same sequence as the column initiation instructions according to rule V3. The types of the 'set...ClField()' instructions depend on the type of the given Attributes, and are analogous to those listed in rule V1. These instructions have two parameters, analogous to those described in rule V3. The DTO table instance is initialised analogously to rule V3.

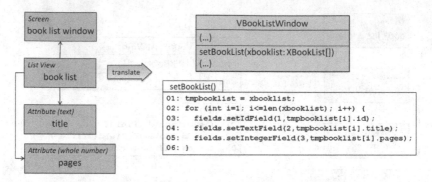

Fig. 4.23 Rule V4: Screens with List Views to column setters

Rule V4 is illustrated in Fig. 4.23. This example presents a List View Notion ('book list') with two Attributes. The code that is produced involves the DTO class ('XBookList') derived from this notion. A table of DTO instances is passed as the parameter and then assigned to a temporary variable ('tmpbooklist'). The 'for' loop iterates over all the instances contained in the 'tmpbooklist' table. For each object, three columns are appended with data. Note that these columns were created according to rule V2 (see Fig. 4.21).

Rule V5. *Every Data View Notion with a relation pointing from a Screen Notion is translated to field getter code.* The relation is in the direction from the Screen Notion to the Data View Notion. First, the translation creates an appropriate getter operation. The operation's name is derived from the Data View name by removing spaces, turning to upper camel case notation and adding the 'get' prefix. If the Data View is a List View, then the getter returns a long integer, otherwise it has no return value and no parameters. For a Simple View, the method code for the above operation consists of several assignment operations. Each assignment pertains to one Attribute Notion pointed at by the Simple View. The assignment sets the attributes of the temporary DTO which was created according to rule V1. The values for the assignment are retrieved from the fields using the 'fields.get...Field()' instructions. The instructions have one parameter—the field number, analogous to that in rule V3. For the List View, the code for the operation consists of just one assignment—the 'return' value is assigned with the 'fields.getIdClField()' instruction for the appropriate column field number.

Rule V5 is illustrated in Fig. 4.24. This example presents a Screen with two related Data Views—'book filter' and 'book list'. This produces two 'get' operations with appropriate names derived from the Data View names. The code for the first operation consists of one assignment, where the temporary DTO's attribute 'title' is set with the value of the appropriate text field, while the code for the second operation returns the value of the respective ID column field.

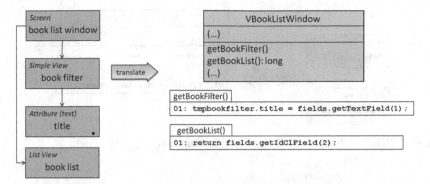

Fig. 4.24 Rule V5: Screens with Views to field getters

> **Rule V6.** *Every Trigger Notion in some relation with a Screen Notion is translated into button initiation code.* There can be three possible situations, (a) The Screen directly points at the Trigger with a relationship, (b) The Trigger is hyperlinked from an SVO sentence that directly follows an SVO sentence where the Screen is hyperlinked, (c) The Trigger is hyperlinked from the first SVO sentence of a use case and that use case is invoked directly after an SVO sentence where the Screen is hyperlinked. For (b) and (c), the sentence that involves the Screen should shift the dialogue state to "actor" and this state should not change until the sentence with the Trigger is reached in control flow. The two sentences can be separated by other sentences that do not change the dialogue state. For situations (a), (b) and (c), the 'init()' operation of the class translated from the Screen notion (see rule G2) is appended. For each relevant Trigger, a 'fields.addButton()' instruction is created and added to the end of the current code. The instruction has one parameter—the button name, which is derived from the Trigger name.

Rule V6 is illustrated in Figs. 4.25, 4.26 and 4.27. Figure 4.25 shows the variant (a). In this variant, the rule is elementary in terms of the source model—a Screen ('new book form') points at a Trigger ('save button'). This results also in a very simple update of the target model—the 'init()' method is appended with one line of code (line 1) which differs from case to case only with the parameter text (here "Save").

Exactly the same code as in Fig. 4.25 is translated from the example model in Fig. 4.27. This situation pertains to version (b) of rule V6 and is more complex. We have the same two domain elements, but the Screen ('new book form') does not necessarily point directly to the Trigger ('save button'). Their relation is determined through the presence of hyperlinks to these two elements in a use case scenario. The scenario has to contain a sentence which hyperlinks to the Screen element. In our example, this is the sentence 'System shows new book form'. This sentence

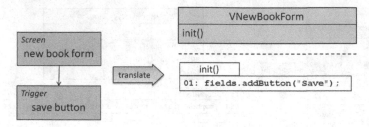

Fig. 4.25 Rule V6a: Screens with Triggers to button initiation

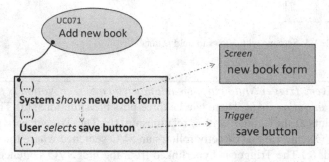

Fig. 4.26 Scenario configuration with Screen and Trigger (for rules V6b, V7b and V8b)

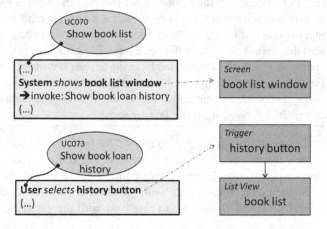

Fig. 4.27 Scenario configuration with Screen, invoke and Trigger (for rules V6c, V7c, V8c)

is a System-to-Screen sentence and it shifts the dialogue state to 'actor'.[2] This is
equivalent to showing some window in the user interface. This sentence can be
followed by any number of sentences that do not shift the dialogue back to 'system'.
These are Actor-to-DataView sentences, similar to 'User enters book data'. Finally,
our scenario reaches an Actor-to-Trigger sentence ('User selects save button'). This

---

[2] Dialogue state is explained in detail in Chap. 2, see Fig. 2.24.

means that the currently shown Screen element ('new book form') has to possess the said 'save button'.

This second variant of rule V6 allows to omit the relations between Screens and Triggers. When developing an RSL model, the developers can concentrate on writing precise scenarios that involve Triggers and do not care about linking these Triggers with the Screen elements in an explicit manner. For the sake of coherence and better comprehension, the links can be introduced into the source model. Moreover, we suggest equipping the RSL editors with an appropriate mechanism to manage (add, remove) these links based on the current configurations of sentences within scenarios.

The same code as for variants (a) and (b) is produced also in variant (c) of rule V6. This is illustrated in Fig. 4.27 which shows two use cases with an invocation relationship. The configuration is somewhat similar to that in rule V6b. However, the System-to-Screen and Actor-to-Trigger sentences are components of two different use cases. The first sentence ('System shows book list window') has to be followed by an invocation sentence. Then the second sentence ('User selects history button') is the first sentence of the invoked use case. The appropriate Trigger ('history button') should—obviously—be present in the current Screen element ('book list window') for these scenarios to be possible. Thus, the appropriate button initiation code has to be added according to the rule.

Rule V7. *Every Trigger Notion (optionally pointing at one or more Simple Views) in some relation with a Screen Notion is translated into event handler code.* There can be three possible situations: (a) The Screen directly points at the Trigger through a relationship, (b) The Trigger is hyperlinked from an SVO sentence that directly follows an SVO sentence where the Screen is hyperlinked, (c) The Trigger is hyperlinked from the first SVO sentence of a use case which is invoked directly after an SVO sentence where the Screen is hyperlinked. The event handling code is inserted into the 'onTrigger()' method of the View class created according to rule G2 from the Screen element. The generated code is an 'if' statement checking the 'trigger_id' to be the name of the current Trigger. If it is, the appropriate operation is called on the Presenter class instance in the form 'instancename.operation(parameters)'. The instance name is the name of the association role created according to rule G5. The operation name refers to the operation created according to rule P4. The parameters are optional and are created only if the Trigger points at one or more Simple Views. The parameters are temporary ('tmp. . .') variables created from the Simple Views according to rule V1. For each parameter, a getter operation (rule V5) is called before the call to the Presenter class instance.

Rule V7 is illustrated in Figs. 4.26 and 4.28. Figure 4.28 shows variant (a) and Fig. 4.26 shows variant (b) where the source models are the same as in rule V6. Figure 4.27 refers to variant (c) but presents a situation with a List View element and is discussed under rule V8. The example in Fig. 4.28 shows a configuration extended from that in Fig. 4.25. The Screen element ('new book form') and the related Trigger element ('save button') are enough to create the appropriate 'if' instruction and condition in the correct 'onTrigger()' method. To create the calls inside the

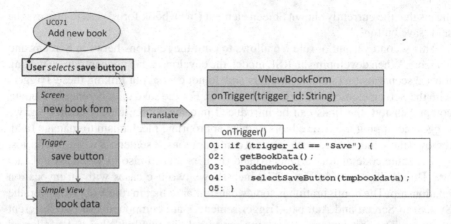

Fig. 4.28 Rule V7a: Screens with Triggers (Simple View) to event handlers

'if' instruction, we need the remaining elements of the source model. The example shows a single Simple View element ('book data') pointed at by the Trigger. This tells us which getter operation should be called ('getBookData()') and which temporary variable ('tmpbookdata') to use as the parameter in the call to the Presenter layer. To determine the Presenter instance name and the Presenter operation name, we need to know the use case and the sentence in which the Trigger is hyperlinked. The use case name ('Add new book') determines the instance name ('paddnewbook'). The sentence contents (the predicate 'selects save button') determine the operation name ('selectsSaveButton()').

Exactly the same code is created for the source model presented in Fig. 4.26 which relates to rule V7b. The discussion of this model was made when discussing rule V6b. Here, we only need to assume the 'book data' element which is pointed at by 'save button' as in Fig. 4.28.

Rule V8. *Every Trigger Notion pointing at one or more List Views, in some relation with a Screen Notion is translated into event handler code.* There can be three possible situations (a, b and c), which are exactly the same as for rule V7. The event handling code is inserted into the 'onTrigger()' method of the View class created according to rule G2 from the Screen element. The generated code is an 'if' statement checking the 'trigger_id' to be the name of the current Trigger. If it is, the appropriate operation is called on the Presenter class instance in the form 'instancename.operation(getter1(),getter2(),...)'. The instance name and the operation name are created as in rule V7. The getters are calls to the operations created according to rule V5 from the List Views.

Rule V8 is illustrated in Figs. 4.26, 4.27 and 4.29. The situation is similar to that illustrating rule V7. The difference is in the contents of the 'if' statement, and in particular—in the parameter of the call to the Presenter operation. In rule V8, the

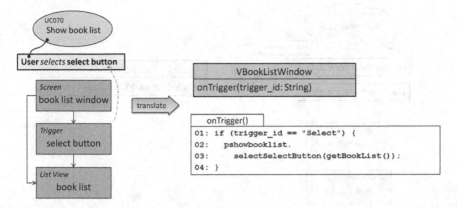

Fig. 4.29   Rule V8a: Screens with Triggers (List View) to event handlers

parameter is always a call to the local getter operation. In our example, the getter is derived from the 'book list' element. Similar code is created for the situations illustrated in Figs. 4.26 (rule V8b) and 4.27 (rule V8c).

When we analyse rules V6, V7 and V8, we notice several constraints that must be set on the source RSL model for the translated code to work. First, we need to make sure that there are no two Triggers with the same name related to a given Screen (in either of the situations a, b or c). Moreover, we need to assure that each Screen element is used only in a specific use case. If it is used in another use case, then the event handler code would have contradicting targets of the calls to the Presenter layer operations. These and other similar restrictions can be removed by extending the RSL definition. The problem of such an extension or RSL and its semantics can be used by the reader as subject for an exercise.

4.4 Semantics Involving the Presenter and Model Layers

The last, and the largest group of rules involves the RSL constructs that translate into the elements of the Presentation layer with some elements of the Model layer. The Presentation layer code covers complete functionality of the application logic. The Model layer is just a skeleton which can be later filled in with code of the domain (business) logic. The presented rules create all the necessary operations of both layers. For the Presentation layer, the rules cover also the method bodies for these operations. As we remember, the classes for which the operations and methods are introduced were created according to the general rules (G1, G3). We also assume the existence of associations created according to rules G5–G7.

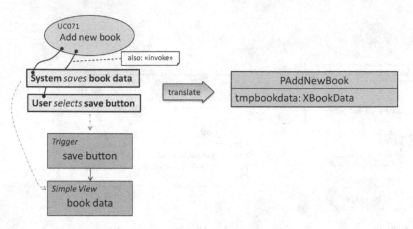

Fig. 4.30 Rule P1: SVO sentences with Simple Views to DTO attributes

---

Rule P1. *Every System-to-SimpleView and Actor-to-Trigger (SimpleView) sentence is translated into a temporary DTO attribute in a Presentation class.* The source configuration involves a use case with a contained or related SVO sentences. There can be three possibilities: (a) SVO sentence of type System-to-SimpleView contained in a scenario of the use case, (b) SVO sentence of type Actor-to-Trigger, where the trigger has a related Simple View, contained in a scenario of the use case, (c) SVO sentence as in point 'b' but contained as the first sentence in a scenario of a use case invoked from the considered use case. Any of these configurations is translated into an attribute typed as the DTO class translated from the Simple View element, according to rule G4. The name of the attribute is identical to that in rule V1.

Rule P1 is illustrated in Fig. 4.30. It shows a use case ('Add new book') and a Presenter class ('PAddNewBook') that was created previously from the use case. We also have two sentences that are contained in some scenarios of this use case. The upper sentence ('System saves book data') hyperlinks directly to a Simple View element ('book data'). The lower sentence ('User selects save button') hyperlinks to a Trigger ('save button') that points to the same Simple View, as the previous sentence. Existence of any of these sentences causes creation of the appropriate attribute ('tmpbookdata') in the mentioned class.

The attribute created using rule P1 is used by some other code created using various rules in this group. Note that System-to-SimpleView sentences necessitate passing a DTO from the Presenter layer to the Model layer (or vice versa), and the Actor-to-Trigger (SimpleView) sentences—passing a DTO from the View layer to the Presenter layer. The temporary attribute can be used to temporarily preserve the DTOs passed by the application logic, between different actions that involve calls to the View layer and the Model layer.

> **Rule P2.** *Every System-to-ListView and System-to-Screen (DataView) sentence is translated into a temporary DTO attribute in a Presentation class.* The source configuration involves a use case with a contained SVO sentences. There can be two possibilities: (a) SVO sentence of the type System-to-ListView contained in a scenario of the use case and (b) SVO sentence of the type System-to-Screen, contained in a scenario of the use case in which the screen is pointed at by a List View or a Simple View. Any of these configurations is translated into an attribute typed as the DTO class translated from the Data View element according to rule G4. For the configurations that involve List Views, the attribute is a DTO table. The name of the attribute is identical to that in rule V1.

Rule P2 is illustrated in Fig. 4.31. The configuration is somewhat similar to that in rule P1. The figure illustrates two cases involving a List View. The first sentence ('System fetches book list') hyperlinks element ('book list'), while the second sentence hyperlinks to a Screen ('book list window') pointed at by the same List View. Existence of any of these sentences causes creation of the appropriate attribute ('tmpbooklist'), which is typed as a DTO table.

As in rule P1, the created attribute is used in some other code. The System-to-ListView sentences necessitate passing a table of DTOs from the Model layer to the Presenter layer. The System-to-Screen (DataView) sentences necessitate passing a DTO (Simple View) or a table of DTOs (List View) from the Presenter layer to the View layer. The temporary attribute can store these values between consecutive calls within the application logic.

> **Rule P3.** *Every Actor-to-Trigger (ListView) sentence is translated into a temporary ID attribute in a Presentation class.* The source configuration involves a use case with a contained SVO sentence. There can be two possibilities: (a) SVO sentence of type Actor-to-Trigger, where the trigger has a related List View, contained in a scenario of the use case and (b) SVO sentence as in point 'a' but contained as the first sentence in a scenario of a use case invoked from the considered use case. Any of these configurations is translated into an attribute typed as long integer. The attribute name is derived from the List View name with spaces removed, 'tmp' added as the prefix and 'id' added as the postfix.

Rule P3 is illustrated in Fig. 4.32. This example is straightforward and involves one sentence that hyperlinks to a Trigger ('history button'). The Trigger points at a List View ('book list') and thus an appropriate ID attribute ('tmpbooklistid') is created. Note that the sentence can be contained in the actual use case, or in any invoked use case. In the second case, it has to be the very first SVO sentence of that invoked use case. The ID attribute can be used to pass information from the View layer about the ID of the selected data object. This ID can then be passed to the Model layer to be used, e.g. for retrieval. This is explained in detail when explaining the code created using the remaining rules.

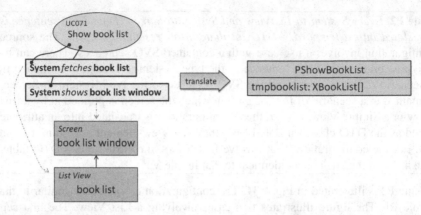

Fig. 4.31 Rule P2: SVO sentences with List Views or Screens to DTO attributes

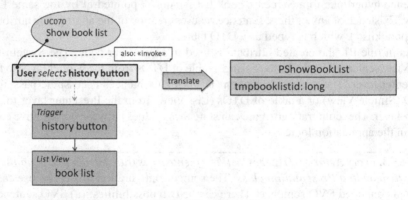

Fig. 4.32 Rule P3: SVO sentences with List Views to list ID attributes

---

Rule P4. *Every Actor-to-Trigger sentence is translated into an event handler operation in a Presentation class.* The source configuration involves a use case with a
related Actor-to-Trigger SVO sentence. The sentence can be contained directly in
the use case or as the first sentence of some use case invoked from the use case.
In both cases, an operation is created in the Presenter class translated previously
from the use case according to rule G1. The operation's name is derived from the
SVO sentence's predicate by removing spaces and turning to camel case notation.
The operation's parameters depend on the Data Views pointed at by the Trigger
hyperlinked by the SVO sentence. If there is no related Data View, no parameters
are created. For a Simple View, a regular DTO parameter is created: the parameter's
type follows rule G4 and the parameter's name is the same as the type, but with all
the letters turned to small. For a List View, an ID parameter of type 'long' is created.
In addition, the method of the created operation is initialised with instructions that
assign the temporary attributes (see rules P1, P3) with the values of the parameters.

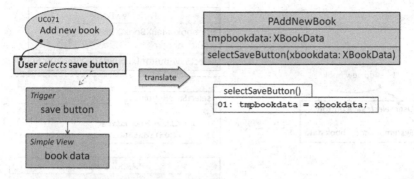

Fig. 4.33 Rule P4: Actor-to-Trigger sentences (Simple View)

Rule P4 is illustrated in Fig. 4.33. The example shows one sentence which is contained in a use case. The predicate part of the sentence ('selects save button') is translated into the name of the operation ('selectsSaveButton'). The Trigger hyperlinked by the predicate ('save button') has a related Simple View ('book data'). Thus, the operation received one parameter whose name and type are derived from the Simple View's name ('xbookdata: XBookData'). This parameter is used in code (line 1) to set the value of the appropriate temporary variable ('tmpbookdata'). This first instruction initialises the variable that is used in the rest of the code for this method, which should be translated according to the remaining rules.

Rule P5. *Every 'non-read' System-to-SimpleView sentence is translated into a call to a Model layer operation.* The sentence should involve an action which is not of type READ (CREATE, VALIDATE, etc.). Each such sentence is translated into a call to the operation whose name is derived from the name of the sentence's predicate by removing spaces and turning into camel case notation. The call is made on the Model layer class instance which is accessed through the role name, translated using rule G6. The call has one parameter which is the temporary variable associated with the Simple View (see rule P1). The call returns a result which is assigned to the temporary variable 'result'. The above code is appended at the end of the operation translated using rule P4, from the last preceding Actor-to-Trigger sentence. This code is synchronised with an operation in the appropriate Model layer class which is created (if not yet created for some previous sentence).

Rule P5 is illustrated in Fig. 4.34. Here, we see a use case with two sentences. The first of these sentences ('User selects save button') determines the operation ('selectSaveButton') whose code will be appended. The second sentence ('System validates book data') determines the code that will be created. We also see that the code uses two attributes ('result' and 'tmpbookdata') created previously using other rules. The created operation call is consistent with the actual operation created in the Model layer class ('MBookData'). The diagram does not show one element necessary to fully understand the new code. We assume that there already exists a

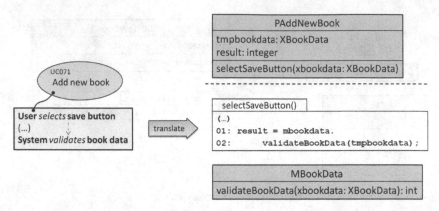

Fig. 4.34 Rule P5: System-to-SimpleView sentences (create, update, validate)

directed association between 'PAddNewBook' and 'MBookData', and the role at the Model side is 'mbookdata'. This allows to use this as the instance name for the operation call.

Rule P6. *Every 'read' System-to-ListView (SimpleView) sentence is translated into a "getter" call to a Model layer operation.* The sentence should involve an action which is of type READ. It should contain two sentence objects (direct and indirect). The first object hyperlinks to a List View and the second—to a Simple View. Each such sentence is translated into a call to the operation whose name is derived from the name of the sentence's predicate up to the direct object (cf. List View), by removing spaces and turning into camel case notation. The call is made on the Model layer instance which is accessed through the role name derived from the List View, translated using rule G6. The call has one parameter which is the temporary variable associated with the Simple View (see rule P1). The call returns a result which is assigned to the temporary variable 'result'. It is followed by a call to a getter operation on the same Model class instance. The name of the getter operation is derived from the List View name by adding the 'get' prefix and turning to camel case notation. The getter returns a table of DTOs derived from the List View according to rule G4. The above code is appended at the end of the operation translated using rule P4, from the last preceding Actor-to-Trigger sentence. This code (two operation calls) is synchronised with two operations in the appropriate Model layer class which are created (if not yet created for some previous sentence).

Rule P6 is illustrated in Fig. 4.35. The situation is similar to that illustrating rule P5. The difference in the source model is that the second sentence is of type READ (uses the verb 'fetch') and it has two objects ('book list' and 'book search criteria'). In code, this results in creating two operations and appropriate two operation calls. The first call ('fetchBookList()') evokes appropriate domain logic that should retrieve the data denoted by the direct object ('XBookList[]') based on the data denoted by the

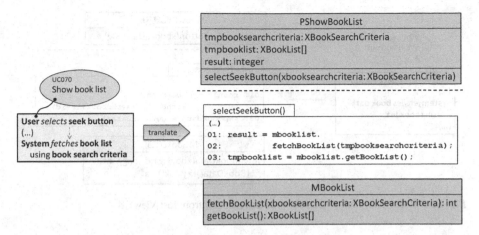

Fig. 4.35 Rule P6: System-to-DataView sentences (read, from Simple View)

indirect object ('XBookSearchCriteria'). The second call ('getBookList()'), passes the retrieved data and stores it locally within the Presenter object.

Rule P7. *Every 'read' System-to-SimpleView (ListView) sentence is translated into a getter call to a Model layer operation.* The sentence should involve an action which is of type READ. It should contain two sentence objects (direct and indirect). The first object hyperlinks to a Simple View and the second to a List View. Each such sentence is translated into a call to the operation whose name is derived from the name of the sentence's predicate up to the direct object (cf. Simple View), by removing spaces and turning into camel case notation. The call is made on the Model layer instance which is accessed through the role name derived from the Simple View, translated using rule G6. The call has one parameter which is the temporary ID variable associated with the List View (see rule P3). The call returns a result which is assigned to the temporary variable 'result'. It is followed by a call to a getter operation on the same Model class instance. The name of the getter operation is derived from the Simple View name by adding the 'get' prefix and turning to camel case notation. The getter returns a DTO derived from the Simple View according to rule G4. The above code is appended at the end of the operation translated using rule P4, from the last preceding Actor-to-Trigger sentence. This code (two operation calls) is synchronised with two operations in the appropriate Model layer class which are created (if not yet created for some previous sentence).

Rule P7 is illustrated in Fig. 4.36. At first sight, the example looks almost identical to that illustrating rule P6. However, we need to note that the second SVO sentence has reversed object types. The first object ('book data') hyperlinks to a Simple View, and the second ('book list') to a List View. This results in creating a different call to the domain logic. It passes an object identifier ('tmpbooklistid'), instead of a full object. The domain logic is supposed to retrieve the appropriate object (typed as

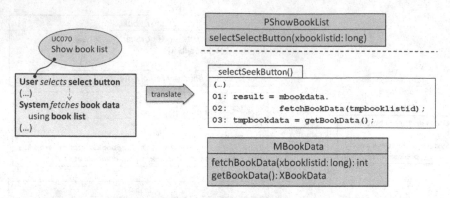

Fig. 4.36 Rule P7: System-to-DataView sentences (read, from List View)

'XBookData'). This object is then passed and stored in the current Presenter, through the getter operation ('getBookData()').

The 'result' passed by the first call, translated with the rules P5–P7 can be used for possible branching of application logic. Thus, the SVO sentences from rule P6 can be followed by condition sentences that define alternative scenarios depending on the result of processing or reading some data from the persistent storage within the Model layer. The appropriate further code is determined by the rule P13.

Rule P8. *Every System-to-Screen sentence is translated into a call to a View layer operation.* The sentence object should hyperlink to a Screen element. Each such sentence is translated into a call to 'close()' (for sentences of type CLOSE) or 'show()' (for other types of sentences), consistent with the rule G0. The call is made on the View layer instance which is accessed through the role name derived from the Screen, translated using rule G5. The call can be preceded by one or more calls to setter operations of the same View layer instance (see rules V3 or V4). Each setter is derived from a Simple View or a List View, that points at the Screen element. The setter name is the same as in rule V3 or V4. The setter has one parameter, and its name refers to the temporary variable created according to rules P1 (Simple View) or P2 (List View). The above code is appended at the end of the operation translated using rule P4, from the last preceding Actor-to-Trigger sentence.

Rule P8 is illustrated in Fig. 4.37. The second sentence ('System shows book list') refers to a Screen ('edit book form') which is pointed at by a Simple View ('book data'). This creates a call (see line 2) to the 'show()' operation of a View layer instance ('veditbookform') which derives from the Screen. This call is inserted into the method ('selectEditButton()') indicated by the first sentence ('User selects edit button'). It is preceded (see line 1) by a call to the setter operation derived from the Simple View element ('book data').

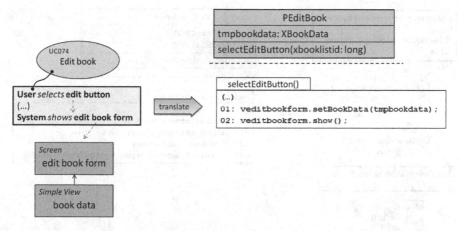

Fig. 4.37 Rule P8: System-to-Screen sentences

Rule P9. *Every invocation sentence in dialogue state 'system' is translated into control passing code within the current event handler method.* The source configuration involves an invocation sentence preceded by an Actor-to-Trigger sentence (and possible other sentences in between that do not change the dialogue state). The translated code is inserted at the end of the method associated with the operation created previously from the Actor-to-Trigger sentence using rule P4. The code first sets the 'returnSentence' attribute (see rule G0) of the containing Presenter class instance. This is set to the identifier of the sentence directly following the invocation sentence. Then the code calls the 'invoke(this)' operation on the instance of the Presenter class derived from the invoked use case (see rule G7). Finally, the code calls the operation associated with the first sentence of the invoked use case (see rule P4). This call is made on the same instance as the call to 'invoke()'.

Rule P9 is illustrated in Fig. 4.38. The source configuration contains several related elements. Everything is centred around the invocation sentence ('**–>invoke:** Show book loan history'). The translated code is inserted into the method created from the nearest preceding Actor-to-System sentence ('User selects discontinue button'). The first created statement marks the sentence following the invocation ('7') as the returning point in the flow of control. Then, control is passed to the Presenter class ('PShowBookLoanHistory') instance related with the invoked use case. First, the pointer to the current Presenter instance ('this') is passed as the parameter of the 'invoke()' operation. Then the appropriate event handler ('selectShowHistoryButton()') of the other instance is called, thus definitely passing control to that other instance. The parameters of this last call are derived from the Data Views associated with the relevant Trigger. In our example, this is a List View ('book list') and thus an ID value ('tmpbooklistid') is used.

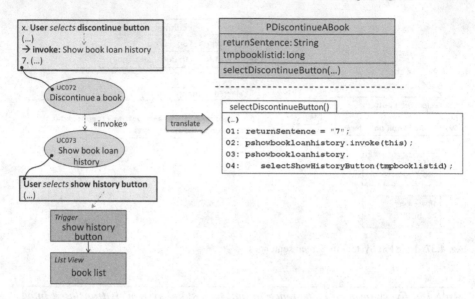

Fig. 4.38 Rule P9: Invocation sentences (dialogue state = system)

Rule P10. *Every invocation sentence in dialogue state 'actor' is translated into control passing code within a dedicated event handler method.* The source configuration involves an invocation sentence preceded by a System-to-Screen sentence (and possible other sentences in between that do not change the dialogue state). This is translated into an operation in the Presenter class derived from the current use case (see rule G1). The operation name is derived from the first sentence of the invoked use case, analogously to that in rule P4. This also pertains to the parameters of this operation. The translated code is inserted at the end of the method associated with this operation. The rules for the contents of this code are identical to those in rule P9.

Rule P10 is illustrated in Fig. 4.39. This example extends the one to rule P9. It involves the same invoked use case. Thus, the generated code is almost identical (except for the return sentence number) to that found in Fig. 4.38. The main difference is in the method in which this code is placed. In rule P10, this is a method of a newly created "proxy" event handler. This proxy ('selectsShowHistoryButton()') calls the identically named operation with exactly the same ID parameter. As in rule P9, this call is preceded with stack-related operations: saving the return sentence (line 1) and setting the pointer to the current Presenter layer instance (line 2).

Rule P10′. The generated code is modified from rule P10 so that the 'returnSentence' parameter is set to −1 (meaning: no return sentence).

Rule P10′ seems as a slight modification of P10 but it changes the way the invocation sentences for the dialogue state 'actor' are interpreted. Setting 'returnSentence'

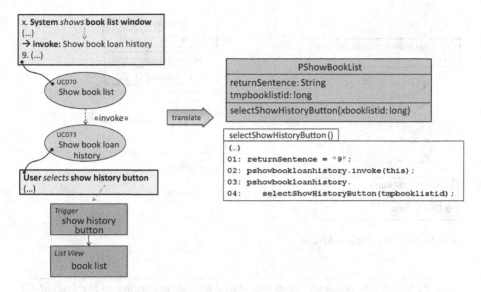

Fig. 4.39   Rule P10: Invocation sentences (dialogue state = actor)

to −1 means that no code is executed after returning control from the invoked Presenter class object (see rules P11 and P12). This in turn means that control goes back to the window that was active before the invocation was started. For the example in Fig. 4.39, the last window shown before the invocation is the 'book list window' (see also rule P8).

Rule P11. *Every final sentence is translated into return of control code.* The final sentence is contained in some invoked use case. Reaching this sentence translates into a call to the local 'return()' operation (see rule G0). It has one parameter: for a "success" final sentence, the value is '0', and for a "failure" final sentence the value is '1'. This call is placed at the end of the method derived from the nearest Actor-to-Trigger sentence that precedes the final sentence (see rule P4). Furthermore, all the invocation sentences that refer to the current use case need to be considered. For each such situation, the 'returned()' method within a relevant Presenter class derived from the invoking use case needs to be updated. The update consists in adding an 'if' statement with a condition that checks the previously set value of the 'returnSentence' attribute (see rules P9 and P10).

Rule P11 is illustrated in Fig. 4.40. The example consists of two use cases related to the «invoke» relationship. One of the use cases contains the final "success" sentence, which is preceded by an Actor-to-Trigger sentence ('User selects OK button'). This configuration determines the method ('selectsOKButton()') in which the 'return()' call is created. The other use case contains the related invocation sentence. Since the following sentence is numbered "9", this number is checked in the 'if' statement created in the relevant 'returned()' method.

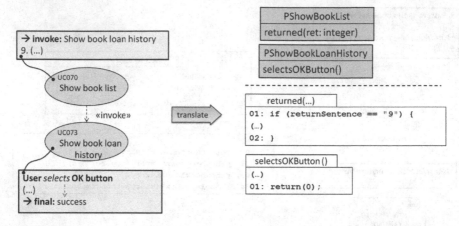

Fig. 4.40 Rule P11: Final sentences

Rule P12. *Every rejoin sentence is translated to code according to the indicated (rejoined) sentence and the following sentences.* When a rejoin sentence is reached it is translated into code that stems from the sentences starting at the point of rejoining. This code is inserted into the method of the Presenter class, into which code was inserted for the sentence preceding the rejoin sentence (rules P4–P10). If this preceding sentence is an invocation sentence, code is inserted into the appropriate 'returned()' method according to rule P11. The inserted code is created as if the rejoin sentence was substituted with the sentence in the rejoining point and all the sentences that follow this sentence until a System-to-Screen or Actor-to-Trigger sentence is reached. This is done according to rules P4–P11.

Rule P12 is illustrated in Fig. 4.41. This example shows two situations involving a rejoin sentence. In the first situation, a rejoin sentence follows an Actor-to-Trigger sentence ('User selects repeat button'). Thus, the current method for inserting code is

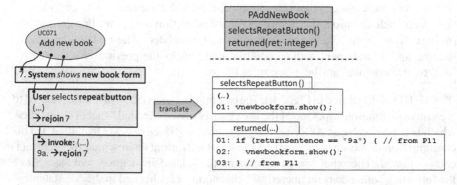

Fig. 4.41 Rule P12: Rejoin sentences

the one that was derived from this sentence ('selectsRepeatButton()'). In the second situation, the rejoin sentence follows an invocation sentence. In this situation, the place for inserting code is the 'returned()' method (see rule P11) inside the appropriate 'if' statement. In both cases the inserted code is derived from the sentence at which the rejoin sentence points ('System shows new book form'). According to rule P8 this creates a call to an appropriate 'show()' operation in a View layer instance ('vnewbookform'). This terminates processing the specific rejoin sentence because it already points at a System-to-Screen sentence.

Rule P13. *Every set of condition sentences for dialogue state 'system' is translated into an 'if-else' statement.* The condition sentences form a set that follows some sentence which initiates and finishes in the dialogue state 'system' (usually, a System-to-DataView sentence). For such a set an 'if-else' statement is created. The number of branches in the statement equals the number of condition sentences in the set. In each branch the condition checks for the value of the 'result' attribute (set according to rules P5–P7). The above statement is appended at the end of the operation translated using rule P4 from the last preceding Actor-to-Trigger sentence.

Rule P13 is illustrated in Fig. 4.42. The presented configuration involves two SVO sentences and a set of two conditions. The first sentence ('User selects save button') determines the method ('selectsSaveButton()') into which the new code is to be appended. The second sentence produces code that sets the 'result' attribute (not shown here, see Fig. 4.34). Finally, the two condition sentences ('book data valid' and 'book data invalid') result in creating an 'if-else' statement with two branches. The first branch contains code created from sentences that follow the first condition sentence, and analogously—the second branch contains code for the second condition sentence.

Relating to rule P13, note that condition sentences which occur in the dialogue state 'actor' (usually after the System-to-Screen sentences) do not necessitate any additional rule. This is because they need to be followed by several Actor-to-Trigger

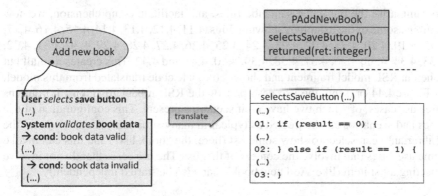

Fig. 4.42 Rule P13: Condition sentences (dialogue state = system)

Fig. 4.43 Rules P1′, P3′,
P4′, P9′ and P10″: source
model variant

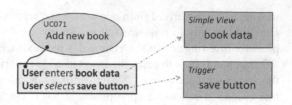

sentences which are already handled through rules V6b, V7b, V8b and P4. Condition
sentences in this situation simply allow to fork scenarios through creating several
buttons with appropriate handling code.

Rules P1′, P3′, P4′, P9′and P10″. *The source model structure in rules P1, P3, P4,
P9 and P10 is modified for Actor-to-Trigger sentences.* The source model is structured so that the Actor-to-Trigger sentences are preceded by Actor-to-DataView
sentences. In such case, the Trigger notions do not need to point at the respective
Data View (List View of Simple View) notions. The relationships between the Triggers and the Data Views are thus substituted by the respective Actor-to-DataView
sentences. The generated target model and code does not change from that in rules
P1, P3 and P4.

The source model for the rules P1′, P3′, P4′, P9′ and P10″ is illustrated in Fig. 4.43.
This example refers to the example for rule P4, but the configuration for the other rules
is similar. As we can see, the configuration involves two sentences, of which the first is
an Actor-to-DataView sentence ('User enters book data') and the second is the Actor-
to-Trigger sentence shown previously in Fig. 4.33. The first sentence hyperlinks to
the same Data View notion as in the example for rule P4. The difference in the
domain model is that the Trigger and the Data View need not be related explicitly.
This relationship is derived from the sequence of sentences in the scenario.

4.5 Summary Example

To summarise the presented semantic rules, and facilitate comprehension, we now
combine some of the examples shown in Figs. 4.11, 4.12, 4.13, 4.14, 4.15, 4.16, 4.17,
4.18, 4.19, 4.20, 4.21, 4.22, 4.23, 4.24, 4.25, 4.26, 4.27, 4.28, 4.29, 4.30, 4.31, 4.32,
4.33, 4.34, 4.35, 4.36, 4.37, 4.38, 4.39, 4.40, 4.41 and 4.42. This creates a small but
coherent RSL model fragment and shows complete code translated from this model.

Figure 4.44 presents the use case part of the RSL model fragment. It contains
three use cases, of which two have their scenarios present. This configuration of use
cases and scenarios can be treated as typical in many situations. An actor (here: the
"Librarian") can select to show some list (here: the "book list") and this can invoke
some use cases that involve the context of this list. The use cases that do not involve
selecting a list item (like 'Add new book') can also be started independently.

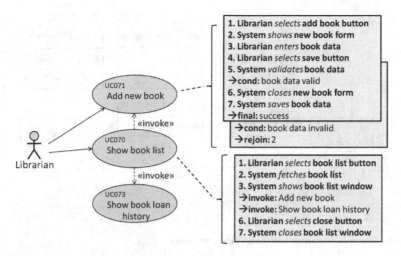

Fig. 4.44 Example use case model (simplified fragment)

The 'Show book list' use case has only one simple scenario. It basically involves fetching the full book list and presenting a window that shows the list. This functionality can be extended to include filtering of the list and other such features. When the window with the list is shown the user can invoke two use cases—'Add new book' and 'Show book loan history'. Alternatively, she can select to close the window, which ends the application. Of the two invoked use cases we present scenarios for only one. To add a book the user has to select a button and this shows a form which can be filled in. After pressing a button on this form the system validates book data and if valid, saves it. If the data are not valid, the form is shown back again. Again, this functionality is very basic and can be extended. One of the obvious extensions would be to allow for cancelling of the operation. Despite this simplicity, our example summarises most of the presented translation rules.

The presented scenarios refer to various domain elements shown in Fig. 4.45. We see the two Screen elements ('new book form' and 'book list window') found in the scenarios, with several associated Trigger elements. Note that the 'add book button' Trigger is not related directly to 'book list window' and the appropriate code is created using the appropriate configuration of scenario sentences. The 'book list button' Trigger is also not related to any Screen, as this is out of the scope of the functionality defined by the three use cases. The Screens and Triggers relate to appropriate Data Views ('book data' and 'book list') These views point to Attributes which should be presented to or entered by the user.

These RSL model elements translate into the code structure presented in Fig. 4.46. All the classes, associations and DTO class attributes are translated using rules G1–G7. We also see that the View layer classes specialise from 'VScreen', and the Presenter layer classes specialise from 'PUseCase'. These two general classes are not shown as their content is constant and already shown in the definition of rule G0.

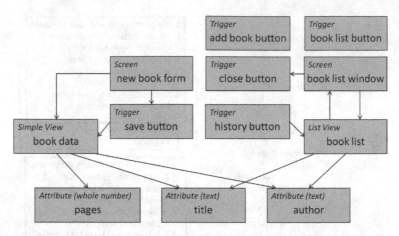

Fig. 4.45 Example domain model (simplified fragment)

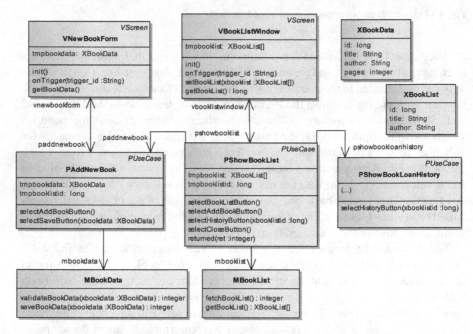

Fig. 4.46 Class model translated from the example RSL model (partial)

The two View layer classes have one temporary attribute each. These were translated using rules V1 and V2. The same attributes are present in the two associated Presenter layer classes as the result of applying rules P1 and P2. In addition, both classes have the same 'tmpbooklistid' attribute which results from applying rule P3. In one of the classes ('PAddNewBook') this is due to the basic variant (P3a), and in the other class ('PShowBookList') due to the invocation variant (P3b).

Note (Fig. 4.45) that 'book data' is connected to 'new book form' with one relationship pointing from the Screen to the Simple View. This results in applying rule V5 and producing the getter operation ('getBookData()') in 'VNewBookForm'. The other Data View element ('book list') is connected to 'book list windows' with two relationships in both directions. This results in applying both rule V5 and V4. Because it is a List View, the setter accepts a table of appropriate DTOs ('XBookList[]') and the getter returns a DTO id (long integer). Along with the getters and setters, appropriate 'init()' operations are created according to rules V1 and V2. Since the Screens have associated Triggers the 'onTrigger()' operations are also created (rules V7, V8).

The operations in the Presenter layer classes are created using rules P4 and P10. Each such operation reflects a single user-evoked event (selecting some Trigger in a use case scenario—rule P4). For the events that involve use case invocations, two identically named operations (one of them a proxy) are added (rules P4 and P10). This is illustrated in Fig. 4.46 by the two 'selectAddBookButton()' operations.

The operations in the Model layer are created using rules P5–P7. Four of such operations are shown in Fig. 4.46. Three of them reflect the appropriate System-to-DataView sentences that indicate some domain logic actions. One of the operations is a getter associated with the 'fetchBookList()' operation. The getter ('getBookList()') allows for transporting data from the Model layer up to the Presenter layer after performing some data processing and retrieval within the 'fetchBookList()' operation.

The class model determines the code skeleton of the final code. This skeleton is filled with code for the View and the Presenter layers. This is illustrated in Figs. 4.47, 4.48, 4.49 and 4.50 which present full code for the four main classes. The two View

```
public class VNewBookForm extends VScreen {
  private XBookData tmpbookdata;
  private PAddNewBook paddnewbook;

  public void init(){
    fields.addLabel("Title"); fields.addTextField();
    fields.addLabel("Author"); fields.addTextField();
    fields.addLabel("Pages"); fields.addIntegerField();
    fields.addButton("Save");
  }

  public void onTrigger(String trigger_id){
    if (trigger_id == "Save") {
      getBookData();
      paddnewbook.selectSaveButton(tmpbookdata);
    }
  }

  public void getBookData(){
    tmpbookdata.title = fields.getTextField(1);
    tmpbookdata.author = fields.getTextField(2);
    tmpbookdata.pages = fields.getIntegerField(3);
  }
}
```

Fig. 4.47 Code of VNewBookForm

```
public class VBookListWindow extends VScreen {
  private XBookList[] tmpbooklist;
  private PShowBookList pshowbooklist;

  public void init(){
    fields.addIdClField(); fields.addTextClField("Title");
    fields.addTextClField("Author"); fields.addButton("Close");
    fields.addButton("Add book");
  }

  public void onTrigger(String trigger_id){
    if (trigger_id == "Close") {
      pshowbooklist.selectCloseButton();
    }
    if (trigger_id == "Add book") {
      pshowbooklist.selectSelectButton(getBookList());
    }
  }

  public void setBookList(XBookList[] xbooklist){
    tmpbooklist = xbooklist;
    for (int i=1; i<=len(xbooklist); i++) {
      fields.setIdField(1,tmpbooklist[i].id);
      fields.setTextField(2,tmpbooklist[i].title);
      fields.setTextField(3,tmpbooklist[i].author);
    }
  }

  public long getBookList(){
    return fields.getIdClField(1);
  }
}
```

Fig. 4.48 Code of VBookListWindow

classes (Figs. 4.47 and 4.48) contain complete code for initiating the UI fields and buttons ('init()') and handling user-evoked events ('onTrigger()') using the rules V1, V3, V6 and V7, V8. This code can be compared with the RSL model in Fig. 4.45. It contains all the field initiation for relevant Attribute elements and button initiation for all the associated Trigger elements. The event handlers contain alternative processing ('if' statements) for each of these initiated buttons.

The View layer code is completed with the contents of the setter and getter methods. Similar to the initiation methods, getters and setters are based on the relevant Attributes in the RSL model. The 'getBookData()' method assigns three fields, which is equivalent to the three Attributes pointed at by 'book data'. The 'setBookList()' method assigns an id column and two fields that are equivalent to the two Attributes pointed at by 'book list'. This code is controlled by the rules V3–V5.

The Presenter layer methods (see Figs. 4.49 and 4.50) are mostly event handlers that contain logic evoked from the View layer's 'onTrigger()' methods. In 'PAddNew-Book' there are two such methods, translated from two Actor-to-Trigger sentences ('Librarian selects add book button' and 'Librarian selects save button') using rule

```
public class PAddNewBook extends PUseCase {
  private XBookData tmpbookdata;
  private long tmpbooklistid;
  private VNewBookForm vnewbookform;
  private MBookData mbookdata;

  public selectAddBookButton(){
    vnewbookform.show();
  }

  public selectSaveButton(XBookData xbookdata){
    tmpbookdata = xbookdata;
    result = mbookdata.validateBookData(tmpbookdata);
    if (result == 0) {
      vnewbookform.close();
      result = mbookdata.saveBookData(tmpbookdata);
      return(0);
    } else if (result == 1) {
      vnewbookform.show();
    }
  }
}
```

Fig. 4.49   Code of PAddNewBook

P4. The contents of these methods are determined by the sentences that follow these two sentences. The first method ('selectAddBookButton()') is simple, because only one sentence needs to be considered here ('System shows new book form'). By applying rule P8 we obtain the presented single call to the 'show()' operation.

The second method ('selectsSaveButton()') is significantly more complex as it involves three SVO sentences, a set of condition sentences, a final sentence and a rejoin sentence. The first SVO sentence ('System validates book data') is translated into a call to the Model layer using rule P5. Then we have a set of condition sentences translated to the 'if-else' statement according to rule P13. One of the two alternatives involves two SVO sentences ('System closes new book form' and 'System saves book data') and a final sentence. Thus, rules P8, P5 and P11 produce the appropriate two external operation calls and a local call to 'return()' in the 'if' part. The other alternative involves a rejoin sentence. This sentence points to sentence no. 2. Thus, according to rule P12 we need to repeat code obtained from sentence 2, which happens to be identical to that in 'selectAddBookButton()'. This code is inserted into the 'else' part.

If the rejoin sentence pointed to sentence 3 ('Librarian enters book data'), the 'else' part of the condition statement would be empty. This would mean that nothing would happen from the point of view of the user. The 'new book form' would still remain open and waiting for user-evoked events. In the actual example, the 'new book form' is shown again. If we assume that 'show()' performed on an already open screen element does nothing, then the two situations would be in fact equivalent.

```
public class PShowBookList extends PUseCase {
  private XBookList[] tmpbooklist;
  private long tmpbooklistid;
  private VBookListWindow vbooklistwindow;
  private PAddNewBook paddnewbook;
  private PShowBookLoanHistory pshowbookloanhistory;
  private MBookList mbooklist;

  public selectBookListButton(){
    result = mbooklist.fetchBookList();
    tmpbooklist = getBookList();
    vbooklistwindow.setBookList(tmpbooklist);
    vbooklistwindow.show();
  }

  public selectAddBookButton(){
    returnSentence = "6";
    paddnewbook.invoke(this);
    paddnewbook.selectAddButton();
  }

  public selectHistoryButton(long xbooklistid){
    tmpbooklistid = xbooklistid;
    returnSentence = "6";
    pshowbookloanhistory.invoke(this);
    pshowbookloanhistory.selectHistoryButton(tmpbooklistid);
  }

  public selectCloseButton(){
    vbooklistwindow.close();
  }

  public void returned(integer ret){
    if (returnSentence == "6"){
    }
  }
}
```

Fig. 4.50 Code of PShowBookList

In 'PShowBookList' there are four event handlers. Two of them ('selectBook ListButton()' and 'selectCloseButton()') are very simple as they involve one or two SVO sentences. Their contents are thus the result of consecutive application of rules P7 and P8. Two other methods ('selectAddBookButton()' and 'selectHistoryButton()') are proxies related with use case invocation (rule P10). The second method additionally involves passing a parameter ('tmpbooklistid'). This is caused by the 'history button' Trigger (see Fig. 4.45) that points at the 'book list' element. This is not the case for the 'add book button' and thus the first method does not involve any parameter passing.

The 'PShowBookList' class contains one additional method—'returned()', because it is involved in use case invocations in the role of the calling class (see rule P11). The code checks for the 'returnSentence' that was set in the two above-mentioned proxy methods. The contents of the condition statement are empty because sentence no. 6 in the 'Show book list' use case is an Actor-to-Trigger. This means that no code needs to be performed after returning from the invocation. This is quite logical. After we perform the logic associated, e.g. with 'Add new book' (the invoked use case), we should place it back in the situation where the 'book list window' is displayed. Note that this is exactly the case when the 'return()' operation is called in 'PAddNewBook'. The 'new book form' element is closed and this retrieves back 'book list window' from the window stack. Thus, there is no need to perform any operation in the 'returned()' method.

Note that the code for the 'returned()' method is not optimal. Also, in several other places code is not optimised. However, with the presented rules we aim at presenting semantics in a comprehensible way and not at producing optimised code. Code optimisation can be the subject of specific transformation programs that would retain this semantics while at the same time producing the actual working code.

Regardless of the above remarks on code optimality, the presented rules give a coherent framework for translating RSL models into code. A careful reader may note some issues not covered by the presented rules. This is caused by the limitations in the presented RSL syntax. For instance, there is no way to order fields in the translated UI elements. However, this can be easily resolved by extending RSL and adding new, or more fine-tuned semantic rules. This chapter should give the basis for doing this. Using the presented approach the reader can also create other similar languages and develop his own translational semantic rules.

Chapter 5
Understanding Model Transformations

The previous chapter explained the rules for transforming models of one kind (written in RSL) to models of another kind (written in UML), and code. In order to implement these rules, we need to write transformation programs. For this purpose, we could use any programming language assuming we can access the model repository and traverse through the source models and create the target models. However, writing a Java program for the purpose of model transformation would then become a quite laborious task due to the lack of necessary constructs to represent model elements that form sophisticated graphs. Thus, instead of a typical programming language, we use a dedicated model transformation language.

5.1 Overview

The purpose of writing model transformations is to help software developers to perform modelling activities. A transformation program can uniformly apply transformation rules to the source model and thus relieve developers from boring, repetitive tasks. In a typical software project environment we have Model Developers (Analysts, Requirements Engineers, Architects, Designers, ...) that use standard model editors. Most often, these are UML modelling tools, but editors for other model-based languages are also used. This includes editors for special-purpose Domain Specific Languages built to specify problems in specific application (business) domains.

Model Developers create their models in these tools and then transform them into —usually more complex—other models. This is illustrated in Fig. 5.1. As we can see, a typical language environment consists of a Model Editor and a Model Storage. If we want models in this language to be transformed, we also need an integrated Transformation Engine. Both the Model Editor and the Transformation Engine can access the Model Storage to update the models. Sometimes, we can operate only within the base language environment. This is when the transformations are **endogenous**, i.e. when they operate only on a single modelling language. In this

© Springer International Publishing Switzerland 2015
M. Śmiałek and W. Nowakowski, *From Requirements to Java in a Snap*,
DOI 10.1007/978-3-319-12838-2_5

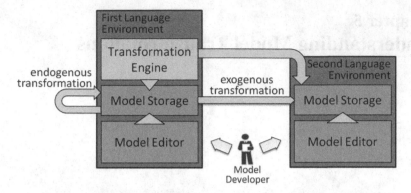

Fig. 5.1 Using model transformations

case, the Model Developer uses a single Model Editor. She first enters the source model manually and then selects and runs an automatic transformation. After this, she can access and further modify the transformed (target) model through the same Model Editor.

It is necessary to note that in many endogenous transformation problems, the target model will overlap with the source model. This is when the purpose of a transformation is to update the source model with additional elements or to change the arrangements of the original elements.

A different situation is when we want to perform an **exogenous** transformation. This kind of transformation turns models written in one language into models written in another language. Thus, it is usual that the Model Developer uses two distinct language environments (see Fig. 5.1), where the Transformation Engine has to have access to the model storage of both environments. From the technical point of view, it is often the case that the Engine operates on a local (unified) storage which is interfaced with storage spaces of the individual language environments.

Performing an exogenous transformation is similar to the task of compiling a program written in a contemporary programming language. We need to parse the input program and then generate an equivalent program in another—more primitive—language. Program parsing consists in lexical and syntactic analysis of linear text. For graphical languages we cannot do linear parsing, instead we perform syntactic analysis through traversing graphs. On output, compilers produce linear code that complies with the operational semantics of the input program constructs. For model transformations the output is not linear code but—again—a graph. Thus, "code generation" in this case consists in producing graph fragments and combining them into the resulting bigger graph. To add to the complexity of this task, the input and output graphs are often adorned with textual elements. These elements can also exhibit some structure and syntax that needs to be reflected when parsing and generating them.

Note that some transformations—especially the endogenous ones—go beyond typical "compilation-type" processing. Namely, they can also modify the source model, which is unlike for any typical compiler. During compilation, compilers build certain internal structures (e.g. abstract syntax trees) that are distinct from the source code, which is not modified. However, when performing graph transformations, we can in fact use both the source and the target graph, and update their contents. As a result, the transformation task is performed through consecutive modifications of the overall graph space.

Both the source and the target graphs have to comply with the definitions of the respective languages. As we know from the previous chapters, this means compliance with the appropriate metamodels, which are also graphs. It would thus be natural to write programs that transform graphs, also in the form of graphs as illustrated in Fig. 5.2. The Transformation Engine runs programs that can traverse through and update graphs stored in the model storage. This model storage is structured in compliance with the appropriate metamodels. The programs use graphs to depict the desired patterns in the source graph and in the target graph.

What is important is that the transformation programs have to comply with the language metamodels. Based on the graphs that metamodels define, they have to specify certain sub-graphs that need to be sought for or created to perform the transformation. Hence, the transformation language syntax has to refer to the metamodel elements and use them throughout most of its constructs. Thus, a crucial issue is how the source and the target language are defined. This moves us back to Chap. 3 and the considerations about the modelling language infrastructures (see Fig. 3.25). For a model transformation language to define its transformations uniformly, it is best to have both the source and the target language defined using the same approach, or—in other words—using the same meta-metamodel. The languages can be completely different in terms of their syntax but the (meta)language to define this syntax has to be the same. Only then will the transformations be able to refer to the source and target graphs in a uniform way. Fortunately, most contemporary modelling languages have their metamodels that comply with this standard metamodelling infrastructure.

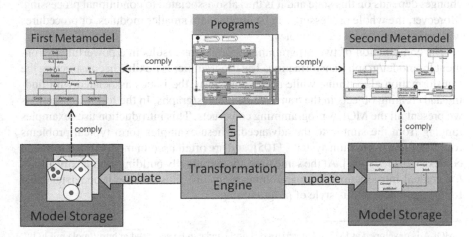

Fig. 5.2 Model transformation internals

Their metamodels are expressed in MOF or MOF-compatible languages (like Ecore). This allows model transformation languages to use these metamodels directly (or after a simple adaptation) within their programming constructs.

In this book we present the model transformation language MOLA[1] [85, 169]. This language has a graphical syntax for model (graph) querying and processing, and uses the MOF[2] notation, familiar to us from the previous chapters. What is important for model-driven requirements is that MOLA can be easily interfaced with the model storage of an RSL editor (ReDSeeDS Engine, see Chap. 7). At the same time, it can produce models in UML and has satisfactory text processing capabilities.

MOLA, analogous to most model transformation languages, combines two programming styles: declarative and imperative. The declarative part is used for querying models and matching graph-based patterns. The imperative part is used for sequencing queries and defining steps for generating the target models.

In general, the purpose of declarative programming is to define the effect of computations without defining its control flow. In other words, we define the "what" instead of defining the "how". For the task of graph transformations, the declarative paradigm is realised through specifying patterns that need to be found or generated in the model graphs. The programmer does not need to specify the algorithm for matching the patterns, but instead the transformation environment does the task internally. As a result of executing a declarative rule, certain objects in the model graph are found and/or updated. These objects are then made available for further processing through references (or variables).

The results of declarative processing can be used by the imperative elements of the language. These elements can define sequences in which declarative rules are to be executed. The imperative parts follow typical constructs of contemporary programming languages. This means that a program is a sequence of statements that change the state of the processing environment. In particular, for model transformations, these changes pertain to the state of the model graphs. The sequence of changes depends on this state and it is thus also associated to conditional processing. Moreover, the whole processing can be divided into smaller modules, or procedures with parameters and local variables.

The combination of two programming paradigms results in a powerful environment for model/graph transformation. The programmer is flexible in constructing the transformation algorithms, while abstracting away the issues associated with finding and creating objects in the transformed models/graphs. In the following sections we present all the MOLA programming constructs. This introduction uses examples ranging from the simple to the advanced. These examples form typical problems for model transformation systems [105], and are often used in model transformation contexts [79, 133, 172]. At the same time, their gradually building complexity allows for gradual introduction of programming elements, thus making it understandable for a person new to this style of programming.

---

[1] MOLA is developed at IMCS, University of Latvia and can be accessed at http://mola.mii.lu.lv/.

[2] In fact, MOLA uses a dialect of MOF, called MOLA-MOF, which slightly varies from the standard but this difference in negligible for our purposes.

5.2 "Hello World" in MOLA—Declarative Processing

We start our MOLA programming tour with the traditional "Hello world" example
[84]. This allows us to present the most basic declarative constructs of MOLA.
The task is to start with an empty model and result in a model that has a single
model element with the text "Hello world". The desired effect is shown in Fig. 5.3
(middle). We assume that before our program executes, the model does not contain
any elements. In our example the empty boxes symbolise the empty diagram window
in the concrete syntax and the empty model repository in the abstract syntax. After
the program executes, the model gets updated with a single object of type 'Greeting'
with its 'text' attribute set with the desired text. In concrete syntax, this can have the
effect of some specifically shaped (e.g. a cloud shape) model element to appear on
the diagram.

The respective MOLA program is shown in the upper part of Fig. 5.3. The program
consists of two parts—the metamodel part and the actual program part. As we can
see, the metamodel is elementary and contains only a single metaclass 'Greeting'
with a single attribute 'text' of type 'String'. 'String' is a predefined type in MOLA
and can hold strings of texts of varying size.

The actual program in MOLA in Fig. 5.3 is self-explanatory. A careful reader can
deduce its meaning by simply examining the MOLA syntax legend at the bottom of
the figure. Let us explain its individual parts. The program execution starts from the
'start symbol' and ends at the 'end symbol'. The sequence of program execution is

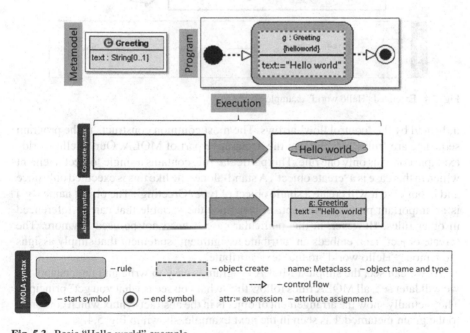

Fig. 5.3 Basic "Hello world" example

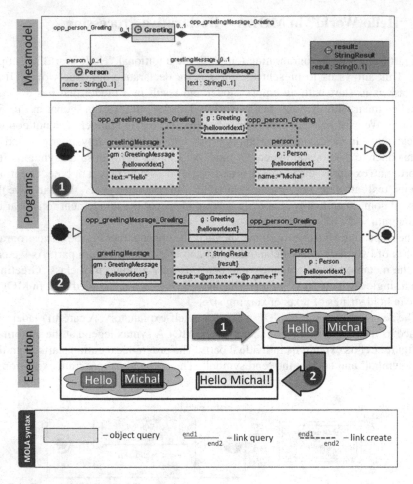

Fig. 5.4 Extended "Hello world" example

indicated by the 'control flow' arrows. The most common constructs in the program sequence are 'rules' which form the declarative part of MOLA. Our "Hello world" example contains only one rule. This particular rule contains a single 'object' element which in this case is a 'create object'. A stand-alone rule like this is executed only once and in our case it will create a single object of type 'Greeting'. The object name ('g') is an important program element, as it defines the variable that can be referenced in other rules. However, in this particular case it need not be used anymore. The 'create object' icon embeds an 'attribute assignment' statement that simply assigns the famous "Hello world" to the 'text' attribute.

As we can see, the simplest MOLA program is easy to write and understand. As we will later see, all MOLA rules follow the "what you see is what you get" principle. They actually show the arrangement of objects in the abstract syntax which conforms to the given metamodel as seen in the next example, shown in Fig. 5.4.

The metamodel is now extended and is composed of two parts. The first part (top-left of Fig. 5.4) is the source language which is defined through three metaclasses. The 'Greetings' elements contain two components: 'Person' and 'GreetingMessage'. Both these elements contain appropriate textual attributes ('name' and 'text', respectively). The second part (top-right) is the target metamodel containing only a single metaclass called 'StringResult'. The task is now to first produce a 'Greeting' composite and then derive a 'StringResult' containing text ('result') concatenated from the texts in the two components of 'Greeting'.

The desired effect (in concrete syntax only) is presented in the "Execution" part of Fig. 5.4. In an empty model, the transformation first creates a cloud-shaped 'Greeting' containing a 'Person' (here: "Michal") and a 'GreetingMessage' (here: "Hello"). Then, this is appended with another (scroll-shaped) element, which is a 'StringResult' containing concatenated text (here: "Hello Michal").

This transformation is composed of two programs. The first program creates the 'Greeting' and its components, while the second creates the 'StringResult'. This task could be developed with only a single program but we have divided it into two programs deliberately to make the description more gradual. To create 'Greeting' we have written a rule that contains several 'object create' constructs that we know from the previous example. These were appended with 'link create' constructs to define the connections between the created objects. Note that these link constructs are always adorned with association end names, which comply with the respective metaassociations in the metamodel.

The second program in Fig. 5.4 introduces query elements of MOLA. The rule contains three 'object queries' linked through 'link queries' constituting a joint query that seeks for elements that are exactly as in this arrangement. Here, the rule seeks one 'Greeting' that is linked with one 'GreetingMessage' and one 'Person'. Note that this rule finds exactly one such pattern in the current model. If there were more model elements linked in this way they would not be considered for processing. Which of the patterns are chosen is not determined, and might be random. Later, we see how to process many patterns in a loop. In our current example we assume that there is only one arrangement like this, so this rule is enough to find it.

After matching the objects, the rule creates a 'StringResult' object and sets its 'result' attribute. This assignment is similar to the one from the previous example but contains a text processing statement that uses the object names from the 'object queries'. It takes the 'gm' object and its 'text' attribute, and the 'p' object and its 'name' attribute. These two texts are concatenated with some additional characters, which produces the final 'result' ("Hello Michal!"). Objects in text processing statements are referred to with the '@' character, and text concatenation is performed with the '+' operator.

The above program assumes that there are only single objects of each kind ('Greeting', 'Person' and 'GreetingMessage') in the original model. However, this is a rare situation and thus we need constructs to process multiple elements. Forinstance, we may want to use a modification of the metamodel from Fig. 5.4, which is presented in Fig. 5.5 (top). The only modification is the multiplicity for the 'person' role. Now, any 'Greeting' can be composed of many 'Persons' (and still up to one 'GreetingMessage'). We would thus want to modify the previous transformation to process many 'Persons', as shown in the "Execution" part of Fig. 5.5. The result would now include many 'StringResults' derived from the appropriate 'Person' names.

To query for many objects in the model, MOLA introduces the for-each loop construct. In concrete notation, it is a thick box drawn around the rules that need to be executed for many model elements. Every for-each loop must have a single loop head object, which is drawn like a query object but with a thick border. When starting to execute a for-each loop the MOLA processor evaluates all the possible objects that match the rule containing the loop head (i.e. the loop head rule). It selects all the objects in the model with the type (metaclass) matching the type of the loop head object. For these objects, it further selects only those that match the query object configuration as specified in the rule. The loop is thus executed as many times as the loop head object is found to be in the exact configuration with the other objects in the model specified in the loop head rule.

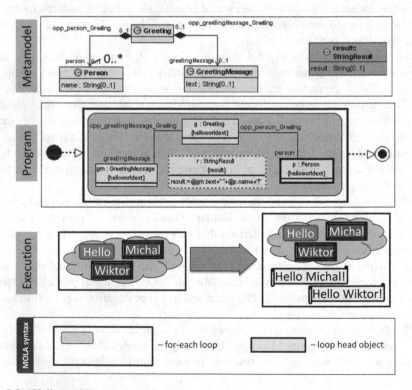

Fig. 5.5 "Hello world" example with a loop

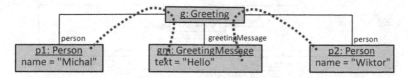

Fig. 5.6 Evaluation of objects in a for-each loop

In our example in Fig. 5.5, the for-each loop is executed twice. This is illustrated in Fig. 5.6 which shows the four objects in the original model (a 'Greeting' with a 'GreetingMessage' and two 'Persons'). Each of the two iterations of the loop execution retrieves three objects as indicated by the dotted aches. Note that within the loop execution, some of the retrieved objects can overlap between loops; only the loop head objects have to be different.

In a given loop, the retrieved objects are given names as determined by the loop head rule. So, in one of the iterations the object referred to as 'p' (see the program in Fig. 5.5) has text equal to "Michal", and in the other—equal to "Wiktor". This results in creating two separate 'StringResult' objects in the final model, with appropriately set 'result' strings.

When constructing MOLA for-each loops we need to remember that they are still declarative programming elements. They do not determine the sequence in which the loops are going to be executed. Thus, normally we should not assume this sequence. Each of the iterations in a loop execution should be treated independently of other iterations.

5.3 Variables and Procedures in MOLA—Imperative Processing

Most non-trivial transformation problems necessitate some kind of sequencing in terms of rule execution. Sometimes, the sequence in which declarative rules are executed is not important. However, in many cases, processing relies on some of the rules changing the state of the model which is then processed by other rules. This leads us to typical imperative processing with variables, control flows and procedures.

To illustrate imperative processing in MOLA, we introduce a more elaborate example than the simple "Hello world". We operate on graphs as defined through the metamodel in Fig. 5.7. 'Graphs' consist of 'Nodes' and 'Edges'. Any 'Edge' connects a source ('src') 'Node' with a target ('trg') 'Node' and thus are directed. In concrete notation, we denote nodes as pentagons and edges as arrows connecting the pentagons. Note that the metamodel allows for "dangling" edges that have missing source and/or target nodes. This is due to the multiplicity of '0..1' set for the 'src' and for the 'trg'.

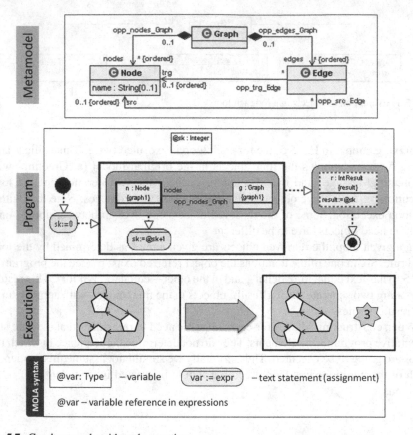

Fig. 5.7 Graph example with node counting

In addition to the graph metamodel we also use the 'IntResult' metaclass (not shown in Fig. 5.7). Objects of this type hold a single 'result' value of type 'Integer'. Their concrete syntax is a star with the integer value placed inside it. This model element allows us to represent results of certain arithmetic calculations pertaining to graphs.

Let us now introduce the first problem associated with the graphs. It is a simple task to count all the nodes in a graph and create an element containing the result of this counting. The expected effect is shown in the "Execution" part of Fig. 5.7.

To perform this calculation we need to use the for-each loop, but we also need an integer type variable that would hold the number of nodes. The program in Fig. 5.7 contains the declaration of such a variable, called 'sk'. As we can see, variable declarations contain the '@' prefix. Variables can be assigned values through text statements with assignment clauses. Considering these explanations, the presented program should be easy to understand. The program starts by setting the initial value of the counter 'sk'. Then control goes to the for-each loop. The loop runs for each of the 'Nodes' contained in a 'Graph'. For each node, the counter is incremented. After all the loops execute, control is shifted to the last rule where an 'IntResult' object is created and its attribute assigned the value of the 'sk' counter. Note that the for-each loop finds any node in the model that is linked with any graph. So, regardless of the number of independent graphs in the model, there will be created a single 'IntResult' with a summary value.

In this example, 'sk' is an explicit variable, which means that it is explicitly declared through a variable declaration construct. In MOLA we can also use implicit variables. These variables are not declared but are introduced as parts of the rules. Any object in a rule has a name (e.g. 'n' or 'g' in our example program). These names can be used in further rules and refer to specific objects found through applying the original rule. We will see how explicit variables can be used in further program examples. Both the explicit and the implicit variables can be used in expressions using the '@' prefix (as in 'sk := @sk + 1').

The first graph problem was a simple one where we only had to count the nodes. Now, we change the problem to count the edges instead of nodes. Furthermore, we count only the edges that form "loops", i.e. that connect nodes with themselves. We also perform calculations separately for each distinct graph in the model. This problem is illustrated in the "Execution" part of Fig. 5.8. There, we can see two distinct graphs, therefore transformation should produce two 'IntResult' objects containing the counted numbers of "loop" edges in each of the graphs.

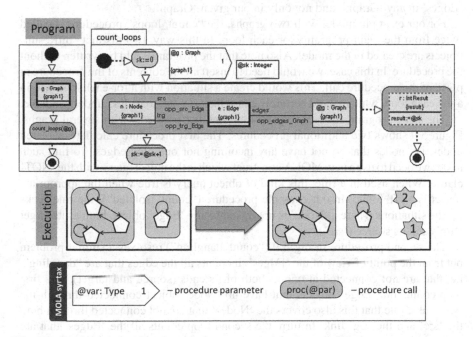

Fig. 5.8 Graph example with edge counting

To handle the problem of separate graphs we introduce a new MOLA construct—the procedure call. The main program (top-left of Fig. 5.8) contains a simple for-each loop that queries for all the 'Graph' objects. Having found such an object in a given loop, the program calls the "count_loops" procedure. This call contains a parameter which is a reference to the found 'Graph' object. As expected, the parameter refers (through the '@' prefix) to the implicitly declared variable that holds the reference to the found object (variable 'g').

The "count_loops" procedure has its parameter declared in a special MOLA construct. The parameter icon contains the name of the parameter, its type (metaclass) and its number. The number is necessary, as there can be more parameters than just one and they need to be logically ordered—physical ordering through positioning in the diagram is not available in MOLA.

As we can see, the structure of the "count_loops" procedure is similar to the structure of the node counting program. The difference lies in the loop head rule. The for-each loop runs through all the 'Edge' objects that connect a 'Node' object with the same object. The rule is very clear that what needs to be found is a set of two objects (a 'Node' and an 'Edge') connected through two links (an 'src' link and a 'trg' link). It is also important that the 'Edge' has to be contained (see the 'edges' link) in a specific 'Graph' object. Namely, it has to be the very object that was passed as the parameter of "count_loops". This is again denoted with the '@' prefix. Note that without the '@' in front of the 'g', the for-each loop would run through all the 'Edges' in any 'Graph', and not only in our given 'Graph'.

For our example model with two graphs, the "count_loops" procedure is called twice from the main programs for-each loop. In this way, two distinct 'IntResult' objects are created in the model. Also note that the program could be written without the procedure. In this case, we would need to insert all the contents of the procedure in place of the procedure call. This would create a situation with a for-each loop within a for-each loop, which would certainly cause the program to be less understandable.

The same program structure can be used in other problems with several graphs. Figure 5.9 shows two additional procedures. The first procedure calculates isolated nodes, i.e. nodes that do not have any incoming nor outgoing edges. To find such nodes we need to use a new MOLA construct which is the object query with the 'NOT' clause. When used in a rule, this kind of object query is true when the appropriate object is NOT found. In our example procedure ("count_isolated"), the rule seeks for the situations where a 'Node' is not linked to any 'Edge' object, both as its target ('trg') and its source ('src').

The second procedure in Fig. 5.9 ("count_dangling") resolves a similar problem but from the point of view of the 'Edges'. It counts all the edges that are "dangling", i.e. that are not connected at one or both of its ends (source and target). The first loop counts the 'Edge' objects that have no 'Node' object connected through the 'src' link. Note that this also covers the 'Nodes' that are not connected through both the 'src' and the 'trg' link. In turn, the second loop counts all the 'Edges' that are

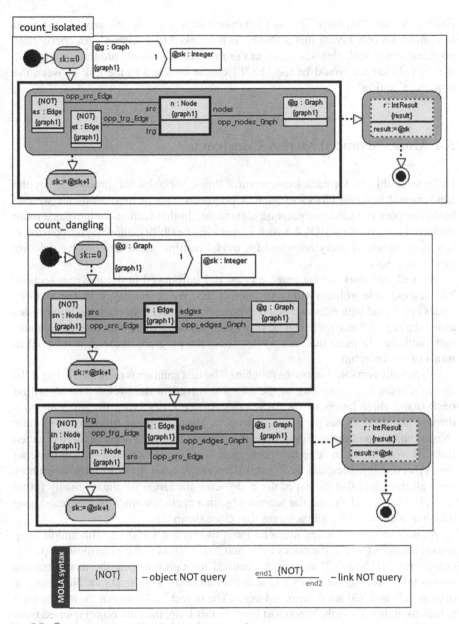

Fig. 5.9 Graph examples with missing edges or nodes

connected with a 'Node' in the role of its source ('src') but not connected to any 'Node' in the role of its target ('trg').

In some situations we would also want to create a rule that determines not the missing objects but the missing links. For instance, we would like to count 'Node' objects that are "orphans", i.e. not contained in any graph. We would thus need to construct a rule saying that a 'Node' is not linked to a 'Graph'. An appropriate program would look almost exactly as our first graph example program in Fig. 5.7; the only difference would be the {NOT} clause attached to the link between the objects 'n' and 'g'.

5.4 More Advanced MOLA Constructs

Rules with objects, for-each loops, control flows, variables and procedures are the fundamental building blocks of MOLA programs. Out of these elements we can build complex model transformation algorithms. In this section we introduce more advanced constructs of MOLA which increase its flexibility, allowing for constructing more advanced query rules and for model manipulations that involve deleting model elements.

We will still work on the graph metamodel introduced in the previous section. The first example problem will be to count cycles. We define a cycle as a set of three nodes connected with edges so that it is possible to traverse through the three nodes along the edges. Since there can be many edges linking two nodes, any three nodes can participate in more than one cycle. Thus, the program becomes non-trivial in terms of its algorithm.

We provide two solutions to the problem. The first solution is presented in Fig. 5.10 and is a brute-force counting of the edges involved in the cycles. The algorithm necessitates three layers of for-each loops. In the outer layer, the program goes through all the edges that participate in a cycle. The appropriate rule consists of three 'Node' objects and three 'Edge' objects connected through appropriately directed links. Having found an edge that participates in a cycle, we need to determine all the cycles that it participates in. For this purpose we enter the inner loop which now finds all the edges that go out of the node being the target for the originally found node. Having found a particular second edge in a cycle, we enter the innermost loop which now searches for all the edges that close the cycle.

As we can see, the loops use references to implicit variables. The middle loop uses references ('@') to the nodes ('n1' and 'n2') found in the outermost loop. The objects for 'n1' and 'n2' are not determined through querying the model but are simply taken as objects already found in the outermost loop head rule. Note that the objects 'n3' and 'e3' are determined anew. The object 'n3' found in the middle loop is then used directly in the innermost loop. In this loop, the only object queried from the model is the loop head ('e3').

The innermost loop also increments the cycle counter 'sk'. This algorithm in fact counts all the edges in all the cycles and, thus, the counted number is three times the number of the actual cycles (each cycle contains three edges). Thus, the last rule which creates the 'IntResult' object divides the final result by 3.

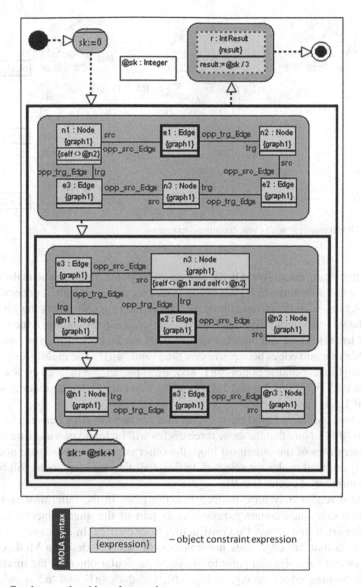

Fig. 5.10 Graph example with cycle counting

To understand better the execution of this algorithm we use the example in Fig. 5.11. This example shows one outermost iteration of the algorithm applied to a specific graph. In this outermost iteration, an edge is found (denoted with a red bold line) and two adjacent nodes (referred as '@n1' and '@n2', also denoted with a red bold border). Of course, this edge and the two nodes are part of at least one cycle (thus they comply with the loop head rule of the outermost loop).

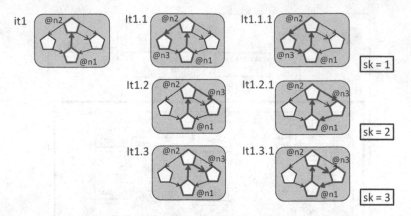

Fig. 5.11 Graph example with cycle counting—execution

With this arrangement found in the outermost loop, the program enters the middle loop. In the first sub-iteration (1.1) the loop finds a second edge with a connected node ('@n3'). Again, with this arrangement of objects the program enters the innermost loop. In the sub-sub-iteration (1.1.1) the cycle is closed and the counter is incremented (here: set to '1'). There are no other iterations of the innermost loop because there are no other relevant edges between nodes '@n3' and '@n1'. The middle loop iterates another two times, because nodes '@n1' and '@n2' participate in three cycles. This is illustrated with iterations 1.2 and 1.3. As in the first case (1.1), the innermost loops (1.2.1 and 1.3.1) run only once.

In this way, we have found three cycles that contain the edge between the nodes "@n1' and '@n2'. Note that the same three cycles will be found two more times each. In other iterations of the outermost loop, the other edges that participate in each of the already counted cycles are selected. In this way, the resulting count will be three times the number of cycles (i.e. 9).

A careful reader may have noticed that the rules in the outermost and in the middle loop contained certain expressions as part of the query objects. This is a MOLA construct that allows for constructing finer queries. In our case, we wanted to make sure that the edge does not connect the same node. In a MOLA query, different object variables can point to the same particular object in the models. So, in case of looping edges (as e.g. in Fig. 5.8), variables 'n1' and 'n2' would point to the same object (the same 'Node' is the source and the target for the 'Edge'). To prevent from counting this we have introduced an object constraint expression. In our example, it refers to the current object ('self') and compares it with another object ('@n2') making sure that they are different ('<>'). Expressions can contain logical operators ('and', 'or') like in the constraint from the middle loop. Expressions can also refer to object attributes, with the syntax identical to that used by us already in the assignment constructs (attributes referenced through the dot '.' operator).

The above algorithm is certainly not optimal from the point of view of processing time. Thus, we change the algorithm to consist of only one loop. This time, it is a

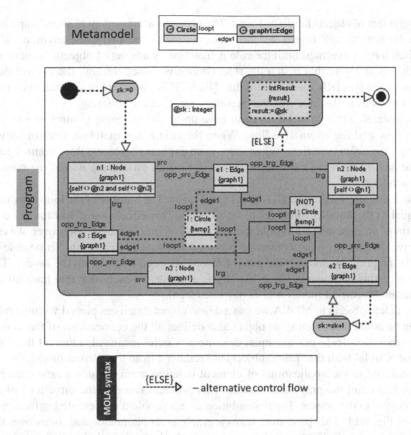

Fig. 5.12 Graph example with cycle counting—alternative solution with a while loop

'while' loop that can be constructed from the MOLA constructs we already know of. However, to implement this new algorithm, we first need to update the metamodel with an additional metclass as shown in Fig. 5.12. The additional metaclass 'Circle' is associated with the already known 'Edge' metaclass. This new metaclass is only a temporary construct that will allow us to mark the cycles already found.

The program is centred around a single rule which uses objects of the newly introduced metaclass. The rule queries for 'Node' and 'Edge' objects that form cycles as in the outermost rule in the previous program. However, in order for matching to occur the 'Edges' in the cycle should not be attached to any 'Circle'; if this is so, the rule creates a new 'Circle' and attaches it to the found 'Edges'.

As we can see, the main rule of this program is not a for-each loop. Thus, it is executed once, whenever flow of control reaches it. When the program begins, the rule finds a random set of objects that fulfil the rule and creates a new 'Circle' attached to the 'Edges'. Then control goes to the next statement which increments the cycle counter 'sk'. The program then loops back to the main rule and this time, some other arrangement of objects has to be found. The previous arrangement is already updated with the new 'Circle' object and thus does not match the query rule anymore. This implicit loop is executed until the rule is matched by any set of objects. If there are no objects anymore that match the rule, control is passed through the control flow arrow that is specially marked with the '{ELSE}' keyword. This alternative control flow moves us to the final rule that sets the 'result' of the counting.

In general, any rule in MOLA can have up to two outgoing control flows—the main flow and the alternative flow. When the rule is not matched, control moves through the alternative flow. When there is no explicit alternative flow, control goes to the final node in the current procedure or finishes processing within the current for-each loop.

Note that the last program has linear complexity. The number of the loop iterations is equal to the number of cycles to be counted. This effectiveness has the price of additional storage needed to hold the temporary 'Circle' objects. Moreover, we can observe that the program cannot be repeated to count cycles again. To be able to repeat the program and receive correct results we need to clean-up the model. The way to do this is shown in Fig. 5.13. This is a simple for-each loop that finds all the circles in the current model and then deletes them.

To delete objects in MOLA we use a delete object statement placed within a rule. It can be noted that deleting an object also deletes all the connections of that object with other objects. In our example, deleting a 'Circle' means also that all the links of that 'Circle' with the 'Edge' objects are removed from the current model.

To illustrate the applications of element deletion we introduce a new example problem around the graph metamodel. This problem reverses the directions of all the 'Edges' in the graphs. The first solution to this problem is presented in the upper part of Fig. 5.14. This procedure takes a graph as its parameter and loops over the edges of this graph. The for-each loop head rule finds the 'Edge' objects that connect nodes. For each of such objects it creates another 'Edge' object which is connected to the two found 'Node' objects, but with reversed links. Of course, the new 'Edge' object is also being linked with the current 'Graph' object.

Note that the above described rule also covers the situation of looping edges, i.e. 'Edge' objects which are linked to the same 'Node' object as its source ('src') and target ('trg'). So, in some iterations the implicit variables 's' and 't' may point to the

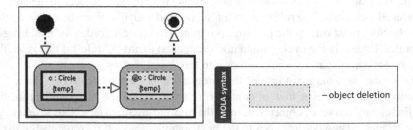

Fig. 5.13 Element deletion example

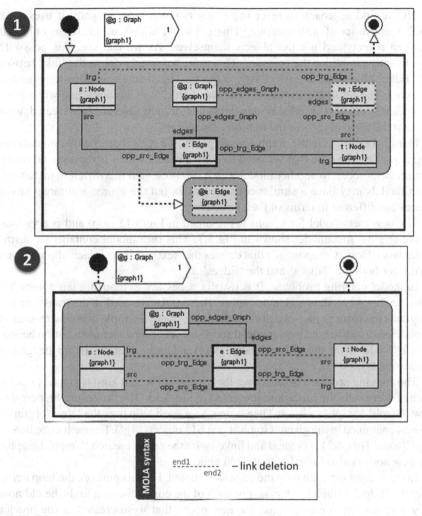

Fig. 5.14 Edge reversal examples with element and link deletion

same object. In this case, the rule will still work correctly and will create a second edge that connects this 'Node' object just like the given 'Edge' but in the opposite direction.

After the new 'Edge' object is created, the old 'Edge' object is deleted. Note that we perform this deletion within the same for-each loop as the old 'Edge' objects are no longer needed. In the previous example with the 'Circle' objects, they could be deleted only after the "while" loop has finished. This was because the 'Circles' were used within this loop to mark the already processed graph cycles. They could be deleted only after the original cycle counting was done.

The second approach to reversing edges is much more elegant. It uses a new MOLA construct of link deletion. This construct allows us to delete only links between objects and not the objects themselves. As we can see, this possibility significantly simplifies the program. This time, we simply delete the links between the 'Edge' object and the two 'Node' objects. This deletion is done together with querying. The MOLA engine first finds the objects with the links, and when found, immediately deletes the links. Within the same rule, new links are then created, which connect the three objects in the opposite direction.

Our final example in the graph domain presents a typical problem of model copying. It is often the case that we need to copy a model which is represented using a certain metamodel, to another model which is represented in a different metamodel. Both models may have a similar concrete syntax but the source and target storage spaces are different in terms of their structure.

The new metamodel for graphs is presented in Fig. 5.15 (top) and is a variation of the original metamodel shown in Fig. 5.7. This metamodel contains an abstract metaclass ('GraphComponent') that defines the 'text' attribute which allows to store names for both the 'Nodes' and the 'Edges'.

In model copying problems, it is usually necessary to maintain temporary links between the old models and their copies. These links are used in the transformation programs to create proper structure of the copy. In our example, the new metamodel is associated with the old metamodel through the additional metaassociation between the old 'Node' (from the 'graph1' metamodel) and the new 'Node' (from the 'graph2' metamodel).

The copying program iterates over the graphs of the first kind ({graph1}) and for each of them calls the procedure presented in Fig. 5.15. The procedure first creates a new 'Graph' {graph2} object. Then it runs a for-each loop over the 'Node' {graph1} objects contained in the given 'Graph' {graph1} object ('@g'). For each node found, a new 'Node' {graph2} is created and linked with the newly created 'Graph' {graph2}; the new node is also linked with the old node.

In the second for-each loop the edges are copied. For this purpose the loop iterates over the 'Edge' {graph1} objects. For each of the edges, the rule finds the old nodes they connect ('sn' and 'tn') and the new nodes that were created in the previous for-each loop ('g2sn' and 'g2tn'). This is where the temporary links between the old and the new nodes are needed without which the program would not be able to determine the structure of the new graph. The new 'Edge' {graph2} object is created and linked with the new 'Nodes' that are temporarily linked to the old 'Nodes'. In this way, the new graph maintains the exact structure as for the old graph.

The new graph preserves the node names from the old graph in the first for-each loop. The statement which creates new 'Nodes' also assigns the 'text' attributes by copying them from the 'name' attributes of the old 'Nodes'. Since the old graph does not cover edge names, the new graph has the edge names set to empty strings. This is done in the second loop when creating the new 'Edge' objects.

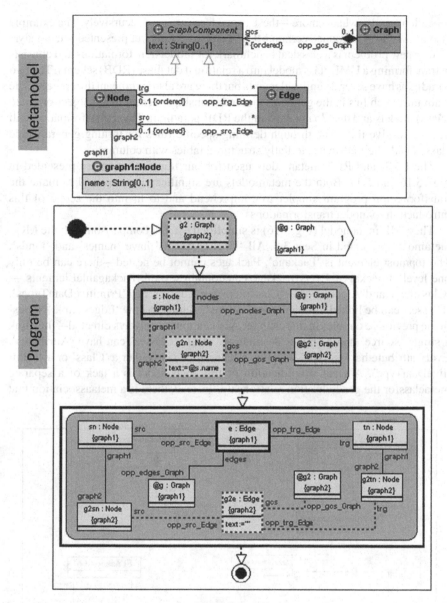

Fig. 5.15   Graph to graph transformation example

5.5 End-to-End Transformation Example

The example MOLA programs in the previous sections were simple and consisted of a maximum of one main program and one additional procedure. Now we present a more sophisticated problem. To solve it, we need to construct several procedures and—what is more—these procedures are used recursively. The example also allows us to introduce certain MOLA constructs not yet presented previously.

Our new problem is a classical benchmark for model transformations and consists in transforming a UML class model into a relational database (RDB) schema. The two paradigms have several similar elements but there are also significant differences. The main mismatch lies in the generalisation relationships present in the object-oriented (class) models and that do not exist in the RDB paradigm. Thus, transformation will need to resolve this issue through defining specific rules for turning generalizable classes with their attributes to flatly structured tables with columns.

The UML and RDB metamodels used for our transformation are presented in Figs. 5.16 and 5.17. Both the metamodels are significantly simplified to make the transformation program simpler to comprehend and to fit into the scope of this introduction to model transformations.

The UML metamodel (Fig. 5.16) is simplified even in comparison with the MOF metamodel presented in Sect. 3.8. All 'UMLElements' have 'names' and 'kinds'. The topmost element is 'Package'. Packages cannot be nested—there can be only one level of packages. Every package can contain several 'PackagableElements'—'Classifiers' and 'Associations'. 'Classifiers' are 'Classes' and 'PrimitiveDataTypes'. 'Classes' can be linked through 'Associations', similar to how 'Edges' link 'Nodes' in the previous examples in this chapter. Associations are always directed—they link a single 'source' and a single 'destination' class. 'Classes' can have 'Attributes'. Every attribute has its 'type' which is a 'Classifier', i.e. either a 'Class' or a 'PrimitiveDataType'. A great simplification of this metamodel is a lack of a separate metaclassfor the generalisation relationship. Instead, there is a metaassociation that

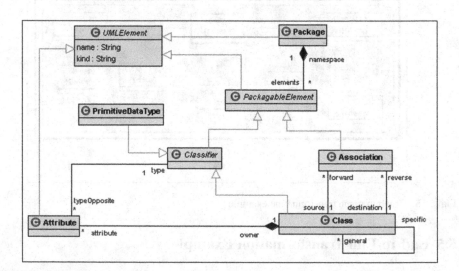

Fig. 5.16 Simplified UML class metamodel

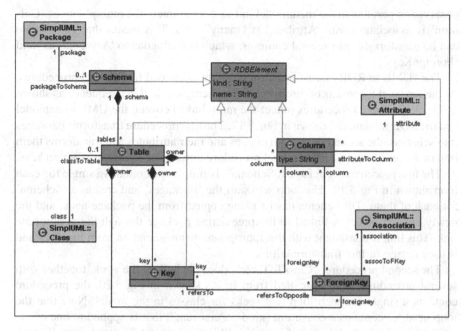

Fig. 5.17 Simplified RDB metamodel

allows for "generalisation links" between classes. One of the classes is 'specific' and the other is 'general'.

The RDB metamodel (Fig. 5.17) is also very simple and consists of only six metaclasses. At the top it defines the generic abstract 'RDBElement' metaclass. Through this metaclass all other RDB elements have 'names' and 'kinds' as the UML class model elements in the previous metamodel. The topmost RDB element is the 'Schema' which consists of 'Tables'. 'Tables' contain 'Columns', 'Keys' and 'ForeignKeys'. The 'Keys' can be associated with 'Columns', and the 'ForeignKeys' link 'Keys' with 'Columns'.

For the models to be well formed, this simple metamodel should also have some constraints defined. The main constraint is that 'ForeignKeys' should link 'Keys' and 'Columns' contained in different 'Table' objects, otherwise the role of the 'ForeingKeys' would not reflect their meaning in typical RDB systems.

Also note that the RDB metamodel is connected with the UML class metamodel. Instances of these metaassociations are used as temporary helpers—traceability links—in the transformation program. As expected, the metaassociations connect the analogous elements in both metamodels. Packages relate to Schemas, Classes to Tables, Columns to Attributes and Associations to Foreign Keys. This reflects the basic transition of elements from the UML class models to the RDB models. Of course, the detailed rules are more complex than this simple transition and we formulate them along the consecutive parts of the presented program. An important observation pertains to the metamodel in Fig. 5.17, namely the multiplicity of 'Column' in association with 'Attribute' is "many" ('*'). This means that an attribute can be transformed into several columns, which is analogous to 'Associations' and 'ForeignKeys'.

The "UML to RDB" transformation program is divided into several procedures. At the top level it consists of three procedures being invoked in a sequence as shown in Fig. 5.18. These procedures reflect the main links between the UML metamodel and the RDB metamodel shown in Fig. 5.17. The first procedure transforms packages into schemas; the second deals with classes and their attributes and transforms them into tables and columns; and the final procedure turns associations into foreign keys.

The first procedure, "PackageToSchema", is simple and contains a single for-each loop shown in Fig. 5.19. The loop seeks all the 'Packages' and creates a 'Schema' for each of them. The schema has its name copied from the package name and the newly created object is linked to the preexisting package through the appropriate link. This link is consistent with the appropriate metaassociation from Fig. 5.17 and is used during further transformations.

The second procedure, "ClassToTable", does the bulk of the work, together with several procedures that are called from it. As shown in Fig. 5.20, the procedure contains a single for-each loop that seeks for classes in the model. Note that the loop head 'c' contains a constraint (kind="Persistent") that is applied to one of the attributes, so only the classes of a specific 'kind' are found. For each such 'Class', the rule retrieves also its containing 'Package' and the 'Schema' that was generated in the previous step. Then the rule creates a 'Table' object and links it appropriately with the 'Schema' object and also creates a temporary traceability link between the 'Table' and the 'Class'.

In addition to generating the 'Table' itself, the rule generates also a primary key and and an associated column. The primary key is an object of type 'Key' where

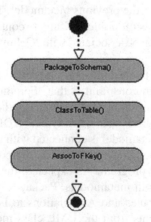

Fig. 5.18 UML to RDB transformation—main procedure

its name is a concatenation of the table name and the "_pk" postfix. The associated 'Column' object is typed as "NUMBER" and named with the "_tid" postfix.

To illustrate the execution of the rule, we use the class model presented in Fig. 5.21. The model consists of four classes, where three of them are in generalisation relationships. The fourth class is used as the type of one of the attributes of another class. The loop head rule in Fig. 5.20 runs through two of the classes—the ones that have their 'kind' set to "Persistent". In concrete syntax this is denoted with the stereotype notation.

Figure 5.22 shows the result of one of the iterations, where the class named "C" produced a table with the same name. The table contains the primary key ("C_pk") and the column holding the table's identifiers ("C_tid"). The primary key points to the column. The figure shows both the concrete and the abstract versions of the model

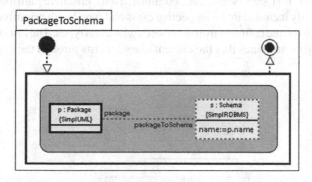

Fig. 5.19 Creating packages from schemas

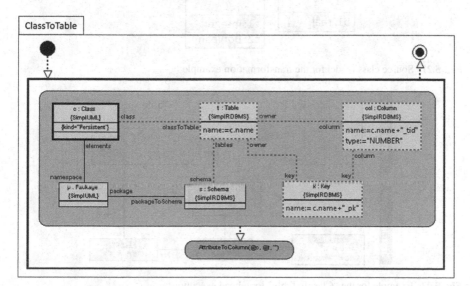

Fig. 5.20 Creating tables from classes

resulting from executing the loop head rule. In concrete syntax, the specific objects are denoted with appropriate stereotypes («Table», «col» and «key»). The abstract syntax shows the resulting arrangement of objects which matches the arrangement of objects in the MOLA rule.

After producing the basic structure of the table the loop in "ClassToTable" calls another procedure—"AttributeToColumn". This procedure shown in Fig. 5.23 has three parameters. These are: the class reference, the table reference and the prefix to be appended to the attribute names. Prefixes are added to the column names derived from attributes that are inherited through generalisation relationships and from the classes used as attribute types. Initially, the prefix is set to an empty string (see Fig. 5.20). The class reference is obviously set to the current class object ('c') and the table reference is set to the newly generated table object ('t').

The "AttributeToColumn" procedure is in fact a sequence of calls to three other procedures. The first step is to create columns from "primitive" attributes, i.e. the attributes directly included in the respective class and typed with primitive types. The second step is to create columns from attributes with class types. The last step is to create columns from attributes that the current class inherits through the generalisation

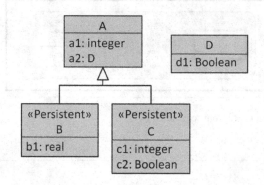

Fig. 5.21 Source class model for the transformation example

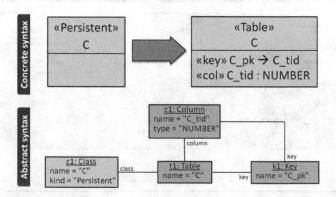

Fig. 5.22 Example for the "ClassToTable" loop head execution

Fig. 5.23 Creating columns from attributes—main procedure

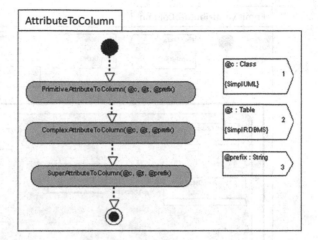

hierarchy. As we can see, all the three calls pass the class reference, the table reference and the prefix. Later, we will also notice that the "AttributeToColumn" procedure is used in implicit recursion; it is called from within two of the three procedures it calls.

The first of the three procedures—"PrimitiveAttributeToColumn" is not recursive, as shown in Fig. 5.24. It processes only the attributes contained in the current class. The procedure's for-each loop seeks the attributes linked to the class passed as the parameter. For each of these attributes it creates a column in the table that was passed as the second attribute. After creating the column the procedure determines the column's 'name' and 'type'. The 'name' is copied from the attribute's name ('@a.name') with the optional prefix added. Note that the procedure introduces a new MOLA construct which is the text statement with a condition. Such conditions (here: @prefix="") are evaluated and can determine the flow of control, using normal and alternative ('{ELSE}') flows.

The column's 'type' is determined within another procedure—"PrimitiveType ToSQL". This procedure accepts a string with the primitive data type name (@p.name) and returns a string with the SQL column type. After this, the column's attributes are assigned the appropriate values in a separate simple rule that ends the loop's internal processing. Note that attribute values can be set also within normal query objects and not only while the object is created. In our example, the object is accessed through a reference (implicit variable 'cl') and then its attributes are set through appropriate assignment statements.

The "PrimitiveTypeToSQL" procedure shown in Fig. 5.25 takes a string ('@primtype') and returns a string ('@sqltype'). The return values in MOLA can be passed through in–out parameters. Normal parameters pass the actual values into the procedure but are not changeable. The in–out parameters can change their values inside a procedure which can then be used outside of the procedure. Apart from

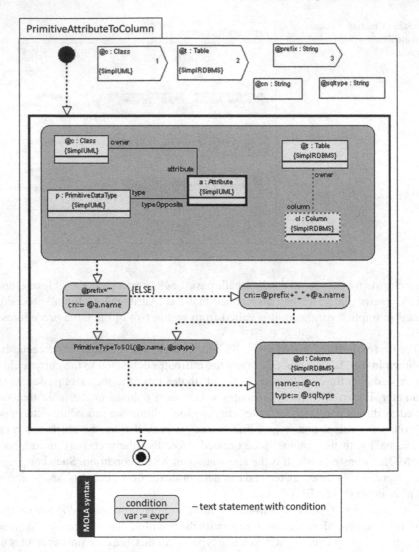

Fig. 5.24 Creating columns from primitive attributes

introducing this new MOLA construct, "PrimitiveTypeToSQL" is very simple. It contains three conditional text statements that set the output string based on the values of the input string.

The last two procedures together produce columns in the current RDB table. To illustrate this, we continue the example from Fig. 5.22. Figure 5.26 shows the situation after executing "PrimitiveAttributeToColumn", applied to the example class "C" and to the respective newly created table. The top-left part of the figure shows the original situation in concrete syntax. In abstract syntax, we have the class ('cl1') and its two

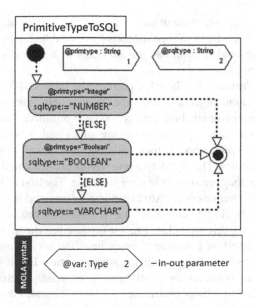

Fig. 5.25 Determining column types

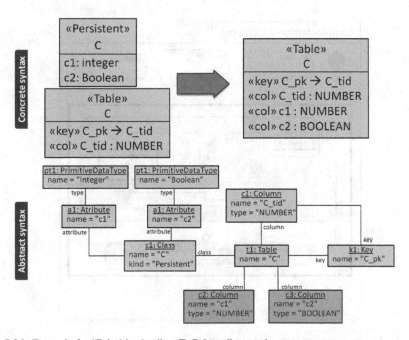

Fig. 5.26 Example for "PrimitiveAttributeToColumn" execution

attributes ('a1' and 'a2' with their names "c1" and "c2"). Both attributes are linked to the appropriate 'PrimitiveDataType' objects ('pt1' and 'pt2'). Note that these two data type objects are singletons and all the attributes with respective primitive types are linked to these objects.

After running "PrimitiveAttributeToColumn" the table ('t1') is appended with two additional 'Column' objects—'co2' and 'co3'. Their 'names' and 'types' are derived from the respective attribute names and their primitive types.

When all the primitive type attributes are processed, control returns to the "AttributeToColumn" procedure. It then calls two procedures to process inherited and class-typed attributes. The respective procedures are presented in Figs. 5.27 and 5.28. As we can see, they are similar in their structure. The first of them ("Complex-AttributeToColumn") iterates over 'Attributes' ('a') contained in the current 'Class' ('c'). The attribute should be "complex", i.e. it should be linked with a 'Class' as its 'type'. After finding this type class ('tc') it is passed as the first parameter to the recursively called "AttributeToColumn" procedure. The second attribute is the current table ('t'); the prefix is set to contain the attribute name. In this way, the columns generated from the complex attribute will have appropriately prefixed names.

The second procedure ("SuperAttributeToColumn") iterates over 'Class' objects ('sc') that are 'general' for the current class ('c'). As in the previous case, after finding the general class, it is passed as the first parameter to the "AttributeToColumn" procedure. The prefix is not changed, as the inherited attributes are treated just like the "owned" attributes.

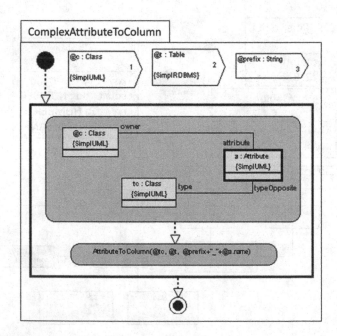

Fig. 5.27 Creating columns from class-typed attributes

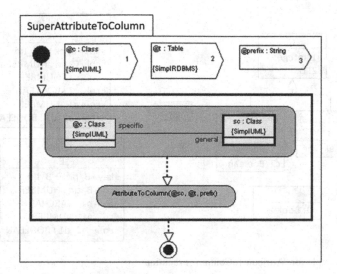

Fig. 5.28 Creating columns from inherited attributes

Both in the case of complex attributes and inherited attributes, the procedures use indirect recursion. The "AttributeToColum" procedure is called for another class: the attribute's type or the super class. However, the table reference is maintained and passed to the recurring procedures. Thus, the primitive attributes within the other class are transformed into further columns of the current table. In case the other class has complex attributes or super classes, the recursion goes even deeper. It ends when there are only primitive attributes left in the class, at the given level of recursion. For the columns generated from complex attributes, the column names have prefixes which may sometimes be multiple when the type classes also have complex attributes.

Finally, note that the set of "...AttributeTo..." procedures handles any situation involving combinations of complex attributes and super classes. For instance, it would properly handle the situation where a super class has complex attributes in which the respective type classes also have super classes with complex attributes, and so on. This is illustrated in Fig. 5.29.

The final procedure is called directly from the main program procedure (see Fig. 5.18). It covers the remaining issue of creating foreign keys from associations. The procedure is called "AssocToFKey" and is presented in Fig. 5.30. It contains a simple for-each loop which queries for all the 'Association' objects. It finds only the associations between the 'Classes' (see 'sc' and 'dc') for which 'Tables' were created in the previous procedures (see 'srcTbl' and 'destTbl'). This eliminates the associations involving classes that are not «Persistent», for which tables were not created.

Recall that according to our simplified UML metamodel, all the associations are directed. Thus the query is simple and can easily determine which 'Class' is the 'source' and which is the 'destination' for a given 'Association'. Whenever a

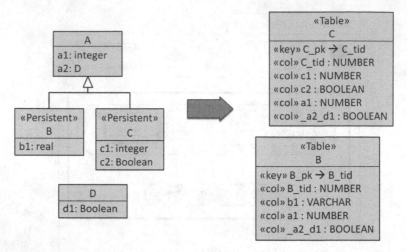

Fig. 5.29 Example for "AttributeToColumn" execution

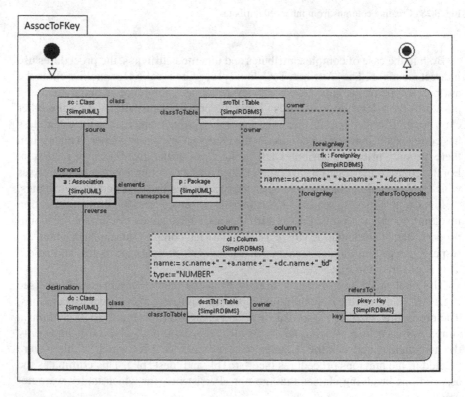

Fig. 5.30 Creating foreign keys from associations

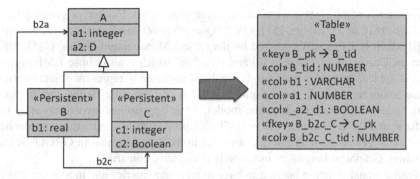

Fig. 5.31 Transformation example with an association

match is found in the for-each loop, the 'Table' generated from the source 'Class' is appended with a 'ForeignKey' and a 'Column'. The names of the new objects are concatenated from the names of the source 'Class', the 'Association' and the target 'Class'. Additionally, the newly created 'ForeignKey' is linked with the primary key ('pkey') of the 'Table' generated from the destination 'Class'.

This processing is illustrated in Fig.5.31. We have extended our example UML model to contain two additional associations ('b2a' and 'b2c'). The result of the transformation is shown on the right (showing only the table generated from class 'B'; the table for class 'C' is not relevant here). The table has two additional elements in relation to the previous example—the appropriately named foreign key («fkey») and column («col»). The foreign key points to the primary key of table 'C'. Note that there is no second pair of «fkey» and «col»because class 'A' is not «Persistent» and thus generation of the respective foreign key is not desired.

Note that the "AssocToFKey" procedure neglects the issue of inherited associations generating foreign keys only for the associations coming directly from the given class and not from the general classes (if any). This would necessitate introducing recursion, as in the attributes. We will leave solving this problem as an exercise for the reader.

With this we conclude the end-to-end example, which resolves a practical problem of UML to RDB transformation. The problem was solved for simplified metamodels. The reader is now encouraged to continue the exercise and modify the solution to comply with the other UML/MOF class metamodels presented in the previous chapters of this book.

5.6 Which Language to Choose?

MOLA is one of many model transformation languages. Besides MOLA, there is a wide variety of model transformation languages to choose from. Generally, these languages can be divided into textual and graphical. Obviously MOLA is a representative of the graphical kind. Other examples include Fujaba[3] originating from the University of Paderborn [51], QVT (Query/View/Transformations) Relations[4] [120] which is a standard managed by the Object Management Group, GROOVE[5] from the University of Twente [59] and Henshin[6] which is an Eclipse-EMF project [11]. Graphical languages use various graphical notations to represent object queries. These notations resemble those found in MOLA and they also define certain notations to denote changes made to the model. Some approaches involve defining the "before" and "after" patterns (as in QVT Relations), while some other approaches denote changes along with the queries (like in MOLA, and also in GROOVE and Henshin). Graphical languages use mostly declarative constructs.

Textual transformation languages have to represent queries and model updates in the form of a serialised text. They also use standard imperative constructs known from typical programming languages. Such languages include QVT-Operational managed by the OMG [120], ATL (Atlas Transformation Language)[7] which was originally developed by INRIA [19, 80], GReTL from the University of Koblenz-Landau [41] and VIATRA2[8] from the Budapest University of Technology and Economics [175]. Such languages offer varying notations to represent model queries and model updates. These notations are combinations of declarative rules and imperative procedures.

In this short overview we do not discuss the above listed languages in detail. The reader is referred to websites and manuals of the respective languages. However, to give the reader some directions we present some brief illustrations which allow for comparison of MOLA with other languages.

Figure 5.32 shows a brief rule written in ATL which creates Tables from Classes [81]. This rule is part of a larger program that transforms a UML class model into an RDB schema, generally equivalent of the end-to-end example from Sect. 5.5. The presented rule shows some of the syntax of the declarative constructs of ATL. For a detailed comparison the interested reader can refer to the ATL documentation and tutorials. We will not explain the notation of ATL but the current example is self-explanatory when related to the equivalent MOLA rule. The example shows that for simple problems the textual and graphical approaches can have similar expressiveness.

When the problem becomes larger and pertains to more than just single objects, the textual notations have to use complex syntax to express graphs of objects as illustrated in Figs. 5.33 and 5.34. These two examples present solutions to the graph edge reversing problem, expressed in GReTL [72] and VIATRA2 [67]. The respective solution in MOLA can be found in Fig. 5.14(2). As we can see, the textual transformations have to somehow represent the layout of the edges and the nodes to

---

[3] http://www.fujaba.de/.

[4] QVT Relations also has a textual syntax variant.

[5] http://groove.cs.utwente.nl/.

[6] http://www.eclipse.org/henshin/.

[7] http://www.eclipse.org/atl/.

[8] www.eclipse.org/viatra2.

```
1. rule PersistentClass2Table{
2.     from
3.           c : SimplUML!Class (
4.                 c.is_persistent
5.           )
6.     to
7.           t : SimplRDB!Table (
8.                 name <- c.name
9.           )
10. }
```

Fig. 5.32 Example rule in ATL versus an equivalent rule in MOLA

```
1. transformation ReverseEdges;
2. MatchReplace ('$[1]') <-- {Edge_LinksToTrg}
3.               ('$[0]') --> {Edge_LinksToSrc} ('$[2]')
4. <== from e : V{Edge_}
5.     reportSet e, endVertex(srcEdge), endVertex(trgEdge),
6.               srcEdge, trgEdge end
7.     where
8.        srcEdge := theElement(edgesFrom{Edge_LinksToSrc}(e)),
9.        trgEdge := theElement(edgesFrom{Edge_LinksToTrg}(e)) ;
```

Fig. 5.33 Example transformation in GReTL for graph node reversing

```
rule reverseEdges() = seq{
  forall Edge with find graphPatterns.Edge( Edge ) do
    let SR = undef , TR = undef in seq{
      try choose Source , SourceRelation with
        find graphPatterns.srcAndRelForEdge
        (Edge , Source , SourceRelation) do seq{
          update SR = SourceRelation;
      }
      try choose Target , TargetRelation with
        find graphPatterns.trgAndRelForEdge
        (Edge , Target , TargetRelation) do seq{
          update TR = TargetRelation;
      }
      if(SR != undef) seq{
        delete(instanceOf(SR,nemf.packages.graph1.Edge.src));
        new(instanceOf(SR,nemf.packages.graph1.Edge.trg));
      }
      if(TR != undef) seq{
        delete(instanceOf(TR,nemf.packages.graph1.Edge.trg));
        new(instanceOf(TR,nemf.packages.graph1.Edge.src));
      }
    }
}
```

Fig. 5.34 Example rule in VIATRA2 for graph node reversing

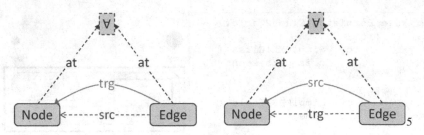

Fig. 5.35 Example rule in GROOVE for graph node reversing

be transformed in serial syntax. They also need to define the changes to the graph based on the directions of the edges and nodes. As in the ATL example we do not explain these two languages as our purpose is only to illustrate expressiveness of text versus graphics. The interested reader can refer to appropriate documentation and tutorials. In general, the best way to understand these programs is to draw the respective graphs when reading/writing the rules. By contrast, the MOLA rule in Fig. 5.14 already offers such a graph drawing, simply as part of the language syntax.

To further understand differences between textual and graphical languages, take a look at Fig. 5.35. It shows the solution to graph edge reversal problem written in GROOVE [58] is to some extent similar to that written in MOLA. The for-each loop is substituted by the 'for-all' operator (∀). Otherwise, the reader should be able to understand this rule easily even without explaining the notation.

The transformation problems can be solved using different notations, however, the main issue is to design the transformation rules. The language to express the rules is a secondary issue and can be left to the preference of developers and other factors—availability of tools (editor, transformation compiler), the transformation compiler performance and the generated transformation performance. An important factor is also the level of integration of the given transformation environment with the modelling environments for the languages involved in the transformations. All this needs to be evaluated before we choose the language and the environment to solve our transformation problems.

MOLA is a natural choice for transformations that process RSL models and is also used in the next chapter. Its graphical syntax complies very well with the complex RSL metamodel and allows to solve complex transformation problems. It is also well integrated with the RSL's modelling environment (the editor and the model repository). However, we need to be aware that graphical languages tend to produce less efficient transformation code and the respective transformations are not well optimised in terms of their performance. A general issue for most transformation languages is their lack of high-level structuring like classes and components in object-oriented and component-based programming. In the next chapter we show how to develop a large model transformation with typical structural constructs like packages and procedures.

Chapter 6
Writing Model Transformations for Requirements

The MOLA transformations presented in the previous chapter were quite elementary and could solve only very simple problems. To fulfil the goal of this book we need to construct a much more sophisticated transformation that operates on the RSL metamodel. This transformation should implement all the rules of RSL semantics presented in Chap. 4. For this purpose, the appropriate MOLA program needs to access RSL models and create UML constructs with embedded textual elements in Java. This means that the MOLA rules in this program should contain various object configurations consistent with the complex RSL and UML metamodels. The RSL models need to be processed ("parsed") in compliance with their runtime semantics and the generated code should be compatible with many detailed aspects of a specific implementation technology. All these issues result in very significant complexity of necessary MOLA code. To assure manageability and comprehension, this code should be properly organised, using typical approaches of structural programming.

6.1 Using the MOLA Tools

Before we start analysing how to approach writing considerably sized MOLA programs, we first need to approach the practical issue of the programming environment. In some cases this may influence the way we structure our code, especially in view of compilation efficiency and debugging.

The MOLA development environment (MOLA Tool) is based on a metamodelling tool development platform called METAclipse [87, 176], which is built on top of the Eclipse framework. It offers a graphical MOLA editor and a MOLA compiler. The environment also offers a debugging facility with a model graph browser, the MOLA Tool offers the typical features of a software development environment. The main difference is that MOLA programs are graphical and operate on graph-based storage.

© Springer International Publishing Switzerland 2015
M. Śmiałek and W. Nowakowski, *From Requirements to Java in a Snap*,
DOI 10.1007/978-3-319-12838-2_6

It is interesting to note that the compiler produces code in another (simpler) transformation language with purely textual syntax called L3 [160]. It is the L3 compiler that produces the final executable code.[1] The type of the resulting executables depends highly on the source and target languages for transformation, and their environments. These executables need to be able to access the model storages and manipulate the models according to the source MOLA program.

6.1.1 Specifying the Metamodel

Before the compiler is executed we first need to enter the MOLA code. As we know from the previous chapters this involves two elements: entering the metamodel and entering the transformation procedures. If we wish to operate on some existing languages (like RSL and UML), the metamodels should be already provided. In fact, MOLA Tool can be installed equipped with a workspace, already containing the metamodels for RSL and a subset of UML. These metamodels are consistent with repositories and editors that handle concrete models. An appropriate environment, compatible with MOLA Tool is presented in Sect. 7.1.

In case we need to transform some Domain Specific Language we develop, the process is more complicated. Together with defining the language's metamodel we need to develop appropriate editors. A good choice for METAclipse and MOLA Tool is the EMF environment, introduced earlier in Sect. 3.8. This environment provides facilities to develop our own graphical editors and model storage. We do not elaborate on this issue further as our transformations operate only within an existing modelling environment for RSL and UML.

Although we do not need to modify the metamodels, we will need to access the metamodel editor frequently. The UML and RSL meatmodels need to be examined when developing transformation procedures. Moreover, we sometimes might want to develop our own diagrams for comprehension purposes without changing the actual metamodel. These diagrams could show some parts of the metamodel, relevant for particular procedures that we develop.

The metamodel editor is shown in Figs. 6.1 and 6.2. The first figure presents a fragment of the RSL metamodel within the MOLA Tool environment. It is contained in the 'RSL' package, which is, in turn, contained in the main 'MetaModel' package. The RSL metamodel is divided into packages according to the division sketched in Sect. 3.2. Within each of the packages we find metamodel diagrams and four types of metamodel elements: metaclasses, metaassociations, generalisations and enumerations. All the elements are visible in the project browser, shown on the left of Fig. 6.1.

---

[1] In fact, the whole process is even more complicated, with the L3 compiler producing code in an intermediate language, called L0.

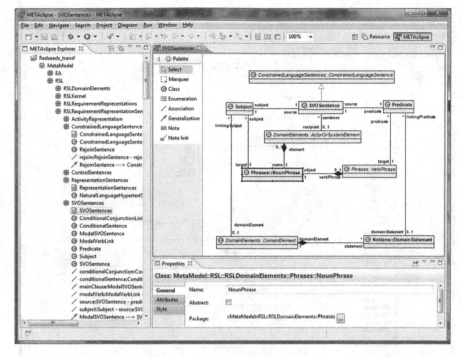

Fig. 6.1 RSL metamodel fragment in MOLA Tool

For the transformations to work correctly, the metamodel must not be changed. However, this does not pertain to diagrams, which can be created and deleted as needed. After creating a new diagram, or modifying an existing one, we can place the existing metamodel elements by selecting them in the project browser and choosing the option to add to the current diagram. When removing elements from being visualised in the diagrams we need to make sure not to delete them from the metamodel.

The same rules for manipulating metamodel elements pertain to the UML metamodel which is shown in part in Fig. 6.2. This part defines the UML's kernel with packages, classes, operations and properties (attributes). While examining the figure we note (see the project browser on the left) that RSL and UML metamodels are placed into two separate major packages and are accompanied by a third package called 'sclkernel'.[2] This third package contains metamodel elements that "connect" the two metamodels and enable their handling within a coherent framework. We use certain elements from 'sclkernel' in the transformation procedures presented further in this chapter.

---

[2] The figure shows also a fourth major package called 'EA'. This package contains a metamodel for interfacing with an external UML tool that supports a significantly simplified UML metamodel and necessitates a separate transformation, not covered in this book.

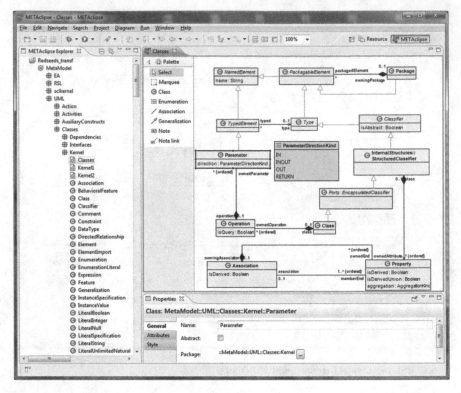

Fig. 6.2 UML metamodel fragment in MOLA Tool

6.1.2 Specifying and Compiling Transformation Programs

The second part of a MOLA Tool project is called 'MolaModel' that contains all
the MOLA procedures grouped within a (potentially) hierarchical package structure.
One such procedure defined in the MOLA Tool environment is shown in Fig. 6.3.
A new procedure is created under a selected package and is shown as an empty
diagram. The procedure in Fig. 6.3 is already filled with content and can be further
edited if necessary. Editing is done using a standard modelling tool approach, where
the program elements are selected from the 'Pallette' box and dragged onto the
procedure diagram.

All the details of various MOLA constructs can be edited in the 'Properties' box
(see bottom). Depending on a specific construct type (procedure, object, text statement, procedure call) the programmer can define or select the various properties like
names, assignment attributes or constraint expressions. In many cases, the programmer is assisted through selection lists that limit the possibility of making a syntax
error or prevents inconsistencies with the metamodel. However, all the expressions
(constrains, assignment expressions) need to be entered by hand and are checked
only during compilation.

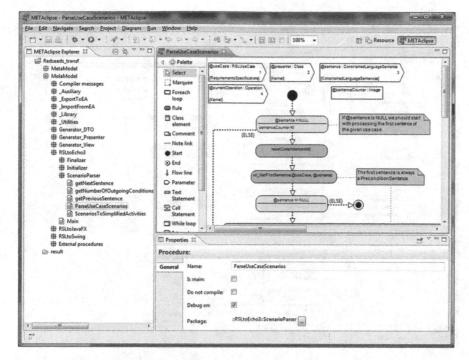

Fig. 6.3 MOLA procedure shown in MOLA Tool

Also note that MOLA Tool supports commenting. Comments can be placed as stand-alone or they can be attached to specific elements within a given procedure. The syntax for comments is similar to that in UML. Obviously, commenting on one's procedures is a good practice just like when using other programming languages.

Some of the procedures in 'MolaModel' constitute compilation units (separately executed transformations). Every such unit has to possess exactly one main procedure (see the 'is main' checkbox in the 'Properties' tab in Fig. 6.3). This is the starting procedure and all other procedures called (directly or indirectly) from here are linked into the final executable program.

Compilation in MOLA Tool is a stepwise process as indicated at the beginning of this section. For large programs it is also a lengthy process and it is thus advised to compile only the packages that have been changed. For example, certain library procedures can be placed in a separate package and precompiled. When used within other units, these procedures do not need to be compiled again and can be linked directly with the final executable.

The compilation process is illustrated in Fig. 6.4. We can prevent any procedure from compiling by using the 'do not compile' checkbox. On the other hand, we need to indicate the compilation unit to be compiled by selecting the 'compile this' checkbox. When this is done, we can select the compiler version depending on the target environment. In our case we use 'JGraLab' as this is the standard repository

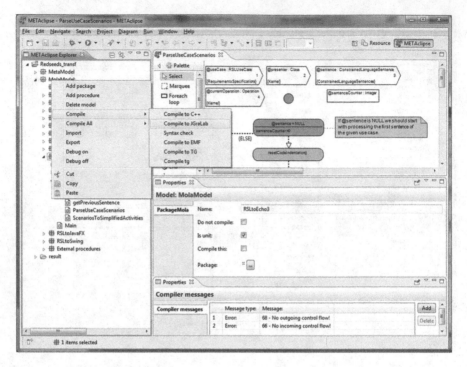

Fig. 6.4 Compilation in MOLA Tool

type for the RSL environment (see Sect. 7.1). Another frequently used choice is 'EMF' for the modelling environments constructed using the Eclipse Modelling Framework.

Detecting compilation errors might sometimes be tricky due to the graphical nature of MOLA. The compiler cannot specify the line number in which an error has occurred, instead it returns a set of compiler messages (see the bottom of Fig. 6.4), and each of them is an active link to a specific MOLA procedure. Within the procedure diagram the elements that cause errors are highlighted (see the upper part of Fig. 6.4). The developer has to bear in mind that sometimes the highlighted elements might not be visible. This is again due to the graphical nature of MOLA procedures—some of the elements might be hidden behind other elements.

Obvious compilation errors associated with the control flow, object configuration and assignments are detected by the upper level compiler, as described above. However, some of the errors are detected only at the level of the L3 compiler. These are mostly errors associated with expressions and their evaluation. Practice shows that detecting such an error is usually not easy because the compiler indicates only an erroneous L3 (or even L0) construct and not the MOLA construct. The only solution is to go through all the recently introduced expressions and seek for incorrect strings or operands. This issue is characteristic of the current MOLA Tool environment and might be improved in the future.

The compilation normally results in producing a 'jar' file that is ready to be transferred to the execution environment. We do not present detailed instructions here because it is specific to the given transformation engine. In general, it consists in copying (manually or automatically) the generated 'jar' into a specific place within the transformation engine configuration. Then the transformation becomes available as one of the options within the appropriate language–workbench interface. The process for the RSL environment is outlined in Sect. 7.1.

6.1.3 Debugging Transformation Programs

Compiled MOLA programs need to be debugged just like programs in any other language. The MOLA compiler offers a debugger feature that allows for producing debug traces. In case some procedure needs to be debugged we need to turn on its debugging by selecting the 'debug on' checkbox (see the bottom of Fig. 6.3).

With debugging turned on the MOLA transformation program produces a debug trace file during its execution. This is illustrated in Figs. 6.5 and 6.6. The first figure presents a fragment of a MOLA procedure and the second figure presents an example trace through this fragment. For brevity, the figure shows only one execution of the procedure, although the actual file contains traces for further executions.

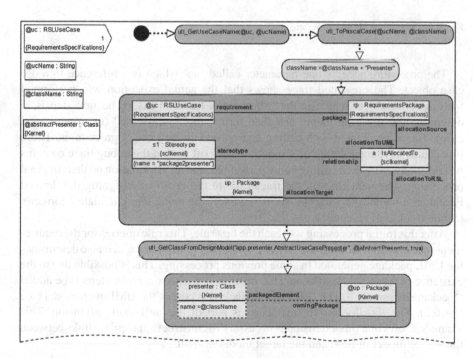

Fig. 6.5 Debugging MOLA programs: example procedure

```
Starting Generator_Presenter_createPresenterBareClass ...
PARAMETERS:
   rsl::rslrequirements::requirementsspecifications::RSLUseCase uc=Show book list
   CALL statement   started ...
      /* utl_GetUseCaseName() */
   CALL statement   ended.
   CALL statement   started ...
      /* utl_ToPascalCase() */
   CALL statement   ended.
   TEXT statement   started ...
      CONSTRAINT {} SATISFIED.
      ASSIGNED: String className=ShowBookListPresenter
   TEXT STATEMENT ended.
   RULE   started ...
      Pattern MATCHED. [...]
      not-changed: [...]::RSLUseCase uc=Show book list
      not-changed: [...]::RequirementsPackage rp=Catalogue management
      not-changed: uml::classes::kernel::Package up=catalogueManagement
      not-changed: sclkernel::IsAllocatedTo a=v2013: sclkernel.IsAllocatedTo
      not-changed: sclkernel::Stereotype s1=v18: sclkernel.Stereotype
   RULE ended.
   CALL statement   started ...
      /* utl_GetClassFromDesignModel() */
   CALL statement   ended.
   RULE   started ...
      Pattern MATCHED. [...]
      CREATED: uml::classes::kernel::Class presenter=ShowBookListPresenter
         ASSIGNED: String name=ShowBookListPresenter
      not-changed: uml::classes::kernel::Package up=catalogueManagement
      CREATED: presenter.owningPackage.up
   RULE ended.
[...]
```

Fig. 6.6 Debugging MOLA programs: debugger trace

The procedure accepts one parameter called 'uc' which is a reference to a use case object. The presented trace shows that the actual execution was performed for a specific object which is the 'Show book list' use case. The first step is to determine the use case name, and then turn it to "Pascal case" (or upper camel case). This is associated with calling appropriate utility ('utl_') procedures. These procedures have their debug information turned off so that the debug trace contains just information on their calling being performed, and no information on their internal processing. The next lines in the trace present the result of assigning the derived Pascal case name to a variable. As we can see, the name was calculated correctly ('ShowBookListPresenter').

After this initial processing we reach the first rule. This rule queries for the requirements package in which our use case is contained. For this package, it also determines the UML package generated in some previous processing. This is possible due to the existence of a special 'IsAllocatedTo' relationship with a specific stereotype added ('package2presenter'). The 'Package' metaclass is part of the UML metamodel (see Fig. 6.2). The 'IsAllocatedTo' metaclass is part of the 'sclkernel' extension. This example shows that this extension is necessary to construct appropriate links between the source model in RSL and the target model in UML.

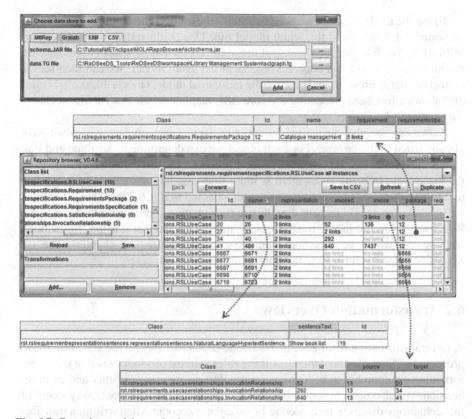

Fig. 6.7 Browsing model repositories

Debugging of a rule consists in providing information about whether the rule's pattern was matched or not. Further helpful information, which we can see in Fig. 6.6, is the information on specific objects that were used for matching. The current trace indicates the five objects that are part of the rule.[3] The trace for the second rule illustrates additional debugging element types, because this rule contains object and link creation. The trace shows that an appropriate 'Class' object was created and its 'name' attribute set with the specific value.

In addition to analysing debugger traces it is often necessary to analyse the current contents of the model repository. This pertains both to the initial (source) and the generated (target) models. To browse the model repository we can use a standalone model browser, which is a simple application illustrated in Fig. 6.7.

Note that the model browser gives much more information than a model editor. The model editor shows only the elements in their concrete syntax which often hides important details. The project browser shows all the elements in their abstract form, including the metaattribute names and their values for specific objects.

---

[3] Note that the trace was slightly abbreviated (marked with [...]), for brevity.

To use the model browser we need to specify the model schema file containing the metamodel definition and the actual model file. This is illustrated in the upper part of Fig. 6.7. The browser then seeks all the metaclasses and lists them together with the numbers of associated concrete objects in the given model. We can then seek a metaclass that interests us and observe the individual model objects. Figure 6.7 (middle) shows a fragment presenting the core RSL metamodel classes ('RSLUseCase', 'InvocationRelationship', etc.)

As we can see, the current model contains 10 use case objects, which we have already listed in the browser. For each object we can determine its attribute and link values. The links to other objects can be followed and their contents examined in the same way. In many cases there is more than one link associated with a given metaassociation. In the case of the use cases selected in Fig. 6.7 there are three links to 'invoke' objects. This means that the use case invokes some three other use cases. When we follow the link to the use case's 'name', we see that it is the 'Show book list' use case which we remember from the examples in previous chapters. The use case is contained in a package together with five other use cases.

6.2 Transformation Overview

A full transformation from RSL to Java code needs to cover all the semantic rules, presented in Chap. 4. The number of these rules (almost 30) indicates that the transformation program has to be highly structured to assure manageability and comprehension. We also need to remember that the semantic rules abstract away many of the technology details, which need to be taken into account when writing a transformation that wants to be useful and produce working code.

The transformation we present in this chapter[4] consists of around 150 MOLA procedures. Our presentation includes some of the most important of these procedures, which cover various techniques for dealing with complex RSL and UML models. Obviously, presenting the full transformation program is out of the scope of this book, as this would double its size and probably bore the reader.

The presented selection should provide enough examples for the reader to be able to write and modify complex transformations involving requirements models. It shows the challenges that have to be faced by the transformation developers. Note that our experience shows that solving these challenges is a very interesting and creative task, giving much satisfaction. The transformation problems at this level of complexity often necessitate non-standard approaches and invention of new algorithms.

The general structure of our transformation is presented in Fig. 6.8. The main compilation unit is the 'RSLtoCode' procedure and processing starts from the 'Main' procedure contained in it. To optimise compilation time the transformation contains

---

[4] The transformation originates from previous simpler transformations operating on RSL. They produced only general architectural (platform-independent) models in UML [86], and some embedded simple code constructs [155, 157].

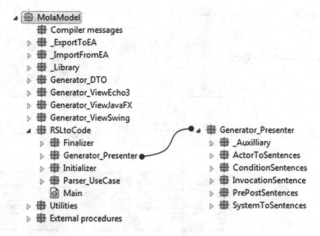

Fig. 6.8 RSL to code transformation structure

several other compilation units external to 'RSLtoCode'. This includes the transformation parts that generate the DTOs and the View layer (the 'Generator_' packages). The transformation is prepared for generating the UI in different technologies (Echo3,[5] JavaFX,[6] Swing[7]).

Other external compilation units contain library and utility procedures that are used in many places within various procedures. These procedures are sometimes quite complex as they traverse through the RSL or UML models to perform standard operations like creating classes and associations, retrieving RSL sentence parts or processing text. An example of one of the simpler utility procedures is given in Fig. 6.9. This procedure accepts a string containing a 'name' (the first parameter) and returns (the second parameter) an object of type 'PrimitiveType' which has this particular name. If the required object does not exist the procedure can create it, if necessary (according to the third parameter). We will notice calls to this and other similar utility procedures in many other places in this chapter.

Figure 6.8 indicates two additional units—'_ExportToEA' and '_ImportFromEA'. These are in fact separate transformations but are used in conjunction with 'RSLtoCode'. These transformations are necessary to interface the 'RSLtoCode' transformation results with a standard UML editor (see Sect. 7.1). Often, such editors implement a different metamodel than the one used by our transformation program (and compliant with the official UML specification [121, 122]). Thus, simple "export" and "import" transformations are needed to switch from one metamodel version to another. The reader might remember a similar problem solved in Sect. 5.4 which pertained to copying graph models, using two different graph metamodels.

---

[5] http://echo.nextapp.com/site/echo3.

[6] http://www.oracle.com/technetwork/java/javase/overview/javafx-overview-2158620.html.

[7] http://docs.oracle.com/javase/tutorial/uiswing/.

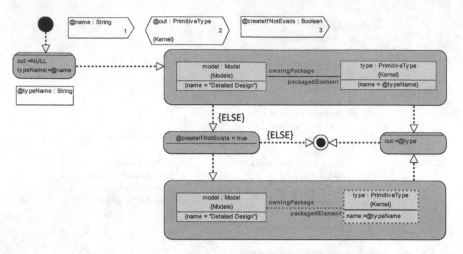

Fig. 6.9 Example utility procedure: 'utl_GetPrimitiveTypeFromDesignModel'

We can find four sub-packages within the main unit of our transformation. We will discuss their contents in detail in the following sections. The most complex is the package responsible for generating the Presenter layer. The respective procedures are divided into groups associated with particular RSL sentence types that produce specific code according to the semantic rules from Chap. 4.

The 'Main' procedure calls several major procedures contained in the above presented packages as shown in Fig. 6.10. The procedure is a simple sequence of five calls that evoke the main steps of the transformation process. These steps are interrupted with four other calls to the procedure called 'showMsg'. This is a special MOLA construct called the external call, which allows to interface with procedures written in C++. There are several external call procedures available by default. The one used here shows an interactive message box and waits

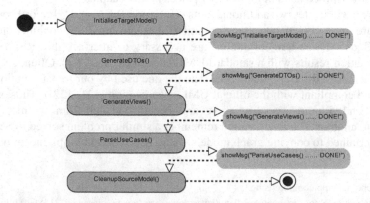

Fig. 6.10 Transformation main procedure

for user intervention. Other available external procedures include a decision box ('yes-no') and a facility to write text to files. Such procedures can be used for debugging purposes or to allow for simple user control over the transformation process.

Transformation starts by initialising the target model. This includes resetting its content after possible previous transformations and building the basic structure with packages and standard classes. Initialisation is based on the general ('G') RSL semantic rules presented in Sect. 4.2. This also pertains to the next step—generating the Data Transfer Objects followed by generating the View layer classes. This part is highly dependent on the specific UI technology and thus we will not present any detail here. As a principle, all the procedures from this part follow the View layer ('V') semantic rules given in Sect. 4.3.

The last major step is to parse use cases and generate the Presenter and Model layer classes. This part does not depend on a specific UI or database access technology but complies with the standard MVP framework patterns. Analogously to the previous steps, all the procedures in this step follow the 'P' rules, presented in Sect. 4.4. The transformation ends by cleaning up the source model from the temporary constructs introduced during processing.

In the following three sections we present some of the important details of three of the above introduced steps. We discuss the various programming solutions and provide some examples of the models produced using the presented procedures. To understand the transformation we need to refer to the RSL and UML metamodels. The RSL metamodel was presented in significant detail in Sect. 3.2., while we have not yet introduced the UML metamodel. However, our transformation uses only a small subset of UML mostly pertaining to class models. In most cases, the MOF metamodel, which comprises classes, should suffice as being a close enough explanation. The reader can refer to Sect. 3.8 (see Fig. 3.24).[8] In cases where the transformation program refers to metaclasses outside of the presented metamodel we will provide the necessary explanations in text.

6.3   Generation of the Basic Structure

One of the first tasks of transformation is to generate the package structure of the target UML model (and eventually—code). Packages were not covered by the semantic rules in Chap. 4 but this is a crucial issue for more complex models that need to group the various resulting classes to assure comprehension and navigability through the generated model. The appropriate procedure ('CreateMVPPackageStructure') is presented in Fig. 6.11 and is evoked as part of the target model initialisation process.

The first rule creates a basic package hierarchy under the already existing 'Detailed Design' model. This main package was created in another procedure, not presented here. All the other packages are created as 'packagedElements' within the model or its sub-packages. Note (see e.g. Fig. 6.2) that most of the UML's metaclasses

---

[8] The reader can also refer to Fig. 6.2 as containing a relevant fragment of the UML metamodel.

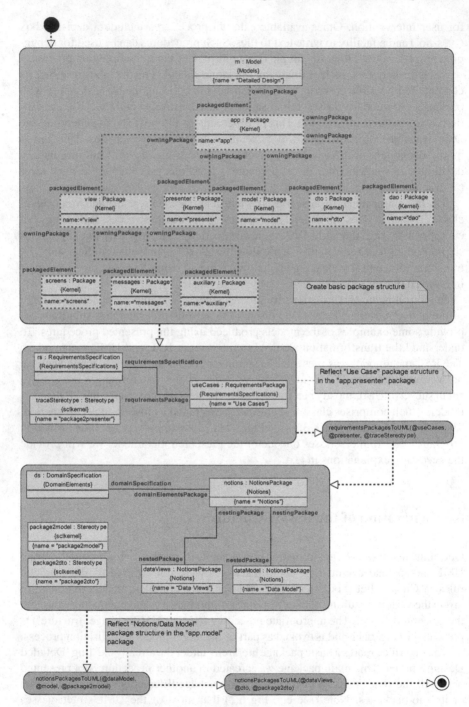

Fig. 6.11 Procedure: 'CreateMVPPackageStructure'

(including 'Package') specialise from the 'PackagableElement' metaclass. In this way, most elements can be connected with a 'Package' element through the links found in this first rule.

The structure generated in the first rule is constant for any source model. However, the model contents to be generated below this hierarchy depend on the structure of the source RSL packages. This is implemented using two procedures ('RequirementsPackagesToUML' and 'NotionsPackagesToUML') that are called from 'CreateMVPPackageStructure'. Each of the three calls to these two procedures creates a variable package structure under the 'presenter', 'model' and 'dto' packages.

Before calling any of the three procedures our current procedure has to prepare the parameters. This is done using two simple query rules. The rules find the appropriate source packages specifically placed within the requirements specification or the domain specification. Transformation assumes that all the use cases to be processed, are placed under the 'Use Cases' requirements package. Similarly, it assumes that concept-type and view-type Notions are placed under 'Notions\Data Model' and 'Notions\Data Views' respectively.

The three procedures are similar, so we concentrate our discussion on 'RequirementsPackagesToUML'. The procedure's code is presented in Fig. 6.12. The first two parameters are obvious—they are the source RSL package and the destination

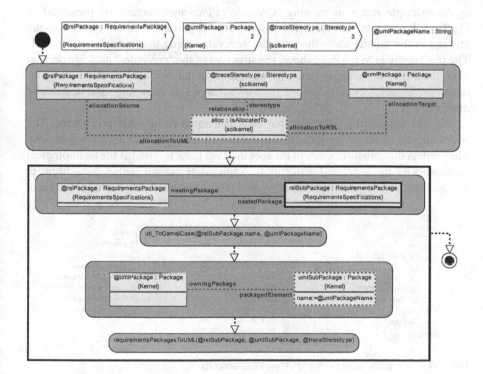

Fig. 6.12 Procedure: 'RequirementsPackagesToUML'

UML package. The third parameter is used to control the creation of a supportive traceability link between the source and the target package. This is done right in the first rule of the procedure. The rule creates a special object of type 'IsAllocatedTo' which links the source element with the target element. This new object is assigned the stereotype passed as the procedure's parameter.

Traceability links are created also in many other places throughout the transformation program. They play an important role in reflecting the structure of the source model in the structure of the target model [185]. We will see this role in some of the procedures discussed later in this chapter. The two relevant metaclasses ('IsAllocatedTo' and 'Stereotype') are part of the supportive 'sclkernel' metamodel, mentioned earlier in Sect. 6.1.

After creating the traceability link, the 'RequirementsPackagesToUML' procedure executes a for-each loop that iterates over all the sub-packages of the source RSL package. For each such package, it creates a new UML sub-package that is contained in the current main UML package. The name of the created UML sub-package is derived from the name of the relevant RSL package and turned into camel case format.

After finishing tasks at the current level of the source RSL package tree, the for-each loop calls 'RequirementsPackagesToUML' in a recursive manner. This enables processing of the next level of the tree. The result of this is a copy of the RSL package tree, reflected in the UML package tree. All the packages are linked through traceability links with their respective copies.

An example result of running 'CreateMVPPackageStructure' is presented in Fig. 6.13. It presents both the constant and variable parts. The tree fragments to the left and in the middle show the structure generated using the first rule in Fig. 6.11. The tree fragment to the right shows the structure of the 'presenter' package derived from the use case packages found in the source model. We can see that it has contained three packages called 'Book reviews', 'Catalogue browsing' and 'Catalogue management'.

We also notice other elements that were generated using other procedures. The additional elements in the left part are related to the particular Java environment. They reflect the actual structure of the specific Java libraries used as the technological framework of the generated application. Appropriate classes within these libraries are used from within the main application classes, generated into the 'app' package.

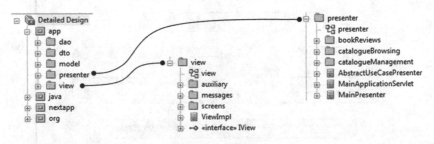

Fig. 6.13 Generation result for the MVP package structure

In order for the final 'app' code to contain proper references and specialisations, its classes must have necessary relationships with the library classes. We discuss this in detail further in this section.

The other additional elements in Fig. 6.13 include several default classes and an interface in the 'view' and 'presenter' layers, together with appropriate diagrams that visualise them. Some of these classes are generated in the next procedure, shown in Figs. 6.14 and 6.15.

The 'CreateAbstractPresenter' procedure is generally responsible for creating a quite elaborated structure of the 'AbstractUseCasePresenter' class. This class is consistent with the semantic rule G0 and is equivalent to the 'PUseCase' class (see Fig. 4.11). However, the contents and environment of 'AbstractUseCasePresenter' have to be extended and somewhat changed due to specific technologies used, and in order to optimise the final code.

Let us now analyse the procedure that creates the generic presenter class. The first part is a sequence of several calls to utility procedures of the kind presented in Fig. 6.9. The first call ('utl_GetClassFromDesignModel') creates the actual class object and places it under the 'presenter' package as illustrated in Fig. 6.13.

The next four calls are associated with the Spring framework used in the target application to manage dependencies between class objects. They create three technology-specific classes referenced from within the definition of 'AbstractUse-CasePresenter'. It should be emphasised that these classes are created only to reflect the contents of the appropriate parts of Spring. These classes will not have their code generated during the transformation, instead the application code will refer to these classes and link ('#include') appropriate library files.

In addition to creating the Spring classes the procedure creates the main View layer interface, named 'IView'. This interface is placed in the 'view' package. The interface has also its implementation class ('ViewImpl') created, as presented in Fig. 6.13. This is done in a similar way in another procedure within the transformation program, which is not discussed here.

The features of the 'AbstractUseCasePresenter' class are generated within two significantly sized rules. The first of the rules (see the bottom part of Fig. 6.15) creates the properties (attributes) and all the properties have appropriate types defined. Also, some of the properties have specific default values added.

Two of the properties reflect the properties present in the semantic rule G0. This is 'invokingPresenter' and 'resumeId'. The actual property names and their types are slightly different than in the rule. The 'resumeId' property (cf. 'returnSentence') is typed as an integer instead of as a String. This will be explained later (see Sect. 6.6) when we discuss the processing of invocation sentences. The 'invokingPresenter' property is typed as 'AbstractUseCasePresenter' (cf. 'PUseCase'), which is consistent with the rule G0.

The 'view' property partially reflects the semantic rule G5. It links the Presenter layer class with an element in the View layer. However, this element is not a specific View layer class, but a common interface ('IView'). It is this common interface, and its implementation class that distributes responsibility between concrete View layer

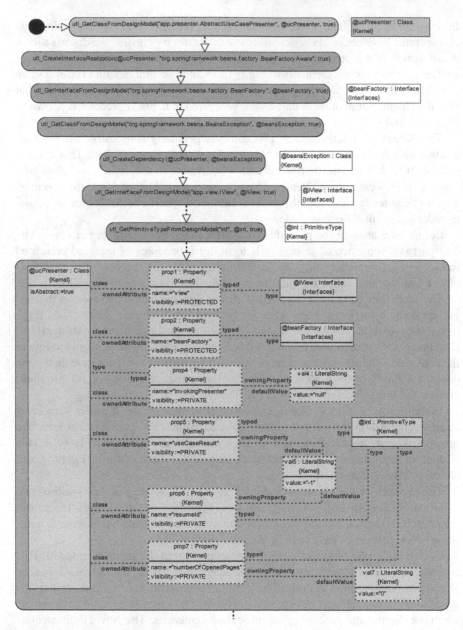

Fig. 6.14   Procedure: 'CreateAbstractPresenter' (part 1)

classes. However, the semantics contained in rule G5 is retained, but implemented differently. This approach allows for good separation of the layers and facilitates switching between different UI technologies.

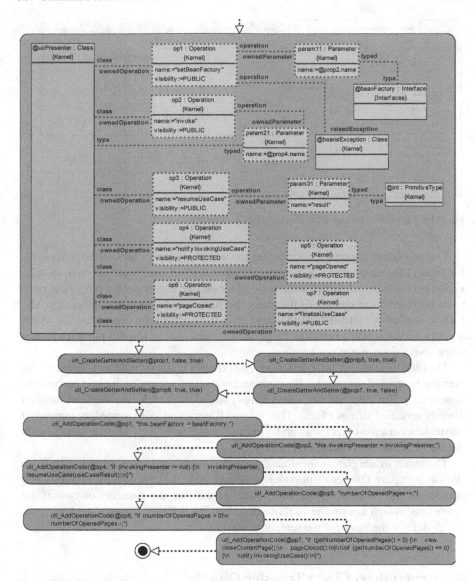

Fig. 6.15 Procedure: 'CreateAbstractPresenter' (part 2)

The second major rule of the 'CreateAbstractPresenter' procedure (see the upper part of Fig. 6.15) creates the operations of 'AbstractUseCasePresenter'. Again, three of these operations reflect the three operations of 'PUseCase' specified in semantic rule G0. These are: 'invoke', 'notifyInvokingUseCase' and 'resumeUseCase'. Apart from changed names the procedures maintain parameters found in Fig. 4.11. The only difference is that 'notifyInvokingUseCase' does not use any parameter, but uses a relevant property of the main class ('resumeId').

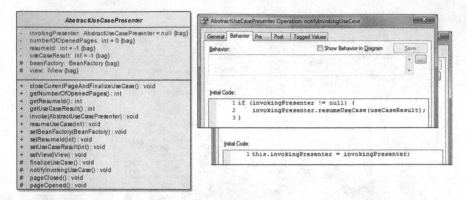

Fig. 6.16 Generation result for the AbstractUseCasePresenter

The procedure continues by creating the necessary getter and setter procedures for some of the properties. The features of 'AbstractUseCasePresenter' have specific visibility constraints defined. Since some of the private and protected properties need to be accessed from outside of the class, the setters and getters are necessary. The calls to the 'utl_CreateGetterAndSetter' procedure accept the properties for which a getter and/or a setter needs to be generated, and two additional parameters that respectively determine their creation.

The final sequence of four procedure calls creates method contents of some of the previously created operations. Since these contents are constant, no text processing is necessary. The appropriate code is simply added to the relevant methods through directly specified strings of text. The 'utl_AddOperationCode' procedure appends a particular operation object with an additional comment object. This comment holds the actual method text expressed in Java.

The result of the 'CreateAbstractPresenter' procedure is presented in Fig. 6.16. We can compare this result in concrete syntax with the procedure's internals that operate on the abstract syntax. Moreover, we can see the contents of two of the operations, which are similar to those found in Fig. 4.10 (cf. 'invoke' and 'return') which defines the basis for the semantic rule G0.

6.4 Generation of Data Transfer Objects

According to rule G4, Data Transfer Objects are translated from View-type notions and associated Attributes. For practical reasons, our transformation program will also generate DTOs for Concept-type notions. Such DTOs can be used to transfer data within the Model layer and for exchanging data with the persistent storage.

The semantic rule G4 is not complex. However, the appropriate realisation of this rule has to consider additionally the package structure generated as described in the previous section. Moreover, we need to remember the good practices in structuring

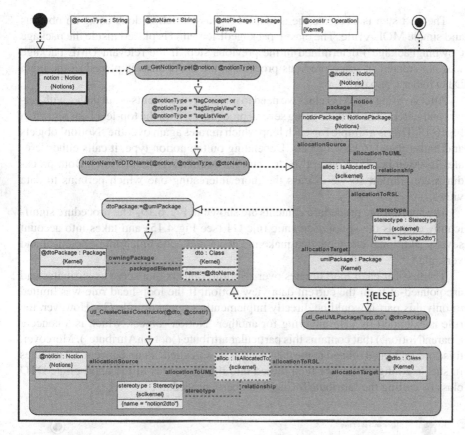

Fig. 6.17   Procedure: 'CreateDTOClasses'

code, and thus the appropriate "getter" and "setter" operations should be also generated.

The first procedure for DTO generation is presented in Fig. 6.17. It contains a
single for-each loop which iterates over all the 'Notions' in the entire model. Since
determining the notion type is not a trivial task we need to call an appropriate utility
procedure ('utl_GetNotionType'). Further processing within the iteration is done
only when the current notion turns out to be a concept or a data view.

The processing starts by determining the DTO name which is done by a call to a
simple text processing procedure. Then the procedure determines the UML package
in which the newly created DTO class will be placed using the 'IsAllocatedTo'
objects (traces) introduced in the previous section. In this situation, we consider the
objects that are adorned with the 'package2dto' stereotype. They were created in one
of the previous procedures in a way similar to that discussed in the previous section.
As we can see, the role of traces is very important as they allow for easy access to
the target model structure from the particular source model elements.

The next step is to create the actual DTO class which is done using an obvious and simple MOLA rule. The class ('packagedElement') is placed inside the package ('owningPackage') determined in the previous step. If the relevant UML package was not created in some previous procedure, the DTO class is placed in the main DTO folder ('app.dto').

After creating the DTO class we need to generate its contents—attributes with getters and setters. This is done using several procedures, with the top-level one shown in Fig. 6.18. This is a simple for-each loop which iterates again over the 'Notion' objects and finds related 'Class' objects. Depending on the notion type, it calls either 'createClassMembersForConcept' or 'createClassMembersForDataView'. Both procedures are similar, so we discuss the more interesting one which pertains to data views.

The appropriate procedure contents are shown in Fig. 6.19. The procedure significantly extends the simple semantic rule G4 (see Fig. 4.15) and takes into account several additional elements that make the generated code much more practical and versatile.

The first for-each loop iterates over 'Notion' objects that serve as attributes and are pointed-at from the current data view notion. If the loop-head rule was limited to only this part it would be directly implementing semantic rule G4. However, the rule is extended by also querying for another 'Notion' object, which is a concept ('parentNotion') that contains this particular attribute ('notionAttribute'). Moreover, this concept is also related to the data view as its so-called "main concept". Attributes in such a configuration are then turned into the properties of the appropriate DTO class by calling the 'attributeToClassMembers' procedure.

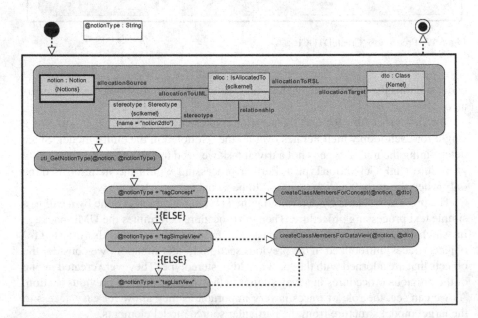

Fig. 6.18 Procedure: 'CreateDTOClassMembers'

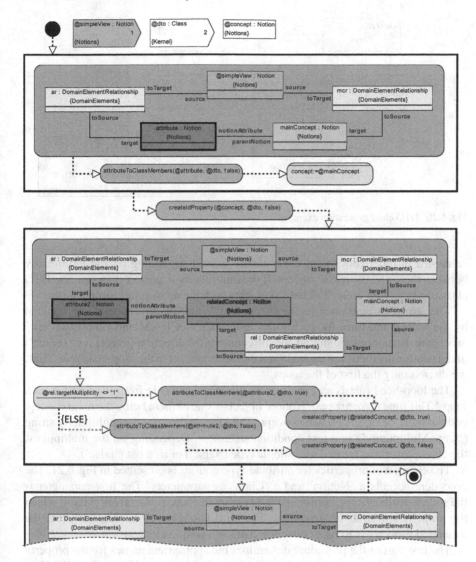

Fig. 6.19 Procedure: 'CreateClassMembersForDataView'

To better understand the reason for determining the "main concept", let us analyse Fig. 6.20. It shows a simple domain model with one simple data view ('book search criteria') and two concepts ('book' and 'author'). The data view relates to attributes contained in both concepts. However, one of the concepts is distinguished by an additional relationship from the data view. This additional semantic adornment provides information that can allow the generator to structure the DTO in a more fine-tuned manner. The attributes contained in the main concept are always unary, i.e. are included in the DTO class as properties with simple types. However, the attributes

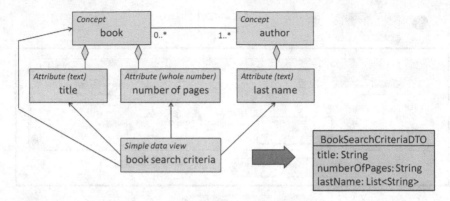

Fig. 6.20 DTO class generation example

contained in other (not main) concepts are treated depending on the multiplicity between them and the main concept. If the multiplicity is greater than one, the DTO class properties are created as lists of objects with the appropriate simple type.

The attributes contained in the "secondary" (non-main) concepts are handled by the second and third for-each loops in the 'CreateClassMembersForDataView' procedure. Both loops are similar and differ only in the direction ('target' vs. 'source') of the relationship between the main and the other concept in the loop-head rule. Thus, we discuss only the first of the loops.

The loop-head rule is an extension of the loop-head rule from the first for-each loop.[9] This time there are two 'Notion' objects—one of them being the main concept and the other being the related concept. The loop determines the multiplicity string ('targetMultiplicity') in a text condition statement. Depending on the multiplicity, the class property is created as a simple type ('false') or as a list ('false').

The creation of properties for attribute-type notions is presented in Fig. 6.21. The procedure accepts a 'Notion' and a 'Class' as parameters. The first parameter is the source attribute-type notion and the second attribute is the target class in which the properties need to be generated. The third parameter determines whether the generated property is to be a collection (list) or a simple element.

The first part of the procedure determines the appropriate names for the property and its getter and setter operations. Then these elements are added to the DTO class using appropriate object creation constructs. The added elements have their metaattributes, like 'visibility', set according to typical programming practice. Moreover, the newly created property is traced ('IsAllocatedTo') from the original attribute-type notion. The third part of the procedure is a series of conditions and text statements which determine the data type for the newly created property and for the parameters of the getter and the setter. This data type depends on the type of the source attribute

---

[9] The differences are clearly visible in the colour version of the procedure's diagram. This is an illustration of additional capability of the MOLA environment to mark objects with different colours. Colouring is an additional valuable way to comment MOLA diagrams for better comprehension.

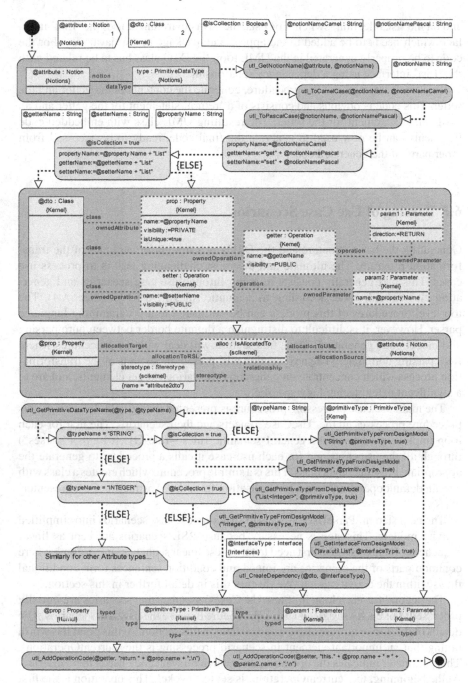

Fig. 6.21 Procedure: 'AttributeToClassMembers'

and on the 'isCollection' switch. For lists, the Java environment uses the 'List' interface which needs to be added to the appropriate package in the 'java' tree. For the
code to be properly generated in the UML tool, the DTO class has to be related with
the 'List' interface using a dependency relationship.

Two final statements of the procedure, generate the contents of the getter and the
setter. This code is obvious and consists of a 'return' statement for the getter and an
assignment statement for the setter. The resulting UML class with embedded code
fragments can be now used to generate the final code, ready to be accessed from
other parts of the generated code.

6.5 Parsing of Use Case Scenarios

Generating the basic structure and the DTOs is a straightforward part of the transformation program. The ultimate and the most challenging task is to process use
cases. This part generally consists in going through use case scenarios and generating classes with code, according to semantic rules P1–P13 (see Sect. 4.4). The
top-level procedures of this process can be compared to a programming language
parser. However, it is difficult to distinguish a definite border between pure parsing
and model/code generation. Thus, this section will deal with the procedures where
RSL parsing dominates. The next section will present these parts of the transformation process which concentrate on generating the various target elements, and are to
a significant extent technology-specific.

The main use case processing procedure is presented in Fig. 6.22. In general, this
procedure processes all the 'UseCase' objects and their scenarios. The first for-each
loop implements one of the general semantic rules—rule G1. It loops ("parses")
through all the use cases and for each use case it calls a procedure to generate the
appropriate Presenter layer class. This is a simple procedure which creates a class with
certain default operations and a generalisation from the 'AbstractUseCasePresenter'
class.

The next step in 'ParseUseCases' is to structure use case scenarios into simplified
activity models. This step is necessary because RSL scenarios are kept as linear
sequences of sentences. We first need to turn these linear sequences into a graph where
common parts of the scenarios are joined and condition sentences form conditional
flows within the activity graph. We discuss this in detail further in this section.

The second for-each loop in 'ParseUseCases' assumes that scenarios are initially
processed. For each use case, it calls a procedure to parse the use case scenarios. The
details of this procedure are also explained later in this section. At this point it is worth
noting that an important element in scenario processing is the 'currentOperation'.
This parameter indicates the operation into which relevant code needs to be inserted.
At the beginning, the 'currentOperation' is set to 'invoke'. This operation is the first
to be called in the running application when the application logic for a given use
case is initiated. This approach is a modification and optimisation of the approach

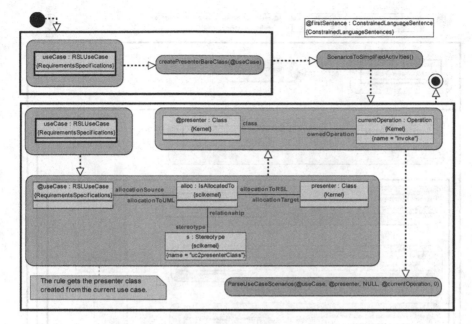

Fig. 6.22 Procedure: 'ParseUseCases'

described by the semantic rules P9 and P10. Two separate calls to 'invoke' and some trigger operations are substituted by a single call to 'invoke'. For this reason, the 'invoke' method contains also code for the first trigger operation and thus is the 'currentOperation' for the initial sentences in the use case scenarios.

Let us now discuss the procedure that preprocesses use case scenarios presented in Fig. 6.23. The procedure is constructed as a set of three embedded for-each loops. The outer loop iterates over use cases, the middle loop iterates over scenarios, and the inner loop iterates over sentences. For each scenario sentence the inner loop creates an activity node—an object of type 'RSLActivityNode'.[10] If the current sentence was already parsed in another scenario, the node is not created again.

The main effect of the procedure is the creation of 'RSLActivityEdge' objects that connect the activity nodes. To illustrate this effect we can refer to the example presented in Fig. 2.28. The activity edges form the arrows that connect nodes that contain sentences. The creation of edges is important for processing alternative flows that result from condition sentences. They would not be necessary in case of only linear processing, because sentences in scenarios are ordered in the repository and thus can be processed in the right sequence by the for-each loop. As we will see, the activity graph will be processed as a tree, in a recursive manner.

---

[10] The RSL's metamodel is extended with a simple activity notation. This part was not presented in Chap. 3 but is self-explanatory in the current context.

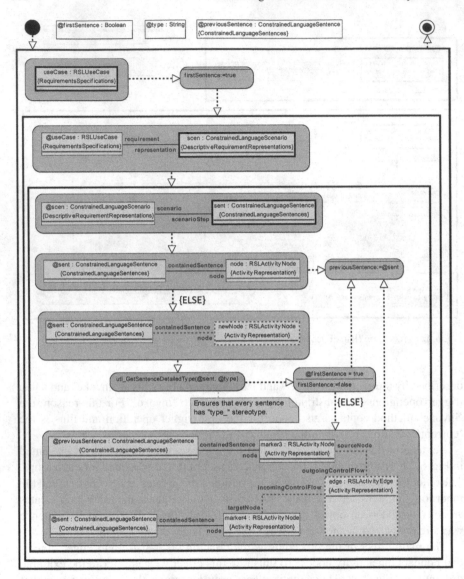

Fig. 6.23 Procedure: 'ScenariosToSimplifiedActivities'

The recursive procedure to parse the activity graph is presented in Fig. 6.24. The recursion is not evident because it is indirect and implemented using another procedure which will be discussed next. The 'ParseUseCaseScenarios' procedure traverses through all the sentences and calls other procedures that perform appropriate processing and generation for each sentence type.

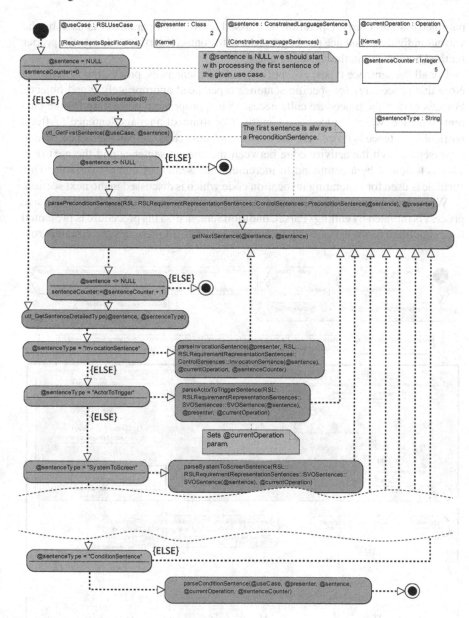

Fig. 6.24 Procedure: 'ParseUseCaseScenarios'

When analysing 'ParseUseCaseScenarios' we need to observe certain issues. The 'sentence' parameter is an important factor in the recursion process. If it is set to NULL, it means that the procedure is called at the beginning of scenario processing. In this case, the precondition sentence needs to be processed first. In other cases, the procedure starts processing from the currently passed 'sentence'. Another important parameter is the 'currentOperation' discussed above. This parameter is used by the various individual sentence parser procedures to control inserting code into the proper method bodies within the presenter class.

For all the sentence types, except for condition sentences, processing is iterative. Note that procedures for specific sentence types need appropriately typed objects. For this reason the procedure calls necessitate appropriate type-casting for the current 'sentence' which is typed as a generic 'ConstrainedLanguageSentence'. After a particular sentence is processed, the iterative process calls 'getNextSentence' which traverses through the activity edge between the current sentence and the next one. This is followed by a command to increment the 'sentenceCounter' variable. This variable is used for generating invocation code which is discussed in the next section.

When a condition sentence is found (see the bottom part of Fig. 6.24), the recursive process is initiated by calling 'ParseConditionSentence'. This procedure is presented (in a simplified form) in Fig. 6.25. Its content generally implements the semantic rule

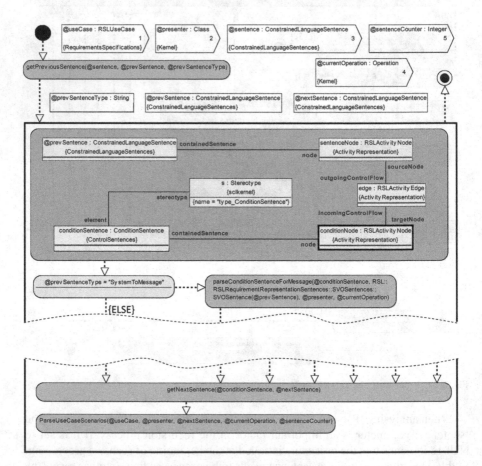

Fig. 6.25 Procedure: 'ParseConditionSentence'

P13. The main goal is to generate an "if-else" statement with full contents, including the conditions and logic for all the statement's branches.

The first important action within the procedure is to determine the type of the sentence that stands prior to the current condition sentence. This is in accordance with rule P13 (see Fig. 4.42) which is applied only when the dialogue state is 'system'. The next step is to iterate over all the condition sentences that follow the "previous" sentence. This allows to generate all the branches of the "if-else" statement. In fact, the loop-head rule iterates over 'RSLActivityNode' objects, but ultimately the related condition sentences are found.

For each condition sentence in the current group of condition sentences, the procedure calls another procedure that generates the appropriate condition code. This generated code is somewhat different for the various "previous" sentence types. Thus, there are different individual procedures for sentences of such types as System-to-Message or System-to-Simple View.

In any case, generation of a particular condition branch is followed by generation of the branch contents. This is done by a recursive call to 'ParseUseCaseScenarios', presented earlier. This time, the procedure is called with the sentence following the current condition sentence, as its parameter. In this way, the following code generation actions will append code to the current "if-else" branch.

When a particular scenario finishes, 'ParseUseCaseScenarios' returns control to the current for-each loop within 'ParseConditionSentence'. The loop continues and starts processing the next condition sentence. In this way, all the alternative scenario branches are processed and the appropriate code generated are within the respective branches of the "if-else" statement. It can be also observed that code is generated within the current operation and the current "if-else", only until the dialogue state in the processed scenario is 'system'. Whenever an Actor-to-Trigger sentence is found, it changes the current operation and the code starts being generated elsewhere, according to the appropriate semantic rules.

6.6 Generation of the Presenter Layer Details

In the previous section we avoided discussing the procedures that generate anything in the target model and code. Processing in the already discussed procedures involved only the source RSL model and traversing through use case scenarios. Here we go into the details of how particular UML elements and Java statements are generated from specific scenario sentence types. We concentrate on three sentence types: Actor-to-Trigger sentences, System-to-Screen sentences and invocation sentences. This allows us to show more details on implementing the semantic rules presented in Chap. 4.

Each of the sentence types is handled by a separate procedure, called from 'ParseUseCaseScenarios' (see Fig. 6.24). The Actor-to-Trigger sentences are processed by 'ParseActorToTriggerSentence'. This is a simple procedure shown in Fig. 6.26 and it partially implements semantic rule P4.

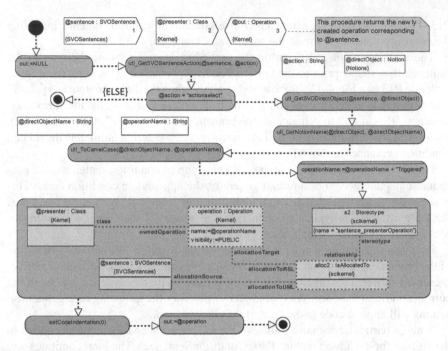

Fig. 6.26 Procedure: 'ParseActorToTriggerSentence'

The procedure accepts two parameters: the current sentence, and the current Presenter layer class. Its main goal is to create and return an event handler operation within the said Presenter class. Note that the procedure does not create any parameters of the new operation because a slightly different method of data passing is used for this implementation of rule P4. Instead of adding parameters to the event handler, separate setter operations and their methods are created in the Presenter class. The procedure for creating these setters is associated with Actor-to-DataView sentences, according to rule P4′ (see Fig. 4.43). This other procedure is quite simple and we do not discuss it here.

Returning to 'ParseActorToTriggerSentence', note that its main functionality is associated with determining the new operation's name and creating the actual operation's object in the target model. Reference to this object is returned ('out') to the calling procedure. In this way, the new operation is now ready to be used as the target for the code generated according to all the other rules that refer to P4.

One of the procedures that generate code for the above new operation is the 'ParseSystemToScreenSentence' shown in Fig. 6.27. This procedure implements rule P8 which covers code generated for System-to-Screen sentences. It needs only two parameters: the current SVO sentence and the current operation (the one created using 'ParseActorToTriggerSentence).

The first part of the procedure determines the name of the procedure to be called on the View layer. Recall from Sect. 6.3 that the View layer is accessible through the 'view' property which points to an 'IView' interface. Thus, the calls to this interface

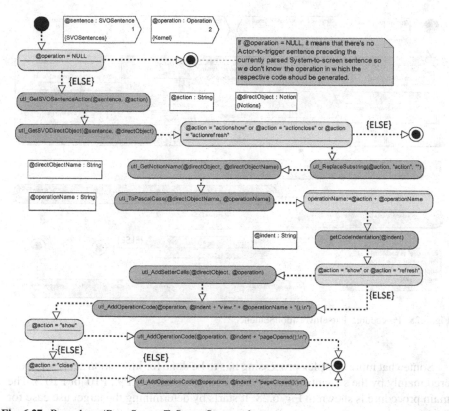

Fig. 6.27 Procedure: 'ParseSystemToScreenSentence'

have to distinguish between individual Screen elements. The actual code will look like: 'view.showEditBookForm()' instead of 'veditbookform.show()'. Note that this approach to structure code is slightly different from the one presented in the semantic rule definition, although it still preserves the actual semantics.

For the 'show' and 'refresh' type actions the call to the UI rendering procedure has to be preceded by data passing—calls to setters with DTO parameters. This is done in the 'utl_AddSetterCalls' procedure which is not discussed in detail. Generally, this procedure analyses the sentence's direct object and looks for all the Data Views associated with the Screen Notion hyperlinked from the direct object. For each such Data View, a call to a setter is generated, according to rule P8.

For the 'show' and 'close' actions the procedure generates calls to 'pageOpened()' and 'pageClosed()'. These two operations control the window stack and change the 'numberOfOpenPages' attribute in the Presenter class object. The appropriate semantic framework for this was discussed in Sect. 4.1 (see the description of 'show' and 'close' in Fig. 4.4). In implementation, the stack is controlled mainly by the Presenter classes.

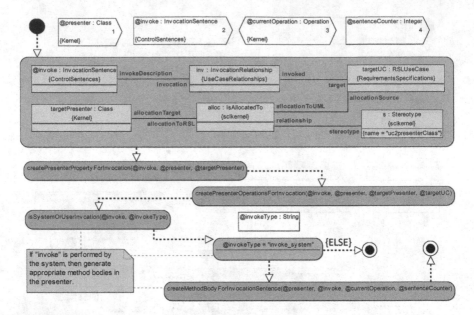

Fig. 6.28   Procedure: 'ParseInvocationSentence'

Somewhat more complex processing has to be done for invocation sentences cov-ered mainly by the semantic rules P9 and P10 (alternatively P9′, P10′ or P10″). The main procedure is shown in Fig. 6.28. It starts by determining the target use case for the current invocation sentence. Recall from Chap. 3 that every 'InvocationSentence' object has a related 'InvocationRelationship' which points at an 'RSLUseCase'. This feature of the RSL's metamodel is used in the introductory rule of 'Parseinvocation-Sentence'. Additionally, the appropriate Presenter class, traced from the target use case (see 'IsAllocatedTo'), is found.

After this the main procedure calls three other procedures. The first two are called unconditionally and the third is called only for the invocation sentences that are in the 'system' state.

The first procedure ('CreatePresenterPropertyForInvocation') updates the target model with a property to access the 'targetPresenter' class object from the current 'presenter' class object. This in fact implements one of the general semantic rules, namely—rule G7 (see Fig. 4.18). The rule is implemented by analysing the scenarios rather than by analysing the use case relationships. In this way there is no need for a separate iterative process that seeks all the 'InvocationRelationship' objects.

The actual procedure that implements G7 is simple and is presented in Fig. 6.29. It first checks if the particular property ('targetProp') was already created when processing some other invocation sentence. If not, then it creates the property together with the respective 'Association' object. In this way the resulting UML model thus becomes more readable due to the existence of the appropriate visual association link

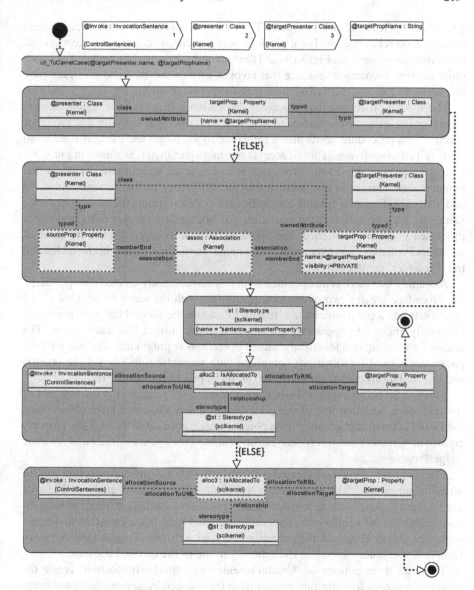

Fig. 6.29 Procedure: 'CreatePresenterPropertyForInvocation'

between the two classes. Note that the code would be the same without the 'Association' object, thus its creation is purely for documentation and readability purposes.

After creating the new property the procedure creates a traceability link ('IsAllocatedTo') between the property and the invocation sentence that was the source for its creation. This traceability link additionally explains the approach to generate properties according to rule G7 by analysing invocation sentences instead of invocation relationships. For a given invocation relationship we can have several invocation sentences (see Fig. 3.19) and thus several traces can be created. The traces point to every invocation sentence that invokes a given use case and they later play an important role in other areas of the transformation program.

The second procedure that processes invocation sentences is 'CreatePresenter-OperationForInvocation'. The previous procedure operated only on the Presenter classes. This procedure needs also a reference to the target use case, as it needs to analyse its first sentences. Thus, it accepts one more parameter, as shown in Fig. 6.30.

In general, the role of the procedure is to create an appropriate operation that contains code similar to that presented in the definitions of the semantic rules, P9 and P10. The first few actions are dedicated to determining the new operation's name and making sure that the operation was not already created for a previously processed invocation sentence. The operation's name is derived from the name of the target Presenter class ('targetPresenter.name') with the 'invoke' prefix added and the 'Presenter' postfix removed.

Assuming that there is no operation with this name already created (see {ELSE}), the procedure creates two overloaded operations with the same name. One of the operations has a parameter called 'resumeId', while the second has no parameters. Obviously, these two operations are attached to the current 'presenter' class. The reason for creating two identically named operations is pragmatic. The one with the parameter is used for situations compliant with semantic rule P9, and the other is used for situations compliant with P10 (or, more precisely—with P10").

This can be better explained when we analyse code generated in the last part of the procedure. The first line of this code creates a new Presenter layer object using the Bean Factory mechanism.[11] This object is made accessible through the property created in 'CreatePresenterPropertyForInvocation' (see again Fig. 6.29 and compare 'targetPropName').

The next lines of code are created within another MOLA procedure called 'addIn-vocationParameters'. This procedure (not presented in detail here) analyses the target use case and generates the appropriate setter operations, and calls to these setter operations. This is done similar to the approach discussed for processing Actor-to-Trigger sentences above. However, the currently analysed Actor-To-Trigger (and Actor-to-DataView) sentences are taken from the beginning of the invoked use case.

The final three actions of 'CreatePresenterOperationForInvocation' create the code that prepares for returning control from the invoked Presenter object and eventually passes this control through calling the 'invoke' operation. The whole code is inserted into the methods of the operations created a few steps earlier. Note that the operation without the parameter simply calls the operation with the parameter, where the actual value of the parameter is −1. This is equivalent to implementing rule P10" which assumes that no resuming of control is necessary and everything is handled by the window stack operations.

---

[11] We will not go into the details of this technology-specific issue.

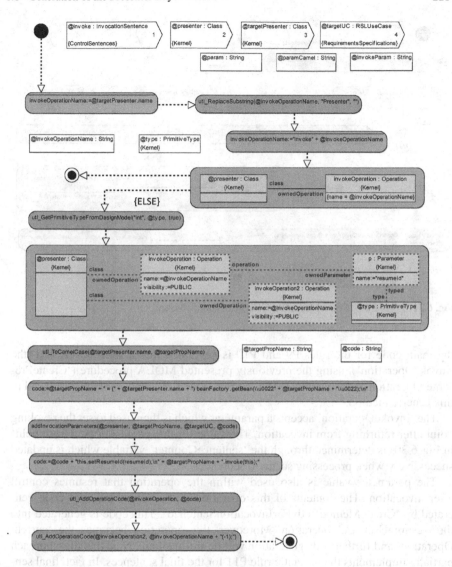

Fig. 6.30 Procedure: 'CreatePresenterOperationsForInvocation'

The third procedure called from 'ParseInvocationSentence' generates additional code which is necessary to handle invocation sentences in the 'system' state. This simple procedure presented in Fig. 6.31 usually generates two pieces of code (see two 'utl_AddOperationCode' calls). The first piece of code is generated in the 'current-Operation'. Note that when the 'system' invocation sentence is processed, the actual invocation call has to be made from the current event handler procedure (i.e. the 'currentOperation') as defined in the semantic rule P9. In the presented implementation,

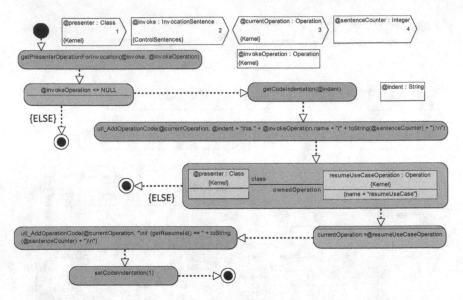

Fig. 6.31 Procedure: 'CreateMethodBodyForInvocationSentence'

the main code for the rules P9 and P10 is generated into a separate method (the 'invokeOperation'), using the previously presented MOLA procedure ('CreatePresenterOperationForInvocation'). The 'currentOperation' code contains just a call to this generic method.

The 'invokeOperation' accepts a parameter which is then used to set the revoking point after returning from invocation. The value for this parameter (see 'resumeId' in Fig. 6.30) is determined through the 'sentenceCounter' variable which is updated successively when processing scenario sentences.

The parameter value is also used within the operation that resumes control after invocation. The contents of this operation is the second piece of code generated by 'CreateMethodBodyForInvocationSentence'. This code is generated into the 'resumeUseCase' operation. Moreover, this operation becomes the 'current Operation' and further code generation will be shifted there. Note that this approach partially implements the semantic rule P11 for the final sentences. In fact, final sentences have to be handled already when processing invocation sentences.

To summarise and better understand the procedures that generate the Presenter layer we can use the simple example shown in Fig. 6.32. The example contains two generated Presenter classes with their features. The classes, obviously, implement the application logic for two use cases in an invocation relationship. We can see the appropriate two invocation operations ('invokeShowBookDetails') generated in the Presenter class for the invoking use case. The invocation involves passing data to the invoking use case, so there were also generated appropriate setter operations

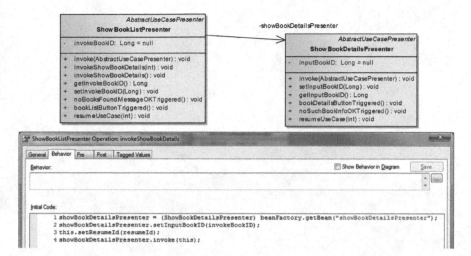

Fig. 6.32 Presenter class generation example

('set...BookID') and properties ('...BookID') both in the invoking and in the invoked Presenter class. These features are used in the code of the 'invokeShowBookDetails' operation which is shown in the lower part of the figure.

Chapter 7
Applying MDRE in Practice

After reading the previous chapters of this book, the reader might wonder how to apply the presented approach in the software engineering practice. It is obvious that in order to use Model-Driven Requirements Engineering, developers will need to update their everyday practices in software development [149]. They will also need to use tools that enable the new and modified practices [153, 166]. In this chapter we present a methodology that provides guidelines in this respect. It encompasses a tool that implements the presented MDRE technology. It also presents necessary modifications to the roles, work products and tasks in a software development project, and especially to standard approaches to requirements engineering [77, 104]. The methodology generally treats the development of new systems, but it is also supplemented with techniques to reuse legacy software and apply patterns to reuse reoccurring behaviour.

7.1 Using the ReDSeeDS Tool

Practicing Model-Driven Requirements Engineering is inherently associated with using a tool that implements the requirements language and the transformations from this language down to code.[1] The tool is fundamental for any methodology associated with applying MDRE in real-life projects. Thus, we start our considerations on practicing MDRE by introducing such a tool. The tool is called ReDSeeDS (Requirements-Driven Software Development System)[2] [156, 158] and it implements all the concepts presented in the previous chapters. Its overview is presented in Fig. 7.1. The actual tool contains an RSL editor, a MOLA transformation engine and a model repository. It also interfaces with MOLA Tool by

---

[1] Note that such tools would significantly extend the capabilities of typical Requirements Engineering tools [29, 104].

[2] http://www.redseeds.eu/.

© Springer International Publishing Switzerland 2015
M. Śmiałek and W. Nowakowski, *From Requirements to Java in a Snap*,
DOI 10.1007/978-3-319-12838-2_7

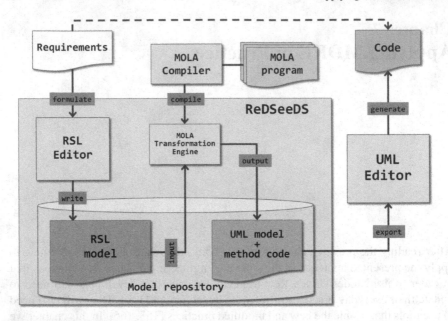

Fig. 7.1 ReDSeeDS overview

accepting compiled MOLA programs, and with an external UML editor to visualise the generated models and to further generate code.

The ReDSeeDS model repository implements the RSL metamodel as described in Chap. 3. This serves as the storage for the RSL models used by the RSL Editor. The editor provides extensive editing capabilities for RSL models and complies with the RSL's concrete syntax. It also supports RSL semantics by providing certain facilities that help in structuring scenarios and domain models for better code generation. The ReDSeeDS repository implements also much of the UML metamodel. It thus allows for storing the results of the transformations as explained in Chap. 6. It is possible to store full class and component models, together with comments that can hold method bodies.[3]

Apart from the capability to edit RSL models, the ReDSeeDS tool can visualise the structure of the generated UML models and show the generated code. It does not contain a full UML viewer/editor because it relies on the existing tools. Currently, it interfaces with Enterprise Architect from Sparx Systems[4] and Modelio from Softeam.[5] Modelio can be used in the open source version. The generated UML models can be easily exported to one of the above UML editors for further

---

[3] The ReDSeeDS repository can also store other UML models like activity models or interaction models. However, these capabilities are not used by the presented transformations.

[4] http://www.sparxsystems.com/.

[5] http://modelio.org/.

processing. Then, standard code generation facilities of the UML tools can be used to generate the final code.

The ReDSeeDS tool is compatible with the executable transformation code, generated from MOLA Tool. The MOLA compiler turns MOLA programs into executable files which form the MOLA Transformation Engine. This code can access the current ReDSeeDS repository and perform all the queries and operations that are available in the MOLA syntax. ReDSeeDS provides an environment to manage and run MOLA executable files (the MOLA Transformation Engine). There are some standard transformations built into ReDSeeDS, available though context menus. However, users can develop their own transformations in MOLA Tool, and integrate them through a special transformation browser.

From the point of view of the tool user (software developer, domain expert), the usage of ReDSeeDS is fairly simple (see again Fig. 7.1). First, we need to formulate our RSL model. Then we select a transformation to execute. The transformation produces a UML model with possible code embedded in comments. We can then export this model to a UML tool and generate code using standard code generation capabilities. For the standard (built-in) transformations, the process is simpler because the UML model export and code generation is evoked from within ReDSeeDS automatically. Following this, the developer can open one of the available programming environments and use the generated code for producing the final system.

We now illustrate this generally presented process with the actual functionality of the ReDSeeDS tool. Our aim here is not to provide a detailed user guide which is already available from the ReDSeeDS website. Instead, we want to provide an insight into the features that seem necessary for the tools that aim at implementing the concepts of MDRE. The main goal for ReDSeeDS is to automate many of the typical tasks and provide an environment that keeps the RSL models coherent.

The first step is to create a new project. In ReDSeeDS, projects are called "software cases", so we select **File –> New** and then **New Software Case Project**. After naming the project we obtain the initial project structure. To define the RSL model we have to fill-in the main Requirements Specification package, together with the contained Domain Specification package.

Within the Requirements Specification we can perform actions as we would expect from a typical CASE tool. We can create new requirements packages and new requirements diagrams. This can be done from the context menu in the project browser tree. In diagrams and in the project browser, we can define new elements like use cases and actors. An example result of such actions is illustrated in Fig. 7.2, which shows an initial use case diagram, created within a project tree. As we can see, we have created a specification for a Library System with one requirements package ("Book management") containing an identically named use case diagram. We have also started creating a use case model.

Note that the actor ("librarian") has been added by the tool to the "Actors" package. This is because according to RSL's definition, actors are part of the Domain Specification. Another observation is that the palette in the use case diagram does not provide the means to add an invocation relationship between use cases. This is

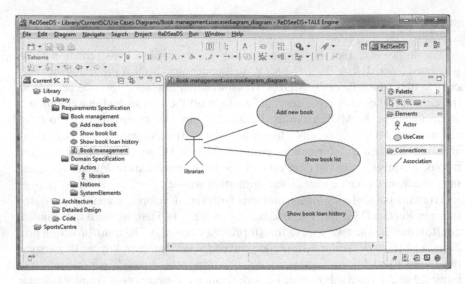

Fig. 7.2 Starting a new ReDSeeDS project

because invocations have to be coherent with the use case scenarios. They appear automatically, as we will show in further description. This is one of the aspects of the tool, which assures coherence of the model and clear separation of concerns, right from the beginning.

After introducing use cases, we can start entering their scenarios as illustrated in Fig. 7.3. We can enter consecutive SVO sentences that are automatically numbered by the editor. We can also introduce condition sentences by selecting the "fork" icon that automatically creates a new scenario which forks from the current scenario after the currently selected sentence. "Forking" a scenario creates its sibling which has exactly the same initial sentences (1–5 in Fig. 7.3). The forked scenario can be ended either with a final sentence or with a rejoin sentence that points to a specific sentence in the original scenario (see sentence 2 in Fig. 7.3).

Directly after entering, the SVO sentences are "raw" and have to be additionally marked. We need to determine the sentence parts (the subject, the verb and the objects) and the sentence type. For some of the sentences we can also specify the type of the action based on certain keyword verbs. As we can see in Fig. 7.3, each SVO sentence can be marked with these two elements (sentence type and action type) which are initially void.[6]

Sentence marking is done semi-automatically. We should select and mark sentence parts by selecting appropriate context menu options. The relevant phrases can be also added to the domain specification if necessary (if not yet present). This can be done

---

[6] The third element is "recipient" which is not used by the presented transformations and will not be discussed.

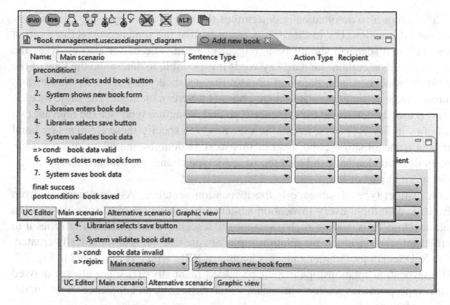

Fig. 7.3   Editing use case scenarios

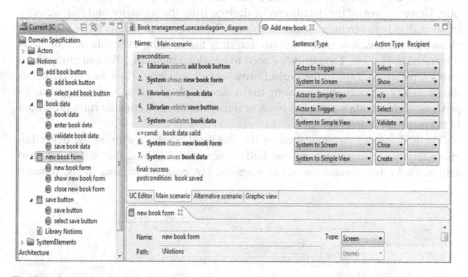

Fig. 7.4   Organising SVO sentences

automatically after selecting the given phrase. An example result of such marking is
shown in Fig. 7.4. The SVO sentences are now appropriately divided into their parts.
Moreover, the domain specification (see the project tree to the left) is automatically
populated with appropriate domain notions and phrases.

The editor also automatically determines the notion types by using certain contextual information. For instance, it is assumed that the sentence object in the first sentence in a scenario should be a Trigger element. The editor also analyses the verbs. Based on certain standard keywords it is possible to determine the type of the element associated with the noun phrase. For instance, the keywords "show" and "close" indicate that the related noun phase is a Screen element. The same mechanism is used to determine the sentence type and the action type (see the relevant two columns in Fig. 7.4). As a result, the user needs to specify these elements by hand only in some situations, and most of this work is done by the editor. If necessary, every domain element can be edited (e.g. its type changed), which is shown in the bottom right part of Fig. 7.4.

A distinct type of sentence is the invocation sentence. As we remember from the RSL definition, every invocation sentence has to be attached to an invocation relationship. Thus, adding such a sentence to a scenario automatically attaches it to a relevant relationship. If the relationship is not present—it is automatically created. The ReDSeeDS tool implements this feature of RSL, which is illustrated in Fig. 7.5. The invocation relationships cannot be added manually. They are always derived from appropriate invocation sentences, which assures strict coherence of the model for invocations.

After specifying the scenarios we obtain an already populated domain specification. However, not all the details can be derived from the scenarios and this includes relationships between notions and attributes. The best way to specify these additional elements is to create notion diagrams and drag the existing elements onto them as illustrated in Fig. 7.6. The attributes need to be added manually. We can group them into a separate package in the project browser (see top-left). Then we can create all the necessary connections according to the desired characteristics of the system. To produce correct code we need to observe the syntactic and semantic rules presented in the previous chapters.

The RSL models are managed by the ReDSeeDS editor with all the hyperlink characteristics stemming from the RSL's metamodel. Thus, the actual scenario sentences do not contain the actual phrases, but point to phrases in the domain

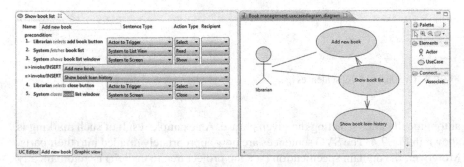

Fig. 7.5 Managing invocations

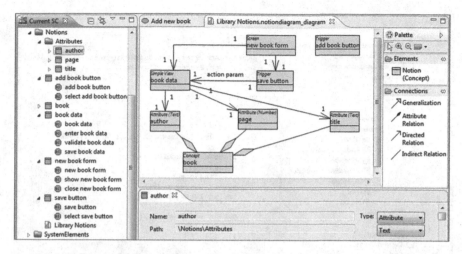

Fig. 7.6 Defining the domain model

specification. This makes it easy to perform changes to the domain elements that get propagated throughout the whole model. For instance, when we change the name of a notion (e.g. from "book data" to "book details"), this change should be reflected in all the SVO sentences that use this notion. The editor does this automatically because the sentences contain hyperlinks that can be easily updated with the new name they point to.

Whenever we judge the RSL model ready, we can run a MOLA program in the transformation engine. This is as simple as selecting an appropriate option in the context menu for the requirements specification. This runs the selected transformation program as that presented in Chap. 6. The target UML model with embedded code is placed in the repository along the source RSL model. Then, the ReDSeeDS system automatically transfers this model to one of the available UML tools. Finally, it evokes the code generator which produces the final code. The result of this process for our example model is presented in Fig. 7.7.

If the RSL model was formed correctly, the resulting code can be compiled and run. The ReDSeeDS tool does not provide facilities to manage the generated UML models and code. It can be used only for browsing the structure, as shown in Fig. 7.7. We can see that the whole MVP structure, together with the DTOs and DAOs is generated. We can update this code in a programming IDE (Integrated Development Environment) of our choice. If we use the Eclipse IDE, ReDSeeDS can already place this code in the right workspace and make it ready for instant compilation.

The ReDSeeDS tool is currently the only implementation of RSL and thus it can be postulated to widen the selection of available tools. It can be noted that any RSL editor would need to have several characteristics that are not present in typical modelling tools. The main effort seems to be in implementing the scenario editor with its grammar enforcement, and strict rules for hypelinking to domain elements. Other RSL constructs should be possible to be implemented using standard profiling

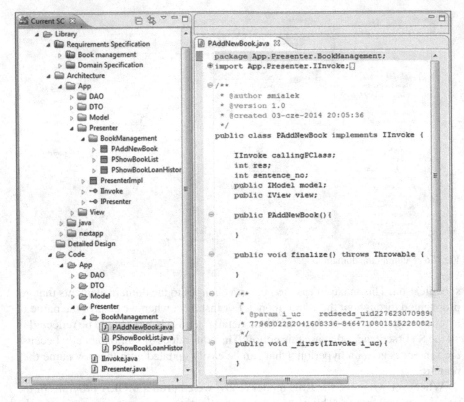

Fig. 7.7 Generating the UML model and code

mechanisms present in many UML tools or standard metamodelling capabilities of language workbenches and DSL environments.

These editing capabilities should be integrated with a model transformation engine. Many UML tools have already implemented some form of such engine or can be integrated with an external model transformation tool. However, we need to make sure that the transformation language is powerful enough to be able to perform complex transformations that involve both declarative and imperative elements. Having assured this we need to implement the semantics of RSL according to the rules presented in Chap. 4. We can use the algorithms presented in Chap. 6 as general guidance. MOLA syntax provides visual documentation which can be easily translated to any other model transformation language.

7.2 Introducing the ReDSeeDS Methodology

Having the necessary tooling environment, we can start applying MDRE in real projects. However, we need to remember that the tool is not enough. This is especially visible in larger projects with many use cases and vast domain models. We need ways to organise the development effort, taking into account all the typical issues of software engineering.

7.2.1 Overview of the ReDSeeDS Process

As we have noted in Chap. 1 (see Sect. 1.4), MDRE can significantly shorten the path from requirements to code and thus promises significant gains in productivity. This book is dedicated to presenting the technology that makes it possible. However, this does not mean an instant solution to all the possible problems. We still face implementing solutions to problems with complex application and domain logic. What is more, the problems and their domains constantly evolve, where this process can often be quite rapid. This is related to quickly changing requirements of contemporary business, industry and generally—the society.

We also need to face the constant development of software and hardware technologies. Software developers can now choose from a plethora of technologies and frameworks where some of them pertain to the overall system architecture, some deal with specific aspects like the user interface, data storage or distributed processing. Moreover, it is often the case that it is necessary to deliver similar or identical applications for different technological platforms. This is especially visible in the case of mobile device applications.

As a result, software developers have to face two simultaneous processes, as illustrated in Fig. 7.8. The first is the process of Software System Evolution. This process involves the evolution of the software applications in terms of their application logic and in terms of the problem domains. Of course, the source of this evolution is new ideas and innovations that expand the user requirements [135]. The second process is the process of Technology Evolution, which involves the evolution of the various technologies with which the software is implemented. The source of this process is the obvious innovation on technological capabilities and features constantly introduced by the technology suppliers.

Both processes overlap and thus are often not properly distinguished. This is associated with distinguishing between the essential complexity and the accidental complexity of systems, mentioned earlier in Sect. 1.1. In MDRE (and often in MDSD in general), this distinction is usually quite clear. This is especially visible in the approach presented in this book. The Software System Evolution process is associated with evolving requirements models (written e.g. in RSL) that reflect changes and innovation in the system's functionality. The Technology Evolution process is associated with evolving transformation programs (written e.g. in MOLA) that transform requirements into code, compliant with the evolving technology.

As Fig. 7.8 illustrates, the two processes do not overlap all the time. Usually, the evolution of a software system is based on a specific technology that is applied constantly throughout some significant span of the system's lifetime. However, at certain moments in that lifetime, a decision needs to be taken to upgrade or even completely change the technology that is applied. This may be associated with certain

Software System   Technology
Evolution   Evolution

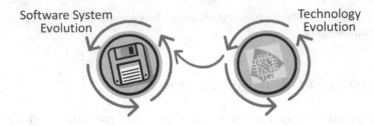

Fig. 7.8 Two major processes of software development

restrictions of the current technology that prevents from implementing some desired functionality. It may also be associated with the technology going out of date and losing proper support from its supplier. At such moments, a Technology Evolution cycle has to be executed to upgrade our development (tooling) framework to some new technology. This upgrade then needs to be applied to the actual system with the use of the upgraded development framework.

These considerations lead us to define more detailed guidelines on how to implement MDRE in practice [101]. We will call this set of guidelines the ReD-SeeDS Methodology [151]. The methodology is (obviously) model-driven and thus it would be natural to present it using models. To do this, we use the Software and Systems Process Engineering Metamodel (SPEM) [119]. It is a popular notation that can be used do denote any kind of software (or system) development methodology.

We shall keep the description simple, and we will use only a subset of the SPEM notation. We introduce SPEM along the actual descriptions as the notation is easy to comprehend without extensive introductions. Using this notation, we present the general guidelines for applying MDRE practices. These guidelines should be easily adaptable to any kind of iterative methodology [8] and include agile methodologies [99] like Scrum [35, 142] and XP [14] and more formal ones [100] like RUP [95] and OpenUP[7] [94].

Figure 7.9 presents an overview of the ReDSeeDS Methodology in terms of the roles, tools and work products. We can distinguish two major roles in the Software System Evolution process: the Requirements Engineer and the Software Developer. In turn, the Technology Evolution process encompasses a single major role of the Transformation Engineer. In larger projects, each of these roles can be played simultaneously by several people, while in smaller projects, one person can play more than one of the roles.

The three roles of the ReDSeeDS Methodology can be mapped onto the roles found in other methodologies. The Requirements Engineer extends the skills of a typical Software Analyst with knowledge of RSL's syntax and semantics. In many situations, also more skilled Domain Experts (End Users) can play the roles of Requirements Engineers. However, the ReDSeeDS' Requirements Engineer has to be rigorous in defining the application logic and the problem domain. Thus, the skills

---

[7] http://epf.eclipse.org/wikis/openup/.

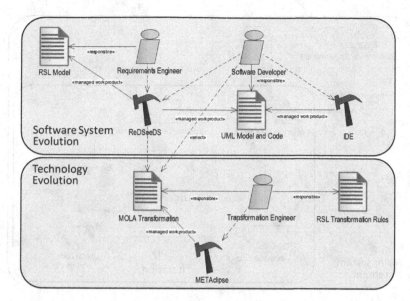

Fig. 7.9 Methodology overview

involve some capabilities of a software programmer. This role can thus be played collectively by people who would traditionally play the roles of Domain Experts, Analysts and Programmers. In turn, the Software Developer is a combination of the typical roles of Software Designer and Programmer. This role should be played by people skilled in the specific technologies and who are capable to finalise the system's implementation.

Normally, the Requirements Engineer tightly cooperates with the Software Developer using the ReDSeeDS tool. The Requirements Engineer is responsible for creating and maintaining the RSL Model, while the Software Developer is responsible for the UML Model and Code that is generated from the RSL Model. These relationships are illustrated in Fig. 7.9 in the SPEM notation. The two work products (RSL model, UML Model and Code) are depicted as document-like icons. The tools are depicted with hammer-like icons. As we can see, in addition to ReDSeeDS, the Software Developer also needs a standard IDE to update, compile and debug code.

The most non-typical role in Fig. 7.9 is the Transformation Engineer. This role should combine skills in model transformation programming with designing software architectures and applying implementation technologies. The programming skills are needed to produce MOLA Transformations using MOLA Tool. However, to develop these transformations, the Transformation Engineer first needs to determine the transformation rules. To do this, the role needs to have detailed knowledge of the target implementation technology and of defining architectural guidelines. We discuss this later in this section.

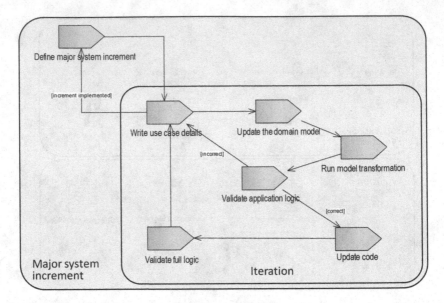

Define major system increment

[increment implemented]

Write use case details

Update the domain model

Run model transformation

[incorrect]

Validate application logic

[correct]

Validate full logic

Update code

Major system
increment

Iteration

Fig. 7.10 Software System Evolution process with MDRE

7.2.2 Software System Evolution Process

Let us now concentrate on the Software System Evolution process. The sequence of tasks in this process is illustrated in Fig. 7.10. We assume that the process is iterative with two cycles. The larger cycle is based on major system increments like new versions or major revisions and the smaller cycle is based on short-term (e.g. one or two week) iterations that result in small increments of the system's functionality.

The overall process consists in defining the major system increment and then conducting consecutive iterations until that increment is implemented. As we will see, each increment is defined through a set of use cases and domain elements. Each iteration starts with writing use case details and updating (refining) the domain model. This is done for a selected part of the overall use case set. After the requirements model details are ready we can run the model transformation. This produces a compilable and executable system that can be validated against the desired application logic. This is only a rough validation to make sure that the source requirements model was prepared correctly. In case of problems this allows for quick corrective actions—returning back to the requirements model and correcting the use case scenario logic and domain element details.

If the logic was defined correctly and the generated code behaves properly, the next step is update this code manually. As we know from the previous chapters, this pertains mainly to the domain logic (e.g. the Model layer) and partially to the presentation (e.g. the View layer). In an ideal situation, only the newly generated methods within these two parts need to be written or modified. However, sometimes the already implemented functionality could have been changed (due to unforeseen changes in the project's scope). This means that some of the already implemented code may necessitate changes. Sometimes, the previously generated methods are substituted by other methods. This can be controlled by the code generation and versioning facilities of the UML tool.

After updating code the next obvious step is to validate it. This should mostly consist in testing the domain logic, which was written manually (not generated). Thus, it generally involves introducing test data, specifying expected results and assuring that these results are correct.[8] We do not go into the details of this part as it should involve normal quality assurance practices, and their discussion is out of the scope of this book. If the validation passed correctly the next iteration cycle can be started. Alternatively, the next iteration may involve correcting code which has caused the errors found during validation.

As we can see, the presented process is kept very simple. Its main purpose is to be easily integrated with the processes of other methodologies, be it agile or more formal. Thus, the process we present does not include the various tasks and techniques found in a fully developed methodology but only provides guidelines on how to integrate MDRE into a standard methodology. In the following paragraphs we present more details, which refer to specific work products and their treatment within the above presented tasks.

We start with explaining the task of defining a major system increment illustrated in Fig. 7.11. By a "major system increment" we mean an increment specified through a substantial set of use cases. This may involve specifying a completely new system or extending the functionality of an existing system. In the second case we assume that the system was already previously specified and developed using RSL. Legacy

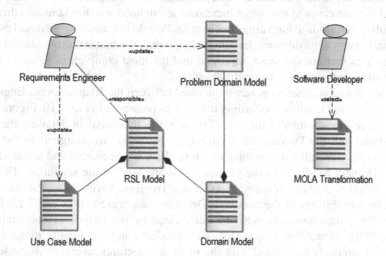

Fig. 7.11 Defining a major system increment

---

[8] It should be noted that this process can be also automated through generation of test cases directly from requirements models [161, 162].

software systems (not developed using RSL) are dealt with in the next section of this chapter.

Defining a major system increment is thus related to creating a new or extending an existing RSL Model by the Requirements Engineer. However, at this stage we do not need the full details. Instead, we only need to define the scope of the major increment. Thus, we concentrate on enlisting use cases and sketching the problem domain. This involves updating the Use Case Model, by adding new use cases or modifying the existing ones without yet specifying the details of their scenarios. Updates to the Domain Model should be limited to the Problem Domain Model. By this we mean specifying the Concepts in the problem domain, their relationships and maybe defining some of their important Attributes.

Defining a major system increment can be accompanied by the decision to update the implementation technology. In the Software System Evolution process we assume that the new technology is already supported by an appropriate MOLA Transformation. Thus, the decision mainly consists in selecting this transformation by the Software Developer, as illustrated in Fig. 7.11. Such a decision has its consequences which need to be considered. It means that many parts of code that was previously manually updated will need to be significantly changed. The new transformation may need to change the code structure to accommodate it to the new implementation technology. Thus, the following iterations will probably involve rewriting some of the already implemented functionalities. The main advantage of the MDRE approach is that the new structure and much of the application logic will be automatically updated. Moreover, the places that need updating will be clearly visible in code and this significantly lowers the barriers that prevent from shifting to the new technology.

After the use cases of the major increment are defined we should assign them to consecutive iterations using various techniques. We do not discuss it in detail as this is normally part of the main methodology. In general, the first iterations should treat the use cases that are the most important and the most complex in terms of their functionality and implementation difficulty.

In each iteration, work is generally divided between the Requirements Engineer and the Software Developer according to the tasks presented in Fig. 7.10. Figure 7.12 shows the responsibilities of the first of these roles. It consists in detailing the Use Case Model and the Domain Model for their parts that are assigned to the current iteration. Generally, this involves writing Use Case Scenarios and updating the System Domain Model with the elements that are used in the scenarios. This, of course, involves defining Screens, Data Views, Triggers, Attributes and so on.

The responsibilities of the Software Developer are presented in Fig. 7.13. First, the developer transforms the RSL Model created by the Requirements Engineer, into the UML Model and Code. This work product can be generally divided into three work products associated with the three architectural layers, as discussed in the previous chapters. The Application Logic should not necessitate any changes to be made by the developer. However, it needs to be validated in terms of the desired functionality. This means compiling and running the whole generated code. This allows for checking if the overall behaviour is appropriate and to check that the RSL Model does not contain any logical errors.

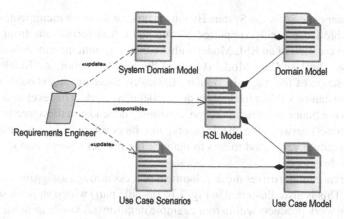

Fig. 7.12 Main responsibilities of the Requirements Engineer in an iteration

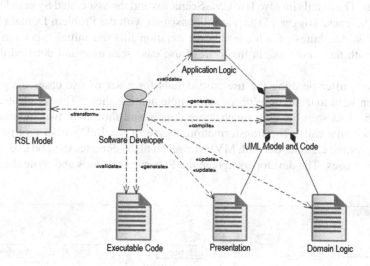

Fig. 7.13 Main responsibilities of the Software Developer in an iteration

Only after assuring that the application logic is correctly defined and generated, it makes sense to update the remaining parts of code. For the Presentation part, it should mainly consist in defining the layouts and look of the various generated windows. In some cases, we would also need to change some of the functionality of the UI elements, not catered for by the automatic transformation program. For the Domain Logic, updates to code are much more substantial. They involve defining database access, implementing necessary data processing, communication with external systems and so on. This forms the main part of the Software Developer's activities. Updates to code are performed within a standard IDE and obviously involves generating (compiler) and validating (debugger) the Executable Code.

In summary, the Software System Evolution process involves incremental delivery of Executable Code highly supported by automatic transformations from the RSL Model. The creation of an RSL Model within a major system increment is illustrated in Fig. 7.14. The Use Case Model (top) and the Problem Domain Model (bottom) define the scope of the major increment. Basically, these models should be treated as stable but can be subject to changes during detailed work. The level of acceptable changes to the major increment's scope, obviously depends on the agreement (e.g. a formal contract) between the clients (users) and the developers. In any case, the two models constitute very good means to manage the project's scope and to negotiate changes in the scope.

The use case model drives the development process through assigning use cases to iterations. This is also illustrated in Fig. 7.14 (middle part) which shows a schematic view on the work products within four example iterations. A single iteration is equivalent to defining the details and implementing the functionality of several selected use cases. The details involve Use Case Scenarios and the associated System Domain Model (Screens, Triggers, Data Views) consistent with the Problem Domain Model (Concepts, Attributes). Each consecutive iteration fills the initial "skeleton" RSL Model with the "muscles" in the form of use case scenarios and detailed domain elements.

Directly after defining the use case details for a set of use cases assigned to the given iteration, the developers start implementing them. This is illustrated in Fig. 7.15. This step involves much more details and thus only two iterations are shown schematically. The transformation engine of the ReDSeeDS tool produces the appropriate class model with MVP classes. It also generates method code for the P and V classes. The developers update the Presenter methods and write the Model

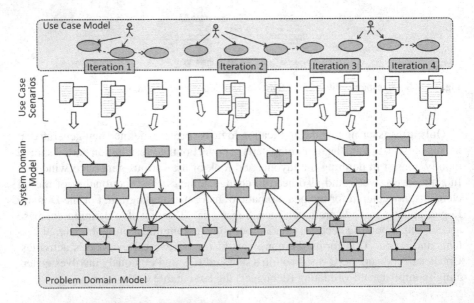

Fig. 7.14 Incremental delivery of RSL Models

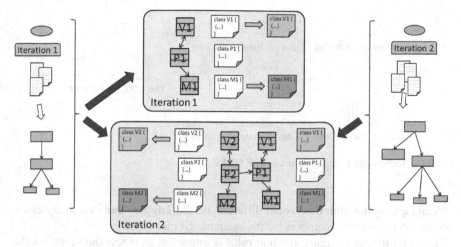

Fig. 7.15 Incremental system delivery using RSL Models

methods. In the next iteration, the engine updates the class model with additional classes (M2, P2, V2) with code for P2 and V2, and the process repeats. Throughout the process, the developers have clear guidance as to where changes and extensions should be performed. This is because of the clear structure of the generated UML model which serves as the "map" of the generated code.

7.2.3 Technology Evolution Process

Note that the amount of additional work associated with updating the generated code depends on the quality of the transformation from RSL to code. This book presents many rules for assuring this quality. However, the details have to be worked out for a given target technology and its specifics. In some cases, the basic RSL syntax may not provide the necessary constructs for translation into a particular technology. This means that the development of a good quality transformation might also need to involve proposing certain extensions to RSL, like attaching tags or defining stereotypes.

This needs to be taken care of by the Technology Evolution process, presented in Fig. 7.16. The important first step is to analyse the target technology, which should involve analysing the best practices for structuring code compliant with this technology, possible ways to structure the user interface, accessing persistent storage and so on. The next step is to define transformation rules from RSL to code in that particular technology. In general, this can extend the set of rules presented in Chap. 4.

Sometimes, in order to raise the quality of the rules, we may need to extend the notation of RSL. For instance, the target technology may introduce several types of Triggers (buttons, menu options, hyperlinks, ...). It thus might be helpful to introduce

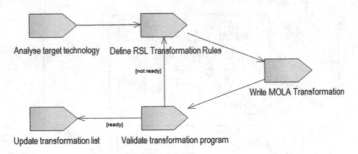

Analyse target technology   Define RSL Transformation Rules

[not ready]

Write MOLA Transformation

[ready]

Update transformation list   Validate transformation program

Fig. 7.16 Technology Evolution process with MDRE

special tagging notation that would differentiate the Triggers and eventually cause generation of code with support for the available UI elements.

Defining the set of transformation rules is important as it sets the scope for the new transformation. It can be seen as a bad practice to jump right into the step of writing a transformation (MOLA) program. Discovering the rules while writing a transformation often leads to poor quality code caused by constant changes and updates due to changing scope and target. In general, we should follow the practices shown in Chap. 6 where the individual procedures of the transformation reflect the transformation rules.

The process of defining transformation rules and writing MOLA transformations can take several iterations before a full transformation is ready. It obviously involves validating the transformation program. We need to make sure that the transformation rules are implemented correctly, mainly in terms of the correctness of the generated code. We need to make sure that the generated code compiles and produces executables that can be instantly validated against typical source RSL Models.

The last step in the Technology Evolution process is to update the transformation list available in the transformation tool (e.g. in ReDSeeDS). This step links the two major processes of the ReDSeeDS Methodology. The new transformation can now be used in the Software Evolution Process and it is up to the particular software development project to decide to switch to using the new transformation. Note that the switch can be associated with only reflecting some small modifications in the previously used technology or refining the transformation rules. It thus may be relatively easy to start using the new transformation. On the other hand, the new transformation may completely change the target code structure due to using a completely new technology that significantly differs from the old one. This is most often associated with making a strategic decision as the switch is associated with a significant investment.

Finally, we can observe that transformations for different technologies can be used simultaneously. We can develop a single RSL Model and implement it using several transformations at the same time. This should significantly facilitate porting a given system onto several target environments, e.g. different operating systems. A common example is the development of applications for mobile devices which could operate on the various mobile platforms available on the market. With the MDRE approach, all the versions share the same RSL Model. The differences between the platforms are reflected through the transformations from RSL to code. The RSL Model evolves along new ideas pertaining to the functionality of our mobile application. The transformations evolve along the changes introduced by the producers of the given platforms.

7.3 Reuse Approaches with Requirements Models

The base ReDSeeDS Methodology assumes that the system is developed using MDRE throughout the whole project. So, it is suitable mostly for new systems, for which requirements can be formulated with RSL and then translated automatically into code. However, in most situations we would prefer not to start formulating requirements models from scratch, but to reuse some behaviour from previous systems [156]. In this section we will present two possible extensions to the standard MDRE process, that allow to deal with this issue.

7.3.1 Applying MDRE to Existing (Legacy) Systems

It is an obvious observation that many software systems still used nowadays were created with old, obsolete technologies. They were developed using traditional methods for years, with many "work-arounds" and "eclectic" programming (to use an euphemism). At some point, a decision has to be made to discontinue their further evolution using the old technologies as it is not economically justified. It becomes necessary to create a system with similar functionality but using new, efficient technologies with modern look-and-feel, acceptable to contemporary users. This includes the rising trend to substitute classical desktop systems with their web-based versions. Unfortunately, recovery of logic from such legacy software is difficult. This is caused by the inability to comprehend and analyse code that became tangled and twisted throughout the years of development. Thus, it is often easier to write the new system from scratch instead of attempting to understand and modify the existing system.

In this section we present a method to recover important elements of legacy software independently of their code structure and details. Instead of analysing and reverse-engineering code, we propose to reverse-engineer the system's user interface [163]. In this solution, the information about the application logic can be extracted from any legacy system by determining its observable behaviour [117]. It can then be stored in the form of requirements (use case) models [134]. This opens all the code generation possibilities that we have described throughout this book and which is summarised in the ReDSeeDS Methodology.

The recovery process illustrated in Fig. 7.17 consists of three major steps: (1) recording test scripts, (2) transforming scripts to RSL and (3) manually correcting RSL models. In the first step, the legacy system is subject to "UI ripping"

[107] (recording the observable behaviour) as available in standard commercial test automation tools. The legacy system users work with it as normal but also record their activity, using the test tool that integrates with the user interface. This produces processable test scripts (e.g. in the XML format). The scripts are then processed by a dedicated module which is part of the ReDSeeDS tool. The module can process test scripts and turn them automatically into RSL models, consisting of use case scenarios and domain notions. These models can be further edited manually by merging scenarios and grouping them into use cases. The final step is to update the extracted RSL models in the RSL Editor. This allows for correcting the domain model (naming etc.), extending the models with new functionality, changing the existing functionality.

To capture the legacy application logic we need to process and store information on all the significant paths through the user interface, including exceptional behavior (e.g. entering invalid data, operation cancellation). Thus, the important requirement of the new tool suite is to be able to record all the possible user-system interaction paths of a legacy system. One of such paths is illustrated in Fig. 7.18. Here we can see a short scenario for entering a new book entry using the JabRef reference manager (jabref.sourceforge.net). We would like to "play-out" many such scenarios through normal usage of the system and to record their steps and the data exchanged with the user (cf. UI ripping). Note that such recording is present in typical test automation tools.

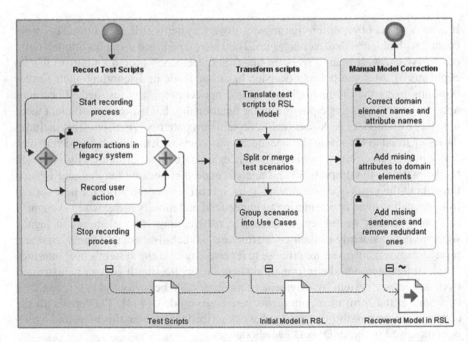

Fig. 7.17 Legacy application logic recovery process

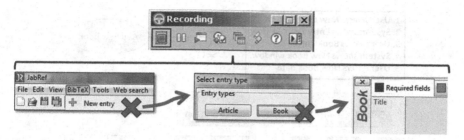

Fig. 7.18 Capturing functionality of a legacy user interface

In our examples we use Rational Functional Tester (RFT) [39] which is suitable for our purposes. In RFT, capturing and simulation of user actions can be performed for various user interface styles and technologies. The captured functionality ("test scripts") is editable and presented together with the UI screens. RFT can also export the test scripts in its proprietary XML format. An example of such a script is presented in Fig. 7.19. The XML file contents reflect some elements of the scenario ("Book" button, "New Book" window) and the data (the "Title" of the new book) from Fig. 7.18.

Obviously, test scripts recorded by RFT need further processing to turn them into RSL models. Their purpose is not to capture application logic units but to capture linear paths through the system behaviour for further repeated automatic test execution. The ReDSeeDS tool has a plug-in called TALE (Tool for Application Logic Extraction) [139] that can automatically turn test scripts into use case scenarios and domain models. The result of such translation for the scenario from Fig. 7.18 is illustrated in Fig. 7.20. The XML file produced by RFT is turned into a scenario containing five SVO sentences supplemented by a domain model containing information on the windows (e.g. "New Book window") and the associated domain elements (e.g. "New Book data" with "Title").

Further processing has to be done manually. The recovered linear scenarios have to be merged into use cases with conditions, alternative paths and invocations as illustrated in Fig. 7.21. The recovered scenarios are displayed in the so-called **Detached scenario list**. Any "detached scenario" can be attached to an existing use case. New

```
...  <testElements xsi:type="com.ibm.rational.test.ft.visualscript:ProxyMethod" name="book" type="GuiTestObject"
role="Button" elementType="TestObject" domain="Java" controlName="Book" topLevelWindow="//@topLevelWindows.2">
        <action name="click">
</testElements>

<testElements xsi:type="com.ibm.rational.test.ft.visualscript:ProxyMethod" name="newBook"
type="TopLevelTestObject" role="Frame" elementType="TestObject" domain="Java" controlName="New Book"
topLevelWindow="//@topLevelWindows.1">
        <action name="inputChars">
            <argument>
                <testelement xsi:type="com.ibm.rational.test.ft.visualscript:Value" value="Title"
                elementType="Value" valueType="String"/>
            </argument>
        </action>  ...
```

Fig. 7.19 Example script with UI recording

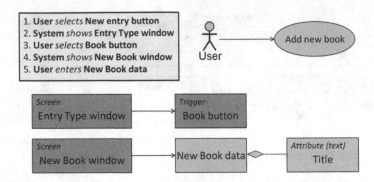

1. **User** *selects* **New entry button**
2. **System** *shows* **Entry Type window**
3. **User** *selects* **Book button**
4. **System** *shows* **New Book window**
5. **User** *enters* **New Book data**

Fig. 7.20 RSL model translated from the recorded script

use cases can be created and freely edited. When attaching a scenario to a use case, the user can choose a reference scenario and point to a correct joining place. This also adds condition sentences to both scenarios. The previously (possibly erroneously) attached scenarios can also be detached back to the unassigned scenario list. The user can also delete scenarios from the list, join them or split them. It is also possible to move scenarios between use cases, merge use cases or notions and automatically find common scenario fragments.

After recovering and editing the legacy application logic and domain we can proceed to generating the target system. For this purpose we can use all the techniques presented in the previous chapters. Having a correct RSL model we can automatically obtain much of the application logic and presentation code. To illustrate the process

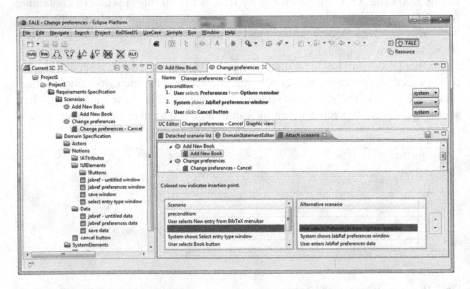

Fig. 7.21 Merging recovered scenarios

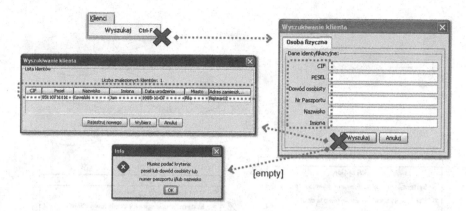

Fig. 7.22 Example of recorded UI behaviour

of recovery and migration to a new technology we use a real case. This is a non-trivial commercial system in the bank loan management domain. The system was developed by a major Polish software provider and was discontinued from further development in 2009, after nearly 10 years of development and commercial usage. The system became obsolete despite it being developed using technologies that are still in use: Java 1.5, Swing[9] for the user interface, WebSphere Application Server[10] and JDBC[11] with Hibernate[12] for database access. The main problem with the system is its use of Swing that is no longer treated as an ergonomic solution. Also, the architectural structure of the system and related code became obsolete and impossible to evolve.

For this reason the only economic way to recover logic from SZOK was to use the TALE tool. The case study covered a significant part of the system's functionality and resulted in a model consisting of 50 full use cases, each with two or more scenarios. The study started with recording test scripts using RFT, illustrated in Fig. 7.22 for one example piece of functionality. This simple example shows two alternative scenarios associated with searching for clients (*pol. wyszukiwanie klienta*[13]). Both scenarios start with selecting an option (Klienci → Wyszukaj; Clients → Search), and then show a search criteria window. One scenario results in showing a client list (*pol. lista klientow*) and the other (when the list is empty) shows an info message.

In the next step of the recovery process, the TALE tool transforms the recorded scripts into an initial RSL model. This model is then manually modified by adding use cases to group the collected scenarios and merging alternative scenarios under appropriate use cases. The result of this activity is illustrated in Fig. 7.23. It shows a small fragment of the use case model with six use cases connected through the «in-

---

[9] http://docs.oracle.com/javase/tutorial/uiswing/.

[10] http://www.ibm.com/software/products/appserv-was/.

[11] http://www.oracle.com/technetwork/java/javase/jdbc/index.html.

[12] http://hibernate.org/.

[13] The system's user interface is entirely in Polish, so we provide some English translations in text.

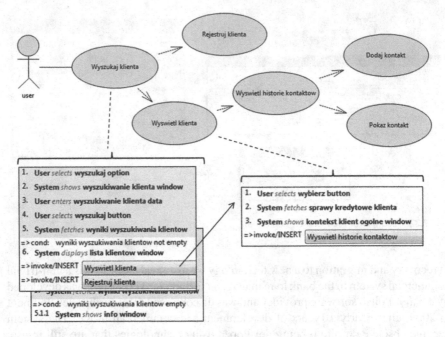

Fig. 7.23 Fragment of the recovered use case model

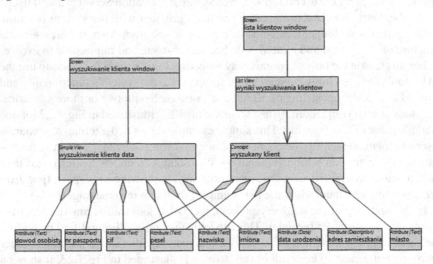

Fig. 7.24 Fragment of the recovered domain model

voke»relationships. Two scenarios generated from the recording, shown in Fig. 7.22, were manually assigned as the contents of the "Wyszukaj klienta" use case. The scenarios were merged and appropriate condition sentences ('cond:') were added. Finally, appropriate invocation sentences were introduced.

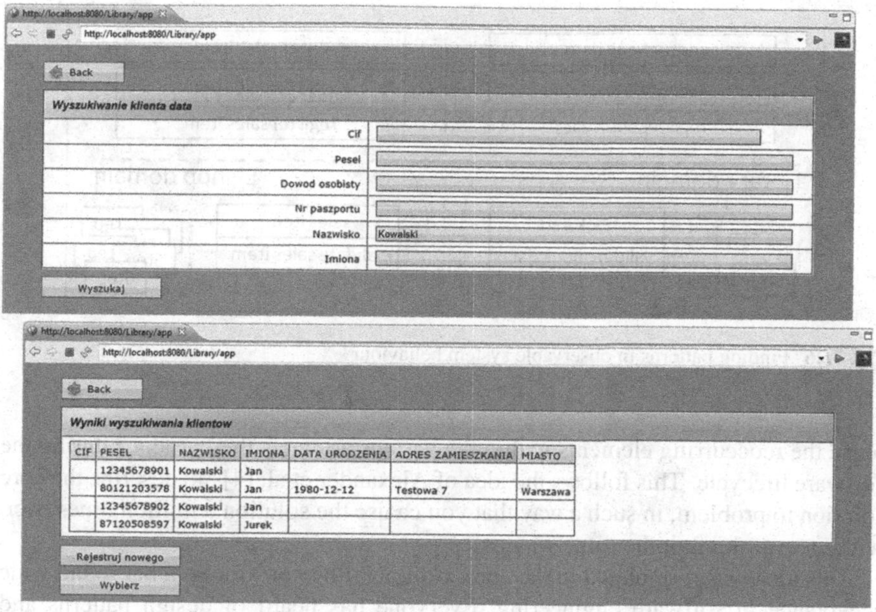

Back

Wyszukiwanie klienta data

Cif	
Pesel	
Dowod osobisty	
Nr paszportu	
Nazwisko	Kowalski
Imiona	

Wyszukaj

Back

Wyniki wyszukiwania klientow

CIF	PESEL	NAZWISKO	IMIONA	DATA URODZENIA	ADRES ZAMIESZKANIA	MIASTO
	12345678901	Kowalski	Jan			
	80121203578	Kowalski	Jan	1980-12-12	Testowa 7	Warszawa
	12345678902	Kowalski	Jan			
	87120508597	Kowalski	Jurek			

Rejestruj nowego

Wybierz

Fig. 7.25 Automatically generated web forms

Together with use case scenarios, also the user interface and domain notions were automatically recovered as illustrated in Fig. 7.24. It shows notions related to two of the windows shown in Fig. 7.22. The notion names reflect also the final step, which is to refine the RSL model to cater for possible modifications and extensions to the system's functionality. Often, the domain model needs manual refactoring due to required renaming of recovered notion names. Some notions were renamed and several use cases "wired" to compose for consistent application logic and navigation between various parts of the user interface.

This finally allowed us to migrate to a new technology using the ReDSeeDS transformation engine. The result of this migration is shown in Fig. 7.25. The shown forms were generated completely automatically from the presented domain model. What is more, the generated system also followed the application logic according to the presented use case scenarios. As part of the case study, the generated code was updated with database access and some simple business logic (data processing).

7.3.2 Reusing Requirements Models Through Patterns

The previous approach to software reuse is based on reverse engineering of existing software. Another widely practiced technique of software reuse is to use patterns. Contemporary software systems present high repeatability in their structure and their logic (behaviour). It is thus an obvious desire of software developers to be able to

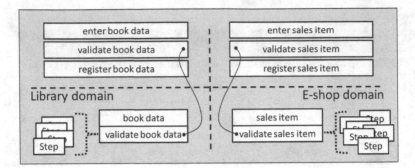

Fig. 7.26 Finding patterns in observable system behaviour

reuse the reoccurring elements within the various artefacts they produce during the software lifecycle. This follows the idea of Alexander et al. [4] "to describe the core solution to problem, in such a way that you ca use the solution a million times over, without ever doing it the same way twice".

This idea was formulated in the context of building construction, but found wide acceptance in software engineering. Everyone has heard of design patterns and architectural frameworks. However, not much can be said about patterns at the level of requirements and specifically—requirements models. The first inspiration came from Alistair Cockburn who proposed the idea of "parameterised use cases" in his seminal book "Writing Effective Use Cases" [34]. This idea consists in creating use cases like "Find a whatever" but was not described in detail. The idea returned in another seminal book "Use Cases: Patterns and Blueprints" by Overgaard and Palmkvist [126]. This book proposes a set of reusable] requirements models, but stops at the level of detail of what we can call the "use case interrelations". It treats arrangements of use cases in use case diagrams but does not go into the details of the "use case contents".

Lack of more detailed patterns can be caused by lack of standard notations for use case internals. However, with the advent of RSL we obtain full capabilities in this respect. In this section we thus present patterns that span all the levels covered by RSL: use cases and their relationships, use case scenarios and domain models. This is associated with capturing repeatable application logic flows, suitable for software systems independent of their problem domains [9].

Figure 7.26 presents an example, illustrating the general idea. It shows two sequences of application logic expressed through two scenarios. The application logic is identical despite the two problem domains being quite different (library vs. e-shop). The two scenarios exhibit the same sequence of user-system interactions and refer to similar domain actions ("validate", "register"). Of course, the domain logic is different (e.g. how to "validate") and should be specified separately for the two systems.

In order to be able to repeat such scenarios in various contexts we would need to abstract over any specific problem domain, extracting pure application logic. This creates patterns that define typical observable behaviour of software in terms of sequences of user-system interactions. However, these patterns involve not only abstract behaviour but also an associated abstract problem domain. This concept is explained in Fig. 7.27. It refers to the already mentioned "Find a whatever" use case concept formulated by Alistair Cockburn. The presented use case model is highly parameterised. The parameters are placed in parentheses as part of actor and use case names, and use case scenarios. Moreover, these parameters ("whatever", used in the use case name and sentence object) refer to specific elements in the domain model (the "whatever" Simple View). This leads us to the following definition of what we call "Software Behaviour Patterns".

A Software Behaviour Pattern (SBP) *is one or more closely related abstract use cases together with their scenarios expressed in RSL notation. These scenarios contain interactions between abstract actor(s) and an abstract system, and system actions defining abstract observable behaviour of the system (abstract events). The events are defined with sentences containing only references to an abstract problem domain. Instantiation of a pattern is performed by substituting references to the abstract domain with references to a specific one.*

This definition contains an important characteristic of SBPs. We prefer them to be associated with an abstract problem domain, easily substitutable by a concrete one. This can be implemented within the ReDSeeDS tool wherein the developers are able to quickly change the names in the domain model, and thus instantly "switching" from one domain to another. In this way, patterns can be quickly created or instantiated. Creation of a pattern consists in changing a concrete domain into an abstract one (e.g. "Add book" –> "Add whatever"), where instantiation is changing in the opposite direction (e.g. "Add whatever" –> "Add sales item").

Based on this mechanism we can create a library of patterns, reusable in many contexts.[14] Here we present one example pattern which can serve as a starting point. This is a classical pattern that uses the well-known CRUD (Create, Read, Update, Delete) approach, presented also in the pattern book by Overgaard and Palmquist.

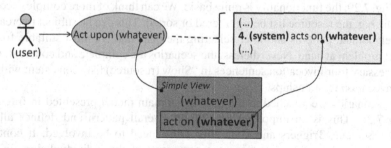

Fig. 7.27 Structure of Software Behaviour Patterns

---

[14] Similarly, a library of anti-patterns can be built [43] and used as guidance to avoid certain commonly made mistakes in use case modelling.

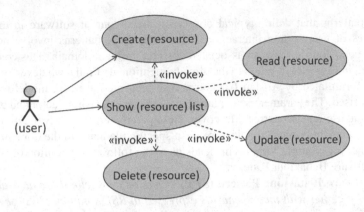

Fig. 7.28 "Manage resources" pattern: use case model

We call our version of the pattern "Manage resources". After Cockburn we could also call it "Manage whatever" but we prefer the more formal name.

The pattern is based on the use case model presented in Fig. 7.28. It involves an abstract "(user)" and five abstract use cases with "(resource)" being the recurring parameter in each of them. The central use case is "Show (resource) list", which invokes the four other use cases which provide the actual CRUD functionality. Note that the "Create" use case is also accessible directly, and not only through an invocation. This is due to creating a "(resource)" that does not necessitate the context needed by the other three invoked use cases. To read, update or delete a "(resource)" we first need to select that resource which is provided by the central use case.

The five use cases are further detailed with appropriate scenarios. Some of them are illustrated in Fig. 7.29. These scenarios are similar to the scenarios found in the examples in the previous chapters, and especially in Sect. 4.5. In fact, we can treat the current "Manage resource" pattern as a generalisation and extension of the presented use case models of the library domain (see e.g. Fig. 4.44).

In Fig. 7.29, the functionality is quite basic. We can think of more complex scenarios with, e.g. the resource list being filtered or sorted. This can be subject to creating more elaborated patterns and later selecting the ones that are most suitable for the current problem at hand. Nevertheless, the scenarios are complete and coherent, with the necessary four invocation sentences in "Show (resource) list" consistent with the four invocation relationships.

The scenarios are attached to the abstract domain model presented in fragment in Fig. 7.30. This is an important part of the overall pattern and defines all the abstract Screens, Triggers and Data Views that need to be involved. It contains all the relationships that determine the semantics of the individual domain elements within the whole model. For instance, note that "update (resource) button" is related with the "(resource) list" while "create (resource) button" is not. This is because the event associated with the first Trigger does not need any context (a resource selected from the list), while the second one does. The model also

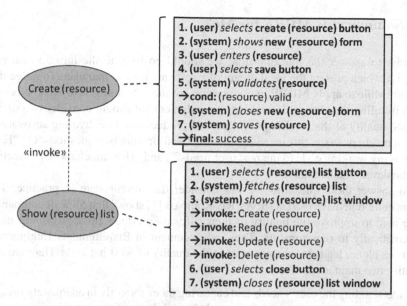

Fig. 7.29 "Manage resources" pattern: selected scenarios

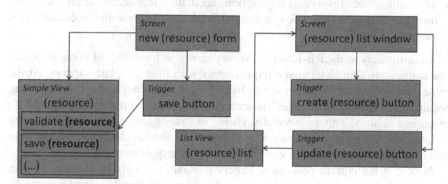

Fig. 7.30 "Manage resources" pattern: domain model fragment

contains all the verb phrases ("validate (resource)" etc.) that provide placeholders for the domain logic to be defined after instantiation. Note that the abstract domain model does not contain any Attributes because they can be determined only for a concrete domain.

7.4 Summary: Is MDRE for Me?

In order to answer the title question, we should go back to the introduction and Sect. 1.1 which present the ideal dream of a software project manager. To judge if it is worthwhile to apply MDRE in our projects, we need to assess how close it brings us to fulfilling this dream. In making this judgment we should consider two major factors: quality of the resulting software and productivity in delivering software to the clients. In practice, this means answering the following two questions: (1) "How close is my working code to the *real* user needs?", and "How much more productive are the development teams?"

To answer these questions we can consider the current state of practice. The recent comprehensive market survey RE-Kompass [1] shows that 58 % of companies were able to improve the quality of their software products by approaching more systematically to requirements. Thus, advancement in Requirements Engineering practices alone, leads to advancement in the quality of working code. Here we can identify two main areas of concern:

- Understanding the user's needs and capturing them correctly in adequately precise and complete descriptions of the intended capabilities of the system;
- Translating these (evolving) descriptions accurately into technical artefacts, and finally to the executable code in a way that leads to software with consistently high quality.

Unfortunately as the RE-Kompass survey shows, at least 70 % of companies still use ambiguous natural language requirements with little template support. At the same time, according to another survey by El Emam and Güneş Koru [45], "too many requirements and scope changes" is seen as one of the two main causes (at 33 %) of project failures. This is especially visible in case of long-term projects, aiming at large, complex and data intensive systems. It is thus evident that the software engineering industry struggles with poor quality of requirements.

Note that the current process is largely manual especially in the area of user and software requirements. RE concentrates on managing largely textual paragraphs text and linking them manually to design. This is why—as the RE-Kompass survey shows—only 35 % companies have experienced productivity increase through applying systematic RE. This causes a lack of stakeholder acceptance for making requirements formally precise—it adds effort but does not result in shorter development and evolution cycles.

To change this we need to turn software requirements into first-class citizens in the software lifecycle. We need to seek ways to make them formally precise (but still comprehensible to business domain experts) and to automate their conversion into working code. MDRE assists us greatly in this quest through its techniques, tools and methodology, as presented in this book.

By introducing automation right at the beginning of the software development process, MDRE promises significant gains in productivity. Of course, this has its limits and MDRE cannot be seen as the universal "silver bullet" from the famous

Fred Brook's paper [26]. There are always cases where high levels of automation are not possible or difficult. However, a high degree of automatic requirements-to-code generation for typical business systems seems perfectly achievable in the wider practice. This includes mainly systems with intensive user-system interaction and relatively standard structures of data processing and storage. For other types of systems, certain aspects of code need to be left for semi-automatic generation and manual completion.

The key to mitigating the problems of software development seems to be shifting our efforts towards the essential complexity (cf. requirements), abstracting away the "accidents", i.e. the technological details. In MDRE, all these details are captured within transformation programs capable of generating various target technological environments (web/mobile/desktop interfaces, database management systems, architectural frameworks, etc.). With a library of such transformations at hand, the various software project stakeholders can concentrate on providing semantically precise functional requirements specifications. As a result, the level of complexity at which developers need to operate decreases dramatically. This has two very significant impacts especially for large and complex systems:

- Complex problems and their solutions have to be handled only at the conceptual level (the essence). This allows for building much more complex systems at a much lower cost associated with their unambiguous specification and implementation.
- The quality of complex systems rises significantly through applying automation in generating code of repeatable high quality, from high-level requirements models.

What is important is that the amount of effort to achieve these impacts in a given organisation might not be very significant. This mostly depends on the current practice in requirements specification. If the development teams have experience with writing good quality use cases and domain models, the effort would mainly consist in shifting to more semantically precise notations of RSL. In other cases, the effort would be obviously higher because it would involve acquiring knowledge on the fundamentals of use case and domain modelling. Of course, when implementing MDRE in our organisation, we should follow the best practices of software process improvement [125]. Generally, this should be a gradual process which improves our practices and raises maturity. This process can go through several levels.

1. *Level 1. No systematic practices in requirements modelling.* At this level, the organisation practices mainly textual requirements with perhaps some elements of modelling like use case diagrams and class diagrams for domain models.
2. *Level 2. Practicing precise requirements models.* At this level, the organisation has codified practices for documenting functional requirements with precise use case models, including detailed use case scenario models. It also codifies practices in documenting domain models which are precisely linked to the functional requirements models.
3. *Level 3. Practicing RSL modelling.* This level is associated with implementing RSL to document all the requirements. It also involves using a dedicated RSL editor to formulate syntactically and semantically precise RSL models. However, no model transformation is yet practiced.

4. *Level 4. Practicing RSL-based development.* At this level, the RSL models are
treated as primary development artefacts. RSL models are transformed to code
using appropriate tools and model transformations. The ReDSeeDS Methodology
is applied and merged into standard practices. However, important parts of code
are developed using standard practices.
5. *Level 5. Practicing requirements-level programming.* This level is associated with
transferring all the essential development activity to creating requirements-level
models. No code is developed using traditional programming languages. Implementation technology is entirely encapsulated in automatic transformations from
requirements to executable code.

As we can see, reaching Level 2 is associated with applying general the best
practices of requirements modelling. Many organisations are already at this level.
Levels 3 and 4 consist of the elements presented in this book. Reaching Level 3
is associated with introducing an RSL Editor to practice, and reaching Level 4 is
associated with practicing the full methodology.

Finally, Level 5 goes significantly beyond the scope of this book, and generally
beyond the current state-of-the-art. However, we think that this is a good direction
of the future research and innovation for MDRE. Shifting from 3GL programming
to "requirements-level programming" could bring productivity gains similar to that
of shifting from assembly language programming to 3GL. This would lead to substituting traditional programming language compilers with requirements model transformation engines. The challenges here seem to be much greater because of the
very large number of dimensions that need to be taken care of by the transformation
engines. This should also involve non-functional requirements which we did not
try to tackle in this book. This issue opens a vast area of potential future research.
Specifically, it may involve studying the influence of non-functional requirements
on requirements-to-code transformations.

Chapter 8
Case Study

So far, we have provided the reader with many technical details on how to achieve fast generation of code from precise requirements models. However, can we claim that such transformations can be done "in a snap" as we promise in the title of the book? In this chapter, we want to demonstrate that this is possible, and a reasonable working application prototype can be obtained very quickly after formulating requirements in RSL. For this purpose, we will present an end-to-end case study example.

8.1 Study Assumptions and Context

As we have learned from Chaps. 2 to 4, in order to obtain working code, we need to specify RSL models very precisely. This precision can be rewarded with instant generation of the system's structure and much of the application logic and user interface code. Yet, an important question is about the efficiency of the approach. How long does it take to formulate a considerably sized RSL model that can produce working code? Can it be more efficient and increase productivity in relation to the "traditional" approaches?

We will approach at answering these questions by presenting a case study example. In this case study, we want to show how far we will get in a very short period of time—in just one working day [148]. Of course, one day is not a "snap". However, in our case study, we will encompass all the steps that include also the formulation of the source RSL model. The time to develop precise requirements is an important factor in judging the effectiveness of our approach.

In the study, we thus make certain assumptions. We want the whole system prototype to be developed by one person in one working day (8 h; one man-day). By a prototype, we mean a system with fully working and verifiable application logic, but without the domain logic and data persistence.[1] We also want to factor out

---

[1] Generation of basic domain logic and data persistence can be made possible by developing an extended transformation—see the discussion section.

© Springer International Publishing Switzerland 2015
M. Śmiałek and W. Nowakowski, *From Requirements to Java in a Snap*,
DOI 10.1007/978-3-319-12838-2_8

the effort to elicit the requirements from the user and to discuss all the possibilities, including the time, to make the final decisions. We treat this as out of scope of our approach and of this case study. Thus, we assume that the initial user requirements are known and either written in natural language or well discussed and understood by the (single) developer.

With well-understood user requirements, the developer has to write a complete RSL model. We assume that the developer is proficient in writing RSL specifications and understands its semantics. We also assume that the developer is proficient in Java and the associated technology platform. This is necessary in order to update the generated Model layer methods with some stub code needed for the prototype to be verified.

Another assumption we make is that we will build a complete end-to-end application during the one day. The application will not just be a part of a larger system. For this reason, we need to keep its size rather modest. Moreover, we want the application to be comparable to some existing demonstrator for a traditional software development technology. This will facilitate assessment of the system generated from RSL and its comparison with the system developed using "traditional" methods.

A suitable example system is the Pet Clinic, which was used as an official example[2] for the Spring Framework [65, 140][3] up to version 2.5. Although this example is no longer maintained and is already over 10 years old, it seems to be well suited for our purposes. We do not care about the actual technology in which it was originally implemented.[4] We want to have a well-defined functionality and problem domain, with an already working system for comparison. The problem domain is a quite standard business domain which is ideal to be specified using the RSL's domain model notation. The functionality contains a significant amount of user–system interaction which can be effectively defined with RSL's scenario notation.

The functionality of the original Pet Clinic system is clear[5] and consists of about a dozen use cases which operate on a simple domain model. Generally, the system is required to handle data of four types: pets, pet owners, veterinarians and visits. The application's functionality consists in browsing through and updating these data. The use cases are interconnected, so browsing through one type of data (e.g. pets) enables operations on some other types of data (e.g. visits for a specific pet).

Based on these general assumptions, the case study provides an RSL model that defines the functionality of the Pet Clinic system. This model was developed within the ReDSeeDS tool's RSL editor and we present direct snapshots of the model made within the tool. The presented model was subject to model transformation which is discussed in Chap. 6. This finally resulted in Java code and UML models. The code was slightly updated manually only by adding some stub code for the methods in the Model layer. This code is clearly marked in further descriptions. Finally, the resulting code was compiled and run.

---

[2] http://docs.spring.io/docs/petclinic.html.

[3] http://spring.io/.

[4] The original source code can be examined at https://github.com/spring-projects/spring-petclinic.

[5] http://www.woehlke.org/p/javaee7-petclinic/.

8.2 Source Model in RSL

8.2.1 General Structure

The RSL model created during the case study consists of 12 use cases, presented in Fig. 8.1. As we can see, four of the use cases are connected to the actor through usage relationships. These use cases should be available for invocation from the

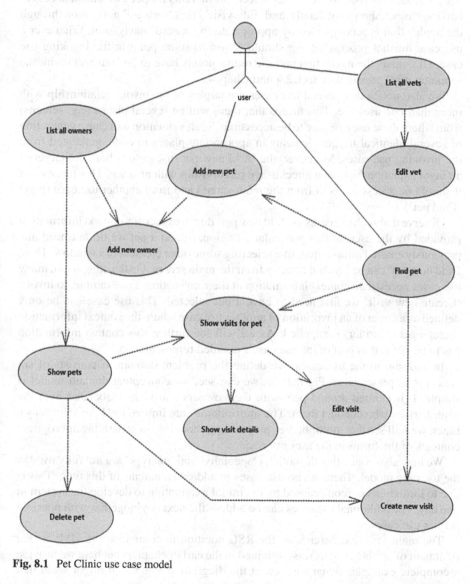

Fig. 8.1 Pet Clinic use case model

main screen of the generated application. Other use cases are interlinked with several invoke relationships that show the overall navigability through the application. We have to remember (see Sect. 7.1) that the invoke relationships are created only when appropriate invocation sentences are present in scenarios. So, the presented diagram shows the status after the scenarios were written (as described further in this section).

To analyse navigation through the use case model, let us start—for example—from the 'Find pet' use case. When we invoke it from the main screen, we should (at some point) obtain access to invoking three other use cases: 'Add new pet', 'Show visits for pet', 'Create new visit'. If we further select 'Show visits for pet', we obtain access to two use cases: 'Show visit details' and 'Edit visit'. This 'forward' navigation through the application is accompanied by appropriate 'backward' navigation. Whenever a use case finishes processing, we should return to some point in the invoking use case. Of course, the navigation and the return points have to be consistent with the semantic rules provided in Sect. 2.4 and Chap. 4.

We also notice that several use cases are targets of the invoke relationship with more than one use case. This means that there will be several places (e.g. screens) from where these use cases are to be accessible. Such a situation will cause generation of several identical trigger elements in appropriate places in code, generated from the invoking use cases. Moreover, the 'Add new pet' use case is both the target of an invoke relationship and a direct usage relationship with an actor. This means that it should be accessible both from the main screen and from another use case (here: 'Find pet').

Observe that such use cases as 'Add new pet' do not expect any context information provided by the user. In this particular situation, to add a pet we do not need any previously entered information, like selecting some other element in a window. Thus, 'Add new pet' can be invoked directly from the main screen. On the other hand, many use cases necessitate context information at their invocation. For example, to invoke 'Create new visit' we first need to have a pet selected. This use case can be only defined as a target of an invocation of another use case where the context information (here: a pet identifier) is supplied. As we will see further, this context information has to be defined as part of the use case's detailed representation.

In addition to the use cases, we define the problem domain. It consists of six concepts as presented in Fig. 8.2. As we can see, the conceptual domain model is simple. It is centred around pets with their owners and visits associated with the veterinarians who conduct them. The multiplicities are limited to '1' or '*' (many). Later, we will see that multiplicities play an important role in generating appropriate contents of the forms in the user interface.

We may also notice that the notions 'specialty' and 'pet type' are not fully used in the use case model. There are no use cases to add/edit elements of this type. This is due to limitations in scope caused by the initial assumption to develop the system in one day. The additional use cases can be added 'the next day' together with possible further use cases.

The main visible difference of the RSL notation in comparison to UML is the treatment of attributes. This was explained in the earlier chapters but here we provide a complete example. When we look at the diagram in Fig. 8.2, it might seem that

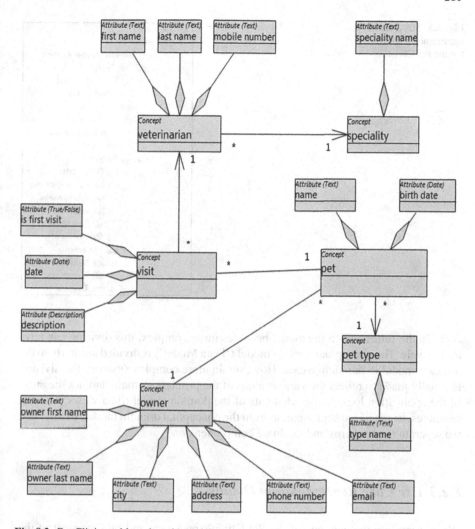

Fig. 8.2 Pet Clinic problem domain model

placing attribute icons outside of the notion icons seems unnecessary and more laborious to maintain. This is perhaps true for the conceptual model alone. However, we will later see that the model needs to define access to individual attributes from other elements like data views. This is not possible with typical UML notation.

The use case model and the conceptual domain model define the overall scope of the system. This needs to be extended with the details of the application logic and system domain elements. The model thus becomes complicated enough to define a package structure that helps in browsing and also organises the structure of the generated code.

The packages for Pet Clinic are presented in Fig. 8.3. We have divided the use cases into three packages which will form three components of the application logic

Fig. 8.3 Structure of the requirements specification for the Pet Clinic

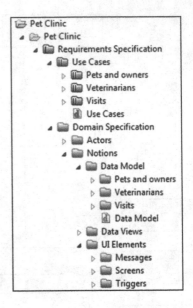

code. In the future, when the model becomes more complex, this division can have more levels. The conceptual domain model ('Data Model') is divided similarly to the use case model in our simple case. However, in more complex systems, the division is usually made to reflect the various areas of the problem domain and not the areas of the application logic. Other elements of the domain model (data views, screens, messages, triggers) are kept separate from the conceptual domain model. In this way, we separate the concerns and facilitate comprehension.

8.2.2 Use Case Representation Details

We now go into the contents of the Pet Clinic's packages and present most of the use case representations and related detailed domain models. For each use case, we provide a set of scenarios and in some cases—a related activity diagram. This is accompanied by an appropriate diagram showing a fragment of the domain model that contains all the related notions.

Note that development of the RSL model details was based on writing use case scenarios in textual form. All the other presented elements were developed along this activity. The activity diagrams were generated automatically by the ReDSeeDS tool and were used only for improving comprehension and validation of the developed application logic. For purposes of better presentation in the book, these diagrams were additionally manually rearranged. The domain model was automatically updated with domain elements when consecutive SVO scenario sentences were introduced. The domain elements were then manually connected through appropriate relationships with multiplicities and other adornments. This was done in diagrams that were also introduced manually.

Our presentation of detailed models starts with the **'Add new pet'** use case as shown in Fig. 8.4. The use case consists of two scenarios that branch after sentence 5. The first five sentences are thus identical in both scenarios and we present them twice just to emphasise this characteristic of RSL and the ReDSeeDS tool. In further presentations we will compress the repeated parts.

The scenarios define typical application logic for adding a new element. They start with an Actor-to-Trigger sentence, which defines the initial interaction of the user (pressing a button). This is followed by a System-to-Screen sentence of type SHOW. Such sentences show some Screen element, together with the associated widgets. To determine the contents of the Screen element we need to examine the associated domain model. In our particular case, the 'new pet form' Screen is related with the 'pet data' Simple View. The relationship is directed towards the Simple View, which means that new data will be entered in the Screen. Initially, the 'new pet form' widgets (e.g. text fields) in the displayed window will be empty or will have default values.

The actual widgets to be present on the 'new pet form' depend on the Attribute elements pointed at by 'pet data'. Figure 8.4 shows these elements together with the Concept elements that contain them (compare with Fig. 8.2). The form contains six fields: two for the 'pet', one for the 'pet type' and three for the 'owner'.

Note that the desired configuration of the fields can sometimes depend on the multiplicities in the conceptual domain model, that—for instance—there can be many ('*') pets associated with an owner, and each pet can have just one owner. So, a form that concentrates on the owner may also need to present a list of that owner's pets. On the other hand, when the form concentrates on one specific pet, an appropriate form would contain also the data of its only owner (and not a list of owners).

Considering the above observation, we may want to extend the syntax and semantics of RSL to distinguish the "main concept" for a particular Data View. This is illustrated in Fig. 8.4, which contains such a relationship between 'pet data' and 'pet'. This is an example of possible extensions that can be made to RSL in relation to the basic semantic rules given in Chap. 4. However, in this case the generated form would have the same fields with or without the additional notation.

Returning to the scenarios of 'Add new pet', note that sentence no. 2 shifts the state of dialogue to the actor. The following sentences should thus allow for entering some data and/or selecting some trigger elements (buttons). The first of these sentences is an invocation sentence. This means that it allows the actor to choose to invoke another use case—'Add new owner'. Alternatively, the actor can choose to enter pet data (sentence 3) and select 'save pet' (sentence 4).

The alternative after sentence 2 can be better seen in the activity variant shown on the right of Fig. 8.4. The invocation sentence returns control back to sentence 2. This means that after performing all the interactions within 'Add new owner', the 'new pet form' is shown again to the user. This variant of semantics is used for invocation

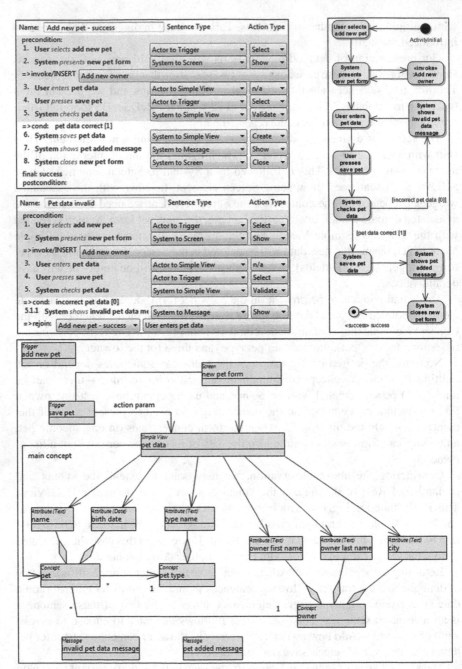

Fig. 8.4 Details for 'Add new pet'

sentences used in the dialogue state 'actor'. As we will later see, different flow of control is used for invocation sentences that are used in the dialogue state 'system'.

Analysing the sentences that follow sentence no. 2, we can determine all the Triggers (buttons) that will be present in the 'new pet form'. The first trigger comes from sentence no. 4—the 'save pet' button. The second trigger has to be derived from the first SVO sentence of the invoked 'Add new owner' use case. This sentence is analogous to the first sentence of 'Add new pet', and thus the second Trigger element in 'new pet form' is the 'add new owner' button.

The Triggers used within a given use case can be also shown in the domain diagram. Figure 8.4 contains the two mentioned Triggers that are related to sentences no. 1 and 4. Note that the first trigger ('add new pet') is not connected with any other element in the diagram. It is not part of any Screen used in the current use case, but is used within the screens that invoke this use case. The second trigger ('save pet') is explicitly associated with the 'new pet form'. This additional connection can be seen as redundant—the appropriate relationship between 'new pet form' and 'save pet' is deduced from sentences no. 2 and 4.

The final element worth noting in relation with the 'new pet form' is the 'action param' relationship between 'save pet' and 'pet data'. This relationship is important when several Data View elements are associated with a given Screen element. In such cases it is often needed to determine which data have to be processed after selecting a given Trigger element. In our current example, the Screen is related with just one Data View ('pet data'). To signal that these data have to be processed after pressing 'save pet', we need to connect these two elements with the 'action param' relationship.

Sentence no. 4 is an Actor-to-Trigger sentence. This means it can be now followed by one or more sentences of type 'System-to'. Sentence no. 5 complies with this rule. It declares some processing of type VALIDATE that operates on 'pet data'. This processing can finish with one of two possible results. Thus, sentence 5 is followed by two condition sentences ('pet data correct' and 'incorrect pet data'). These two sentences are responsible for splitting the use case representation into two scenarios. This splitting of control flow can be determined by examining the presented activity diagram.

The main ('success') scenario finishes with three SVO sentences that follow checking 'pet data'. They are followed by the 'final' sentence which passes control back to the invoking logic—either the 'Find pet' use case or the main application screen (see Fig. 8.1). The alternative scenario finishes with one SVO sentence followed by a 'rejoin' that shifts control back to sentence no. 3.

When analysing the final SVO sentences of 'Add new pet' we should remember that Message elements have slightly different semantics than Screen elements. They offer a "shortcut" where there is no need for additional 'Actor-to-Trigger' sentences and for a sentence that closes the Message element (cf. sentence no. 8 for 'new pet form'). In our simple case (sentences 7 and 5.1.1), the messages need just an acknowledgement from the user. Pressing of the appropriate 'OK' button and closing the message window is implicitly assumed in the scenario.

What cannot be assumed for the Message elements is the contents of the message defined in Fig. 8.5. The appropriate text is given as part of the element's description

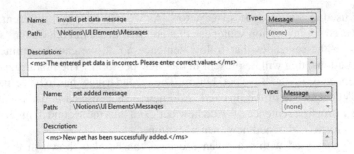

Fig. 8.5 Extended notation for message text

field using special marking. This is another example of extending RSL's syntax and semantics on top of the rules given in Chap. 4. We can also imagine an even more complex extension, where the text is not constant but determined through some attributes taken from the associated Data View elements.

The 'Add new pet' use case contains standard functionality for adding new data elements to the system's repository. Its logic contains many elements used in other use cases. Thus, in further descriptions, we discuss only certain additional aspects, characteristic for other types of functionality. This includes searching for data, listing data elements, showing and editing data items.

The **'Find pet'** and **'List all owners'** use cases are two examples of application logic for data searching whose scenarios and associated domain elements are shown in Figs. 8.6 and 8.7, respectively. Both use cases have three scenarios; one of them finishes with success, one with failure, and one with a rejoin sentence. The alternative scenarios are controlled with two pairs of condition sentences. The first pair works like that for 'Add new pet'. The second pair is similar, but it works based on the result of a 'System-to-Message' sentence ('System shows no pets found message' and 'System shows add new owner dialog'). The condition pairs in this situation determine also the buttons present in the message windows. For instance, the 'no pets found message' have two buttons: 'YES' and 'NO'.

Both use cases eventually present a Screen element that contains a list of data elements—either a 'pet list' or an 'owner list'. In both cases, a List View element is related with the respective Screen element, and the relationship is directed towards the Screen. This of course means that some existing data (taken from the system's repository) will be displayed. Somewhat more elaborate domain model—worth mentioning—was needed for the 'Find pet' use case (Fig. 8.6). The displayed list widget will contain six columns that are determined by the attributes pointed at by the 'pet list'. Some of these attributes are used to search for the pets and are pointed at by another Data View, 'pet search criteria'.

The next typical situation, shown in Figs. 8.6 and 8.7, is the invocation of various use cases ('Create new visit', 'Add new pet' and so on) after displaying the screens with the appropriate element lists ('pet list screen' or 'owner list screen'). The above invocation operations usually depend on selecting an item in the list, and then pressing

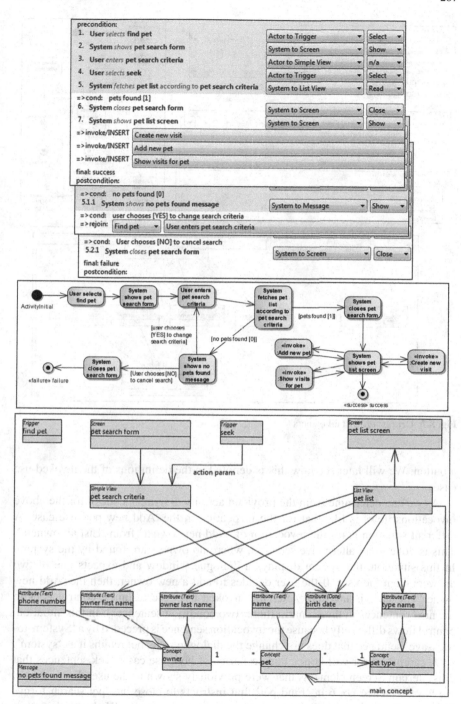

Fig. 8.6 Details for 'Find pet'

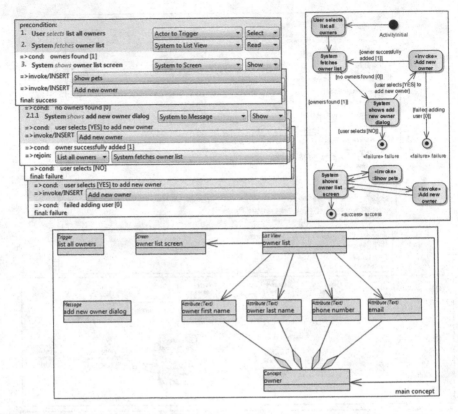

Fig. 8.7 Details for 'List all owners'

a button. We will later see how this is denoted in the definitions of the invoked use cases.

As we can determine from the provided activity diagrams, control for the above invocations flows is like that for the invocation in the 'Add new pet' use case. A different situation is for the invocation of 'Add new owner' from 'List all owners'. This is done in an alternative scenario, where no owners are found by the system. In this situation, the system displays a dialogue window and expects one of two answers from the user. If the user decides to add a new owner, then the 'Add new owner' use case is invoked. After the invoked use case resumes, control goes to the next sentences in the scenario (here: two condition sentences). In this situation, control flows differently because the invocation sentence is preceded by a 'System-to-Message' sentence that does not change the dialogue state, but retains it as 'system'.

A careful reader will notice that scenarios of both use cases lack sentences that close certain Screen elements that were previously shown to the user. For instance, we have sentence no. 6 in 'Find pet' that instructs to close the 'pet search form'. However, there is no analogous sentence for 'pet list screen'. We know that there is no need to explicitly close a Message element, but Screen elements necessitate closing.

This is not an error if we apply yet another extension of scenario semantics. We assume that every Screen element has a standard 'Back' button. This means that we do not need to add explicit sentences to press such buttons and close the respective screens. Of course, this simplifies scenarios in many situations where the default functionality is to go back to the "previous" Screen element. As we remember, RSL semantics maintains a stack of Screen elements that are "uncovered" whenever some element on top of the stack is closed. The application of this extended semantics is illustrated in sentence no. 7 for 'Find pet' and sentence no. 3 for 'List all owners'. These sentences are not followed by any Actor-to-Trigger sentence and a CLOSE sentence. However, such sentences are assumed and appropriate screen elements and logic are generated in the target application code.

The **'Show pets'** use case, shown in Fig. 8.8, is also a variant of data searching functionality. In contains simpler logic than the previous two use cases and its purpose is to show a list of all the pets for a selected pet owner. With this use case, we introduce an additional element that is needed in many situations where use cases invoke one another. To show the pet list, we first need to know the context, i.e. the pet owner.

This context is emphasised through specifying a precondition. It contains a declaration of a use case "parameter", which is the ID of the owner selected from the 'owner list'. This declaration can be used for checking consistency of the use case model. The use case can be invoked only within some context where an owner ID can be determined (e.g. selected by the user from a displayed owner list). The parameter in the precondition is consistent with the first sentence of the scenario, which is of type Actor-to-ListView. This sentence refers to a screen element that has to be present in the invoking use case. In our example, the 'List all owners' use case can invoke 'Show pets' after the user selects an owner in the 'owner list' shown in the 'owner list screen'.

The second sentence of the scenario is of type Actor-to-Trigger, which normally starts the use case logic. This sentence determines the Trigger element that will be contained in the Screen element that invokes this use case. So, in our example, the 'owner list screen' will contain the 'show pets' button.

A similar starting logic is defined for the **'Delete pet'** use case, presented in Fig. 8.9. In this case, the 'delete pet' button will be present in the 'owner's pet screen', displayed within 'Show pets'. The remaining logic of this use case is self-explanatory as it contains just one alternative based on user's decision.

More elaborated is the logic for the **'Create new visit'** use case presented in Fig. 8.10. An interesting new element present in this use case is a Screen with opposite relations to Data Views. The 'new visit form' is related with two elements: 'pet data' and 'visit data'. The first element is already known from the 'Add new pet' use case (see Fig. 8.4 which contains the full definition). In this previous situation, 'pet data' was to be entered by the user, and thus the relation was directed towards the respective Screen element. In the current situation, the intention is to only show 'pet data' on the screen and not modify it. Thus, the relation is directed towards 'new pet form'.

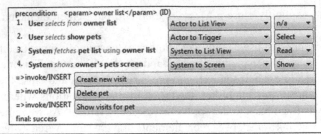

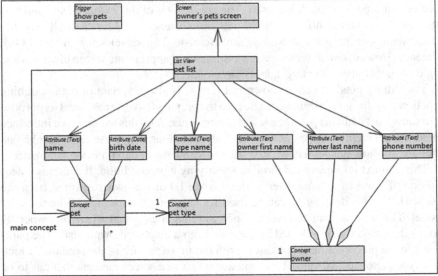

Fig. 8.8 Details for 'Show pets'

Fig. 8.9 Details for 'Delete pet'

To present 'pet data' in the 'new visit form', we need to indicate the actual data element (a specific pet). Thus, sentence no. 4 ('System shows new visit form') has to be preceded by a sentence which retrieves a single 'pet data' element. This is an SVO sentence with two objects. The first (direct) object identifies the data element,

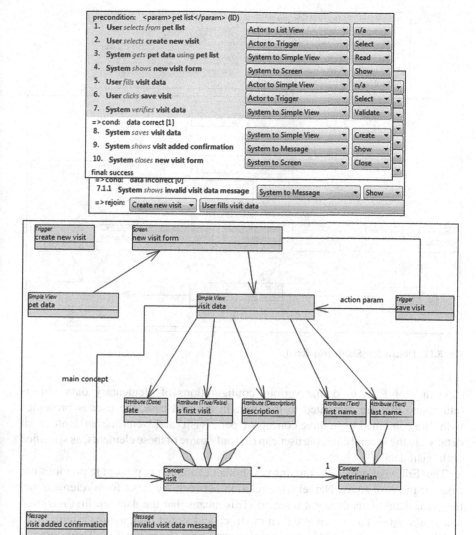

Fig. 8.10 Details for 'Create new visit'

and the second (indirect) object identifies the selection criterion. In this case, the criterion is based on the ID of the pet selected from the 'pet list' element.

The 'new visit form' element is related also to 'visit data'. This time, the appropriate screen widgets are initially empty as for the 'new pet form' in 'Add new pet'. These data are entered by the user and used in sentences no. 7 and 8 to perform appropriate domain logic operations (VALIDATE and CREATE).

Our discussion of use case details is complemented with the definitions of 'Show visit details' and 'Edit visit', shown in Figs. 8.11 and 8.12. These use cases illustrate the standard logic for manipulating simple data elements. We also notice the

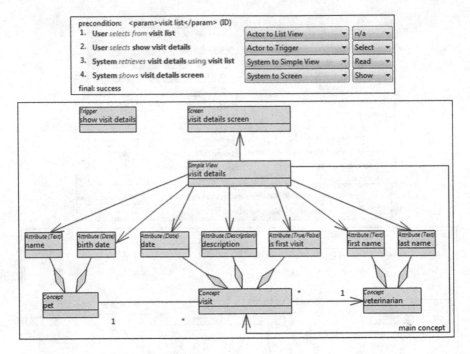

Fig. 8.11 Details for 'Show visit details'

capability of RSL to define various configurations of elementary data objects (attributes) that are presented to the user. In the first case, the user is presented with data combined from three concepts ('pet', 'visit' and 'veterinarian') into 'visit details'. In the second case, the user can edit only some of these elements, as specified with 'visit data'.

The 'Edit visit' use case contains yet another element, not present in previous use cases of the case study. Namely, the relation between the 'visit form' element and the 'visit data' element is not directed. This means that the data are first retrieved and presented on the screen and then modified and stored back in the system.

We do not present the four remaining use cases from Fig. 8.1. Their logic is practically identical to the ones already presented. For instance, the 'Add new owner' use case is similar to the 'Add new pet' use case. In fact, we can treat them as two instances of the same software behaviour pattern (see Sect. 7.3.2)—'Add new (resource)'.

8.3 General Architecture of the Generated System

After the RSL model is finished, we run the transformation presented in Chap. 6. This results in generating fully compilable Java code of the Pet Clinic application.

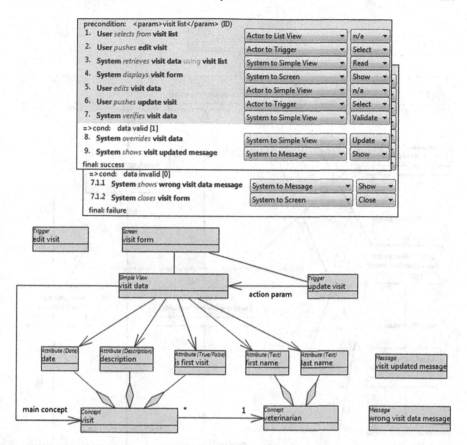

Fig. 8.12 Details for 'Edit visit'

The general structure of this code is presented through UML class diagrams in Figs. 8.13 and 8.14. In fact, the UML class model is generated together with (or rather: prior to) the Java code. The presented diagrams are only manually arranged for a more comprehensible presentation in the book.

Note that the two class diagrams concentrate on the Presenter layer classes and their relationships with the interfaces of the View layer and of the Model layer. The Presenter classes are arranged on the diagrams to show how they were generated from the use case model shown in Fig. 8.1. Note the navigable associations between the Presenter classes that reflect the «invoke» relationships between use cases.

All Presenter classes relate to the respective Model layer interfaces. These interfaces are generated based on the domain model and its packages, as presented in Fig. 8.3. There are three interfaces that originate from the three packages in the Data Model package of the Pet Clinic's domain model.

Figures 8.13 and 8.14 also emphasise that the Presenter classes are all specialisations of 'AbstractUseCasePresenter'. Through this class, all the Presenters inherit

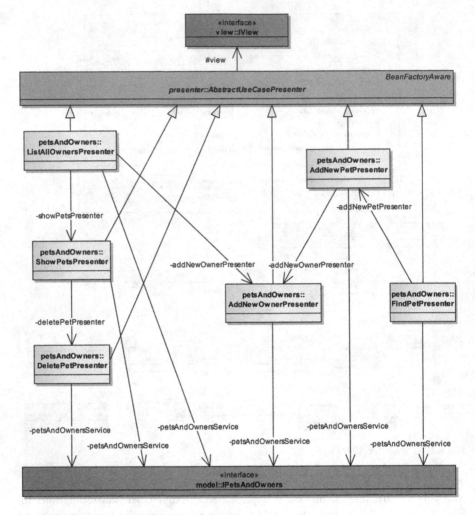

Fig. 8.13 General structure for pets and owners

the relationship with the 'IView' interface. The transformation generates only one, commonly used, interface to the View layer. This interface dispatches messages to the various UI elements.

The implementation of 'IView' and the Model interfaces is illustrated in Fig. 8.15. This is only a small fragment of the whole model, showing some of the classes that participate in two selected use cases ('Find pet' and 'Create new visit'). We show only this fragment because of the high total number of View layer classes. The configuration of other classes is similar, so the presented fragment is a good representation and illustration of the overall approach.

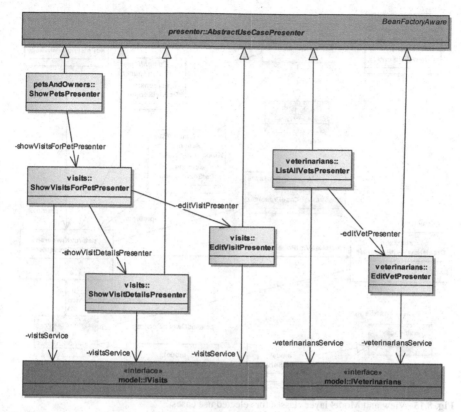

Fig. 8.14 General structure for visits and veterinarians

The 'IView' interface is implemented by the 'ViewImpl' class that uses other classes that represent specific UI elements originating from RSL's Screens and Messages. We can thus compare the window classes in Fig. 8.15 with appropriate RSL elements in Figs. 8.6 and 8.10. These classes are instantiated at appropriate moments within the code of 'ViewImpl'. Their code in turn refers to the appropriate Presenter classes to call specific code that handles user interactions.

The user interactions are supposed to result in execution of appropriate domain logic code. This code is centred around the implementations of the Model layer interfaces (e.g. 'IVisits' and 'IPetsAndOwners'). The respective classes that implement these interfaces (e.g. 'VisitsService' and 'PetsAndOwnersService') are generated with empty methods. It is up to the developers to fill the generated operations with method code. As we will later see, in our case study, we have filled the methods with simple stub code that returns constant test data.

Data are transferred between the layers using Data Transfer Objects defined with DTO classes as illustrated in Figs. 8.16 and 8.17. Again, we limit ourselves to the two already mentioned use cases. Other DTO classes have a similar structure. In general, DTOs transfer all the necessary data elements that are declared as their attributes.

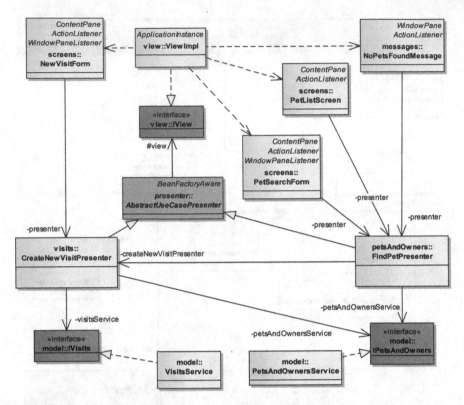

Fig. 8.15   View and Model layer classes for selected use cases

The class attributes reflect the Attribute elements in the RSL model associated with the respective Data Views (compare with Figs. 8.4, 8.6 and 8.10). For each of the class attributes, the transformation also generates a getter and a setter operation.

The example in Fig. 8.16 contains two DTO classes that are used to transfer data within the logic that realises the 'Create new visit' use case. Note that the two DTOs are used to declare appropriate attributes within the Presenter class ('CreateNewVisitPresenter') and the View class ('NewVisitForm'). In the model, these attributes are represented as associations, navigable towards the DTO classes. The role names ('petDataDTO' and 'visitDataDTO') reflect the names of respective fields that will be generated in Java code. These fields are used as temporary buffers to hold DTO values at specific moments in the application logic. These values can be accessed through getter and setter operations. Figure 8.16 shows them for one of the DTO classes. The other classes also have such operations but they were compressed for brevity.

Another important element to note is the multiplicity of the associations. Normally, the multiplicity is set to '1' (being default for UML, it is not shown in the diagrams). However, the DTOs that originate from List Views need to hold and transfer multiple objects of a specific type. Thus, they are declared with multiplicities of

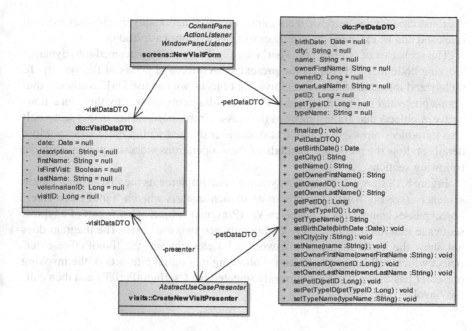

Fig. 8.16 DTO classes for 'Create new visit'

'0..*' and the 'PetListItemDTO' objects are held as lists within 'FindPetPresenter' and 'PetListScreen'.

To transfer data, DTOs are used as parameter types of appropriate operations within all the architectural layers. Here, we illustrate this by analysing the system dynamics and showing how data flows through these layers. We use the 'Create new

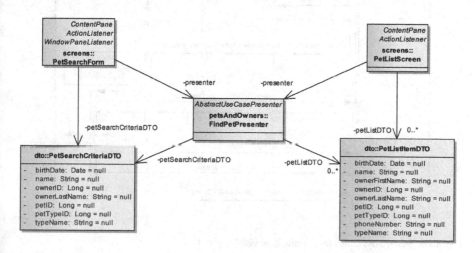

Fig. 8.17 DTO classes for 'Find pet'

visit' use case for this purpose. It contains a typical functionality that follows uniform rules and can be extended also to other use cases of our case study.

The scenarios of 'Create new visit' (see Fig. 8.10) are transformed into dynamic working code that involves all the presented architectural layers of the system. To understand interactions between individual objects, we can use UML sequence diagrams presented in Figs. 8.18 and 8.19. These diagrams show only the interactions between objects that are instances of the classes introduced earlier in this section. It also introduces messages that reflect operations defined within these classes. More details on how the particular methods of these operations work are presented in the following sections.

Figure 8.18 shows the system's dynamics that implements the first seven scenario sentences (see Fig. 8.10). The presented sequence starts when a 'FindPetPresenter' object passes control to a 'CreateNewVisitPresenter' object. This is part of a typical sequence that implements an invocation between two use cases. The diagram does not show the initial interaction between a UI element and the 'FindPetPresenter' object which will be discussed later. Following this initial interaction, the invoking presenter passes the ID of the currently selected pet ('setInputPetID') and then calls the 'invoke' operation.

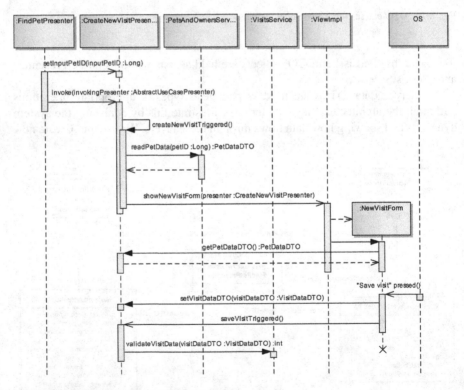

Fig. 8.18 System dynamics for 'Create new visit'—part 1

The next step is to read the pet data based on the pet's ID by calling 'readPetData' on the appropriate Model layer object. The call is made from the 'createNewVisitTriggered' method generated from sentences 2 and 3 to handle the initial user interaction. After reading pet data, the method asks the View layer object to show the appropriate form. The 'ViewImpl' object creates the 'NewVisitForm' object which then renders the form on the screen. This is preceded by reading pet data which is used to fill in the respective widgets in the form.

Further sequence is executed when the user selects the 'save visit' button (see sentence 6 in the scenario). This is associated with passing the visit data down to the Presenter and Model layers. Thus, the appropriate event handler first calls 'setVisitDataDTO' on the related Presenter layer object ('CreateNewVisitPresenter'), and then calls 'saveVisitTriggered', finally passing control to the Presenter layer.

This starts the sequence of messages that derive from scenario sentences from no. 7 onward, presented in Fig. 8.19. The first step is to validate the data just entered by the user. This is done by the appropriate Model layer object ('VisitsService'). Based on the result of the validation, one of two possible scenarios can happen. The sequence diagram presents only the main scenario ('ret == 1').

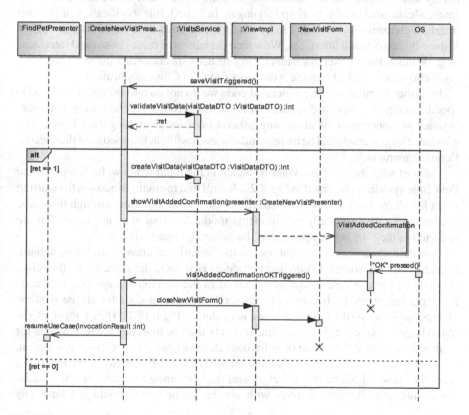

Fig. 8.19 System dynamics for 'Create new visit'—part 2

If the data are valid, the Presenter layer decides to call 'createVisitData' which should update persistent storage with the new data. This is followed by a sequence that presents the confirmation message on the screen and closes the new visit form. The final step is to resume control back to the invoking Presenter object ('resumeUse-Case').

The above-presented sequence reflects the contents of code generated automatically by transformation. It reflects the sematic rules defined in Chap. 4. The presented general architecture and system dynamics can be applied to various technological contexts. In the following sections, we present details of the generated code that are specific to the technology framework used in this case study.

8.4 User Interface Code

To generate the detailed user interface code, we have to decide on the specific UI technology. In our case study we use Echo3[6] as a representation of several contemporary technologies that are compatible with the MVP framework and are based on Java code, instead of, e.g. markup languages. In Echo3, full specification of the user interface elements and layouts can be made within Java code based on appropriate framework classes and interfaces. We notice the names of these classes and interfaces (e.g. 'WindowPane', 'ActionListener') in Fig. 8.15 specialised/realised by the View layer classes that reflect specific windows of the Pet Clinic application.

In further discussion of the generated code we do not go into the details of Echo3-specific code; the interested reader can refer to appropriate Echo3 documentation. Instead, we concentrate on discussing general rules for generating the UI code. The presented fragments should be understandable even without knowledge of the specific Echo3 constructs.

We start with the simplest window, which is the main window. Its layout for the Pet Clinic system is presented in Fig. 8.20. Recall that the main window is the starting point for all the use cases that are directly related with the actors through the usage relationship. Our case study requirements model has four such use cases that are reflected in the four buttons present in the generated main window.

The main window code concentrates on the 'MainPage' class generated by default, regardless of the source requirements model. However, the contents of this class depends on the use case model as discussed in the previous paragraph. This code is simple and short. It also shows the general structure of code for all the window classes, so it is worthwhile to discuss it in detail. Figure 8.21 shows most of the 'MainPage' class' code. We have removed only the few lines that are responsible for setting the layout and the style of individual elements not relevant to our discussion.

As we can see, 'MainPage' is situated within the UI framework by inheriting from the standard 'ContentPane' class and implementing the standard 'ActionListener' interface. Readers familiar with similar frameworks should not have any

---

[6] http://echo.nextapp.com/site/echo3.

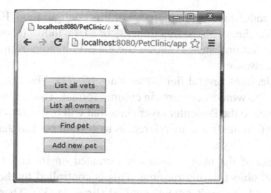

Fig. 8.20 Pet Clinic application main page

```
01:public class MainPage extends ContentPane implements ActionListener {
02:  private Column column; private MainPresenter presenter;
03:  private Button listAllVetsButton; private Button listAllOwnersButton;
04:  private Button findPetButton; private Button addNewPetButton;
05:  public MainPage(MainPresenter presenter){
06:    this.presenter = presenter;
07:    column = new Column(); /* ... */ add(column);
08:    addContent();
09:  }
10:  public void actionPerformed(ActionEvent e){
11:    if (e.getActionCommand().equals("listAllVetsButton")) {
12:      presenter.invokeListAllVets();
13:    }
14:    if (e.getActionCommand().equals("listAllOwnersButton")) {
15:      presenter.invokeListAllOwners();
16:    }
17:    if (e.getActionCommand().equals("findPetButton")) {
18:      presenter.invokeFindPet();
19:    }
20:    if (e.getActionCommand().equals("addNewPetButton")) {
21:      presenter.invokeAddNewPet();
22:    }
23:  }
24:  private void addContent(){
25:    listAllVetsButton = new Button("List all vets");
26:    listAllVetsButton.setStyleName("Button.Default");
27:    listAllVetsButton.setActionCommand("listAllVetsButton");
28:    listAllVetsButton.addActionListener(this);
29:    column.add(listAllVetsButton);
30:    listAllOwnersButton = new Button("List all owners");
31:    /* ... */ column.add(listAllOwnersButton);
32:    findPetButton = new Button("Find pet");
33:    /* ... */ column.add(findPetButton);
34:    addNewPetButton = new Button("Add new pet");
35:    /* ... */ column.add(addNewPetButton);
36:  }
37:}
```

Fig. 8.21 'MainPage' code

problem with understanding the purpose of this configuration. Extending 'Content-Pane' equips our class with the functionality of a UI window (showing, closing, etc.). Implementing 'ActionListener' allows the class to handle events coming from the user (button presses, etc.).

The class declares several fields (see lines 02–04). The first field ('column') is used to lay out the window contents in column format. The second field ('presenter') holds a reference to the Presenter layer class that will respond to user-related events. The remaining four fields declare references to the four buttons that need to be present in the window.

The contents of the main window are created on instantiation (creation) of a 'MainWindow' object during runtime. This is controlled by the class' constructor (lines 05–09) and the 'addContent' method (lines 24–37). These two methods are simple and their code is self-explanatory. The 'presenter' object is supplied to the 'MainPage' object as the parameter of the constructor by the application's overall dependency creation framework. After setting the presenter and creating the overall window layout, the 'addContent' method creates the four button objects. For each of the objects, the label text and style is defined and the appropriate event handling operation are indicated.

The events related to the four buttons are handled by the standard 'actionPer-formed' method (lines 10–23). As we can see, the code inside this method is very obvious. It has four condition statements that determine which button was pressed. Depending on this, an appropriate operation is called on the associated 'presenter' object. In the next section, we see how this is handled by the Presenter layer.

The simple code of 'MainPage' has to be extended for more complex form windows that are part of the Pet Clinic's user interface. The amount of code raises dramatically for even simple forms, so we show only the most interesting excerpts. We base our analysis of typical form window code on the 'Pet search form' window, whose layout is shown in Fig. 8.22. The window contains only two fields, which is consistent with the appropriate definition of the source domain model shown in Fig. 8.6. The first field is a purely textual field, and the second field is a date field. Also, the form contains two buttons; the first is the 'Back' button generated by default in all the windows (except the main one) and the second is derived from the 'Find pet' use case scenarios (see again Fig. 8.6) which indicate (sentence 4) that the 'Pet search form' should allow to select the 'Seek' button. This simple form is implemented with the code shown partially in Figs. 8.23, 8.24 and 8.25.

Figure 8.23 introduces the declaration of the 'PetSearchForm' class and its fields. The field declaration is significantly extended in comparison to that contained in the 'MainPage' class. The declarations of the two buttons (lines 03 and 16) and the 'presenter' (line 15) are similar to those in 'MainPage'. The declarations of the two form fields necessitate additional class field declarations, where each form field has an associated 'Label' and a 'TextField' (lines 08–10). The date field has additional associated fields that hold the date setting button and the calendar dialogue for selecting the date (lines 11–12).

Figure 8.24 presents the most important parts of the code that initiates the contents of 'PetSearchForm' objects. This code is much more elaborate than that for 'Main-Page', but follows the same general rules. It contains more sophisticated formatting

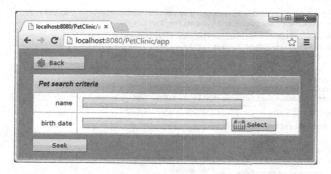

Fig. 8.22 'Pet search form' in the 'Find pet' use case

```
01:public class PetSearchForm extends ContentPane
02:    implements ActionListener, WindowPaneListener {

03:    private Button _closeButton;
04:    private Column column; private Grid grid;
05:    private GridLayoutData gridLayout;
06:    private ResourceBundle labels;

07:    private Label petSearchCriteriaHeaderLabel;

08:    private Label nameLabel; private TextField nameTextField;

09:    private Label birthDateLabel;
10:    private TextField birthDateTextField;
11:    private Button birthDateButton;
12:    private DateSelectionDialog dateSelectionDialog;
13:    private TextField _currentDateTextField = null

14:    private PetSearchCriteriaDTO petSearchCriteriaDTO = null;

15:    private FindPetPresenter presenter;

16:    private Button seekButton;

17:    /* ... */
18:}
```

Fig. 8.23 'PetSearchForm' attributes

that includes the 'column' and the 'grid' objects. For clarity, we have removed some of the code related to setting field styles and layouts. What is left is–generally—the consecutive creation of window widgets that represent individual labels, text fields and buttons. All these elements were derived automatically based on detailed platform-specific transformation rules for the View layer. Of course, the developers might want to change these default characteristics. To do this, they would need to either change the generated code manually or update the transformation program. We discuss this in the last section of this chapter.

Code presented in Fig. 8.25 is independent of the window layouts and is responsible for handling events that come from active window elements. In our example, these are the three buttons of 'Pet search form'. The 'actionPerformed' method is structured similar to that in the 'MainPage' class and contains three condition statements for each of the buttons. Pressing the standard 'Close' button (lines 02–04) results in calling a standard procedure that closes the current window and finalises the use case. This finalisation is associated with checking if the current window was

```
01:public PetSearchForm(FindPetPresenter presenter, ResourceBundle labels){
02:   this.presenter = presenter; this.labels = labels;

03:   column = new Column(); column.setInsets(new Insets(30, 15));
04:   column.setCellSpacing(new Extent(10));
05:   column.setStyleName("Column.ContentPane"); add(column);

06:   _closeButton = new Button(labels.getString("Button.Back"));
07:   _closeButton.setStyleName("Button.Back");
08:   _closeButton.setActionCommand("_closeButton");
09:   _closeButton.addActionListener(this); column.add(_closeButton);

10:   addContent();

11:   petSearchCriteriaDTO = new PetSearchCriteriaDTO();
12:}

13:private void addContent(){
14:   grid = new Grid(2); /* ... */ column.add(grid);

15:   petSearchCriteriaHeaderLabel =
16:      newLabel(labels.getString("HeaderLabel.petSearchCriteria"));
17:   gridLayout = new GridLayoutData(); /* ... */
18:   petSearchCriteriaHeaderLabel.setLayoutData(gridLayout);
19:   petSearchCriteriaHeaderLabel.setStyleName("Label.Header");
20:   grid.add(petSearchCriteriaHeaderLabel);

21:   nameLabel = new Label("name "); /* ... */ grid.add(nameLabel);
22:   nameTextField = new TextField(); /* ... */ grid.add(nameTextField);

23:   birthDateLabel = new Label("birth date "); /* ... */  grid.add(birthDateLabel);
24:   Row birthDateRow = new Row(); /* ... */ grid.add(birthDateRow);
25:   Column birthDateCol1 = new Column(); /* ... */ birthDateRow.add(birthDateCol1);
26:   Column birthDateCol2 = new Column(); /* ... */ birthDateRow.add(birthDateCol2);
27:   birthDateTextField = new TextField(); /* ... */ birthDateCol1.add(birthDateTextField);

28:   birthDateButton = new Button(labels.getString("Button.Select"));
29:   birthDateButton.setStyleName("Button.Calendar");
30:   birthDateButton.setActionCommand("birthDateButton");
31:   birthDateButton.addActionListener(this); birthDateCol2.add(birthDateButton);

32:   seekButton = new Button(labels.getString("Button.seek"));
33:   seekButton.setStyleName("Button.Default");
34:   seekButton.setActionCommand("seekButton");
35:   seekButton.addActionListener(this); column.add(seekButton);
36:}
```

Fig. 8.24 'PetSearchForm' content population

the only opened within the current use case's logic and if so—resuming the invoking use case logic.

When the user presses the 'Select' button for the 'birth date' field (lines 05–10), the event handler evokes standard code that opens a date selection dialogue. The dialogue places the selected date in the appropriate field of the 'PetSearchForm' object. Finally, pressing the 'Seek' button (lines 11–15) results in calling further application logic according to the current use case's scenario. In our case, this logic is contained in the method of the 'seekPetTriggered' operation, which is called in line 14. Calling further application logic should be associated with passing data entered in the form as is done in lines 12 and 13. The 'populateDTOs' method (lines 17–28) collects data from individual form fields and places them into an appropriate DTO ('petSearchCriteriaDTO'). These data are also initially validated using simple standard validation rules.

The 'Pet search form' contains only simple data and reacts to user interactions by passing this data to the Presenter. The next window of the 'Find pet' use case is the 'Pet list screen' (see once again Fig. 8.6). This time, the window has to handle multiple data elements (lists) and inform about the selected items when invoking

```
01:public void actionPerformed(ActionEvent e){
02:   if (e.getActionCommand().equals("_closeButton")) {
03:     presenter.closeCurrentPageAndFinalizeUseCase();
04:   }
05:   if (e.getActionCommand().equals("birthDateButton")) {
06:     dateSelectionDialog = new DateSelectionDialog(labels);
07:     dateSelectionDialog.addWindowPaneListener(this);
08:     this.add(dateSelectionDialog);
09:     _currentDateTextField = birthDateTextField;
10:   }
11:   if (e.getActionCommand().equals("seekButton")) {
12:     populateDTOs();
13:     presenter.setPetSearchCriteriaDTO(petSearchCriteriaDTO);
14:     presenter.seekTriggered();
15:   }
16:}

17:private void populateDTOs() {
18:   if (nameTextField.getText() != null)
19:     petSearchCriteriaDTO.setName(nameTextField.getText());
20:   if (birthDateTextField.getText() != null) {
21:     Date date = null;
22:     SimpleDateFormat dateFormat = new SimpleDateFormat("yyyy-MM-dd");
23:     try {
24:       date = dateFormat.parse(birthDateTextField.getText());
25:     } catch (ParseException e) { e.printStackTrace(); }
26:     petSearchCriteriaDTO.setBirthDate(date);
27:   }
28:}
```

Fig. 8.25 'PetSearchForm' event handling and data passing

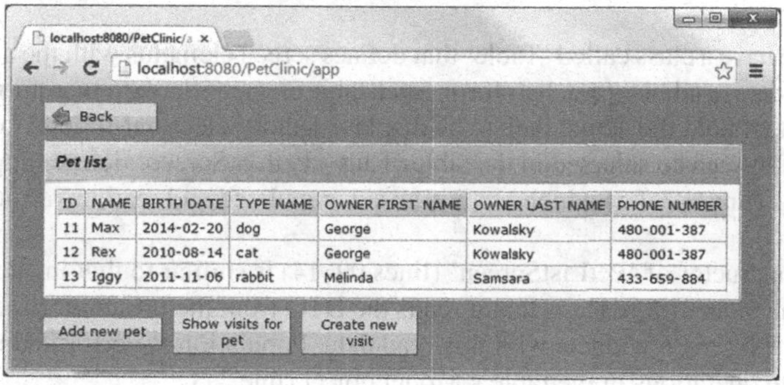

Fig. 8.26 'Pet list screen' in the 'Find pet' use case

logic defined through other use cases. The window's layout illustrated in Fig. 8.26 contains a list with several columns that reflect Attribute elements associated with the 'pet list' Data View in the source RSL model. Moreover, it contains three buttons derived from the three use cases which—according to the use case scenario—can be invoked when the 'Pet list screen' is displayed.

Figure 8.27 presents some interesting excerpts of the 'PetListScreen' class' code and shows only the elements that are characteristic for handling lists. Otherwise, the code is similar to that of 'PetSearchForm'. The first elements worth noting are the fields responsible for holding and supporting the widget that shows the pet list data. In

```
01:public class PetListScreen extends ContentPane implements ActionListener {
02:  /* ... */
03:    private Table petListTable;
04:    private DefaultListSelectionModel petListSelectionModel;
05:    private PetListTableModel petListTableModel;
06:  /* ... */
07:    private List<PetListItemDTO> petListDTO = null;
08:  /* ... */
09:    public PetListScreen(FindPetPresenter presenter, ResourceBundle labels){
10:      /* ... */
11:      addContent();

12:      petListDTO = presenter.getPetListDTO();
13:      populateControls();
14:    }

15:    public void actionPerformed(ActionEvent e){
16:      /* ... */
17:      if (e.getActionCommand().equals("createNewVisitButton")) {
18:        int row = petListSelectionModel.getMinSelectedIndex();
19:        if (row != -1) {
20:          long petID = petListTableModel.getRow(row).getPetID();
21:          presenter.setInvokePetID(petID); presenter.invokeCreateNewVisit();
22:        }
23:      }
24:    }

25:    private void populateControls() {
26:      if (petListDTO != null)
27:        petListTableModel.addRows(petListDTO);
28:    }
29:}
```

Fig. 8.27 'PetListScreen' code fragments

Echo3, we have a class called 'Table' that defines screen elements with the capability to present data in tabular (e.g. list) form. Such table elements have to be equipped with 'Models' that hold the actual data to be displayed and 'SelectionModels' that define the way items can be selected in the table. Thus, 'PetListScreen' defines appropriate three fields (lines 03–05) which are initialised, populated and read in various places in code.

The constructor of 'PetListScreen' (lines 09–14) is similar to that in 'PetSearch-Form'. The main difference is that it reads the DTO from the presenter (line 12) and populates the screen widgets with this read data. Population is performed using the appropriate operations in the table's Model object (line 27).

Note that the event handler code has to handle the selections within the pet list made by the user. This is illustrated by the code that responds to pressing the 'Create new visit' button. This is the starting point of the 'Create new visit' use case and the generated code follows the logic of the first two sentences in this invoked use case. The first step is thus to determine the row that is selected by the user (line 18). Following this, it is necessary to get the ID value of the selected pet (line 20) and pass it to the associated Presenter object (line 21). Only then, the appropriate invocation sequence can be called (line 21).

After invoking the 'Create new visit' use case we eventually reach the 'New visit form'. This window is presented in Fig. 8.28 and illustrates the situation where some data ('Pet data') are displayed and some data ('Visit data') are to be entered by the user.

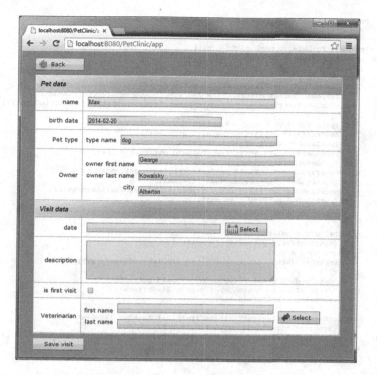

Fig. 8.28 'New visit form' in the 'Create new visit' use case

Appropriate code that handles this situation is presented in Fig. 8.29. The 'NewVis-itForm' class declares two fields (lines 04–05) to refer to the two data objects that should be handled by the window. The first object is used to populate the window's widget controls (lines 07–22). This is done in a straightforward code which goes through all the attributes of 'petDataDTO' and sets related controls (in this case—text fields). The second object is used to transfer data down to the Presenter and is populated with data from the related widget controls (lines 23–35). This is done similarly as in the 'PetSearchForm' class.

The generated code of the View layer contains 13 classes that reflect the Screen elements and 16 classes that reflect the Message elements. It is out of the scope of this book to discuss all of them.[7] Their code is in general similar to that already presented.

Figure 8.30 shows some additional element types that were generated from the Pet Clinic's RSL model. Notice that the date fields present in the forms have associated 'Select' buttons that open the appropriate date selection windows using standard Echo3 date selection functionality. Moreover, message windows are defined as popup windows. Their code is similar to that of "normal" windows but differs in setting specific switches that control the window's behaviour.

---

[7] The full code can be accessed from the book's website: http://www.redseeds.eu/fromrtoj.

```
01: public class NewVisitForm extends ContentPane implements ActionListener,
02: WindowPaneListener {
03: /* ... */
04:    private PetDataDTO petDataDTO = null;
05:    private VisitDataDTO visitDataDTO = null;
06: /* ... */
07:    private void populateControls() {
08:        if (petDataDTO.getBirthDate() != null) {
09:           SimpleDateFormat dateFormat = new SimpleDateFormat("yyyy-MM-dd");
10:           birthDateTextField.setText(dateFormat.format(petDataDTO.getBirthDate()));
11:        }
12:        if (petDataDTO.getName() != null)
13:           nameTextField.setText(petDataDTO.getName());
14:        if (petDataDTO.getTypeName() != null)
15:           typeNameTextField.setText(petDataDTO.getTypeName());
16:        if (petDataDTO.getOwnerFirstName() != null)
17:           ownerFirstNameTextField.setText(petDataDTO.getOwnerFirstName());
18:        if (petDataDTO.getOwnerLastName() != null)
19:           ownerLastNameTextField.setText(petDataDTO.getOwnerLastName());
20:        if (petDataDTO.getCity() != null)
21:           cityTextField.setText(petDataDTO.getCity());
22:    }

23:    private void populateDTOs() {
24:        if (dateTextField.getText() != null) {
25:           Date date = null;
26:           SimpleDateFormat dateFormat = new SimpleDateFormat("yyyy-MM-dd");
27:           try {
28:               date = dateFormat.parse(dateTextField.getText());
29:           } catch (ParseException e) { e.printStackTrace(); }
30:           visitDataDTO.setDate(date);
31:        }
32:        visitDataDTO.setIsFirstVisit(isFirstVisitCheckBox.isSelected());
33:        if (descriptionTextArea.getText() != null)
34:           visitDataDTO.setDescription(descriptionTextArea.getText());
35:    }
36:}
```

Fig. 8.29 'NewVisitForm' code fragments

Finally, the generated code offers 'Select' buttons for some of the fields (here: 'Pet type' and 'Owner'). This functionality is yet another extension of the RSL's semantics. The 'Select' buttons are generated for the attribute groups contained in the Concepts that are not the 'main concept' for the given Screen element (compare with Fig. 8.4). After pressing one of these buttons, the application searches through appropriate tables and allows to populate the form's fields with a selected item (e.g. the 'pet type'). This is a reasonable assumption, because these groups of attributes reflect data related to the main Concept and thus should be consistent with the objects already existing in the persistent storage.

8.5 Application Logic Code

The application logic can be made independent of any specific technology and based on plain Java classes. Yet, our example transformation generates code that uses some elements of the Spring framework to manage dependencies between objects in the dynamic system. In our examples we find several places that use instances of the

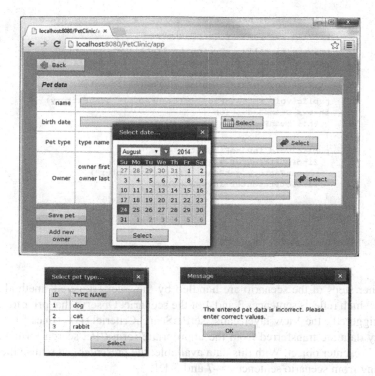

Fig. 8.30 UI elements in the 'Add new pet' use case

'BeanFactory' class that facilitates creating objects dynamically and managing their references. Otherwise, the presented code uses only standard Java constructs.

The influences of the Spring framework dominate in the central class of the Presenter layer which is the 'MainPresenter'. Some excerpts of its generated code are shown in Fig. 8.31. As mentioned in the previous section, the 'MainPresenter' object handles the user interface events that happen in the related 'MainWindow' object. In the presented example, we show only one of such handler methods (lines 11–14) responsible for starting the logic that implements the 'Find pet' use case whose contents are very basic. First, it gets a reference to the appropriate Presenter object (lines 12 and 13) and then calls its 'invoke' operation (line 14).

To see what happens when 'invoke' is called, let us analyse the code of the appropriate presenter class, shown in Fig. 8.32. It is best to analyse this code by comparing it with the use case's scenarios in Fig. 8.6. The 'invoke' method (lines 19–21) is simple as it generally calls the 'findPetTriggered' operation which is responsible for handling the first user interaction (sentence 1 of the scenario). According to the use case's scenario (sentence 2), the handler should show the 'Pet search form' which is exactly what it requests (line 14) by calling an appropriate operation of the 'IView' interface (note that the declaration of the 'view' field is present in 'AbstractUseCasePresenter').

```
01:public class MainPresenter implements BeanFactoryAware {
02:    private BeanFactory beanFactory;
03:    private ListAllVetsPresenter listAllVetsPresenter;
04:    private ListAllOwnersPresenter listAllOwnersPresenter;
05:    private FindPetPresenter findPetPresenter;
06:    private AddNewPetPresenter addNewPetPresenter;
07:    public void setBeanFactory(BeanFactory beanFactory)
08:    throws BeansException {
09:       this.beanFactory = beanFactory;
10:    }
11:    public void invokeFindPet() {
12:       findPetPresenter = (FindPetPresenter)
13:          beanFactory.getBean("findPetPresenter");
14:       findPetPresenter.invoke(null);
15:    }
16:    /* ... */
17:}
```

Fig. 8.31 'MainPresenter' code fragments

Further steps of the scenario are handled by the 'seekTriggered' method (lines 37–47) which reflects sentences 3 and 4 of the scenario. Observe that prior to calling 'seekTriggered', the View layer calls 'setPetSearchCriteriaDTO' (lines 51–54). In this way data are transferred from the appropriate form ('Pet search form') to the current Presenter object. With this data available, the presenter can realise the logic stemming from scenario sentences 5–7 and 5.1.1.

The first step is to read 'pet list' data, based on the 'pet search criteria'. This is implemented through a call to the relevant Model layer operation (line 38). The next lines implement the condition sentences that fork the use case's logic into two alternative scenarios. We have two 'if' statements that detect the result of 'readPetList'. Based on this, either the 'pet list screen' or the 'no pets found' message is shown.

The invocation sentences that follow sentence 7 are handled by three methods, where we show only the 'invokeCreateNewVisit' method (lines 22–27). The other two methods are similar. In general, the contents of these methods follow the approach already discussed for the 'MainPresenter'. The only addition is that—where necessary—appropriate ID data (see 'invokePetID', line 25) is passed to the invoked Presenter object. This ID data is previously set by the View layer object using an appropriate setter (see lines 48–50).

'FindPetPresenter' code is complemented by two methods that handle two possible events from the user, coming from the 'no pets found' message window. The first handler (lines 31–34) responds to pressing 'NO' which results in closing the 'pet search form' and finalising the use case. The second handler (response to 'YES') is empty, because the logic returns to the already active 'pet search form' (the 'no pets found' message is already closed upon pressing a button). Thus, no further actions in code are needed.

Very similar code to that of 'FindPetPresenter' is generated for the other Presenter layer classes. Figure 8.33 shows fragments of code for 'CreateNewVisitPresenter'.

```
01:public class FindPetPresenter extends AbstractUseCasePresenter {
02:   private IPetsAndOwners petsAndOwnersService;

03:   private Long invokePetID = null;
04:   private List<PetListItemDTO> petListDTO = null;
05:   private PetSearchCriteriaDTO petSearchCriteriaDTO = null;
06:   private CreateNewVisitPresenter createNewVisitPresenter;
07:   private AddNewPetPresenter addNewPetPresenter;
08:   private ShowVisitsForPetPresenter showVisitsForPetPresenter;

09:   public FindPetPresenter(){
10:     petsAndOwnersService =
11:       (IPetsAndOwners) beanFactory.getBean("petsAndOwnersService");
12:   }

13:   public void findPetTriggered(){
14:     view.showPetSearchForm(this);  pageOpened();
15:   }

16:   public List<PetListItemDTO> getPetListDTO(){
17:     return this.petListDTO;
18:   }

19:   public void invoke(AbstractUseCasePresenter invokingPresenter){
20:     super.invoke(invokingPresenter); findPetTriggered();
21:   }

22:   public void invokeCreateNewVisit(int resumeId){
23:     createNewVisitPresenter = (CreateNewVisitPresenter)
24:       beanFactory.getBean("createNewVisitPresenter");
25:     createNewVisitPresenter.setInputPetID(invokePetID);
26:     this.setResumeId(resumeId);  createNewVisitPresenter.invoke(this);
27:   }

28:   public void invokeCreateNewVisit(){
29:     invokeCreateNewVisit(-1);
30:   }

31:   public void noPetsFoundMessageNOTriggered(){
32:     view.closePetSearchForm(); pageClosed();
33:     setUseCaseResult(0); finalizeUseCase();
34:   }

35:   public void noPetsFoundMessageYESTriggered(){
36:   }

37:   public void seekTriggered(){
38:     petListDTO = petsAndOwnersService.readPetList(petSearchCriteriaDTO);
39:     if (!petListDTO.isEmpty()) { /* pets found [1] */
40:       view.closePetSearchForm(); pageClosed();
41:       view.showPetListScreen(this); pageOpened();
42:       setUseCaseResult(1); finalizeUseCase();
43:     }
44:     else if (petListDTO.isEmpty()) { /* no pets found [0] */
45:       view.showNoPetsFoundMessage(this);
46:     }
47:   }

48:   public void setInvokePetID(Long invokePetID){
49:     this.invokePetID = invokePetID;
50:   }

51:   public void setPetSearchCriteriaDTO
52:     (PetSearchCriteriaDTO petSearchCriteriaDTO){
53:     this.petSearchCriteriaDTO = petSearchCriteriaDTO;
54:   }
55:   /* ... */
56:}
```

Fig. 8.32 'FindPetPresenter' code fragments

```
01:public class CreateNewVisitPresenter extends AbstractUseCasePresenter {
02:    private IVisits visitsService;
03:    private IPetsAndOwners petsAndOwnersService;

04:    private Long inputPetID = null;
05:    private PetDataDTO petDataDTO = null;
06:    private VisitDataDTO visitDataDTO = null;

07:    public CreateNewVisitPresenter(){
08:      visitsService = (IVisits) beanFactory.getBean("visitsService");
09:      petsAndOwnersService =
10:         (IPetsAndOwners) beanFactory.getBean("petsAndOwnersService");
11:    }

12:    public PetDataDTO getPetDataDTO(){
13:      return this.petDataDTO;
14:    }

15:    public void invalidVisitDataMessageOKTriggered(){
16:    }

17:    public void invoke(AbstractUseCasePresenter invokingPresenter){
18:      super.invoke(invokingPresenter); createNewVisitTriggered();
19:    }

20:    public void createNewVisitTriggered(){
21:      petDataDTO = petsAndOwnersService.readPetData(inputPetID);
22:      view.showNewVisitForm(this);
23:      pageOpened();
24:    }

25:    public void saveVisitTriggered(){
26:      int result;
27:      result = visitsService.validateVisitData(visitDataDTO);
28:      if (result == 1) { /* data correct [1] */
29:        visitsService.createVisitData(visitDataDTO);
30:        view.showVisitAddedConfirmation(this);
31:      }
32:      else if (result == 0) { /* data incorrect [0] */
33:        view.showInvalidVisitDataMessage(this);
34:      }
35:    }

36:    public void setInputPetID(Long inputPetID){
37:      this.inputPetID = inputPetID;
38:    }

39:    public void setVisitDataDTO(VisitDataDTO visitDataDTO){
40:      this.visitDataDTO = visitDataDTO;
41:    }

42:    public void visitAddedConfirmationOKTriggered(){
43:      view.closeNewVisitForm(); pageClosed(); setUseCaseResult(1);
44:      finalizeUseCase();
45:    }
46:    /* ... */
47:}
```

Fig. 8.33 'CreateNewVisitPresenter' code fragments

As we can see, this code follows the same scheme as in 'FindPetPresenter'. This should be obvious if we consider that it has been generated automatically using uniform semantic rules of RSL. Similar to the discussion in the previous paragraphs, we can compare code in Fig. 8.33 with the respective use case scenarios in Fig. 8.10. Full code of the other Presenter classes and the whole Pet Clinic application can be found at the book's website.

In discussing the Pet Clinic's code, we did not yet introduce the details of the Model layer classes. This layer is generated with empty methods because they could not be derived from RSL models using the semantic rules as in Chap. 4. Thus, the Model layer code contains just method headers, so it would not be interesting to include it in our discussion. It can be easily deduced from the Presenter layer code that contains calls to appropriate operations on the Model layer interfaces. In the case study examples, we have used manually created stubs that return appropriate data. This allowed to populate the presented forms and lists with example contents.

8.6 Discussion

The presented case study shows most of the potential of Model-Driven Requirements Engineering based on RSL. We were able to obtain a fully functional prototype of a simple system in only one working day. It took around 5 h to develop detailed scenarios and the domain model for the dozen use cases of the Pet Clinic system. Additional 1–2 h had to be spent on correcting errors in the application logic within the scenarios. The rest of our experimental working day was used for developing simple stubs for the Model layer.

Of course, the complexity of the Pet Clinic system is not impressive. Typical business systems normally implement tens or even hundreds of use cases of the size presented in the study. However, we can argue that the effort to develop the Pet Clinic system can be extrapolated onto larger systems. A good example is the SZOK system, briefly introduced in Sect. 7.3. This system consists of several tens of use cases formulated in RSL and it was redeveloped using the presented application logic reuse method. Our experience shows that developing such a system is proportional in effort to developing a small system with around a dozen use cases.

This can be explained by the fact that the complexity of application logic rises proportionally with the number of use cases. Use case models do not contain complex dependencies and architectures that could cause exponential growth of their complexity in the function of the number of use cases. What is more, also the growth in complexity of the domain model does not exhibit characteristics of an exponential function but rather rises proportionally with the growth in the number of use cases. This second observation can be explained by the fact that the domain models are formed into "islands" of interdependent domain elements (Concepts, Screens, Triggers, etc.), concentrated around specific use cases. This is well illustrated in Figs. 8.4, 8.5, 8.6, 8.7, 8.8, 8.9, 8.10, 8.11 and 8.12. Note that each use case introduces somewhat the same number of new domain elements. The number of new domain elements and relationships between them does not seem to show any dependency on the current number of use cases in the model. Of course, the above observations necessitate more detailed studies and collection of more empirical data, which can be an interesting direction of future research effort.

Most importantly, the results of the case study show significant shift in complexity of the development artefacts. At the level of RSL models, we have to handle

10–30 sentences per use case and around 5–15 domain elements with related attributes. When we transform this into Java code, we obtain much more complex configuration with several classes, operations and many lines of Java code. This can be illustrated, e.g. for the 'Find pets' use case presented in detail in the previous sections. The application logic of this use case contains 19 sentences (including 9 SVO sentence, 4 condition sentences, 3 invocation sentences and 3 final/rejoin sentences). These sentences refer to 10 domain elements (3 Concepts, 2 Screens, 1 Message, 2 Triggers and 2 Data Views) with 6 Attributes. It thus totals to 35 development "items".

This can be compared with the size of the generated Java code which is necessary to implement the RSL model and is semantically equivalent. This code involves 7 classes (1 Presenter class, 4 View classes, 2 DTOs) and 2 interfaces. In total, these units are composed of 61 fields, 85 operation declarations with full signatures (parameters, etc.) and 306 lines of method content code.[8] Thus, in total, the developers need to handle 461 "items". Moreover, these items are much more technology-oriented than the items in the RSL model. Similar figures can be given for the other use cases of our study.

As we can see, the RSL model contains an order of magnitude less (35 vs. 461) elements to be specified and managed by developers. This very significant reduction in complexity can be compared with the shift from assembly to 3GL programming. Every instruction in a 3G language (like Java) is equivalent to several instructions in assembly/machine code or some other code, executable directly by the computer (or through a virtual machine). We can thus conclude that Model-Driven Requirements Engineering promises a similar reduction in complexity as achieved by the introduction of contemporary third generation programming languages. Yet, this statement deserves the backing of more elaborate experimental studies which form another interesting research agenda.

When analysing the benefits of using formal requirements models, we need to consider also the effort needed to formulate requirements in a typical software development process. Models written in RSL reflect software requirements that need to be formulated anyway. This can be done in less formal notations and involve somewhat less effort. However, the application logic and the data items that need to be manipulated through the user interface need to be specified with full precision at some point, in all cases. This is preferably done by skilled requirements analysts together with the end-users. However, in many projects, very detailed decisions about the application logic, are made arbitrarily by the programmers already at implementation time. This often leads to poor user satisfaction and change requests pertaining to the "finished" system.

Software development based on RSL (and MDRE in general) has the potential to significantly improve the above-presented situation. First, we note that writing RSL models is similar to developing 3GL code but at a much higher level of abstraction. It has to be precise and any change in the model has its consequences in the resulting

---

[8] Note that the calculated lines of code include only the effective method contents, without the method signatures, comments, empty lines, closing brackets and import statements.

application. Thus, the cost of introducing RSL is that development of requirements models is more difficult and time-consuming than writing requirements traditionally. Specifically, writing—for instance—a use case scenario in RSL takes more time than writing an informal use case scenario using natural language. This is one side of the issue.

On the other hand, we should remember that writing RSL "code" combines two activities into one. It is—at the same time—requirements formulation and writing effective code. Thus, the effort to write requirements in RSL pays off in savings associated with treating requirements as first-class citizens in the software development process. The RSL specification can be thoroughly discussed with end-users and brought to a precise level. Requirements specifications with a comparable level of detail can be found as contractual artefacts in many software development projects. The breakthrough advantage of RSL is that precise requirements can be instantly turned into a running application that can be examined by end-users and validated against their expectations.

The remaining issue is that the system generated from an RSL model is not fully functional. As pointed out in Sect. 8.1, we did not expect to construct a fully operational system for the Pet Clinic but only a prototype that contained full user interface and application logic (flow of control through the user interface). The developers still have to undertake activities at the Java level to implement the business domain logic and data persistence operations. These activities are significantly facilitated by the fact that the generated code has clear, uniform structure and is equipped with a visual "map" in the form of the generated UML class model. The developers simply need to implement methods for the already generated Model layer operations, as required by the Presenter layer classes.

The necessity to develop code at the 3GL level raises an idea to extend RSL to be able to also specify the business domain logic (data processing) and operations for data persistence. This would eliminate the need to write Java code almost completely (except for some potential optimisation issues). This idea extends to specifying the layout and detailed look-and-feel of the user interface. Currently, the transformations generate very rudimentary windows with basic widgets, laid out in a standard way. We would certainly appreciate having much more control over how the user interface behaves and looks.

The above idea to extend RSL in various direction opens a very wide area of research and innovation. We can already indicate several potential directions of improving RSL by equipping it with more detailed syntax and developing more advanced transformations.

- *Generation of the database.* This extension necessitates defining detailed semantic rules for transformations that would turn RSL domain models (Concepts, Attributes, etc.) to database schemas. It may also need to involve some changes in the RSL's syntax that would allow for controlling the generation process.
- *Generation of CRUD domain logic.* This extension is related with developing detailed semantics for the System-to-DataView SVO sentences which evoke specific domain logic operations. The sentences with standard CRUD operation types

(see Sect. 2.3.3) can be turned into appropriate data persistence code using a selected data persistence framework.

- *Combining RSL with 3GL code for domain logic.* The domain logic can be specified directly in a 3G language like Java. However, instead of manually weaving this code into the code generated from RSL, we can think of linking Java procedures to individual SVO sentences. This would allow the transformation to weave the explicit Java code automatically into the code generated from RSL.
- *Combining RSL with Domain Specific Languages.* This approach is similar to the previous one, but instead of using Java we use a DSL. In this way, the domain logic is specified in a less technology-specific language. This approach necessitates that the RSL-based transformation is combined with a DSL-based transformation.
- *Extending RSL syntax for UI elements.* This includes a wide set of possible extensions. One of them involves adding the syntax to reflect form layouts and generally—positions of various elements in windows. With such an extension, the RSL editor could be combined with a window layout editor that would allow for designing window layouts to be generated in the resulting code. Another possible extension consists in adding initial field validation. This would involve extending the syntax of RSL with a notation to define various data formats which would be the basis for generating the validation code.
- *Defining access policies.* The RSL semantics can be extended by defining policies to access data and application logic. This can be initially based on the existing syntax for relationships between actors and use cases. However, to implement more detailed security rules, it will be perhaps necessary to define special syntax for use case preconditions and equip RSL with data access adornments attached to domain elements (Concepts).

The above-indicated directions for RSL certainly do not exhaust all the possibilities. In general, we envision a significant potential to turn requirements modelling languages into fully capable general-purpose programming languages. Such languages would be able to hide the complexity of the underlying specific technology frameworks. The developers would then be able to concentrate on the essential complexity of the problem at hand and the logic of the application, as seen by end-users. At the same time, development activities could become more accessible to less technical people and end-users could be more explicitly involved in the development of software systems through direct cooperation with professional developers in formulating requirements-level "programs".

We hope that the presented case study and the whole book will inspire readers and give them the motivation to follow the research directions proposed. We believe that the current results, presented in this book already show that development of languages like RSL can lead to a significant rise in the productivity of software development teams.

Appendix A
Summary of RSL Syntax

This appendix presents a concise reference of the RSL syntax. The syntax is divided into three parts: Requirements (with use cases and packages), Scenarios and sentences, and Domain elements. Each of the RSL elements is explained in terms of its concrete syntax, abstract syntax and semantics. For the concrete syntax, examples with relations to other RSL elements are given.

A.1 Requirements

Requirement

Concrete Syntax and Example

Generic *Requirement* is depicted as a rectangle with two additional vertical lines on its left. *Requirements* 'ID' is written in the top left corner of the box. *Requirements* 'name' is written in the centre of the rectangle. Additionally, *Requirements* can be presented with minimised icons in tree structures (see 'Requirements Package').

FRO75	CR251	QR251
Editing the user lists	Network throughput limit	Response time of entry gate

Abstract Syntax

Requirements 'name' is a 'Hyperlinked Sentence'. *Requirement* is detailed with one or more 'Requirement Representation'. *Requirements* can be related with other *Requirements* through 'Requirement Relationships'. They can be grouped into 'Requirements Packages'. *Requirement* is the superclass for 'Use Case'.

© Springer International Publishing Switzerland 2015
M. Śmiałek and W. Nowakowski, *From Requirements to Java in a Snap*,
DOI 10.1007/978-3-319-12838-2

Semantics

Requirement is understood as a placeholder for one or more 'Requirement Representations'. It is treated as a concise way to symbolise this representation. Requirement is very general and it can express every kind of required feature of the system to be built.

Use Case

Concrete Syntax and Example

Use Case concrete syntax is an extension of UML's concrete syntax for use cases: "A use case is shown as an ellipse, either containing the name of the use case or with the name of the use case placed below the ellipse." As for any Requirement, every Use Case icon can present an 'ID'. Additionally, Use Cases can be presented with minimised icons in tree structures (see 'Requirements Package').

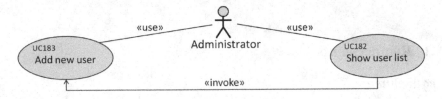

Abstract Syntax

Use Case is a specialisation of 'Requirement'. Instances of *Use Case* can be related with each other by 'Invocation Relationships'. *Use Case* can contain several 'Participation' relationships and can be pointed to by 'Usage' relationships. These relationships relate it with 'Actors'. It can contain 'representations', which usually are 'Constrained Language Scenarios'.

Semantics

Use Case derives its meaning from that defined in UML: "A use case is the specification of a set of actions performed by a system, which yields an observable result that is, typically, of value for one or more actors or other stakeholders of the system." This definition is analogous to the one specified in Sect. 1.2.2. The semantics in RSL is extended by stating that *Use Case* is a special kind of Requirement, thus being a placeholder for its 'representations'. These 'representations' describe the observable behaviour (set of actor-system interactions) for the *Use Case*.

Attribute

Concrete Syntax and Example

Attribute is expressed through its name and (possibly multiple) values in the following textual syntax:

```
attribute name '=' value [',' value]
```

When showing *Attributes* on requirements diagrams, the above syntax can be placed in a "note" (similar to a UML Comment), i.e. in a rectangle with a corner bent and connected to the appropriate RSL element (requirement or domain element) with a dashed line.

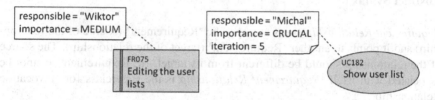

Abstract Syntax

Attribute can be a component of any 'Requirement', 'Use Case' or 'Domain Element'. *Attribute* can have multiple 'AttributeValues' associated with it.

Semantics

Attributes are entities that contain properties of various RSL elements. These properties do not define the requirements or the domain as such but they define the RSL elements' external features, usually associated with the software development project. Attributes are thus containers for external (e.g. project-related) value(s), which should be attached to RSL elements.

Requirement Relationship

Concrete Syntax and Example

Requirement Relationship is drawn as a dashed line connecting two 'Requirements'. An open arrowhead is drawn on the end of the line indicating the target of the relationship. The line can be labeled with a stereotype determining the type of the relationship (see 'Invocation Relationship'). The line may consist of many orthogonal or oblique segments.

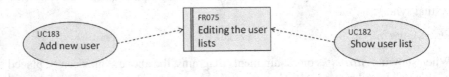

Abstract Syntax

Requirement Relationship starts at a specific 'Requirement' (source of the relationship) and it points to another 'Requirement' (target of the relationship). The source of the relationship should be different from its target—a 'Requirement' cannot be associated with itself. *Requirement Relationship* is the superclass for 'Invocation Relationship'.

Semantics

Requirement Relationship denotes a conceptual relation between two requirements. The nature of this relation (e.g. similarity, conflict, trace, fulfillment) is specified by a stereotype that can be associated with the *Requirement Relationship*.

Invocation Relationship

Concrete Syntax and Example

Invocation Relationship is denoted similarly to the 'Requirement Relationship'. The dashed line has to be adorned with the «invoke» stereotype notation. The line has an open arrowhead at one of the ends.

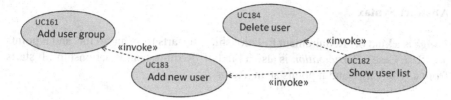

Abstract Syntax

Invocation Relationship is a kind of 'Requirement Relationship'. The source and the target elements are always 'Use Cases'. *Invocation Relationship* points at an 'Invocation Sentence', which must be contained in a 'Requirement Representation' of the 'Use Case' which is the source of the relationship.

Semantics

Invocation Relationship substitutes the UML's «include» and «extend» relationships and unifies their disadvantageous semantics. *Invocation Relationship* denotes that another 'Use Case' can be invoked from within the currently performed 'Use Case'. After executing one of the final 'Sentences' in the invoked 'Use Case', the flow of control returns to the invoking use case right after the point of invocation. The exact point of invocation and the use case to be invoked are defined by a special kind of scenario sentence—the 'Invocation Sentence'.

Usage and Participation

Concrete Syntax and Example

The concrete syntax of *Usage* and *Participation* is a solid line drawn between an 'Actor' and a 'Use Case'. *Usage* is adorned with the «use» stereotype notation, and *Participation* is adorned with «participate». Alternatively, *Usage* can be drawn as an arrow pointing towards a 'Use Case', and *Participation* points in the opposite direction.

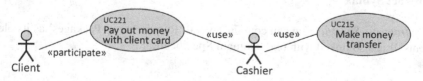

Abstract Syntax

Usage is a kind of 'Requirement Relationship'. It starts from an 'Actor' and it points at a 'Use Case'. *Participation* is also a kind of 'Requirement Relationship'. It starts from a 'Use Case' and it points at an 'Actor'.

Semantics

Usage indicates that a given 'Actor' initiates a particular 'Use Case'. This 'Actor' is the primary actor for this 'Use Case', i.e. one that starts the use case to reach the use case's goal. *Participation* indicates that a given 'Actor' is a secondary 'Actor' for a particular 'Use Case'. It means that this actor does not initiate the use case but interacts with the system while the use case instance is running. This interaction is started by the system asking the actor to perform some actions.

Requirements Specification

Concrete Syntax and Example

Concrete syntax for *Requirements Specifications* is almost the same as for UML's 'Packages': "A package is shown as a large rectangle with a small rectangle (a 'tab') attached to the left side of the top of the large rectangle." Their names are placed inside the large rectangle. In addition to concrete syntax for plain Packages, *Requirements Specification* icons have one thick vertical line on their left. They can also be presented in a Project Tree structure with a minimised icon being the root of the requirements specification tree.

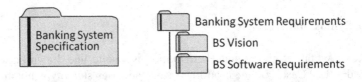

Abstract Syntax

Requirements Specification can contain several 'Requirements Packages' as its elements. It is also linked with one 'Domain Specification'.

Semantics

Requirements Specification is the main container of the requirements part of an RSL model. It can contain all the requirements-related elements for a given project— 'Requirements' grouped into appropriate 'Requirements Packages'. It can be treated as an equivalent of a 'Model' (cf. requirements model) in UML.

Requirements Package

Concrete Syntax and Example

The syntax for *Requirements Packages* is similar to that for 'Requirements Specifications'. The icon has two thin vertical lines on the left. *Requirements Packages* can be presented in Project Trees with minimised icons.

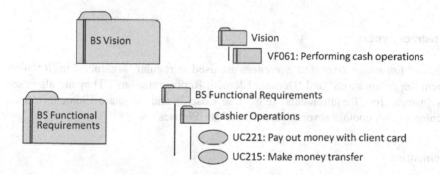

Abstract Syntax

Requirements Package can have owned members which are 'Requirements' and 'Use Cases'. It can also have nested 'Requirements Packages'. Every *Requirements Package* is part of a 'Requirements Specification' or another *Requirements Package*.

Semantics

Requirements Package is the basic grouping element within the requirements part of an RSL model. It can contain 'Requirements' (and 'Use Cases' as their specialisations) as well as nested 'Requirements Packages'.

A.2   Sentences and Scenarios

Natural Language Hypertext Sentence

Concrete Syntax and Example

Natural Language Hypertext Sentence is expressed as a string of free natural language texts. This text can contain several 'Hyperlinks'. These hyperlinks point to various 'Phrases' and are marked by underlining and blue colour of the font. Another variant for representing hyperlinks within *Natural Language Hypertext Sentences* is to insert them in double square brackets.

The system shall allow the *cashier* to *withdraw cash* on behalf of the *bank client*.

```
To acknowledge, the [[bank client]] has to [[swipe : the : bank card]].
```

Abstract Syntax

Natural Language Hypertext Sentences are used as regular 'sentences' in 'Requirement Representations' and 'Domain Element Representations'. They are also used as 'names' for 'Requirements' (e.g. 'Use Cases') and 'Domain Elements'. Such sentences can contain several 'Hyperlinks' to 'Phrases'.

Semantics

Natural Language Hypertext Sentence can be used in the most generic, natural language descriptions and names of various RSL elements. They extend free text with inserted wiki-like 'Hyperlinks'. In this way, a coherent connection to 'Phrases' contained in the domain vocabulary is made possible.

Precondition and Postcondition Sentences

Concrete Syntax and Example

Precondition and *Postcondition* sentences are similar in their concrete syntax to 'Natural Language Hypertext Sentences'. They can contain 'Hyperlinks' but generally they contain free text. *Precondition* and *Postcondition* sentences start with the **Pre:** or **Post:** keyword respectively. In activity (graphical) notation, *Preconditions* are denoted as initial nodes with attached notes containing the main sentence text. Similarly, *Postconditions* are denoted as final nodes.

Pre: *balance* of the *bank account* is greater than 0

Post: [cash amount] is subtracted from the [bank account] [balance]

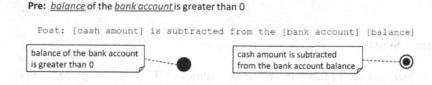

Abstract Syntax

Precondition and *Postcondition* sentences are contained in 'Constrained Language Scenarios'. The *Precondition* is always the first sentence in a scenario, and the *Postcondition* is always the last. All the 'Constrained Language Scenarios' in a 'Use Case' must begin with the same *Precondition*. The *Postconditions* are different for each scenario in a 'Use Case'. Every scenario can have at most one *Postcondition* and exactly one *Precondition*.

Semantics

Precondition sentence defines the condition that enables execution of all the 'Constrained Language Scenarios' in a given 'Use Case'. When the condition is not met, the associated 'Use Case' cannot start execution. This might be equivalent to, e.g. an inactive menu option that starts this 'Use Case'.

Postcondition sentence specifies the condition that must be met at the end of execution of a given 'Constrained Language Scenario'. This condition normally determines the final system state in relation to the system state at the *Precondition*. The state can be changed or unchanged, depending on whether the 'Use Case' execution, denoted with the given *Postcondition*, is successful or not.

Final Sentence

Concrete Syntax and Example

Final Sentence is tightly related to 'Postcondition' sentences. Every 'Postcondition' must be preceded with a final sentence. The sentence begins with the →**final:** keyword followed by either the *success* or the *failure* keyword which denote the result. In activity (graphical) notation, one of the two result keywords is attached in a note, to a final node.

Abstract Syntax

Final Sentences are in fact parts of 'Postconditions'. They always precede 'Postconditions' within 'Constrained Language Scenarios'. They have an attribute that determines whether the scenario ends with success or failure.

Semantics

Such sentences denote end of execution of a scenario. After reaching a *Final Sentence*, the given 'Use Case' terminates and control is passed to the invoking use case or to the operating system (the application terminates).

Rejoin Sentence

Concrete Syntax and Example

Rejoin Sentences are denoted with the →**rejoin:** keyword. After the keyword, they include the name of another 'Constrained Language Scenario' and the text of the 'Scenario Sentence' to be rejoined. Another variant of representation is to give just the sequence number of the rejoined 'Scenario Sentence'. *Rejoin Sentences* are always placed at the end of scenarios. This means that—when applied—they substitute the 'Final Sentence'-'Postcondition' pairs. In activity (graphical) notation, *Rejoin Sentences* are represented by control flow arrows that point at the sentence to be rejoined. These arrows can be adorned with the «rejoin» stereotype notation.

Abstract Syntax

Rejoin Sentences are contained in 'Constrained Language Scenarios'. They are always the last sentences in scenarios (alternatively to 'Final Sentences' and 'Postconditions'). Every scenario can have at most one *Rejoin Sentence*.

Semantics

Rejoin Sentence returns the flow of control to a sentence in another 'Constrained Language Scenario' of the current 'Use Case'. It is not allowed to rejoin to a sentence contained within some other 'Use Case'. Whenever a 'Rejoin Sentence' is reached, control is passed to the indicated other sentence and execution continues from this other sentence.

Condition Sentence

Concrete Syntax and Example

Condition Sentences start with the →**cond:** keyword. Their remainder complies with the syntax of a generic 'Natural Language Hypertext Sentence'. They can contain 'Hyperlinks' but generally they contain free text. Condition sentences have to follow 'SVO Sentences' in a 'Constrained Language Scenario'. In activity (graphical) notation, *Condition Sentences* are represented by control flow arrows with attached guards (conditions in square brackets). The actual condition is contained in the guard text.

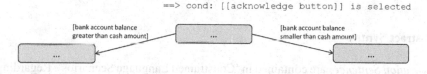

Abstract Syntax

Condition Sentences are contained in 'Constrained Language Scenarios'. Every such sentence has at least one alternative 'Condition Sentence', contained in another scenario of the same 'Use Case'. Regarding the sentence ordering in a scenario, no *Condition Sentence* can follow a precondition (i.e. it cannot be the first executing sentence in a scenario).

Semantics

Condition Sentence is a special kind of scenario sentence that controls the flow of scenario execution. Sentences that follow a *Condition Sentence* in a given 'Constrained Language Scenario' can be executed only if the condition expressed by this sentence is met. When this condition is not met, another (parallel) *Condition Sentence*, being part of another scenario of this 'Use Case', is evaluated. Control goes to the scenario for which the condition is evaluated to true.

Invocation Sentence

Concrete Syntax and Example

Invocation Sentences start with the →**invoke:** keyword. After the keyword, they include the name of another 'Use Case', to be invoked with this sentence. In activity (graphical) notation, *Invocation Sentences* are denoted as actions with the «invoke» stereotype. An invoke action is connected to 'SVO Sentences' through control flow notation. It can also be followed by a 'Rejoin Sentence' denoted with a control flow with the appropriate stereotype.

→**invoke:** Print cash withdrawal receipt

                                              ==> invoke: [[Show : account history]]

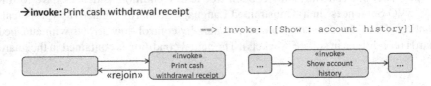

Abstract Syntax

Invovation Sentences are contained in 'Constrained Language Scenarios'. Regarding the sentence ordering in a scenario, no *Invocation Sentence* can follow a precondition (i.e. it cannot be the first executing sentence in a scenario). Every *Invocation Sentence* has to be linked to an 'Invocation Relationship'. This relationship has to connect the containing 'Use Case' (as the 'source') with some other 'Use Case' (as the 'target').

Semantics

Invocation Sentence has the procedure call semantics. It denotes invocation of another 'Use Case' with its scenarios at the point marked with this sentence. After executing all the scenario steps of the invoked use case, the flow of execution returns to the invoking scenario of the current 'Use Case'. This means executing the sentence that immediately follows the *Invocation Sentence*.

SVO Sentence

Concrete Syntax and Example

SVO Sentence contains a sequence of terms that point to 'Domain Elements' and 'Phrases'. It starts with a subject (S) which is a noun and points to either an 'Actor' or a 'System Element'. The subject is followed by a verb (V) which points to one of the 'Phrase' verbs. This is followed by an object (O), which is a noun pointing at one of the domain vocabulary 'Notions'. In its variant, an *SVO Sentence* can also contain a preposition with another (indirect) object. These elements have to be denoted in hyperlink notation. The first hyperlink is the subject and the second hyperlink is the predicate (the rest of the sentence). They can be either underlined or denoted with double square brackets. In activity (graphical) notation, *SVO Sentences* are denoted as actions which are linked with other sentences with control flow arrows.

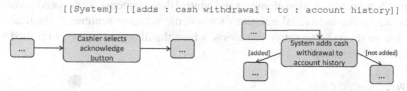

Abstract Syntax

SVO Sentences are contained in 'Constrained Language Scenarios'. They can be placed in any order in relation to other sentences. The only restriction is that they cannot be the first or the last sentences in scenarios, as this is reserved for 'Preconditions', 'Postcondition'-'Final Sentence' pairs and 'Rejoin Sentences'. Every *SVO Sentence* contains one 'subject' and one 'predicate'. Both are 'Hyperlinks' to appropriate elements in the domain model ('Actor'/'System Element' or 'Verb Phrase', respectively).

Semantics

Each *SVO Sentence* denotes a single interaction between the considered system and an actor. It can denote an action performed by the actor or by the system, depending on the sentence's 'subject'. The actions can pertain to various 'Notions' from the domain model. Depending on the type of the 'subject' and the type of the 'Notion' that constitutes the direct 'object', the sentence can have different interpretations. Possible ordering of different types of *SVO Sentences* is determined through changing the dialogue state between the system and one of the participating actors. More details on this can be found in Sect. 2.4.3.

Constrained Language Scenario

Concrete Syntax and Example

Constrained Language Scenarios are sequences of constrained language sentences. Each scenario starts with a 'Precondition' and ends with a 'Postcondition'-'Final Sentence' pair (or a 'Rejoin Sentence'). The first sentence after the 'Precondition' has to be an 'SVO Sentence' that has an 'Actor' as its 'subject'. The ordering of the remaining sentences should follow specific rules assigned to each sentence type. 'SVO Sentences' and some 'Invocation Sentences' are numbered. In activity (graphical) notation, a scenario is part of an activity—a graph of actions linked through control flow arrows. Action elements and control flow elements are denoted according to the respective individual notations for specific scenario sentences. Each activity can denote several alternative scenarios, where the alternatives are controlled with 'Condition Sentences'.

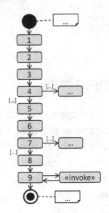

Pre: *balance* of the *bank account* is greater than 0
1. **Cashier** selects **withdraw cash option**
2. **System** shows **cash withdrawal form**
3. **Cashier** enters **cash withdrawal data**
4. **Cashier** selects **acknowledge button**
→ **cond:** *balance* greater that *cash amount*
5. **System** shows **swipe card message**
6. **Client** swipes **bank card**
7. **System** validates **bank card data**
→ **cond:** *bank card* OK
8. **System** performs **cash withdrawal** with **cash withdrawal data**
9. **System** shows **OK message**
→ **invoke:** *Print cash withdrawal receipt*
→**final:** success
Post: *cash amount* is subtracted from the *balance*

Abstract Syntax

Each *Constrained Language Scenario* contains one 'Precondition' and either one 'Postcondition' (with a 'Final Sentence') or one 'Rejoin Sentence'. It also contains an ordered list of other types of sentences: 'SVO Sentences', 'Condition Sentences' and 'Invocation Sentences'. *Constrained Language Sentences* are representations of 'Use Cases'.

Semantics

Scenarios have control flow semantics defined according to the description in Sect. 2.4.3.

A.3 Domain Elements

Notion

Concrete Syntax and Example

Notions are represented as rectangles with the notion names placed inside them (centred and and aligned to the top). The *Notion* icon can also indicate the notion type. This can be done through stereotype notation or through placing the type name in the top-left corner. When the *Notion* type is 'attribute', the appropriate name of the data type is placed in brackets. Typical data types are: "text", "whole number", "real number", "true/false", "date" and "secret text".

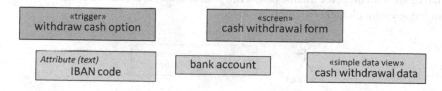

Abstract Syntax

Notions are kinds of 'Domain Elements'. They consist of 'domain statements' which are represented by 'Phrases'. *Notions* can be related through 'Domain Element Relationships'. Some *Notions* can have an associated 'Primitive Data Type' and thus they can serve the role of *Notion* attributes. If a *Notion* is an attribute, it can be only in 'Domain Element Relationships' with other *Notions* which indicate its role as an attribute. The *Notion* names are represented as 'Noun Phrases'. *Notions* can be related with other *Notions* as sources or targets of 'Notion Specialisations'. *Notions* are contained in specific kind of 'Domain Element Packages' ('Notion Packages')

Semantics

Notions are the core elements in domain specifications. They represent the domain vocabulary used within all the other elements of RSL models. All the 'Phrases' (noun phrases, verb phrases) that are part of various constrained language requirements representations are grouped within notions. Notions can be of several types which have different meanings:

- **concepts**—elements of the problem domain vocabulary,
- **attributes**—atomic data elements, contained in concepts,
- **simple data views**—elements that group attributes for presentation,
- **list data views**—like simple data views but presentation in the form of a list,
- **screens**—user interface elements that present or modify data,
- **triggers**—user interface elements that allow users to trigger events,
- **messages** and **confirmations**—standard user interface elements for presenting simple messages.

Actor and System Element

Concrete Syntax and Example

The syntax for *Actors* is identical to that found in UML. They are denoted by stick man figure with the actor's name below it. *System Elements* are denoted like 'Notions' but the «system element» stereotype added.

Cashier

«system element»
Banking System

Abstract Syntax

Actors and *System Elements* are kinds of 'Domain Elements'. They are contained in specific 'Domain Element Packages' ('Actor Packages' or 'System Element Packages'). Their names are represented as 'Noun Phrases'.

Semantics

Actors represent roles played by objects (people, systems) outside of the currently modelled system. They can interact with the current system, where this interaction is specified mostly through 'Use Case' scenarios ('Constrained Language Scenarios'). *System Elements* represent parts of the currently modelled system. In particular, this system itself is a *System Element*.

Phrase

Concrete Syntax and Example

Phrases can consist of a single noun ('Noun Phrases') or additionally contain a verb ('Verb Phrases'). Verb phrases can have one noun (direct object) or two nouns (an additional indirect object) separated by a preposition. *Phrases* have purely textual form with phrase parts being distinguished by bolding or underlining. When presented as parts of 'Notions', *Phrases* are shown within rectangle frames placed inside the 'Notion' icon.

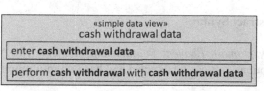

Abstract Syntax

Phrases are composed of 'Term Links' which refer to terms in the global terminology. Noun phrases contain a single 'Noun Link'. Simple verb phrases contain an additional 'Verb Link'. Complex verb phrases add another 'Noun Link' and a 'Preposition Link'. *Phrases* can be contained in domain statements within 'Notions', can serve as names of various RSL elements and can be referred to from various requirement and domain representation sentences ('Constrained Language Sentences', 'Natural Language Hypertext Sentences').

Semantics

Phrases denote various constrained language expressions, used in other parts of RSL models. Verb phrases denote actions, and noun phrases denote names.

Domain Element Relationship

Concrete Syntax and Example

Domain Element Relationships are denoted with lines that connect 'Notions'. Their notation is similar to that of UML's associations. *Domain Element Relationships* can be directed, and this is denoted with an arrow. Relationships pointed from concept-type 'Notions' towards attribute-type 'Notions' can be denoted using aggregation notation (a diamond placed at the aggregate end). Relationships can be adorned with multiplicities at each of the ends. Multiplicity notation is identical to that in UML.

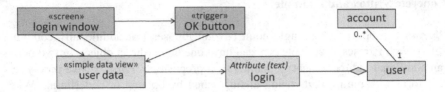

Abstract Syntax

Any *Domain Element Relationship* connects two 'Domain Elements' (usually— 'Notions'). It can be directed and has two multiplicity strings.

Semantics

A *Domain Element Relationship* denotes that two 'Domain Elements' ('Notions') are in some conceptual relation. The meaning of this relation depends on the notion types at both its ends:

- concept and concept (undirected)—conceptual (ontological) link between two elements of the vocabulary,
- concept to attribute (directed)—containment of an attribute (atomic data) in a concept,
- data view to attribute (directed)—inclusion of an attribute in a data view for its presentation,
- screen to data view (directed)—presentation of the data view (its related attributes) in the screen,
- data view to screen (directed)—updating of the data view (its related attributes) when presented in the screen,
- screen to trigger (directed)—presentation of the trigger in the screen,
- trigger to data view (directed)—data view is affected by the trigger.

Domain Specification

Concrete Syntax and Example

Concrete syntax for *Domain Specifications* is derived from UML's 'Packages' (see 'Requirements Specification'). Their names are placed inside additional rectangles within the large rectangles. They can also be presented in a Project Tree structure with a minimised icon being the root of the domain specification tree.

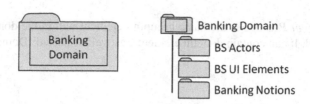

Abstract Syntax

Domain Specification can contain several 'Domain Element Packages' as its elements. It is also linked with one 'Requirements Specification'.

Semantics

Domain Specification is the main container of the domain part of an RSL model. It can contain all the domain-related elements for a given project—'Notions', 'Actors' and 'System Elements' grouped in appropriate 'Domain Element Packages'. It can be treated as an equivalent of a 'Model' (cf. domain model) in UML.

Domain Element Package

Concrete Syntax and Example

The syntax for *Domain Element Packages* is identical to that for UML's Packages. The icon has no additional adornments. *Domain Element Packages* can be presented in Project Trees with minimised icons.

Abstract Syntax

Domain Element Packages can be classified as 'Actor Packages', 'Notion Packages' and 'System Element Packages'. The respective types of packages can hold 'Actors', 'Notions' or 'System Elements'. They can also have nested 'Domain Element Packages' of the appropriate types. Every *Domain Element Package* is part of a 'Domain Specification' or another *Domain Element Package*.

Semantics

Domain Element Package is the basic grouping element within the domain part of an RSL model. It can contain domain elements, as well as nested 'Domain Element Packages'.

Appendix B
Summary of MOLA Syntax

This appendix presents a concise reference of the transformation part of the MOLA syntax. It does not present the MOLA syntax for defining metamodels (MOLA-MOF). The syntax is divided into three parts: Expressions, Rules and control flow, Procedures. Expressions are presented in terms of their textual syntax with several annotated examples. Other elements are explained in terms of their concrete graphical syntax, abstract syntax and semantics. For the concrete syntax, examples with relations to other MOLA elements are given.

B.1 Expressions

Like for any programming language, MOLA uses identifiers in its expressions and element names. Identifiers can contain small and capital letters ('a'–'z', 'A'–'Z'), digits (0–9) and the underscore ('_'). No other symbols are allowed. The identifiers cannot start with digits.

Pointer and Attribute Expressions

Syntax

Pointers refer to metaclass instances (model objects) in a model. *Pointers* have identifiers which refer to 'Object' elements or 'Variables'. Normally, the prefix '@' has to be used before the name of a *Pointer*. The prefix may be omitted only if the pointer is used in the constraint of a pattern 'Rule' and it points to a non-reference object element within the same 'Rule'. If the pointer is used in an 'Object' element and it points to that particular object, then the keyword self must be used. If the pointer is empty, the keyword NULL is used. Pointers can be down-casted by using metaclass identifiers and the pointer names in parentheses.

© Springer International Publishing Switzerland 2015
M. Śmiałek and W. Nowakowski, *From Requirements to Java in a Snap*,
DOI 10.1007/978-3-319-12838-2

Pointers can be appended with attribute specifications. To access attribute values, dot notation is used.

Examples

`@node`—pointer to a model object
`@node.name`—pointer to an attribute value in a model object
`@node.outgoing`—a pointer to a set of model objects that represent the (possibly many) edges outgoing from the node
`Graph::SpecialNode(@node)`—pointer down-casted to a specialised metaclass.

Integer Expressions

Syntax

Integer expressions return integer values. They consist of integer constants, attribute specifications of type Integer, variables of type Integer and standard functions. Standard arithmetical operations ('+', '−' and '*') and parentheses can be used. Standard functions are: `toInteger`, `size`, and `indexOf`.

Examples

`toInteger(@num_string)`—converts the string in a variable into an integer value
`@node.outgoing->size()`—gives the size of the set of 'outgoing' edges (i.e. the number of outgoing edges)
`(size(@node.name) + 1) * 5`—the size of the node's name incremented by 1, and then multiplied by 5
`indexOf("a","name")`—finds the position of the string 'a' in the string 'name'; returns 2.

Boolean Expressions

Syntax

Boolean expressions return Boolean values. They consist of Boolean constants (*true* or *false*), attribute specifications of type Boolean, variables of type Boolean and standard functions. Standard functions are: `isTypeOf`, `isKindOf`, `isEmpty`, `notEmpty`.

Examples

@node.isTypeOf(Node) —returns *true* if the model object 'node' is exactly typed with the metaclass 'Node'

@node.isKindOf(GraphElement) —returns *true* if the model object 'node' is typed with the metaclass 'GraphElement' or one of its subclasses

@node.outgoing->isEmpty() —returns *true* if there is no element in the set of 'outgoing' edges (no outgoing edge for the node exists)

@node.name->notEmpty() —returns *true* if the node has its name set (not empty).

String Expressions

Syntax

String expressions return text string values. They consist of string constants (contained in quotation marks), attribute specifications of type String, variables of type String and standard functions. Standard functions are: toString, substring, toLower, toUpper. String expressions can contain string concatenations denoted by the + symbol.

Examples

toString(57+5) —returns a string of text characters: "62"

substring("The MOLA",5) + substring("?!&%$",2,1) —returns a concatenation of two substrings, the first one starting with the 5th character, the second one starting with the 2nd character and being 1 character long; returns "MOLA!"

toLower(@node.name) —returns some 'name' in just lowercase characters (eg. "node1")

"->" + toUpper(@node.name) + "<-" —returns a concatenation of strings with some 'name' in uppercase (e.g. "->NODE1<-").

Constraint Expressions

Syntax

Constraint expressions consist of simple constraints which use 'Pointer', 'Integer', 'Boolean' or 'String' expressions. A simple constraint uses relational symbols to define conditions: = (equal), <> (unequal), < (less, strong subset), <= (less or equal, weak subset), > (greater, strong superset), >= (greater or equal, weak superset). The = and <> symbols are used to compare two expressions of the same type. The other symbols can be used only to compare the results of 'Integer' expressions or sets.

Constraint expressions return Boolean values. They can consist of a single 'Boolean' expression, or a constraint expression, or several such expressions connected with the logical operands or, and, not. Parentheses can be used in case of more complex expressions.

Examples

(size(@node.name)>5) and not @node.isFinal—returns *true* if the node's name is longer than 5 characters and is not a final node (the 'isFinal' attribute value is *false*)

((@cur_node <> NULL) and @ended) or not @ended—returns *true* if the '@cur_node' variable was initialised and the '@ended' variable is *true* or if the '@ended' variable is false.

Assignments

Syntax

Assignments are composed of the left-hand sides and right-hand sides with the := symbol between them. For assignments being parts of 'Text Statements', the left-hand side is either a pointer to an 'Object's' attribute or a variable pointer or a parameter pointer. For assignments being parts of 'Objects', the left-hand side is a pointer to an attribute of that 'Object'. The right-hand side is an expression. The data type of the left-hand side has to be the same as the data type of the right-hand side.

Examples

name := "C" + @r.name—the 'name' of the current 'Object' is set to the 'name' of some other object ('@r') with a prefix ("C") concatenated at the beginning

@tmp_name := @r.name + " " + @v.content—the '@tmp_name' variable (or parameter) is set to the concatenation of three strings.

B.2   Rules and Control Flow

Object

Concrete Syntax and Example

Objects[1] are shown as rectangles with up to three compartments. They can be placed only inside 'Rules'. The upper compartment contains the name of the *Object* and the type name. For reference *Objects*, their names are prefixed with the @ symbol. The upper compartment can also contain the {NOT} annotation. It can also contain the full name of the *Object* type's package, which is shown below the class element name in curly brackets. The middle compartment can contain constraints (also in curly brackets), which are normally constraints involving this *Object's* attribute values. The bottom compartment can contain the list of attribute 'Assignments' (one per line).

There are four types of *Objects*: object queries, object creates, object deletes and loop variables. Object queries have normal (solid) border. Object creates have thick, red dashed/dotted border. Object deletes have thin dashed border. Loop variables have solid thick border.

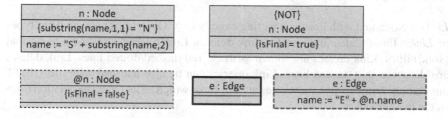

Abstract Syntax

Every *Object* contains a 'name', and refers to a specific metaclass in the metamodel, as its 'type'. It also defines its 'action type' which can be *normal, delete, create* or *loop variable*. *Objects* contain 'constraint' expressions, and can have several 'assignments' associated. They also define the existence of the NOT annotation and can be associated with other *Objects* as their reference objects. *Object* is always part of some 'Rule' and can be connected through 'Links' to other *Objects* contained in the same rule.

---

[1] In official MOLA reference objects are called 'class elements'.

Semantics

An *Object* represents a particular metaclass instance (exactly one) in the model. It has a name—an identifier that can be used to refer to this instance in the current MOLA procedure. Every *Object* has to have its type specified, which is one of the classes from the metamodel. *Objects* are of two kinds—reference and non-reference. A non-reference *Object* gets the pointer to a particular instance when a pattern has been matched or a create instance operation has been performed in the rule owning the class element (during the execution of the rule). A reference *Object* gets the pointer to a particular instance before the execution of the rule. It refers to an element that already has some value. It can be a parameter, a variable or an already matched *Object*. Reference objects can be only those with the action types of *normal* (query) and *delete*. The semantics of *Objects* during rule execution is explained in the description of 'Rules'.

Link

Concrete Syntax and Example

Links are denoted with lines connecting exactly two 'Objects'. There are three types of *Links*: link queries, link creates, link deletes. Link queries are shown as normal (solid) lines. Link creates are shown as thick, red dashed/dotted lines. Link deletes are shown as thin dashed lines. Link queries can be also adorned with the {NOT} annotation. *Links* always show roles at both ends, which reflect metaassociation roles in the metamodel.

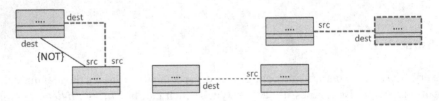

Abstract Syntax

Every *Link* is connected to a metaassociation in the metamodel. *Link* ends are named exactly as the metaassociation ends. A *Link* can be placed between two 'Objects' whose types are the same as the metaclasses connected through the metaassociation. *Links* are always contained in 'Rules'.

Semantics

A *Link* represents a particular metaassociation instance in the model. The metaassociation must be valid for the metaclasses that the connecting 'Objects' correspond to. The semantics of *Links* during rule execution is explained in the description of 'Rules'.

Rule

Concrete Syntax and Example

Rules are shown as gray rectangles with rounded corners. The *Rule* box contains at least one 'Object' and any number of 'Links'.

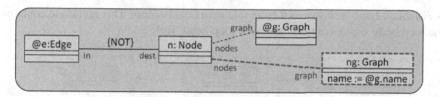

Abstract Syntax

Every *Rule* is contained in some 'Procedure' or a loop. It can be a regular rule or a loop head. In the second case, it has to contain exactly one loop variable 'Object'. A *Rule* can have any number of incoming 'Control Flows', except for a loop head rule, which has no incoming flows. A *Rule* can have up to two outgoing 'Control Flows'. It is possible to have no outgoing flows only for the rules contained in loops. If there are two outgoing flows, one of them must be an alternative flow ({ELSE}).

Semantics

A *Rule* is a kind of a decision statement with side effects. A rule execution consists of four steps: (1) pattern matching, (2) instance and link creation, (3) attribute value assignment, (4) instance and link deletion.

Pattern matching is performed for query, delete and loop variable 'Objects' and 'Links' contained in a *Rule*. A pattern is matched, when a set of metaclass and metaassociation instances are found in the model that are formed in exactly the same configuration as the elements in the pattern. If reference 'Objects' are used in a pattern, the pattern must consist of the instances referenced by them. Additionally, all the constraints set on the pattern's 'Objects' have to be met. If the pattern is not met (no set of instances conforming to the pattern is found), the *Rule* is evaluated to *false*, otherwise it is evaluated to *true*. Note: for normal rules, the pattern is matched once—the first available matching set of instances is evaluated.

After a pattern is matched, all the actions defined in the rule are performed. First, new instances are created based on create 'Objects' and create 'Links'. Then, all the attribute assignments are performed. Finally, appropriate instances are deleted based on delete 'Objects' and delete 'Links'. After executing a *Rule*, one of the 'Control Flows' is followed—depending on the result of pattern evaluation (normal flow for *true* and {ELSE} for *false*).

For-Each Loop

Concrete Syntax and Example

A *For-Each Loop* is shown as a rectangle with bold borders. This rectangle contains the loop body which contains at least a loop head 'Rule'.

Abstract Syntax

Every *For-Each Loop* is contained in a 'Procedure' or in another loop. It contains one loop head 'Rule' and can contain other 'Rules', 'Text Statements' and 'Procedure Calls'. A *For-Each Loop* has at least one incoming 'Control Flow' and at most one outgoing 'Control Flow'. The outgoing control flow can be absent if the loop is contained in another loop.

Semantics

The *For-Each Loop* has the semantics of the iterator. It iterates through all the instances of the model specified by the loop variable 'Object'. This is a special 'Object' contained in the loop head rule. For each of the iterated loop variable instances, the pattern in the loop head 'Rule' is matched. For every match, the loop body is executed.

Text Statement

Concrete Syntax and Example

Text Statements are shown as yellow rectangles with rounded corners. The rectangle is divided into two horizontal parts. The upper compartment contains a 'Constraint' expression. The lower compartment contains a list of 'Assignments'. One of the compartment contents can be absent.

Abstract Syntax

Every *Text Statement* is contained in some 'Procedure' or a loop. It can own one 'Constraint' and several 'Assignments'. A *Text Statement* always has one incoming and at most two outgoing 'Control Flows'. It is possible to have no outgoing flows only for the statements contained in loops. If there are two outgoing flows, one of them must be an alternative flow ('ELSE').

Semantics

A *Text Statement* is kind of a decision statement with side effects. Execution of *Text Statements* starts with the evaluation of the contained 'Constraint'. When it is met, the 'Assignments' are executed. After executing a *Text Statement*, one of the 'Control Flows' is followed—depending on the result of pattern evaluation (normal flow for *true* and {ELSE} for *false*).

Start and End

Concrete Syntax and Example

The *Start* element is shown as a small solid black circle. The *End* element is shown as a circle with a smaller solid circle inside. This notation is identical to that of end nodes and start nodes in UML's Activity notation.

Abstract Syntax

Start and *End* elements are contained in 'Procedures'. There is exactly one *Start* element in every 'Procedure' and at least one *End* element. A *Start* element has one outgoing 'Control Flow' and no incoming ones. An *End* element can have many incoming 'Control Flows' (at least one) and no outgoing ones.

Semantics

Start element is the entry point of execution for every 'Procedure'. All other statements must be reachable through 'Control Flows' from the *Start* element. Whenever a 'Control Flow' reaches an *End* element, the containing 'Procedure' terminates its execution and passes control to the calling 'Procedure' (or the program terminates if it is the main procedure).

Control Flow

Concrete Syntax and Example

Control Flows are shown as dashed lines with hollow triangular arrow heads. They connect 'Rules', 'Text Statements' and loops. A *Control Flow* can have the {ELSE} adornment.

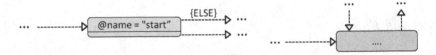

Abstract Syntax

Every *Control Flow* connects two statements. One of them is the source of the flow, and the other is the target. A *Control Flow* can be normal or alternative ({ELSE}).

Semantics

A *Control Flow* passes control from the source statement to the target statement. Statements determine which outgoing *Control Flow* should be followed (normal or alternative) according to specific rules for the particular statement type. The rules are explained in the statement descriptions (see 'Rule' and 'Text Statement'). If a given statement has no alternative *Control Flow*, and an alternative flow is to be followed, control is passed to the 'End' element or the loop's iteration end.

B.3 Procedures

Variable

Concrete Syntax and Example

Variables are shown as white rectangles. The upper part of the rectangle contains the variable name preceded by the @ symbol, and the variable type preceded by the : symbol. The lower part of the rectangle contains the name of the package that contains the metaclass defining the variable type. The package name is included in curly brackets.

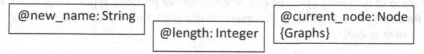

Abstract Syntax

A *Variable* is contained in a specific 'Procedure'. It has the variable 'name' and the name of its 'type'. The type can be either one of primitive types (*Integer*, *String* or *Boolean*) or a metaclass.

Semantics

Variables can hold primitive values or pointers to instances in the model. Their values can be set through 'Assignments' or when referenced through 'Objects' in rules (when typed with metaclasses). *Variables* can be used as 'Objects' in rule patterns and in expressions.

Parameter

Concrete Syntax and Example

Parameters are shown as white convex flags (arrow-shaped pentagons) or as white hexagons shaped into double arrows. The first variant is used for the *in* paramenters, and the second—for the *in-out* parameters. The upper part of the parameter symbol contains the parameter name preceded by the @ symbol, and the parameter type preceded by the : symbol. The lower part of the parameter symbol contains the name of the package that contains the metaclass defining the parameter type. The package name is included in curly brackets. Additionally, the parameter symbol has to contain the parameter number, placed on its right side.

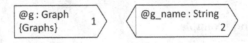

Abstract Syntax

A *Parameter* is contained in a specific 'Procedure'. It has the parameter 'name' and the name of its 'type'. The type can be either one of primitive types (*Integer*, *String* or *Boolean*) or a metaclass. A *Parameter* also has its 'number' and indication of its kind: *in* or *in-out*.

Semantics

Parameters define the types and order of arguments (call parameters) that must be supplied when the containing 'Procedure' is called. The order of parameters is determined by parameter numbers. Parameter numbering must be started from one. Every *Parameter* has its value set when the containing 'Procedure' is started. Principles of parameter passing are identical to those found in traditional programming languages. The *in* parameters are passed by value, and the *in-out* parameters are passed by reference. Note that in case of pointer-type parameters (typed with metaclasses), changes done to the pointed model instances are permanent, regardless of whether the parameter is passed by value or by reference. *Parameters* can be used and changed exactly in the same way as 'Variables'.

Procedure

Concrete Syntax and Example

Procedures in MOLA are represented as diagrams containing all the contents defined with other MOLA constructs. A *Procedure* can be also represented in project trees using a distinct icon accompanied by the *Procedure* name.

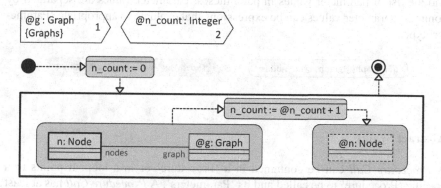

Abstract Syntax

Every *Procedure* has to be contained in a specific 'Package'. It contains 'Parameters', 'Variables' and program statements. A MOLA *Procedure* has a name and an indicator of whether it is a main procedure in the MOLA program.

Semantics

MOLA programs start by executing the main *Procedure*. Other procedures in a MOLA program are called through 'Procedure Calls'. When a procedure starts executing, its parameter values are set with the passed values. Then, its statements are executed, beginning with the 'Start' element. After reaching the 'End' element, the procedure passes control to the calling procedure. It the current *Procedure* is the main procedure, the MOLA program terminates.

Procedure Call

Concrete Syntax and Example

Procedure Calls are shown as rectangles with rounded corners. Calls to MOLA procedures are coloured green (khaki), and calls to external procedures are coloured yellow (with red/pink border). The rectangle contains the name of the 'Procedure', and the list of parameter values in parentheses. Parameter values are separated by commas. Parameter values can be expressions that evaluate to appropriate 'Parameter' types.

init_graph(@graph, @no_nodes)   showMsg("Node:" + @node.name)

Abstract Syntax

A *Procedure Call* can be contained in a 'Procedure' or in a loop. It points to a specific 'Procedure' to be called and its 'Parameters'. A *Procedure Call* has at least one incoming and at most one outgoing 'Control Flow'. It is possible to have no outgoing flow only for the calls contained in loops.

Semantics

Procedure Calls are used to call MOLA or external 'Procedures'. Call parameters must be supplied according to the order and types that are specified by the definition of the called 'Procedure'. If a parameter is the *in* kind, then the corresponding call parameter can be any expression evaluated to the same type as the parameter (the parameter is passed by value). If a parameter is the *in-out* kind, then the corresponding call parameter must be a 'Variable' or a 'Parameter' (but not an 'Object' reference) of the same type as the parameter (the parameter is passed by reference). The next statement (determined by the outgoing 'Control Flow') is executed when the called procedure finishes its execution. The outgoing flow can be absent if the call statement is owned by a loop. Then the next iteration of the loop is executed.

Package

Concrete Syntax and Example

Packages are shown in project trees as distinct icons accompanied by the *Package* names. All the elements in a *Package* (usually—'Procedures') can be shown as child nodes in the project tree.

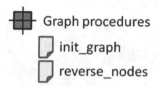

Abstract Syntax

A *Package* contains other *Packages* and 'Procedures'. It has a 'name' and can be defined as a *unit*. A special *Package* is the 'Model' which is the root of the project tree for a given project.

Semantics

Packages are the main grouping elements in MOLA programs. They are also compilation units. When a *Package* is defined as *unit*, then it recompiles every time any contained 'Procedure' is changed. All the directly contained 'Procedures' and those contained in child *Packages* are recompiled for a *unit*.

Literature

1. Sebastian Adam, Christian Wuench, and Matthias Koch. Ergebnisberight RE-Kompass. Technical report, Fraunhofer IESE, HOOD GmbH, 2013. http://www.re-kompass.de/.
2. Steve Adolph, Paul Bramble, Alistair Cockburn, and Andy Pols. *Patterns for Effective Use Cases*. Addison Wesley, 2002.
3. Alfred V. Aho, Monica S. Lam, Ravi Sethi, and Jeffrey D. Ullman. *Compilers: Principles, Techniques, and Tools*. Addison-Wesley, 2 edition, 2006.
4. Christopher Alexander, Sara Ishikawa, and Murray Silverstein. *A Pattern Language: Towns, Buildings, Construction*. Oxford University Press, August 1977.
5. Ian F. Alexander and Richard Stevens. *Writing Better Requirements*. Addison Wesley Professional, 2002.
6. Jésus Almendros-Jiménez and Luis Iribarne. Describing use-case relationships with sequence diagrams. *The Computer Journal*, 50(1):116–128, 2007.
7. Thomas A. Alspaugh and Annie I. Antón. Scenario support for effective requirements. *Information and Software Technology*, 50:2, 2008.
8. Scott Ambler. Agile Modeling: *Effective Practices for eXtreme Programming and the Unified Process*. Wiley, 2002.
9. Albert Ambroziewicz and Michał Śmiałek. Application logic patterns—reusable elements of user-system interaction. *Lecture Notes in Computer Science*, 6394:241–255, 2010. Model Driven Engineering Languages and Systems, MODELS'10.
10. Bente Anda and Dag I. K. Sjøberg. Investigating the role of use cases in the construction of class diagrams. *Empirical Software Engineering*, 10:285–309, 2005.
11. Thorsten Arendt, Enrico Biermann, Stefan Jurack, Christian Krause, and Gabriele Taentzer. Henshin: Advanced concepts and tools for in-place EMF model transformations. In Dorina C. Petriu, Nicolas Rouquette, and Øystein Haugen, editors, *Model Driven Engineering Languages and Systems*, volume 6394 of *Lecture Notes in Computer Science*, pages 121–135. Springer, 2010.
12. Hernán Astudillo, Gonzalo Génova, Michał Śmiałek, Juan Llorens Morillo, Pierre Metz, and Rubén Prieto-Díaz. Use cases in model-driven software engineering. *Lecture Notes in Computer Science*, 3844:262–271, 2006.
13. Joy Beatty and Anthony Chen. *Visual Models for Software Requirements: An RML Handbook*. Developer Best Practices. Microsoft Press, 2012.
14. Kent Beck and Cynthia Andres. *Extreme Programming Explained: Embrace Change*. Addison-Wesley, 2 edition, 2004.

© Springer International Publishing Switzerland 2015
M. Śmiałek and W. Nowakowski, *From Requirements to Java in a Snap*,
DOI 10.1007/978-3-319-12838-2

15. Brian Berenbach. A 25 year retrospective on model-driven requirements engineering. In *Model-Driven Requirements Engineering Workshop (MoDRE), 2012 IEEE*, pages 87–91, 2012.

16. Brian Berenbach, Florian Schneider, and Helmut Naughton. The use of a requirements modeling language for industrial applications. In *20th IEEE International Requirements Engineering Conference (RE)*, pages 285–290, Sept 2012.

17. Brian A. Berenbach. Comparison of UML and text based requirements engineering. In *Companion to the 19th Annual ACM SIGPLAN Conference on Object-oriented Programming Systems*, Languages, and Applications, OOPSLA '04, pages 247–252, 2004.

18. Sami Beydeda, Matthias Book, and Volker Gruhn, editors. *Model-Driven Software Development*. Springer, 2005.

19. Jean Bézivin, Grégoire Dupé, Frédéric Jouault, Gilles Pitette, and Jamal Eddine Rougui. First experiments with the ATL model transformation language: Transforming XSLT into XQuery. In *2nd OOPSLA Workshop on Generative Techniques in the context of Model Driven Architecture*, 2003.

20. Robert Biddle, James Noble, and Ewan Tempero. Essential use cases and responsibility in object-oriented development. *Australian Computer Science Communications*, 24(1):7–16, January 2002.

21. Dines Bjôrner. *Software Engineering 3: Domains, Requirements, and Software Design*. Texts in Theoretical Computer Science. An EATCS Series. Springer, 2006.

22. Dines Bjôrner. Rôle of domain engineering in software development. why current requirements engineering is flawed! *Lecture Notes in Computer Science*, 5947:2–34, 2010. PSI 2009.

23. Jacek Bojarski, Tomasz Straszak, Albert Ambroziewicz, and Wiktor Nowakowski. Transition from precisely defined requirements into draft architecture as an MDA realisation. In Michał Śmiałek, Kizito Mukasa, Markus Nick, and Jürgen Falb, editors, *2nd International Workshop on Model Reuse Strategies (MoRSe 2008)*, pages 35–42. Fraunhofer IRB Verlag, 2008.

24. Grady Booch, James Rumbaugh, and Ivar Jacobson. *The Unified Modeling Language User Guide*. Addison-Wesley, 2 edition, 2005.

25. Marco Brambilla, Jordi Cabot, and Manuel Wimmer. *Model-driven Software Engineering in Practice*. Morgan & Claypool, 2012.

26. Frederic P. Brooks. No silver bullet: Essence and accidents of software engineering. *IEEE Computer*, 20(4):10–19, April 1987.

27. Frederic P. Brooks. *The Mythical Man-Month, Anniversary Edition: Essays On Software Engineering*. Pearson Education, 1995.

28. Frank Budinsky. *Eclipse Modeling Framework: A Developer's Guide*. The Eclipse series. Addison-Wesley, 2004.

29. Juan M. Carrillo de Gea, Joaquín Nicolás, José L. Fernández Alemán, Ambrosio Toval, Christof Ebert, and Aurora Vizcaíno. Requirements engineering tools. *Software, IEEE*, 28(4):86–91, 2011.

30. Juan M. Carrillo de Gea, Joaquín Nicolás, José L. Fernández Alemán, Ambrosio Toval, Christof Ebert, and Aurora Vizcaíno. Requirements engineering tools: Capabilities, survey and assessment. *Information and Software Technology*, 54(10):1142–1157, 2012.

31. J. Carter and W. B. Gardner. Mise en scene: Converting scenarios to CSP traces in support of requirements-based programming. In *31st IEEE Software Engineering Workshop (SEW'07)*, pages 41–52, 2007.

32. Murali Chemuturi. *Requirements Engineering and Management for Software Development Projects*. Springer, 2012.

33. Betty H. C. Cheng and Joanne M. Atlee. Research directions in requirements engineering. In *Future of Software Engineering*, 2007. FOSE '07, pages 285–303, May 2007.

34. Alistair Cockburn. *Writing Effective Use Cases*. Addison-Wesley, 2000.

35. Mike Cohn. *Succeeding with Agile: Software Development Using Scrum*. Addison-Wesley, 2009.

36. Steve Cook, Gareth Jones, Stuart Kent, and Alan Cameron Wills. *Domain-Specific Development with Visual Studio DSL Tools*. Addison-Wesley, 2007.

37. Alexandre R. S. Correia, Juliano M. Iyoda, and Carla T. L. L. Silva. From requirements to ready to run software: A brief thought on how to mechanize the software development process. *International Journal in Foundations of Computer Science & Technology*, 4(3):17–26, 2014.

38. Krzysztof Czarnecki and Simon Helsen. Feature-based survey of model transformation approaches. *IBM Systems Journal*, 45(3):621–645, 2006.

39. Chip Davis, Daniel Chirillo, Daniel Gouveia, Fariz Saracevic, Jeffrey B Bocarsley, Larry Quesada, Lee B Thomas, and Marc van Lint. *Software Test Engineering with IBM Rational Functional Tester: The Definitive Resource.* IBM Press, 2009.

40. Remco C de Boer and Hans van Vliet. On the similarity between requirements and architecture. *The Journal of Systems and Software*, 82:544–550, 2009.

41. Jürgen Ebert and Tassilo Horn. Gretl: An extensible, operational, graph-based transformation language. *Software and Systems Modeling*, 13(1):301–321, February 2014.

42. Bruce Eckel. *Thinking in Java.* Prentice Hall Professional, 2003.

43. Mohamed El-Attar and James Miller. Improving the quality of use case models using antipatterns. *Software and Systems Modeling*, 9:141–160, 2010.

44. Mohamed El-Attar and James Miller. Constructing high quality use case models: a systematic review of current practices. *Requirements Engineering*, pages 1–15, 2011.

45. Khaled El Emam and A.Güneş Koru. A replicated survey of it software project failures. *IEEE Software*, 25(5):84–90, Sept 2008.

46. Sebastian Erdweg, Tijs van der Storm, Markus Volter, Meinte Boersma, Remi Bosman, William R. Cook, Albert Gerritsen, Angelo Hulshout, Steven Kelly, Alex Loh, Gabriel D. P. Konat, Pedro J. Molina, Martin Palatnik, Risto Pohjonen, Eugen Schindler, Klemens Schindler, Riccardo Solmi, Vlad A. Vergu, Eelco Visser, Kevin van der Vlist, Guido H. Wachsmuth, and Jimi van der Woning. The state of the art in language workbenches. In Martin Erwig, Richard F. Paige, and Eric van Wyk, editors, *Software Language Engineering*, volume 8225 of *Lecture Notes in Computer Science*, pages 197–217. Springer, 2013.

47. Eric Evans. *Domain Driven Design: Tackling Complexity in the Heart of Software.* Addison-Wesley, 2004.

48. Joerg Evermann and Yair Wand. Toward formalizing domain modeling semantics in language syntax. *IEEE Transactions on Software Engineering*, 31(1):21–37, January 2005.

49. Christiane Fellbaum, editor. *WordNet: An Electronic Lexical Database.* MIT Press, 1998.

50. Anthony Finkelstein and Wolfgang Emmerich. The future of requirements management tools. In G. Quirchmayr, R. Wagner, and M. Wimmer, editors, *Information Systems in Public Administration and Law.* Oesterrechische Computer Gesselschaft, 2000.

51. Thorsten Fischer, Jörg Niere, Lars Torunski, and Albert Zündorf. Story diagrams: A new graph rewrite language based on the unified modeling language and java. In Gregor Engels and Grzegorz Rozenberg, editors, *Theory and Application of Graph Transformations*, volume 1764 of *Lecture Notes in Computer Science*, pages 296–309. Springer, 1998.

52. Martin Fowler. *UML Distilled: A Brief Guide to the Standard Object Modeling Language.* Addison-Wesley, 3 edition, 2004.

53. Martin Fowler. Language workbenches: The killer-app for domain specific languages?, June 2005. http://www.martinfowler.com/articles/languageWorkbench.html.

54. Martin Fowler and Rebecca Parsons. *Domain-Specific Languages.* Addison-Wesley, 2010.

55. Xaview Franch and Pere Botella. Putting non-functional requirements into software architecture. In *Ninth International Workshop on Software Specification and Design*, pages 60–67, Apr 1998.

56. David S. Frankel. *Model Driven Architecture: Applying MDA to Enterprise Computing.* OMG. Wiley, 2003.

57. Gonzalo Génova, Juan Llorens, and Victor Quintana. Digging into use case relationships. *Lecture Notes in Computer Science*, 2460:115–127, 2002. UML'02.

58. Amir Hossein Ghamarian, Maarten de Mol, Arend Rensink, and Eduardo Zambon. Saying hello world with GROOVE—a solution to the TTC 2011 instructive case. In *TTC*, number 74 in Electronic Proceedings in Theoretical Computer Science, pages 215–222, 2011.

59. Amir Hossein Ghamarian, Maarten de Mol, Arend Rensink, Eduardo Zambon, and Maria Zimakova. Modelling and analysis using GROOVE. *International Journal on Software Tools for Technology Transfer*, 14(1):15–40, 2012.
60. Hassan Gomaa. *Designing Software Product Lines with UML: From Use Cases to Pattern-Based Software Architectures*. Addison Wesley, 2004.
61. Ian M. Graham. Task scripts, use cases and scenarios in object-oriented analysis. *Object-Oriented Systems*, 3(3):123–142, 1996.
62. Jack Greenfield and Keith Short. *Software Factories. Assembling Applications with Patterns, Models, Frameworks and Tools*. Wiley, Indianapolis, Indiana, 2004.
63. Sol Greenspan, John Mylopoulos, and Alex Borgida. Capturing More World Knowledge in the Requirements Specification. In *Proc. 6th International Conference on Software Engineering*, pages 225–234. IEEE Computer Society Press, 1982.
64. Sol Greenspan, John Mylopoulos, and Alex Borgida. On formal requirements modeling languages: RML revisited. In *Proc. 16th International Conference on Software Engineering*, pages 135–147. IEEE Computer Society Press, 1994.
65. Felipe Gutierrez. *Introducing Spring Framework: A Primer*. Apress, 2014.
66. Michael Guttman and Jordi Parodi. *Real-Life MDA: Solving Business Problems with Model Driven Architecture*. The MK/OMG Press. Morgan Kaufman, 2006.
67. Ábel Hegedüs, Zoltán Ujhelyi, and Gábor Bergmann. Saying hello world with VIATRA2—a solution to the TTC 2011 instructive case. In *TTC*, number 74 in Electronic Proceedings in Theoretical Computer Science, pages 302–324, 2011.
68. Jonas Helming, Maximilian Koegel, Florian Schneider, Michael Haeger, Christine Kaminski, Bernd Bruegge, and Brian Berenbach. Towards a unified Requirements Modeling Language. In *Requirements Engineering Visualization (REV), 2010 Fifth International Workshop on*, pages 53–57, Sept 2010.
69. Michael G. Hinchey and James L. Rash. A formal approach to requirements-based programming. In *Proc. 12th IEEE International Conference and Workshops on the Engineering of Computer-Based Systems (ECBS'05)*, 2005.
70. Robert Hirschfeld, Michael Perscheid, and Michael Haupt. Explicit use-case representation in object-oriented programming languages. In *Proceedings of the 7th Symposium on Dynamic Languages*, DLS '11, pages 51–60, 2011.
71. Matthias Hoffmann, Nikolaus Kuhn, Matthias Weber, and Margot Bittner. Requirements for requirements management tools. In *12th IEEE International Requirements Engineering Conference*, pages 301–308, Sept 2004.
72. Tassilo Horn. Saying hello world with GReTL - a solution to the TTC 2011 instructive case. In *TTC*, number 74 in Electronic Proceedings in Theoretical Computer Science, pages 295–301, 2011.
73. Heinrich Hussmann, Gerrit Meixner, and Detlef Zuehlke. *Model-Driven Development of Advanced User Interfaces*. Studies in Computational Intelligence. Springer, 2011.
74. ISO/IEC. 9126:2001: Software engineering—Product quality, 2001.
75. ISO/IEC. 19502:2005: Information technology—Meta Object Facility (MOF), 2005.
76. ISO/IEC. 25010:2011: Systems and software engineering—Systems and software Quality Requirements and Evaluation (SQuaRE)—System and software quality models, 2011.
77. ISO/IEC/IEEE. 29148:2011: Systems and software engineering—Life cycle processes - Requirements engineering, 2011.
78. Ivar Jacobson, Magnus Christerson, Patrick Jonsson, and Gunnar Övergaard. *Object-Oriented Software Engineering: A Use Case Driven Approach*. Addison-Wesley, Reading, 1992.
79. Edgar Jakumeit, Sebastian Buchwald, Dennis Wagelaar, Li Dan, Ábel Hegedüs, Markus Herrmannsdörfer, Tassilo Horn, Elina Kalnina, Christian Krause, and Kevin Lano. A survey and comparison of transformation tools based on the transformation tool contest. *Science of Computer Programming*, 85:41–99, 2014.
80. Frederic Jouault, Freddy Allilaire, Jean Bezivin, and Ivan Kurtev. ATL: A model transformation tool. *Science of Computer Programming*, 72(1–2):31–39, 2008. Special Issue on Experimental Software and Toolkits (EST).

81. Frederic Jouault and Ivan Kurtev. Transforming models with ATL. In Jean-Michel Bruel, editor, *Satellite Events at the MoDELS 2005 Conference*, volume 3844 of *Lecture Notes in Computer Science*, pages 128–138. Springer, 2006.
82. Hermann Kaindl. Using hypertext for semiformal representation in requirements engineering practice. *The New Review of Hypermedia and Multimedia*, 2:149–173, 1996.
83. Hermann Kaindl, Michał Śmiałek, Patrick Wagner, Davor Svetinovic, Albert Ambroziewicz, Jacek Bojarski, Wiktor Nowakowski, Tomasz Straszak, Hannes Schwarz, Daniel Bildhauer, John P. Brogan, Kizito Ssamula Mukasa, Katharina Wolter, and Thorsten Krebs. Requirements specification language definition. Project Deliverable D2.4.2, ReDSeeDS Project, 2009. http://www.redseeds.eu.
84. Elina Kalnina, Audris Kalnins, Agris Sostaks, Janis Iraids, and Edgars Celms. Saying hello world with MOLA—a solution to the TTC 2011 instructive case. In *TTC*, number 74 in Electronic Proceedings in Theoretical Computer Science, pages 237–252, 2011.
85. Audris Kalnins, Janis Barzdins, and Edgars Celms. Model transformation language MOLA. *Lecture Notes in Computer Science*, 3599:14–28, 2004. MDAFA'04.
86. Audris Kalnins, Agris Sostaks, Edgars Celms, Elina Kalnina, Jacek Bojarski, Wiktor Nowakowski, Volker Riediger, Hannes Schwarz, Daniel Bildhauer, and Jurgen Falb. Reuse-oriented modelling and transformation language definition. Project Deliverable D3.2.2, ReDSeeDS Project, 2009. http://www.redseeds.eu.
87. Audris Kalnins, Oskars Vilitis, Edgars Celms, Elina Kalnina, Agris Sostaks, and Janis Barzdins. Building tools by model transformations in Eclipse. In *Proceedings of DSM'07*, pages 194–207. Jyvaskyla University Printing House, 2007.
88. Lennart C. L. Kats, Richard G. Vogelij, Karl Trygve Kalleberg, and Eelco Visser. Software development environments on the web: A research agenda. In *Proceedings of the ACM International Symposium on New Ideas, New Paradigms, and Reflections on Programming and Software*, Onward! '12, pages 99–116, 2012.
89. Steven Kelly and Juha-Pekka Tolvanen. *Domain-Specific Modeling: Enabling Full Code Generation*. Wiley, 2008.
90. Suntae Kim, Dae-Kyoo Kim, Lunjin Lu, and Sooyong Park. Quality-driven architecture development using architectural tactics. *Journal of Systems and Software*, 82(8):1211–1231, 2009.
91. Anneke G. Kleppe. *Software Language Engineering: Creating Domain-Specific Languages Using Metamodels*. Addison-Wesley Professional, 2008.
92. Anneke G. Kleppe, Jos B. Warmer, and Wim Bast. *MDA Explained, The Model Driven Architecture: Practice and Promise*. Addison-Wesley, Boston, 2003.
93. Gerald Kotonya and Ian Sommerville. *Requirements engineering: processes and techniques*. Worldwide series in computer science. Wiley, 1998.
94. Per Kroll and Bruce MacIsaac. *Agility and Discipline Made Easy: Practices from OpenUP and RUP*. Addison-Wesley, 2006.
95. Philippe Kruchten. *The Rational Unified Process: An Introduction*. Addison-Wesley, 3 edition, 2003.
96. Daryll Kulak and Eamonn Guiney. *Use Cases: Requirements in Context*. Addison Wesley, 2 edition, 2012.
97. Miguel A. Laguna, José M. Marqués, and Yania Crespo. On the semantics of the extend relationship in use case models: Open-closed principle or clairvoyance? *Lecture Notes in Computer Science*, 6051:409–423, 2010. CAiSE 2010.
98. Kevin Lano, editor. *UML 2 Semantics and Applications*. Wiley, 2009.
99. Dean Leffingwell. *Agile Software Requirements: Lean Requirements Practices for Teams, Programs, and the Enterprise*. Addison-Wesley, 2010.
100. Dean Leffingwell and Don Widrig. *Managing Software Requirements: A Unified Approach*. Addison-Wesley object technology series. Addison-Wesley, 2000.
101. Grzegorz Loniewski, Ausias Armesto, and Emilio Insfran. Incorporating model-driven techniques into requirements engineering for the service-oriented development process. In Jolita Ralyté, Isabelle Mirbel, and Rébecca Deneckère, editors, *Engineering Methods in the Service-Oriented Context*, volume 351 of *IFIP Advances in Information and Communication Technology*, pages 102–107. Springer, 2011.

102. Grzegorz Loniewski, Emilio Insfran, and Silvia Abrahão. A systematic review of the use of Requirements Engineering techniques in Model-Driven Development. In Dorina C. Petriu, Nicolas Rouquette, and Øystein Haugen, editors, *Model Driven Engineering Languages and Systems*, volume 6395 of *Lecture Notes in Computer Science*, pages 213–227. Springer, 2010.

103. Leszek Maciaszek. *Requirements Analysis and System Design*. Addison-Wesley, 3 edition, 2007.

104. Raimundas Matulevicius. *Process Support for Requirements Engineering: A Requirements Engineering Tool Evaluation Approach*. PhD thesis, Norwegian University of Science and Technology NTNU, 2005.

105. Steffen Mazanek. HelloWorld! An instructive case for the transformation tool contest. In Pieter van Gorp, Steffen Mazanek, and Louis M Rose, editors, *TTC*, number 74 in Electronic Proceedings in Theoretical Computer Science, pages 22–26, 2011.

106. Stephen J. Mellor, Kendall Scott, Axel Uhl, and Dirk Weise. *MDA Distilled: Principles of Model-Driven Architecture*. Addison-Wesley object technology series. Addison-Wesley, 2004.

107. Atif M. Memon, Ishan Banerjee, and Adithya Nagarajan. GUI ripping: Reverse engineering of graphical user interfaces for testing. In *Proceedings of the 10th Working Conference on Reverse Engineering*, pages 260–269, November 2003.

108. Pierre Metz, John O'Brien, and Wolfgang Weber. Against use case interleaving. *Lecture Notes in Computer Science*, 2185:472–486, 2001. UML'01.

109. Pierre Metz, John O'Brien, and Wolfgang Weber. Specifying use case interaction: Types of alternative courses. *Journal of Object Technology*, 2(2):111–131, March-April 2003.

110. Pierre Metz, John O'Brien, and Wolfgang Weber. Specifying use case interaction: Clarifying extension points and rejoin points. *Journal of Object Technology*, 3(5):87–102, May-June 2004.

111. Joaquin Miller and Jishnu Mukerji, editors. *MDA Guide Version 1.0.1, omg/03-06-01*. Object Management Group, 2003.

112. Parastoo Mohagheghi, Wasif Gilani, Alin Stefanescu, and Miguel A. Fernandez. An empirical study of the state of the practice and acceptance of model-driven engineering in four industrial cases. *Empirical Software Engineering*, 18(1):89–116, 2013.

113. Parastoo Mohagheghi, Wasif Gilani, Alin Stefanescu, Miguel A. Fernandez, Bjorn Nordmoen, and Mathias Fritzsche. Where does model-driven engineering help? Experiences from three industrial cases. *Software & Systems Modeling*, 12(3):619–639, 2011.

114. Ana Moreira, Gunter Mussbacher, Joao Araujo, Nelly Bencomo, and Pablo Sanchez, editors. *International Workshop on Model-Driven Requirements Engineering (MoDRE)*, Rio de Janeiro, Brasil, 2013. IEEE.

115. Ana Moreira, Gunter Mussbacher, Joao Araujo, and Pablo Sanchez, editors. *Model-Driven Requirements Engineering Workshop (MoDRE)*, Trento, Italy, 2011. IEEE.

116. Gunter Mussbacher, Joao Araujo, and Pablo Sanchez, editors. *Model-Driven Requirements Engineering Workshop (MoDRE)*, Chicago, IL, USA, 2012. IEEE.

117. Wiktor Nowakowski, Michał Śmiałek, Albert Ambroziewicz, Norbert Jarzębowski, and Tomasz Straszak. Recovery and migration of application logic from legacy systems. *Computer Science*, 13(4):53–70, 2012.

118. Wiktor Nowakowski, Michał Śmiałek, Albert Ambroziewicz, and Tomasz Straszak. Requirements-level language and tools for capturing software system essence. *Computer Science and Information Systems*, 10(4):1499–1524, 2013.

119. Object Management Group. *Software and Systems Process Engineering Metamodel specification (SPEM), version 2.0, formal/2008-04-01*, 2008.

120. Object Management Group. *MOF 2.0 Query / View / Transformation Specification, v. 1.1, formal/2011-01-01*, 2011.

121. Object Management Group. *Unified Modeling Language, Part 1: Infrastructure, version 2.4.1, formal/2012-05-06*, 2012.

122. Object Management Group. *Unified Modeling Language, Part 2: Superstructure, version 2.4.1, formal/2012-05-07*, 2012.

123. Object Management Group. *OMG Meta Object Facility (MOF) Core Specification, version 2.4.1, formal/2013-06-01*, 2013.
124. Object Management Group. *XML Metadata Interchange (XMI), version 2.4.2, formal/2014-04-04*, 2014.
125. Gerard O'Regan. *Introduction to Software Process Improvement*. Springer, 2010.
126. Gunnard Övergaard and Karin Palmkvist. *Use Cases: Patterns and Blueprints*. Addison-Wesley, 2005.
127. Oscar Pastor and Juan Carlos Molina. *Model-Driven Architecture in Practice: A Software Production Environment Based on Conceptual Modeling*. Springer, 2007.
128. Tom Pender. *UML Bible*. Wiley, 2003.
129. Marian Petre. UML in practice. In *Proceedings of the 2013 International Conference on Software Engineering*, ICSE '13, pages 722–731, Piscataway, NJ, USA, 2013. IEEE Press.
130. Klaus Pohl. *Requirements Engineering: Fundamentals, Principles, and Techniques*. Springer, 2010.
131. Klaus Pohl, Günter Böckle, and Frank J. van der Linden. *Software Product Line Engineering: Foundations, Principles and Techniques*. Springer, 2005.
132. Roger S. Pressman. *Software Engineering: A Practitioner's Approach*. McGraw-Hill series in computer science. McGraw-Hill Higher Education, 7 edition, 2010.
133. Arend Rensink and Pieter Van Gorp. Graph transformation tool contest 2008. *International Journal on Software Tools for Technology Transfer*, 12(3–4):171–181, 2010.
134. Julien Repond, Philippe Dugerdil, and Pietro Descombes. Use-case and scenario metamodeling for automated processing in a reverse engineering tool. In *Proceedings of the 4th India Software Engineering Conference*, ISEC '11, pages 135–144. ACM, 2011.
135. J. Rilling, W. J. Meng, R. Witte, and P. Charland. Story-driven approach to software evolution. *IET Software*, 2(4):304–320, 2008.
136. Suzanne Robertson and James Robertson. *Mastering the Requirements Process: Getting Requirements Right*. Addison Wesley, 2012.
137. Dough Rosenberg and Kendall Scott. *Use Case Driven Object Modeling with UML*. Addison Wesley, 1999.
138. Jean-Claude Royer and Hugo Arboleda. *Model-Driven and Software Product Line Engineering*. ISTE. Wiley, 2013.
139. Kamil Rybiński, Sławomir Blatkiewicz, Norbert Jarzębowski, Wiktor Nowakowski, and Michał Śmiałek. TALE: Tool for application logic extraction. In *4th International Workshop on Academic Software Development Tools and Techniques*, 2013.
140. Ashich Sarin and J Sharma. *Getting started with Spring Framework: a hands-on guide to begin developing applications using Spring Framework*. CreateSpace Independent Publishing Platform, 2 edition, 2014.
141. Geri Schneider and Jason P. Winters. *Applying Use Cases: A Practical Guide*. Addison-Wesley, 2 edition, 2001.
142. Ken Schwaber and Mike Beedle. *Agile Software Development with Scrum*. Prentice Hall, 2001.
143. Anthony J. H. Simons. Use cases considered harmful. In *Proceedings of the 29th Conference on Technology of Object-Oriented Languages and Systems-TOOLS Europe'99*, pages 194–203. IEEE Computer Society Press, June 1999.
144. Daniel Sinnig, Patrice Chalin, and Ferhat Khendek. LTS semantics for use case models. In *Proceedings of the 2009 ACM Symposium on Applied Computing, SAC '09*, pages 365–370. ACM, 2009.
145. Fábio Levy Siqueira and Paulo Sérgio Muniz Silva. An essential textual use case meta-model based on an analysis of existing proposals. In Maria Lencastre, Hugo Estrada-Esquivel, and Eduardo Figueiredo, editors, *Anais do WER11—Workshop em Engenharia de Requisitos*, pages 419–430, April 2011.
146. Kenneth Slonneger and Barry L. Kurtz. *Formal Syntax and Semantics of Programming Languages*. Addison-Wesley, 1995.

147. Michał Śmiałek. Accommodating informality with necessary precision in use case scenarios. *Journal of Object Technology*, 4(6):59–67, August 2005.
148. Michał Śmiałek. From user stories to code in one day? *Lecture Notes in Computer Science*, 3556:38–47, 2005. XP'05.
149. Michał Śmiałek. *Software Development with Reusable Requirements-Based Cases*. Publishing House of the Warsaw University of Technology, 2007.
150. Michał Śmiałek. Requirements-level programming for rapid software evolution. In Janis Barzdins and Marite Kirikova, editors, *Databases and Information Systems VI: Selected Papers from the Ninth International Baltic Conference, DB&IS 2010*, chapter 3, pages 37–51. IOS Press, 2011.
151. Michał Śmiałek, Albert Ambroziewicz, Wiktor Nowakowski, J. Bojarski, T. Straszak, K. Wolter, L. Hotz, K. Mukasa, A. Jedlitschka, D. Bildhauer, K. Falkowski, J. Haas, T. Horn, V. Riediger, H. Schwarz, A. Kalnins, E. Kalnina, A. Sostaks, E. Celms, M. Rein, S. Drejewicz, J. Knab, J. Falb, Ö. Tüfekçi, and I. Çokkeçeci. Case-driven software development: Comprehensive approach to produce and reuse model-based software cases. Project Deliverable D8.2.2, ReDSeeDS Project, 2009. http://www.redseeds.eu.
152. Michał Śmiałek, Jacek Bojarski, Wiktor Nowakowski, Albert Ambroziewicz, and Tomasz Straszak. Complementary use case scenario representations based on domain vocabularies. *Lecture Notes in Computer Science*, 4735:544–558, 2007. MODELS'07.
153. Michał Śmiałek, Jacek Bojarski, Wiktor Nowakowski, and Tomasz Straszak. Scenario construction tool based on extended UML metamodel. *Lecture Notes in Computer Science*, 3713:414–429, 2005. MODELS'05.
154. Michał Śmiałek, Norbert Jarzębowski, and Wiktor Nowakowski. Runtime semantics of use case stories. In *2012 IEEE Symposium on Visual Languages and Human-Centric Computing (VL/HCC)*, pages 159–162. IEEE, 2012.
155. Michał Śmiałek, Norbert Jarzębowski, and Wiktor Nowakowski. Translation of use case scenarios to Java code. *Computer Science*, 13(4):35–52, 2012.
156. Michał Śmiałek, Audris Kalnins, Albert Ambroziewicz, Tomasz Straszak, and Katharina Wolter. Comprehensive system for systematic case-driven software reuse. *Lecture Notes in Computer Science*, 5901:697–708, 2010. SOFSEM'10.
157. Michał Śmiałek, Wiktor Nowakowski, Norbert Jarzębowski, and Albert Ambroziewicz. From use cases and their relationships to code. In *Second IEEE International Workshop on Model-Driven Requirements Engineering, MoDRE 2012*, pages 9–18. IEEE, 2012.
158. Michał Śmiałek and Tomasz Straszak. Facilitating transition from requirements to code with the ReDSeeDS tool. In *20th IEEE International Requirements Engineering Conference (RE)*, pages 321–322. IEEE, 2012.
159. Ian Sommerville. *Software Engineering*. International computer science series. Addison-Wesley, 8 edition, 2007.
160. Agris Sostaks and Audris Kalnins. The implementation of MOLA to L3 compiler. *Scientific Papers University of Latvia*, 733:140–178, 2008. Computer Science and Information Technologies.
161. Tomasz Straszak and Michał Śmiałek. *Advances in Software Development*, chapter Acceptance test generation based on detailed use case models, pages 116–126. Polish Information Processing Society, 2013.
162. Tomasz Straszak and Michał Śmiałek. Automating acceptance testing with tool support. In *Federated Conference on Computer Science and Information Systems (FedCSIS)*. IEEE, 2014.
163. E. Stroulia, M. El-Ramly, P. Iglinski, and P. Sorenson. User interface reverse engineering in support of interface migration to the web. *Automated Software Engineering*, 10(3):271–301, 2003.
164. Alistair G. Sutcliffe. *User-Centred Requirements Engineering*. Springer, 2002.
165. Alistair G. Sutcliffe and Neil A. M. Maiden. The domain theory for requirements engineering. *IEEE Transactions on Software Engineering*, 24(3):174–196, 1998.
166. Alistair G. Sutcliffe, Neil A. M. Maiden, Shailey Minocha, and Darrel Manuel. Supporting scenario-based requirements engineering. *IEEE Transactions on Software Engineering*, 24(12):1072–1088, December 1998.

167. Dave Thomas. MDA: Revenge of the modelers or UML utopia? *IEEE Software*, 21(3):22–24, 2004.
168. Laurence Tratt. Model transformations and tool integration. *Software & Systems Modeling*, 4(2):112–122, 2005.
169. University of Latvia. *The MOLA Language, Reference Manual, Version 2.0 final*, 2007.
170. Klaas G. van den Berg and Anthony J. H. Simons. Control flow semantics of use cases in UML. *Information and Software Technology*, 41(10):651–659, 1999.
171. Frank J. van der Linden, Klaus Schmid, and Eelco Rommes. *Software Product Lines in Action: The Best Industrial Practice in Product Line Engineering*. Springer, 2007.
172. Pieter Van Gorp, Steffen Mazanek, and Louis M. Rose, editors. *Proceedings Fifth Transformation Tool Contest, TTC 2011*, volume 74 of *Electronic Proceedings in Theoretical Computer Science*, Zürich, Switzerland, June 2011.
173. Axel van Lamsweerde. *Requirements Engineering: From System Goals to UML Models to Software Specifications*. Wiley, 2009.
174. Jonne van Wijngaarden and Eelco Visser. Program transformation mechanics: A classification of mechanisms for program transformation with a survey of existing transformation systems. Technical Report UU-CS-2003-048, Institute of Information and Computing Sciences, Utrecht University, 2003.
175. Daniel Varro and Andras Balogh. The model transformation language of the VIATRA2 framework. *Science of Computer Programming*, 68(3):214–234, 2007. Special Issue on Model Transformation.
176. Oskars Vilitis and Audris Kalnins. Technical solutions for the transformation-driven graphical tool building platform METAclipse. *Scientific Papers University of Latvia*, 733:179–212, 2008. Computer Science and Information Technologies.
177. Aliya Virani. *A Scenario-based Model-driven Engineering Framework*. The University of Texas at San Antonio, 2008.
178. Markus Völter, Thomas Stahl, Jorn Bettin, Arno Haase, and Simon Helsen. *Model-Driven Software Development: Technology, Engineering, Management*. Wiley, 2013.
179. Viliam Šimko, Petr Hnětynka, and Tomáš Bureš. From textual use-cases to component-based applications. *Studies in Computational Intelligence*, 295:23–37, 2010.
180. Gerald M Weinberg. *Understanding the professional programmer*. Dorset House Publishing, 1988.
181. Jon Whittle. Precise specification of use case scenarios. *Lecture Notes in Computer Science*, 4422:170–184, 2007. FASE'07.
182. Karl Wiegers. Automating requirements management. *Software Development*, 7(7):1–5, 1999.
183. Karl Wiegers and Joy Beatty. *Software Requirements*. Developer Best Practices. Microsoft Press, 3 edition, 2013.
184. Wikipedia. List of Unified Modeling Language tools. http://en.wikipedia.org/wiki/List_of_UML_tools, last accessed in July, 2014.
185. Stefan Winkler and Jens von Pilgrim. A survey of traceability in requirements engineering and model-driven development. *Software & Systems Modeling*, 9(4):529–565, 2010.
186. Yingzhou Zhang and Baowen Xu. A survey of semantic description frameworks for programming languages. *ACM SIGPLAN Notices*, 39(3):14–30, 2004.
187. Iyad Zikra, Janis Stirna, and Jelena Zdravkovic. Analyzing the integration between requirements and models in Model Driven Development. In Terry Halpin, Selmin Nurcan, John Krogstie, Pnina Soffer, Erik Proper, Rainer Schmidt, and Ilia Bider, editors, *Enterprise, Business-Process and Information Systems Modeling*, volume 81 of *Lecture Notes in Business Information Processing*, pages 342–356. Springer, 2011.

Index

© Springer International Publishing Switzerland 2015
M. Śmiałek and W. Nowakowski, *From Requirements to Java in a Snap*,
DOI 10.1007/978-3-319-12838-2

Printed in the United States
By Bookmasters